Queen Emma and Queen Edith

FOR BILL

Queen Emma and Queen Edith

Queenship and Women's Power in Eleventh-Century England

Pauline Stafford

BLACKWELL
Publishers

First published 1997

2 4 6 8 10 9 7 5 3 1

Blackwell Publishers Ltd
108 Cowley Road
Oxford OX4 1JF
UK

Blackwell Publishers Inc.
350 Main Street
Malden, MA 02148
USA

British Library Cataloguing in Publication Data

A CIP catalogue record for this book is available from the British Library.

Library of Congress Cataloging in Publication Data

Stafford, Pauline.
 Queen Emma and Queen Edith: queenship and women's power in eleventh-century England/Pauline Stafford.
  p. cm.
 Includes bibliographical references and index.
 ISBN 0-631-16679-3
 1. Emma, Queen, consort of Canute I, King of England, d. 1052. 2. Edith, Queen, consort of Edward, King of England, ca. 1020–1075. 3. Great Britain – History – Anglo-Saxon period, 449–1066. 4. Women – England – History – Middle Ages, 500–1500. 5. Great Britain – Kings and rulers – Succession. 6. Power (Social sciences) – England – History. 7. Social history – Medieval, 500–1500. 8. Queens – Great Britain – Biography. 9. Anglo-Saxons – Queens – Biography. 10 Eleventh century. I. Title.
DA160.S73 1997
942.01′9′0922 – dc20
[B]   96-38246
                                                               CIP

ISBN 0-631-16679-3

Typeset in 10 on 12 pt Sabon
by Best-set Typesetter Ltd, Hong Kong
Printed in Great Britain by Hartnolls Limited, Bodmin, Cornwall

This book is printed on acid-free paper

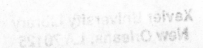

Contents

Figures

Preface

On the Wednesday of Ember week, during Lent 1072, a small group gathered in the upper room of the westworks of the new stone church of Wilton nunnery. There was a bishop, half a dozen priests and deacons, rather more lay nobles, two goldsmiths and a couple of cooks. All but the bishops and one of the goldsmiths were English; all, without exception, were survivors of the pre-1066 English regime. They were transacting a gift of land by one of the nobles to the church of Wells, and the scribe of the charter recorded the event, not in Latin, but in Old English. At the centre of the group, and the principal witness to the proceedings, was a middle-aged woman. She was, as the recorder of the events described her, Edith 'the Lady, the widow of King Edward'. This is the last recorded public appearance of Queen Edith, the last pre-Norman Conquest English queen. The choir had just sung the psalm for this Wednesday in Lent 'Remember thy mercies O Lord'. There is no knowing what Edith was prompted to recall; it is the purpose of this book to supply the story of seventy years of queenship on which she might have reminisced.

The two women with whom it is concerned are Emma, the Norman woman who came to England in 1002 as the bride of King Æthelred II (the Unready), and her daughter-in-law Edith, who married Edward, the future Confessor, son of Emma and Æthelred and the last native English king. The careers of these two queens span a turbulent period in English history, involving two foreign conquests, the second by the Normans in 1066 a permanent one, and a protracted succession problem of which the Conquest of 1066 was the dramatic outcome. The part played in all this by both queens is a central concern of this book. It is not, however, its intention to retell the eleventh century with the queens added in. Instead it is a retelling from a perspective focused on these queens which will, it is hoped, provide new insight into that century.

This is not a conventional biography. The materials do not exist to permit such a biography for eleventh-century English men let alone women, though Emma and Edith are especially well served by two almost unique sources which they themselves commissioned, the *Encomium Emmae Reginae* and the *Life of King Edward who rests at Westminster*. These are rare works of political apologia from the English eleventh century, and are in themselves compelling reasons to explore the lives of the women for whom they were produced. Neither, however, provides the basis for a sustained biography of either queen. This problem of sources is a challenge and an opportunity. It focuses attention on what little we know about eleventh-century political actors, male as well as female, and invites a detailed consideration of the sources of this knowledge, with a view to asking not merely who wrote and when, but to what purposes, from what perspectives, and especially to tell what overall tale. It is the structure of the narratives which people chose to write at the time and soon after which determines the structure of the lives which can be told. The story of Emma and Edith is thus told three times in three different ways in what follows: once briefly as a set of facts as far as possible without interpretation in the prologue to Part I; secondly through the various contemporary and near-contemporary chronicles of the eleventh century in which Emma and Edith feature, which form the bulk of Part I; and finally in my own reconstructed and interpreted late twentieth-century narrative in Part III. This final narrative is as close as the book comes to a biography of these women. It draws heavily on the sources from Part I, and on the wider comparative framework which study of tenth- and eleventh-century powerful women more generally can provide and especially on recent work informed by the concerns and interests of women's history. It also derives insight from Part II. Part II is a study of the structures of eleventh- and, since a longer perspective is necessary, tenth-century English queenship. The problems of eleventh-century biography compel a consideration of the deeper structures which underlie and shape even if they do not determine all individual lives. Neither Emma nor Edith can properly be understood without attention to the structures and frameworks within which they lived and to the roles and identities which they, as individual women, combined. The sum total of those roles and structures is the 'Queenship' of the title; Emma and Edith the 'Queens'.

The book is a study of eleventh-century English queens and queenship, but it stops well short of the end of the eleventh century, with the death of Edith in 1075. It therefore excludes the third eleventh-century English queen, Mathilda. This exclusion has been made with some regret. It might appear to reinforce the idea of 1066 and the coming of the Normans as a sharp turning point, a thesis by which I am far from convinced; many of the conditions of English queenship remained constant across this divide. The reasons were largely pragmatic. The inclusion of Mathilda would have required more consideration of Norman inheritance and family, which would have extended an already lengthy book. Whatever the common threads across 1066, later writers often felt the date significant, and exploration of the differing interpretations of two pre-conquest English queens in these sources raised interesting comparisons to which the Norman queen would have been extraneous. And finally Emma and Edith were an especially interesting pairing because of the works of self-presentation they commissioned. The decision to stop in 1075 is, nonetheless, a rather arbitrary one, and one with which I still feel some unease.

In the writing of this book there was a recurrent problem of terminology posed by the term 'queen'. It is only with the queen as the king's wife or mother, not as a female king, 'rex femineus', that this book is concerned; with the exception of Æthelflæd at the beginning of the tenth century there were no regnant queens in the period it touches on. 'Queen', even in this more restricted sense, is both a general term, denoting all the various identities of the king's wife, and one with a specific meaning, denoting a consecrated Queen and a partner in or parallel to the official and public duties of the King. I have tried to maintain this distinction of meaning by using the capitalized form 'Queen' only in the latter sense and as a title, as e.g. Queen Emma. 'Queen' and 'Queenship' have thus been restricted to discussions of the official, quasi-kingly role and identity of the 'queen'; 'queen' has been used to describe kings' wives and mothers more generally, whether or not they were consecrated and had this official role.

Finally I have called Emma by her Norman name, and not 'Ælfgifu' the name she was given when she married Æthelred and by which she was always known in England before 1066. This is for several reasons: to avoid confusion, since Ælfgifu is a common name in the English royal family; because it is the name by which she is most generally known in English historiography, but especially because Emma was her own given name in Normandy.

Acknowledgements

Much of the research and all the writing of this book took place during my tenure of a British Academy Research Readership from 1994 to 1996, and I owe a major debt of gratitude to the British Academy for providing me with this unique opportunity without which this book would probably not have been written and certainly not in this form. Thanks are also due to the staff of the Interlibrary loans section of the University of Huddersfield, of the Brotherton Library in Leeds, and of the Manuscript Room at the British Library for unfailing courtesy under whatever pressure.

The book is the fruit of a long-standing interest in the history of the tenth and eleventh centuries and in the history of powerful women. Over the years I have incurred innumerable debts for help and inspiration in pursuit of these interests; it is impossible to acknowledge them all, and in many ways invidious to single out a few. I owe, however, particular thanks to those who have answered questions, provided information or allowed me to see work in advance of publication in the course of the writing of this book: to Simon Keynes for providing me with a copy of his invaluable Atlas of Attestations to pre-1066 charters; to Julia Crick, for letting me see her work on nunneries, and to George Garnett for his on the Third Coronation *Ordo*; to Erin Barrett for discussion of the iconography of the royal couple; to Tim Thornton for advice on the fifteenth- and sixteenth-century court for comparative purposes; to Lesley Coote for references to Henry of Huntingdon and prophecy; to Michelle Brown for advice on the dating of manuscripts of the *ordines*; to David Bates for critical scrutiny of the Norman genealogy, and to Katharine Keats-Rohan for allowing me to see her own unpublished work on this subject. Most of all my thanks are due to Susan Kelly, for an advance copy of her edition of the Shaftesbury charters and for her working copies of the charters of 975–1066, an interim supplement to Birch, and of her forthcoming second edition of *Sawyer's Handlist of Anglo-Saxon Charters*. All historians of early England will owe her a huge debt when this finally appears, and those who have had the benefit of it in advance an even larger one.

Some debts are more general than these. I shall always be grateful to Stuart Airlie for first prompting me to pull together my thoughts on Emma and Edith by asking me to address staff and students in Glasgow; they remain the audience for Emma and Edith in their earlier incarnations of whom I have the fondest memories. My own students have given me much stimulus, not least those whose horror at Emma's lack of maternal feeling forced me to think hard about eleventh-century motherhood. Three people in particular have been a source of friendship and sustenance, intellectual and other, over many years: Nicholas Brooks, Janet Nelson, who also read the chapter on 'Queenship', and Susan Reynolds. My thanks are due to all of them. Finally my husband has been an unfailing support. He read the whole manuscript in draft and clarified it at many points, and provided encouragement when it was most needed. This book owes more to him than to anyone else, and it is to him that it is dedicated.

Part I

The Stories

Prologue

Shorn of interpretation and judgement, the bones of Emma's and Edith's lives are bare and sparse.

Emma was one of the nine known children of Richard I of Normandy; almost certainly his daughter by his Danish-descended wife Gunnor and thus the sister of Richard II, who became duke of Normandy after his father in 996, and of Robert Archbishop of Rouen. She was the aunt of dukes Richard III and Robert and great-aunt of Duke William, better known in England as the Conqueror. In 1002 she came to England to marry King Æthelred II, the Unready. Emma was not the English king's first wife. He had been married before, once if not twice, and already had a large family of six sons and at least four daughters. At the time of the marriage Emma's French/Norman name was changed for an English one, Ælfgifu. She bore Æthelred three children: two sons and a daughter, Edward, the future Confessor, Alfred and Godgifu.

Emma's marriage took place against the background of the Scandinavian attacks which plagued Æthelred's England. These culminated in Swein of Denmark's conquest of England in 1013. Emma, her sons and later her husband then took refuge at the Norman court with her brother Richard II. After Swein's death early in 1014, Æthelred returned to rule briefly until his own death in 1016. An armed struggle for the throne ensued between Æthelred's eldest surviving son, Emma's stepson, Edmund Ironside, and Swein's son, Cnut. Fierce fighting, the division of the kingdom, then Edmund's death made Cnut king of all England by the end of 1016.

In 1017 Cnut, the Danish conqueror, married Emma, Æthelred's widow. By this second husband she had two more children, a son Harthacnut and a daughter, Gunnhild, who in 1036 married Henry III, then king of the Romans, future emperor. Again Emma was not a first wife. Cnut already had a union with an English noble woman, Ælfgifu, daughter of a former ealdorman of York, a union which his marriage to Emma may not have terminated. Before or after 1016 Ælfgifu bore him two sons, Swein and Harold Harefoot. Cnut's reign is the second stage of Emma's career in England, and is marked by most references to her in charters and similar documents.

The death of Cnut late in 1035 put an end to this phase and inaugurated a third, dominated by questions concerning the succession to his several kingdoms of Denmark, Norway and England, particularly concerning that to the English throne. During his lifetime Cnut had sent his son Swein and Swein's mother Ælfgifu to act as regents in Norway, and despatched Harthacnut to be regent in Denmark. At the time of his father's death, Harold Harefoot was the only son in England. From late 1035 until 1037 the English throne was once again at issue. Harthacnut remained in Denmark, whilst Harold collected support in England. At first Emma remained at Winchester, with Cnut's military household and in possession of the royal treasure; Godwine earl of Wessex was close to her. In 1036 her sons by Æthelred, Edward and Alfred, returned to England from their refuge in Normandy. Alfred was captured, blinded and died in circumstances which left suspicion attached to both Godwine and Harold. Edward, who had gone to his mother at Winchester, now returned quickly to Normandy. In 1037 Emma's stepson Harold became king of the English and she was exiled to Flanders; there she lived, enjoying the hospitality of Count Baldwin, until 1039.

In that year her son Harthacnut joined her, and in 1040, on the death of Harold Harefoot, mother and son, accompanied by a fleet, returned to England where Harthacnut was accepted as king. Emma now entered the final stage of her life, as queen-mother. In 1041 Edward was recalled from Normandy, and associated in some way in rule; after Harthacnut's premature death in 1042, he became king in turn. A year later, in 1043, Edward deprived his mother of much treasure and land. Although Emma was restored to court by 1044, little or no evidence has survived of her activity after this and she disappears from view after 1045. Emma probably lived the rest of her life at Winchester, where she died on 6 March 1052. She was buried there in the Old Minster alongside her second husband, Cnut.

The bones of Edith's life are even barer. She was one of the nine or more children of Earl Godwine of Wessex and the Danish noblewoman Gytha, the sister of jarls Ulf and Eilaf, whom Godwine married after Cnut's conquest of England. Through her mother's brother, Ulf, Edith was cousin to Swein Estrithson, later king of Denmark. She was raised at the royally-connected nunnery of Wilton. Edith's family survived the return of the English dynasty when Edward succeeded to the throne in 1042 with their standing confirmed: her father remained earl of Wessex, effectively of England south of the Thames, and her brothers Harold and Swein were given earldoms in 1043. On 23 January 1045, Edith married King Edward, Emma's son. The marriage was childless. In 1051 she was sent from court and deprived of lands and treasure. Her fall was connected with her husband's moves against her family as a whole. 1051 saw royal accusations against her father, Godwine, and his flight from England with her mother Gytha and her brothers. In 1052 Edith and all her family were restored, and a number of Frenchmen fled the country, among them Archbishop Robert of Jumièges. Godwine died in 1053.

During the 1050s and early 1060s Edith's four brothers, Harold, Tostig, Leofwine and Gyrth, came to control most of the English earldoms. Edith's appearances in charters and similar documents are concentrated now. During these years the childless Edward invited back to England the surviving family of his half brother, Edmund Ironside.

On the night of 4–5 January 1066, Edward died, leaving the succession to the English throne once again in doubt. Harold, Edith's brother, became king, whilst another brother, Tostig, was in exile as a consequence of the Northern rebellion of 1065. Tostig, along with the Norwegian King Harold Hardrada, returned to attack Harold in autumn 1066. Almost simultaneously William of Normandy, great-nephew of Emma, attacked in the south. At the battles of Stamford Bridge and Hastings Edith's four brothers were killed. On Christmas day 1066 William was crowned king of the English.

Edith outlived her husband by over nine years, one of the most prominent English survivors of the Norman Conquest. She died at Winchester on 19 December 1075 and was taken for burial, at William's command, to Westminster Abbey, where she lay alongside her husband Edward in the church he had built there.

The bare skeletons assembled above were made from bones disarticulated from many plots. The eleventh-century English story as now told is a twofold tale of conquest and succession, dominated in retrospect by the Norman Conquest of 1066. Before that fateful date there was not one but several English narratives as well as Norman and Scandinavian ones. After 1066 new tales were added, and old ones reformed. Emma's and Edith's stories were told as part of these many tales and their retelling. In addition both women contributed their own eleventh-century narratives, in the *Encomium Emmae* and the *Life of King Edward*. The aim of this book is to add to the skeletons and put flesh on their bones. Its starting point is the stories and story-tellers who told the tale of early eleventh-century England, delineated its patterns and described its dramatis personae; not merely the dominant narratives imposed by 1066 but the alternative tales, the re-tellings, editings, and omissions. The study of Emma and Edith must begin by asking who told their story and why, by establishing which voices have become dominant and which forgotten, and by marking not only the shapes but the silences of the narratives which have survived.

1

Emma and Edith in the Narratives of the Eleventh Century

The narratives of the eleventh century tell of its dramas: conquests, succession disputes and the tumbling of the great. They were told by English, Normans and Scandinavians, recounted by contemporaries and retold later; still living tales as late as 1200 AD and beyond. They were told exultantly in triumph and bitterly in defeat, occasionally in a considered attempt at balance. They were told as chronicle and explanation, as legitimation and apologia, as celebration, as nostalgia and as romance.

1 English Narratives pre-1066

The English stories preserved in the Anglo-Saxon Chronicles and written before 1066 were contemporary with Emma's and Edith's own lives. These chronicles are a complex series of narratives written at various times and places. Most of the surviving chronicles are later copies and compilations of originally independent accounts which are now often difficult to identify, date, or place. One of the first and most important was the narrative of Æthelred's reign. This is the fullest account of an English king since Alfred. It was a retrospective produced at some date between 1016 and 1023,[1] at the end of the reign, and after the flight of the king and his family to Normandy in 1013. It was a story of defeat and conquest, written in the midst of both, and its author told a tale imbued with a strong sense of England and the English.[2] Through

[1] Keynes 1978, especially p 231, cf Clark 1971, pp 224–30. This account survives in all three major versions of the eleventh-century Anglo-Saxon Chronicles, MSS C, D and E.
[2] A sense present in other works of these years, see e.g. Archbishop Wulfstan of York's Sermon of the Wolf to the English preached in 1014, strongly concerned with the English, and given this title in the principal and earliest manuscripts, including in BL Cotton Nero A i, the manuscript associated with Wulfstan himself.

this retrospect Emma entered English history. Æthelred's earlier wife or wives were, like most tenth-century English queens, never referred to.[3] This chronicler's story, and the circumstances which prompted it, gave Emma a special importance.

Her first significance was as a Norman. Her arrival in 1002 was noted, as was her return to Nomandy along with the young princes in 1013. It was her arrival not her marriage, the link she established with Richard and his son, which was significant to a perspective late in Æthelred's reign. In 1002 and 1013 she was identified as 'Richard's daughter' not primarily as 'Æthelred's wife'. The Norman alliance she embodied was part of the tale of English versus Danes which was one of the chronicler's themes; its significance was especially clear at the end of the reign. Her brother had provided refuge for members of the English royal family in 1013–14; as late as 1016 and after he was still harbouring the surviving sons of Æthelred, the last traceable remnants of the old dynasty. The Danish conquest of 1013, and its results for the English royal family, prompted the chronicler to write and also brought Emma into the story now told, setting her apart from most earlier English queens.

It was an English narrative and for its author Emma was 'Richard's daughter', but she was not 'Norman', nor 'French'; she was an English queen, the woman whom he remembered as the 'Lady/*Hlæfdige*'.[4] Though the Chronicler was aware of the French identity of her reeve, whom he fingered for the betrayal of Exeter in 1003, Emma's foreignness went unremarked. Emma's meaning and identity for this writer were those appropriate to his view of 1013–17, and the role he saw her filling in these years. In 1017 Emma married Cnut, the conqueror of her first husband Æthelred. The marriage took place mid-year, but for the chronicler it was the culmination of events. His record of 1017 is not a strict chronology, it leads to this critical point. Emma had become the wife of a conqueror. Hostilities ended in traditional fashion with the taking of a woman who was important both to Cnut and to the story teller.[5] By the time he wrote, Emma was a link not merely with Normandy but with the English past; the widow of the dead king of the English and their queen,

---

[3] Except by MS D which mentions Edmund's second wife, Æthelflæd, s.a. 946, St Ælfgifu, his first wife, s.a. 955, and the marriage of Ælfthryth and Edgar, s.a. 965. It is unfortunately impossible to be certain whether D, in its present form a late manuscript, is here making later insertions, and thus to decide to whom, why and when these women appeared important.

[4] She is '*seo hlæfdige*' in 1002 and 1013; see below pp 56–9 for discussion of this title.

[5] It is difficult to place this story within the years 1016–23. The writer of the entry for 1016 already knew that Cnut was king, which arguably dates this entry to 1017, the likeliest date for its original composition. The shorter entries for 1018 and 1019 would then have been added later to a story already largely complete.

the Lady.[6] The Chronicler never named her.[7] A contemporary did not need to; more importantly what mattered for him were her separate identities which linked her with Normans, English and conquerors, as daughter, widow, wife and Lady:[8] Cnut took as a wife 'the widow of Æthelred, Richard's daughter'. The events of 1013–17 ensured that Emma had a part when the tale of Æthelred's reign was told. The story encourages a closer scrutiny of these years, preparing us to see them as a crux in Emma's life, and signals the importance of her Norman birth and acquired English identity. But the shape it gives to the earliest stages of her life is that imposed by retrospective priorities.

There is no sustained contemporary English narrative of the reign of Cnut. Emma would later provide her own in the *Encomium*. She is virtually absent from what other fragments of history remain. When those fragments concerned the reconciliation of English and Danes the queen who embodied it might be mentioned. She was recorded, along with the young Harthacnut, at the translation of the bones of Ælfheah, the English archbishop martyred by the Danes, an event which sought to expiate the brutalities of the Danish conquest.[9] It was, however, Cnut's death and the struggles that followed it that prompted a second major English story of the eleventh century, or rather a series of them. Whilst the first had been a tale of conquest, these were of disputed succession. They are more difficult to date and place than was Æthelred's chronicle.[10] All of them had a place for Emma. Conquest included woman and wife as link, continuity and peace-binder; succession to the throne was family conflict writ large as national politics. Even more than the conquest of 1013–17 such a story featured women, and had its own roles for widow, mother and queen.

[6] *ASC*, MS E underlined her queenliness by saying that Cnut took her as '*cwen*' not as 'wife', as in MSS C and D. E is a later copy and may here be influenced by Emma's significance during Cnut's reign. '*Cwen*' is E's normal title for king's wives, though it uses '*hlæfdige*' in 918, 1002, 1013, 1048, 1052 and 1075.

[7] Only the later MS F names her as Ælfgifu *and* Emma in 1002, 1013 and 1017.

[8] *Encomium*, pp 55–6, A. Campbell suggests contemporaries failed to give her name because they were unsure which one to call her by. I think the significance goes beyond this.

[9] *ASC*, MS D 1023 is the only version of the chronicles to mention this, and as the record stands it is likely to be post 1066, since it calls her 'Imma' a name virtually unused in England before that date.

[10] *ASC*, MS C may be a continuous narrative put together as late as 1042, possibly close to the court, and thus affected by the return and succession of Edward the Confessor. There is evidence of retrospective knowledge throughout its account: in 1035 Emma stays at Winchester 'as long as she might'; 1036 is written with the knowledge that Harold would win, and the poem of this year has a cult already growing around the dead Alfred; in 1037 Baldwin kept Emma 'as long as she had need' which seems to assume knowledge of the 1040 return; 1040 is aware of Harthacnut's death in 1042 'he did nothing kingly as long as he lived', and the same awareness is present in 1041. This may mean that the writer wrote on more than one occasion, always with a year or more's retrospect. The open

The clearest narrative was that told by the author of manuscript C of
the Anglo-Saxon Chronicle, perhaps close to the southern court itself. It
was a tale of drama and wickedness: of the claims of a usurper, Harold;
of the murder of a prince, Alfred; of the deprivation and driving out of
a queen, Emma, in the bitterness of winter; of her return with her son,
Harthacnut, who then ruled harshly; all ending happily with the accession of the rightful heir, Edward, in 1042. A mother and her sons are
central to this story. Emma is presented as Alfred's mother in 1036;
Harthacnut's in 1037, when his tardiness results in her exile, and again
in 1039, when he goes to her in Flanders; Edward's when he returns in
1041. But Emma must also be a Queen; the narrative plays on her royal
dignity and rights. She is Lady when she sits at Winchester with Cnut's
treasures in 1035–6; the exile of 1037 is all the more dramatic for being
that of a Queen/*cwen*. This first story is sympathetic to Emma as a
mother and indignant for her as a Queen.

There is another less coherent and possibly earlier tale in the E manuscript of the Anglo-Saxon Chronicle. It is less polished, less rounded in its
ending, a story not of triumphant right but of bitter dispute. Emma's role
in it is simply a family one as mother and widow: Harthacnut's mother,
not the impartial Lady, in 1036; Cnut's widow, not a royal Queen in
1037. Her rival, Cnut's other wife Ælfgifu, has her own dignity in this
story. Dismissively referred to as 'the other Ælfgifu' in the first tale, she
is here named as the daughter of ealdorman Ælfhelm, just as Emma is
identified as 'Earl Richard's daughter' in 1041. In this tale the rights and
wrongs are less clear, Emma's own position not obviously justified. The
partiality of her family position eclipses her queenly status. The chroniclers disagree in their interpretations of these years, but converge in
affirming Emma's importance during them. Few earlier English queens

hostility to Godwine in the 1036 entry suggests a date c. 1040 (just possibly a late as 1051).
There must be a strong presumption that the whole narrative is a retrospect from c. 1042/
3. This MS was copied at Abingdon in 1043, *ASC MS C*, ed. Conner, Introduction, though
the argument that this section was also composed there is less convincing; these entries have
no connection with Abingdon, ibid pp lxxviii–lxxix . The D chronicler combined more than
one account of these years: one identical with C, and another which makes Harold succeed
Cnut as his undoubted son and without problem in 1036 – a statement which might fit a)
the strictly contemporary circumstances, before division developed b) a Northern perspective, or c) a date in Harold's own reign. It omits all reference to Godwine's involvement in
1036, suggesting it was finally put together after Godwine's return to favour in the 1040s.
E's account of these years is extremely difficult to date. Unlike C it does not anticipate
Edward's succession. Yet nor does it seem to be a strictly contemporary, year-by-year
account, since 1035–7 are telescoped together, and 1037's references to Emma's stay with
Baldwin refer to her treatment 'as long as she was there', which assumes the return in 1040.
Its account of 1036–7 gives the most confused picture of these shifting events, and perhaps
thus the nearest in date. It is possible that its story is to be dated to the reign of Harthacnut;
Conner argues for substantial augmentation and editing of E's exemplar after it moved to
St Augustine's c. 1044, *ASC MS C*, ed. Conner, pp lvii–lviii.

had achieved such prominence in the laconic stories of the chroniclers. Only the early tenth-century Æthelflæd of Mercia, in her own court record, rivals and surpasses Emma now. The account of Æthelflæd was adulatory, that of Emma divided and uncertain. Guided by contemporary perceptions, we would seek Emma's greatest prominence now; warned by their differences of interpretation we should be aware of the difficulty of judging her situation and actions.

When Emma's son Edward returned from Normandy in 1041, the E Chronicler was reminded of Emma's own Norman ancestry. 'In this same year Edward, son of King Æthelred, came to this land from France. He was the brother of King Hardacnut. They were both sons of Ælfgifu, who was Earl Richard's daughter'. It was a fact irrelevant to those who recorded her death in 1052. At that point the English chroniclers crystallized her life into a series of identities: the mother of kings, the wife now widow of kings, still the Lady, albeit a dowager one.[11] The Norman birth which brought her into England and into the first English story seemed marginal now. For chroniclers who had no inkling of 1066, her Normanness was now eclipsed.[12] Her life was summed up in family roles and identities, in *royal* family and queenly ones. Such roles should be as central to us as they seemed to contemporaries. The challenge will be to recover their rich contemporary meanings and thereby in turn reconstruct her life.

The record of an early English queen's death is uncommon. That of Emma's may indicate her significance: by 1052 this great woman had a part in any narrative. Her temporary fall in 1043 had been worthy of remark in its own right.[13] But 1051–2 were special years; chroniclers were moved to prolixity by their events; the chances of inclusion were enhanced. Emma's death occurred in the midst of the upheavals which saw the exile and return of Earl Godwine and his family. The resulting stories included a rare appearance of Edith.

Edith had made a brief debut at the time of her marriage. The union of the king with the 'daughter of Earl Godwine' was noteworthy to the

---

[11] See *ASC*, MSS D, E, D and C respectively.

[12] Yet another indication that Normans and Normandy meant little or nothing to those who were writing English chronicles c. 1051–2, whatever they may or may not have meant to the king.

[13] Possibly outside of any wider narratives. It is not clear whether C's version here should be seen as a continuation of its 1035–42 story; it gives an account of the fall of Emma which gives least excuse to Edward, and implicates Stigand as a bad counsellor of the queen, which might be interpreted as a continuation of its earlier sympathy with Emma. Conner, *ASC MS C*, p xxvi sees it as an annal composed separately as the last act of copying up of MS C. D, by contrast, makes the event more dramatic and accuses Emma of failing to look to Edward's interests both before and after his accession. It is not clear that it belongs in a longer story D is telling here. E omits the annal, perhaps because of the connection of St Augustine's and Emma's reinstatement, *ASC, MS C*, ed. Conner, p lviii.

author of the story in manuscript C, who had openly accused the earl of Alfred's murder in 1036. Edith entered the historical record as Godwine's daughter, and it was Godwine's fall and return in 1051–2 which prompted the only other references to her in the pre-1066 stories. As in 1035–42, dramatic events provoked different tales. The virtually contemporary author of manuscript E produced a narrative of high drama, a story of national events, though from a distinctly South East English perspective.[14] For him the dismissal of Edith by the king was witness to the enormity of the situation. One calamity recalled another; the fall of Emma in 1043 may be mentioned in the story because of the parallel it offered to that of Edith.[15] It was the fall of a Lady, of a *consecrated* Queen; no other pre-1066 English chronicler specifically remarks on the consecration of queens. The details of queens' lives are often revealed only to heighten a narrative. For the author of E, Edith's exile from court was the crowning act of a dramatic year, just as her restoration in 1052 completed the domestic reconciliation which left the blame firmly on Archbishop Robert and the Frenchmen, now outlawed. This high drama, told to explain the actions of the people of the South East, is matched by a more muted story, perhaps closer and more sensitive to the king, in manuscript C. Here Edith is Godwine's daughter, not the Queen; her fall is not even mentioned, only her restoration along with her family in 1052. The drama of a Queen's exile did not fit this careful account of the reconciliation of Godwine and the king.[16] Nor was Edith's queenliness central to the third narrator of 1051–2, the writer of manuscript D. For him it was an occasion for comment on fate and the fall of the great. This might have included the queen, but in fact centred on Godwine; Edith is merely a part of the earl's greatness, pulled down by his fall and restored with him. In the stories told in England pre-1066 Edith, unlike Emma, had no central place.

D may already have had an eye on 1066 when it centred on Godwine in 1052.[17] The conquest of that year quickly cast its shadow back over the earlier stories. At some stage an erasure was made in the record of Emma's death in C. Whatever was there in the pre-1066 manuscript was

---

[14] *ASC*, MS E, see Stafford 1989a, p 84.

[15] E uses very similar phraseology to describe both; it may be that the events of 1051–2 prompted this Chronicler's whole account of the years from 1043 onwards, in which he borrowed from C and D or their sources. In this Chronicle the earlier reference to the marriage of Edith may thus be part of the 1052 story.

[16] C's account reads almost like the declaration of the legal judgement, using phrases like 'swa full and swa forð . . .' and speaking of the Frenchmen who 'unlage rærdon and undom demdon and unrædræddon'. Conner, *ASC MS C*, pp lxiii–vi and lxxix–lxxx suggests that the annals 1049–57 were added to MS C at Abingdon in 1057. He suggests that they were composed there at that date, but there are very few Abingdon connections of these annals.

[17] This Chronicle in its final form was written late in the eleventh century.

replaced by the name 'Imme', her Norman not her English name; the change was surely made after 1066. Just as Edith's brother *King* Harold disappeared to be replaced by the usurping oath-breaker *Earl* Harold,[18] so *Ælfgifu*, became *Emma*.[19] Emma's Norman birth had been present in the earlier English stories, often important, but always subject to English concerns. 1066 changed identities, retold stories, brought in new ones, altered history. Before 1066 there were English stories; after they would be reworked in the light of that year and of the tales the Normans told.

2 Eleventh-Century Norman Narratives

Emma's first possible appearance in narratives from her native Normandy was both anonymous and unflattering. The Norman Latin poem, *Semiramis*, is a dramatic satire of the early eleventh century.[20] It presents a queen/whore drawn willingly into an abominable marriage with a horned adulterous bull, who turns out to be Jupiter. If, as seems likely, Emma is Semiramis, the bull is Cnut and their marriage the subject of the poem's critical satire, the occasion for the first surviving Norman comment on Emma. The work is scarcely official. Its anonymous cast included Emma's brother Archbishop Robert of Rouen as a 'weak, pompous and rather pitiful' necromancer.[21] Its author used Emma to criticize her male relatives; her independence is their weakness. The 1017 marriage attracted contemporary censure in some Norman circles, but that critical tone was lost as the later and more official Norman versions of the eleventh century took shape. This wilful and active woman was not the Emma who was to emerge from the Norman narratives.

William of Jumièges furnished the basis of the major Norman story, and William of Poitiers gave it its full, watertight and legalistic shape. Jumièges' narrative was put together in the 1050s, and added to after 1066.[22] The English were incidental to its glorification of Norman rulers. Emma features because of the connections she brought to the family through her marriages to two kings, her motherhood of two more, and through her daughter's splendid match; Gunnhild married Henry king of

---

[18] Garnett 1986b.

[19] The change was rapid, and was marked in official documents like Domesday Book, where Emma is always called by her Norman never her English name, even though she had held the land under that name. When a manuscript of the Anglo-Saxon Chronicle, like MS F, or later John of Worcester, give her English and her French names one should suspect a deliberate statement about the pre-1066 past on their part.

[20] van Houts 1992.

[21] van Houts 1992, p 21.

[22] William of Jumièges, van Houts ed., vol I, pp xxxii–v and xlv–l. It is difficult to be certain whether the earlier sections were revised or added to after 1066.

the Romans, future emperor.[23] Any doubts about the 1017 marriage were swallowed in this glittering genealogy. The Norman line was glorified through her and her children, including her daughter: glorified by its capacity to provide a refuge for her, her husband and sons in time of need in 1013, but equally glorified by its victory against her husband Æthelred.[24] Emma's husband Æthelred is no hero in Jumièges' account, rather the criminal king of the St Brice day massacre of the Danes in England, an event so detestable that even pagans were shocked by it.[25] William of Jumièges wrote at the monastery of Jumièges, where Archbishop Robert, the man outlawed from England in 1052, lived until his death in 1055. Robert's memories of England were mixed, and this Æthelred may be part of the tale told by Robert of the misdeeds of the people who had expelled him. It was perhaps from Robert that William had the story of the murder of Alfred, at once the tragic fate of a young man reared at the Norman court, and also the terrible deed of which Robert accused Godwine in 1051.[26] But Alfred's mother Emma had little place in Robert's tale. In the Norman narratives written in the 1050s, she is the mother of Edward the Confessor; and the link which leads to Edward's return to England at Harthacnut's request;[27] but she played no active part.

The role Emma had been given was, however, easily adaptable to the justification of the Norman Conquest of 1066. By the mid 1070s if not before the Normans had perfected the case to be read before the bar of late eleventh-century opinion. It is fully expounded by William of Poitiers. Emma's part is small, but now explicitly bound into the Norman case. The daughter of Richard I, she was also the *genitrix*, the blood-mother, of Edward the Confessor and Alfred,[28] and the origin of William the Conqueror's blood claim. 'If a claim by blood (*ratio sanguinis*) be sought, it should be noted that King Edward was linked by the closest consanguinity to the son (i.e. William) of Duke Robert, whose aunt was Emma, sister of Richard II, daughter of Richard I, the genitrix of Edward.'[29] Emma had a brief incarnation as the independent-minded queen Semiramis, but she entered the official Norman story to glorify the

---

[23] Ibid Bk IV cap 18 and Bk V cap 8.

[24] Ibid Bk V cap 6 and cap 4.

[25] Ibid Bk V caps 6 and 7. Depending on whether William reworked this after 1066, it may also be a further justification of a conquest of a criminous people; the St Brice massacre is specifically cited as justification of Swein's conquest of 1013. Jumièges may also here betray the influence of Northern sources; he elsewhere takes a line closer to them than to English ones, see below, n 73.

[26] Ibid Bk VII caps 5 and 6 and cf 16 where Jumièges brings his two stories together.

[27] Ibid Bk V cap 8 and VII cap 6.

[28] William of Poitiers, p 2, Æthelred is the *genitor* – the terms with their emphasis on biological birth and inheritance are not casually chosen.

[29] Ibid p 220–2.

dukes, and stayed to legitimize the king-duke, however dubiously. This is Emma, the origin of the Norman Conquest, the conduit through which Norman blood and ultimately Norman dukes entered England and its story.

Whilst the Norman narratives of 1066 rendered Emma ever more passive, they brought Edith to life. The *Song of the Battle of Hastings* tells of the battle and its immediate aftermath.[30] After the victory at Hastings William extended his conquest town by town. In some he inspired terror, but when it came to Winchester, held by Edith as her dower, his approach was more tempered. Judging that it would be a disgrace to take it from her, he asked only for tribute and loyalty.[31] Edith debated his offers and sent the keys and tribute. Edith is an occasion to stress William's kingly attributes of mercy and justice. William of Poitiers also presents an active Edith, both as sister of Harold and widow of Edward. Utterly unlike her brother in her way of life, she fought against him in an appropriately feminine way with pleas and counsel. She preferred that the English be ruled by William, whom her husband had made his heir. Poitiers uses Harold's family relationships to blacken him: he is the murderer of his own brother Tostig, rejected by his own sister, Edith. As Edward's widow, she bore the wishes of her husband, who had adopted William, the wise, just and strong, to succeed him.[32] Edith came to life only to be a part of Norman justifications for 1066. The resulting pro-Norman English queen must be treated with the caution all aspects of the Norman case require. Yet that case is intriguingly suggestive. The widow's extension of her husband's identity had to be accorded full recognition. The feminine woman incapable of arms who confronted Harold became the woman of 'virile discretion' when she preferred William as ruler of the English. In her active recognition of William's claims she must display manly attributes; only such a sex change could resolve the conundrum of female passivity and a woman's action. The bald English stories often contented themselves with women's identities, leaving us to tease out their content. The elaborate Norman defence sometimes required female action and motivation, revealing both the power and the contradictions of these gendered identities. In doing so they beg questions about the silences which normally enshroud Emma's or Edith's activity, inviting attempts to unmask it. They serve as a reminder that the contradictions which faced chroniclers when presenting women's action, faced Emma and Edith throughout their political lives.

---

[30] There has been much debate over the date of the *Carmen*, but see now van Houts 1989, arguing persuasively for Lent–Autumn 1067 and vindicating Guy of Amiens' authorship.
[31] *Carmen*, p 40.
[32] William of Poitiers, p 166.

3 Post-1066 Narratives

After 1066 all stories of the earlier eleventh century were overcast by the knowledge of the Norman Conquest to come. The Norman stories of which Emma and Edith were a part changed little after 1066. As the stories of the battle and its justification became less detailed, Edith disappeared, and Emma remained only as the passive link-woman of marriage politics.[33] But as the English told and retold the story of the eleventh century in response to 1066, both women were caught up in the analyses.

The reporting of Edith's own death was affected by these responses. It can scarcely have seemed a coincidence to the fatalistic English Chronicler that the death of 'the Lady . . . King Edward's wife' in 1075 ended a year which had seen the fall of the last surviving great English noble, Earl Waltheof.[34] In the early twelfth century, John of Worcester noted her death with a mixture of nostalgia and defiance; she was 'sister of King Harold, former Queen of the English'. Pro-Harold Worcester defiantly remembered her as the sister of *King* Harold, as did Henry of Huntingdon in the East Midlands in the 1130s.[35] But English memories of Edith and the Norman Conquest were mixed. John of Worcester, or his English sources, placed her at the beginning of the chain of events which led ineluctably to Hastings. It was she who engineered the death of the Northumbrian nobles at the southern court, which triggered the Northern rebellion, dividing English resistance in 1066.[36] She did it 'on behalf of her brother Tostig'. Tostig and Edith were associated by the Norman story in the vilification of Harold and the justice of William's claim. After 1066 some English saw these siblings joined in a less holy alliance, with a disastrous outcome. Other narratives linked Edith ever more closely with her father. John of Worcester had already closely identified Edith and Godwine; her fall was explicitly due to the king's wrath against him.[37] Henry of Huntingdon incorporated Edith's marriage into the Norman view of Godwine's plots to control the simple and innocent Edward, and reversed the ages of Edward and Alfred in the process.[38] Godwine planned to marry his daughter to Edward, here the younger son, because he was more guileless; hence Godwine's role in

---

[33] Even in Wace, for example, there is little development of Emma, except a reference to her counsel of Cnut to make Harthacnut king of Denmark, Wace, Vol II lines 4623–7.

[34] *ASC* MSS D and E s.a. 1075 – D calls her Edward's '*geresta*' – not his widow but his wife.

[35] FI Wig s.a. 1075; Henry of Huntingdon, p 192. On Worcester's sympathy with Harold see Mason 1990, pp 65–7, 219–21 and Williams 1995, p 169.

[36] FI Wig s.a. 1065.

[37] FI Wig s.a. 1051.

[38] Henry of Huntingdon, p 191.

the murder of the more belligerent older brother, Alfred. William of Malmesbury suggested that Edward and Edith were childless because Edward extended to his wife his hatred of her family.[39] Godwine and his sons were debatable figures after 1066, and Edith shared some of their fate. The daughter of Godwine, Lady of the English and widow of the pro-Norman Edward was an ambiguous figure. Edith remained useful to the Normans. William of Malmesbury told of Edith's death largely to stress William the Conqueror's piety, and in particular his respect for the marriage bond, which had been called into question.[40] But elsewhere his Edith is prophetic; she foretold the death of Walcher of Durham, tall and ruddy-faced, he would make a 'beautiful martyr'.[41] If there are hints of a cult here, it is difficult to know whether it is Norman, English or both. Edith was certainly undergoing romanticization if not sanctification in some late eleventh- and early twelfth-century English hands. John of Worcester added poignancy to the story of her exile to Wherwell by having her sent there with but 'one maidservant, and without honour'.[42] Edith carried blame for the Conquest but she could still express English feeling.

Emma, by contrast, became firmly linked with the Normans and the Conquest. Eadmer remembered her as the sister of Richard of Normandy and noted her death before the return of Godwine and the sending of hostages to William of Normandy. For him Harold's ill-fated quest to free the hostages precipitated William's Conquest; what little he remembered of Emma was chiefly in connection with their despatch into Norman custody. Orderic Vitalis and Henry of Huntingdon in the twelfth century explicitly made Emma the origin of the Norman Conquest. The English-born Orderic echoed Eadmer's sense of English outrage. When Mathilda daughter of Henry I went to Germany to marry the emperor's son, she was accompanied by many Normans, who hoped through the union to rise to the height of power in the Roman Empire and to acquire the highest dignities for themselves. 'Thus their predecessors in England had dominated through Emma, daughter of Duke Richard, and in Apulia had oppressed the genuine heirs through Sichelgaita daughter of Gaimar duke of Salerno.'[43] For Orderic the marriage led to oppression and, by association, to the dispossession of true heirs. Wise men, like the emperor, sent such camp followers packing. Orderic's position, half English

---

[39] William of Malmesbury, *DGRA*, Bk 2 cap 197, Vol I p 239; Roger of Wendover later reinterpreted Edward's action, or inaction, in the light of a thirteenth-century view of the dignity of monarchy: Edward would not have wished to produce heirs from the blood of a traitor to corrupt the royal seed, vol I, p 588.

[40] William of Malmesbury, *DGRA*, Bk 3 cap 273, Vol II p 332.

[41] Ibid Bk 3 cap 271, vol II p 331.

[42] FI Wig s.a. 1051.

[43] Orderic Vitalis, vol VI, Book 11 cap 38, pp 166–8.

half Norman, and a twelfth-century monk to boot, made him peculiarly sensitive to marriage, to marriage as the transfer of inheritance and as a type of conquest, though it failed to make him aware of the difficult position into which such unions could place a woman like Emma. Henry of Huntingdon was equally sure of the significance of the marriage, but more convinced of the justice of its final outcome. He divided Æthelred's reign between two books. Book Six told the story of the Norman Conquest and its origins; and Emma's marriage to Æthelred inaugurates it. With a union aimed to alleviate problems with the Danes, the English king merely set in train the inexorable series of events which led to 1066: 'from this union of a king of the English and a daughter of the duke, the Normans ... claimed and acquired England.' Henry's view of the Conquest and thus of Emma was still coloured by a 'lingering perception of ... the down-trodden English, oppressed by the French',[44] though for him the Norman claim and acquisition was just 'according to the law of peoples (*ius gentium*)'.[45] Emma was an essentially Norman woman in these accounts; the jewel of the Normans, a wife and mother of kings at her death, but also a Norman-born woman.[46] In many eyes, 1066 drove a wedge between Emma and her English identities. William of Malmesbury was a sophisticated historian, an interpreter of events, a teller of many tales not merely of one. His Emma is a complex figure whose significance for the English he understood. Cnut married her to placate the English, precisely because of her meaning to them. Whilst offering obedience to their accustomed 'Lady', they might be less inclined to sigh under Danish domination.[47] But the Emma who predominates in Malmesbury's judgements was never truly English: never attached to her philandering and idle English husband, and even worse, transferring her hatred of him to her English sons; ready to abandon the memory of her husband, and tolerate the exile of her sons to warm herself in the bed of him who had attacked the one and put to flight the other; a clear partisan of Harthacnut and her Danish family in 1035.[48] Such judgements were easily built on the bald annals of the earlier English chroniclers; Malmesbury was too good a historian to force his evidence. But judgements they were, and Malmesbury may here echo wider English feeling against Emma in the wake of 1066.

---

[44] Gillingham 1995, p 89.
[45] Henry of Huntingdon, p 173. This section of Henry, and Emma's marriage, had a curious after-life as a late medieval prophetic text, in which guise it is found in Oxford Bodleian, MS Fairfax 20 and College of Arms MS Arundel XXIX. I am grateful to Lesley Coote for bringing this to my attention and providing the references.
[46] Henry of Huntingdon, pp 174 and 193.
[47] William of Malmesbury, *DGRA*, Bk II cap 181, Vol I, p 219.
[48] Ibid, Bk II cap 165, Vol I, p 191; cap 180, p 218; cap 196, p 237.

Yet Emma's English identity lived on after 1066 in a different type of narrative. When the story of the English eleventh century and its conquests was replaced by or merged with those of individual religious houses and of royal patronage, a different woman emerged. The Conquest forged in a man like Eadmer a fierce English feeling. When he remembered Emma in relation to 1066, he could see only the Norman woman. But when at the Council of Bari he saw the bishop of Benevento wearing a cloak of splendid English work, his pride led him to recall another Emma, the great and powerful queen of the English, whose reputation for generosity to the church brought suppliants to her court even from Italy itself.[49] His reaction to 1066 placed the same woman differently depending on whether the dominant feeling was of bitter regret or defiant pride; there was some of the same contradiction in John of Worcester's views of Edith.

These men reacted to Emma and Edith not only as Englishmen after 1066, but as monks. Chronicles of religious houses, telling of their vicissitudes and of the patronage they received, had their own narratives and created their own roles. The heroes were the patron saints, their houses and the successful defenders of those houses; the villains their despoilers. The laity attracted praise or censure depending on whether they gave to or took from particular houses. The sharper lay/clerical distinctions by the twelfth century accentuated this and the dead were especially open to stereotyping and remoulding to suit current needs. Emma and Edith were remembered in these largely monastic tales, Emma on the whole as a great patroness, Edith in more dubious guise. Abingdon told contradictory stories of Edith. In one she was a queen, a courteous and refined lady, who was moved by the meagre rations she observed the children eating to give the abbey land from which their morning food could be provided. She enters a story which is essentially one of disputed land as a royal benefactor, a *coup de grace* against objectors to the abbey's holdings; but the twelfth-century monastic storyteller could not resist portraying her as an elegant laywoman with little understanding of the primitive rigours of the monastic calling.[50] Abingdon also remembered her as an imperious Lady who came to take away their treasures.[51] The Conquest, its deprivations and disputes, is the background of both tales. This is house history, essentially in-house history, spawning and tolerating internal contradiction as readily as did the divided response to 1066.

The post-1066 stories take us further from the lives of Emma and Edith, and subject both to increasingly anachronistic judgements which

---

[49] Eadmer, *Historia Novorum*, p 107ff.
[50] *Chron Abing*, vol I, pp 459–61; '*urbana*' is the word I have translated as 'courteous, refined, elegant'.
[51] *Chron Abing*, vol I, p 485.

must be used with caution, if at all. They are not, however, irrelevant to an understanding of those lives. The woman who is both patron and despoiler reveals the politics of giving and of clientage.[52] The woman who was Norman daughter, English queen and Danish wife had different meanings in life as well as in death, easily masked by celebratory descriptions of her as 'wife and mother of kings'.

It was not merely reaction to 1066 and the imperatives of monastic history which shaped the twelfth-century Emma and Edith. Chivalric Romance was another twelfth-century genre. In Emma, than whom there could be no fairer woman,[53] in the beautiful young Edith,[54] we meet its stock faces. Chroniclers who wrote in this vein often stood closer to lay practice than their monastic counterparts. They were often more sensitive to court practice and readier to admit women to the accepted role of wifely counsellor.[55] Wace has Emma counsel in favour of sending Harthacnut to rule Denmark.[56] Gaimar elaborates Emma's counsel in a story of a good and loving mother, fearful that the obviously rightful claims of Edward and Alfred will be overridden, who advises Cnut to dispose of, though not to harm, the other surviving sons of Æthelred.[57] But neither Wace nor Gaimar elaborate much on either woman: it is Ælfthryth, Emma's mother-in-law, not Emma or Edith, whom Gaimar develops.[58] It is, however, to a late twelfth-century chivalric chronicler, Richard of Devizes, that we owe the most famous later development of Emma's story and one of the fullest accounts of Emma or Edith.

Richard is the source of the tale of Emma and the burning plough-shares. Writing at the end of the twelfth century, Richard was interested in the court, marriage and queens. In the *Annals of Winchester* he extended that interest back to the eleventh century, to Emma,[59] or more correctly to Emma-and-Edith, since Richard tells a tale in which the fall of both queens has run together.[60] Richard's Emma was a powerful

---

[52] See below pp 148–52 for further comment on patronage and the representation of patrons, and particularly of Emma and Edith in relation to 1066.

[53] Gaimar, line 4202 on Emma.

[54] Wace, Vol II, line 4742 on Edith.

[55] Roger of Wendover also had Emma as a counsellor, developing Malmesbury's points about Emma's role in reconciling the English into her specific advice to Cnut to send back his fleet and mercenaries, vol I, pp 548 and 550; in this he was followed in the fourteenth century by Richard of Cirencester, pp 176–7.

[56] Wace, Vol II, line 4623ff.

[57] Gaimar, lines 4481ff and 4523ff.

[58] On Gaimar's and other stories of Ælfthryth, Wright 1939, Bell 1926, Freeman 1875, and Stafford 1993.

[59] Appleby 1963 on date and authorship, and Gransden 1974, pp 248–51 on Richard's interest in court life, and especially in women. Ælfthryth, for example, is given detailed treatment here.

[60] Freeman, vol 2, Note H, 2nd ed, pp 569–71 developing this point.

woman, regent for Cnut during his absence.[61] On Cnut's death she was forced into exile by Harold, only to return, as in other stories, with Harthacnut. In the troubles of these years no one spoke of Edward and Alfred 'because neither did their mother herself'.[62] Godwine, knowing of her lack of feelings for her sons, and planning the accession of his own son Harold, tempted Alfred back to England and murdered him. Meanwhile Emma stayed at Winchester, content with her son who was reigning, and intent on her dalliance with Ælfwine, bishop of Winchester, a familiarity which so absorbed her that she neither wept for the death of one son, Alfred, nor cared for the fate of the other, Edward. She ruled alongside Harthacnut, and at his death endowed Winchester in his memory. With her consent the care of the kingdom was given to Godwine. Edward, bereft of help in Normandy where the dukes were dead and the young William staying with the French king, and without hope of help from his mother, decided to approach his manifest enemy. In return for a promise that he would marry Godwine's daughter and maintain his power, Edward was helped by Godwine to the throne. For his mother he felt no affection, though nor did he yet act openly against her. The innocent king fell under the influence of Archbishop Robert, who established such an ascendancy that Edward would have believed that a black crow was white if Robert had told him so. Together he and Robert plotted the fall of Godwine, the deprivation of Emma and the exile of her and the bishop, she from court to Wherwell, he beyond the boundaries of Winchester. Emma's imprisonment was lax. From it she could write to the bishops of England, presenting herself as a wronged mother attacked by her son, a queen attacked by a king who had also laid his hand upon the lord's anointed.[63] The bishops were won over, but not Robert. He spoke of a mother who was a wild beast not a woman, who consented to the death of Alfred and plotted the poisoning of Edward himself, and who named her own paramour as the lord's anointed. She might be allowed to clear herself, but only by walking barefoot over nine burning ploughshares, four for herself and five for the bishop, the ordeal to be carried out in the cathedral at Winchester itself. Should she succeed Robert would take on all guilt and be deprived of honour.

The story builds to its dramatic climax on the floor of the cathedral. From all over England great crowds gathered; the king and his great men assembled, only Robert was missing, feigning illness and poised at Dover ready to flee. The queen was brought from Wherwell the day before, and spent a prayerful vigil before the tomb of St Swithun. During her wakeful night she slept long enough for the saint to appear to her and promise his aid. Next morning she was brought before her son, and invoked God as witness to her innocence. Putting aside her outer garments, she was led by two weeping bishops to the burning ploughshares. The crowds wailed and called upon St Swithun. Emma prayed to the God who liberated Susannah and the children in the fiery furnace; then walked across without harm, hurt or sensation. Edward fell prostrate and begged her forgiveness. He was beaten by the rods of the bishops, and given three blows by his sorrowing mother. The bishop and queen were restored, the tears of the crowd turned to laughter, and both queen and bishop rendered due recognition to the role of St Swithun in their deliverance by each granting him nine manors, one for each ploughshare.

The story is far from any simple record of eleventh-century events.[64] The Emma delivered by prayers to St Swithun is a more dramatic form of the Emma who had called on St Mildrith in Goscelin's late eleventh-century Canterbury story. She too had been restored by a saint's intervention after a false accusation, in this case of attempting to aid Magnus of Norway in a bid for the English throne.[65] Swithun and Mildrith were English saints saving an English queen. At Winchester, where Richard wrote, some elements of accusations against Emma or Edith in 1043 or 1051 may have been preserved. But they are preserved in a story which brings together eleventh-century facts[66] and twelfth-century romanticization with hagiographical traditions into a somewhat inconsistent tale of false accusation and innocence exonerated. There are stock elements from earlier stories, like Godwine's guilt; stock elements of the story of queens, adultery with court bishops if not burning ploughshares,[67] and both were combined with post-Conquest stories of the English saints. This strange tale is a final reminder of how little trace

[64] It has no internal historical coherence, mixing together the events and contemporaries of 1043 (Emma and Ælfwine) with those of 1051 (Godwine and Robert); for scepticism concerning it see e.g. Freeman, vol 2, Note H, 2nd ed and Harmer, *Writs*, p 384 and n 1.
[65] Goscelin, *Translation*, pp 176–8.
[66] At least four of the ploughshare manors can be associated independently with Emma or Edith: Hayling Island, Wargrave, Wycombe, Edith's man held Sewell attached to the royal manor of Houghton, and if *Bergefeld* is Burghfield, it too was queen's land, see Appendices 1 and 2, including Wulfweard. Hayling Island was a subject of long dispute, as was Wargrave, which was granted to the Old Minster by Stephen and Henry II, see Harmer 1938, pp 349–51; this may provide a context for some details of the story. Such agreement with known eleventh-century queens' lands argues more than coincidence. There was more than one version of the story. The *Annals of Winchester* did not know the name of the manors and left a blank. The names were, however, entered in an abbreviated version, without speeches, found in the fifteenth century in Thomas Rudbourne's *Historia Major Wintoniensis*, p 235.
[67] For accusations of queens see Stafford 1983; Cunigund, wife of Emperor Henry II, is alleged in the late twelfth-century lives concerned with her canonization to have cleared herself by walking over burning ploughshares: *Lexikon des Mittelalters*, vol 5, p 1571 and Folz 1992, pp 82–93 at p 87. Richard of Devizes is a contemporary and this may be the

Emma or Edith's political activity left in the narratives of the eleventh and twelfth centuries. Whether at Winchester or in Kent it was the attacks on both queens which captured the eleventh- and twelfth-century imagination. The dramas of their lives could still inspire writers a century and more after their deaths; dramas not of their exercise of power, but of their fall from it.

4 Northern Narratives

The eleventh-century Norman and English stories became the building blocks of later English history. A third set of eleventh-century narratives, the Northern and Scandinavian ones, did not.[68] Scandinavian political rule in England did not survive the eleventh century; these stories would not be incorporated into the tale of the English eleventh century in the way that Norman ones were. But during the first half of the eleventh century Scandinavian involvement in England was far more significant than Norman. From surviving Northern fragments it is clear that Emma played a part, albeit a restricted one, in the Northern narratives of the first conquest of eleventh-century England, that of England by the Danes.

Like the Normans after 1066, the Danes after 1016 celebrated and justified their conquest. The English battles of Æthelred's reign, and especially the siege and later taking of London were important in Northern celebration, and news of them spread to their German neighbours. It is in London that Emma makes her first appearance. Thietmar of Merseburg had heard of events in London within a year or so of 1017.[69] His Emma is a queen worn down by attack, suing for peace only to be offered the grim choice between the lives of her companions and those of her sons. The queen's predicament, the threats of murder and ransoms were part of this German chronicler's condemnation of the Danish Swein and his evil brood. For later native Scandinavian kings' sagas and contemporary skalds, battles and seige were the glory and also the testing

source of his story. However, Richardis, wife of the ninth-century Emperor Charles the Fat, also offered to clear herself by walking over burning ploughshares, Regino of Prum, *MGH Scriptores* I, p 597. Her cult revived in the mid eleventh century and her bones were translated in 1049. Such stories could thus have been current in Emma's and Edith's lifetimes, though the surviving eleventh- and twelfth-century records of the cult had lost all reference to the ploughshares, Folz 1992, pp 50–1.

[68] Apart from Adam of Bremen and Thietmar, none of the Northern sources which include Emma survive in works older than the end of the twelfth century. But the skaldic verse they preserve dates back to Cnut's own reign, and the kings' sagas arguably have a long oral tradition behind them, see A. Campbell 1971, Frank 1994, Poole 1987. On the dating of the historical sources and the kings' sagas see Kristjánsson 1992 and especially Anderson 1985.

[69] Thietmar of Merseburg, Bk VII caps 36–43, esp cap 40.

point of Northern heroes, and London and its Lady had a different significance. In the skaldic verse sung at Cnut's court Emma was an unnamed and enigmatic 'chaste widow' within the stones of London, who watched Cnut attack it, '(to see) how the Danish leader, eager for victory, valiantly assails the city's garrison. . . . each morning on the bank of the Thames, the lady sees swords stained with blood.'[70] In later tellings, she attempted to escape the city, and was captured and brought to Cnut, sometimes by his followers, sometimes by Jarl Thorkell.[71] This story had no place for Emma the dominant dowager.[72] Here Emma appears as the female witness of male valour, as part of the prize and loot of victory, and also of the exchange of women by which peace was secured. In all versions Emma, London and the final stages of English resistance are closely related.[73] We do not have to accept all the meanings given to that association to see that Emma, like London, was important to English and Danes alike in 1016, even to allow that her presence there may have been significant.

In the sober pages of Northern chroniclers, marriage and peace and the links made through marriage were where Emma fitted. For Adam of Bremen Cnut took Emma along with the kingdom, and as the sister of the count of Normandy. Cnut exchanged women with Richard, giving the count his sister Margaret (Estrith) and taking Emma, as pledge of the peace between them, and as a way of making English and Normans more faithful to the Danes.[74] Adam's chronology of Estrith's marriages is wrong, but it was a mistake necessitated by his recurring view of the use of women to bind peace; Gunnhild, the daughter of Cnut and Emma who married Henry III, was given as a pledge of friendship between Conrad and Cnut.[75] Like William of Jumièges, Adam viewed women and marriage as part of an understanding and explanation of history in dynastic terms. Emma is mentioned in a series of marriages by which Adam elucidates the links between England, Normandy and Denmark through the unions of Cnut, Richard of Normandy, Emma, Estrith, Ulf and Godwine. It is an authentic eleventh-century view of marriage and its political role, one which is essential to an understand-

---

[70] In Liðsmannaflokkr, printed Poole, 1987, pp 282–3.
[71] *Knytlinga Saga*, p 107 cap 9; and Supplement to Jómsvikinga saga, printed *Encomium*, pp 92–3.
[72] Frank 1994, p 112 suggests that in this role she 'did not go over big with the housecarls'.
[73] Outside Scandinavia and Germany, the only source to place Emma in London and to relate her capture to that of the city is William of Jumièges. It is tempting to link his interpretation to these Northern tales, perhaps available in Normandy in the eleventh century. Cf van Houts 1983, p 117, pointing out that only Jumièges, Adam of Bremen and the *Encomium Emmae* record the struggle for power in Denmark which succeeded Swein's death. See also above n 25.
[74] Adam of Bremen, Bk 2 cap 54, pp 114–15.
[75] Ibid cap 56, pp 116–17.

ing of the lives of Emma and Edith even if it fails to elucidate the powers
and problems of the women thus exchanged.

Emma lived on in Scandinavian history in this guise, as a genealogical
marker.[76] She served to place Harthacnut in the events after 1035 and to
stress his legitimacy.[77] She helped explain the choice of Edward over
Estrith's son Swein in 1042.[78] But she is scarcely more significant than her
daughter Gunnhild, whose marriage to an emperor's son reflected glory
on the Danish dynasty. The succession struggle which gave Emma such
importance in the English stories was even more irrelevant to the Danes
than to the Normans. And in the North, as with the Normans, the
passage of time saw her recede more and more. Her motherhood was
extended to include earlier sons of Æthelred,[79] and became so all-
embracing that even her arch-rival Harold Harefoot became her own
son.[80] Once the link in a dynastic net, who explained its complicated
patterns, she was now a convenient parent under whose skirts its intrica-
cies could be swept by writers to whose narratives such complications
were no longer relevant.

Ironically it was Emma's female rival, Ælfgifu of Northampton,
whose memory stayed green, or rather black, in the North. She was
already the tyrannical ruler of Norway in eleventh-century skaldic
verse.[81] Saga gave her and her son responsibility for harsh Danish rule in
Norway. Though suggesting that the blame was unfairly heaped on
Ælfgifu alone, St Olaf's saga nonetheless cast her in the role of Doubting
Woman. When St Olaf's preserved body was disinterred, it is she who
demanded that it be put to the proof of fire.[82] Ælfgifu was remembered
in the North as a female ruler, however unflatteringly; traces of Emma in
that guise are rare. Olaf's saga places Emma behind the ill-judged actions
of Ulf and Harthacnut in the 1020s.[83] She had supposedly written and
surreptitiously sealed the letter allegedly from Cnut by which Ulf urged
Harthacnut to take the title of King, thereby provoking the attack of the
kings of Norway and Sweden on his weakness. She afterwards acted as
a mediator between son and father, advising Harthacnut to bow to his

---

[76] E.g. Saxo Grammaticus, Bk 10 cap 14, p 28, derived from Adam of Bremen, see Saxo,
ed Christiansen, p 169 n 99.
[77] Adam of Bremen, cap 74, p 134 – Adam distinguishes the birth of Harold Harefoot and
Swein as sons of a concubine, whereas Harthacnut is the son of a *regina*.
[78] Ibid cap 78, p 136; cf Saxo, Bk 10 cap 21, pp 46–7.
[79] *Historia Norwegiae*, p 123 makes her Edmund's mother, as does *St Olaf's Saga*,
p 129.
[80] She is not even mentioned by Sven Aggeson; *St Olaf's Saga*, p 133 makes Harold as well
as Gunnhild and Harthacnut her children.
[81] *Agrip*, pp 32–3, and cf Theodric the monk, cap 21, pp 44–5.
[82] *St Olaf's Saga*, pp 385–6 and 388–9.
[83] *St Olaf's Saga*, pp 305ff.

father's wishes. All this is a prelude to the battle of the Holy River,[84] and Emma is usefully positioned as an interfering woman whose actions precipitate trouble, just as Edith stood at the origin of the Northern revolt for John of Worcester. But no other memory, however distorted, of Emma as an active queen survived in the North. It is unfortunate that Cnut's saga, if it ever existed, has not survived; with it has gone even a late twelfth- or thirteenth-century reworking of a king's story in which Emma might have featured,[85] though there is no reason to feel that it would have centred Emma in this role. Her rival Ælfgifu ruled in the North as a regent, and left a memory accordingly. There is little to suggest that Emma was ever active there, and English internal politics were of little concern to the Northern stories. It is the Norman Conquest, with its marginalization of Cnut's reign and its aftermath in the *English* historical story, which has deprived us of any detailed memory of Emma as ruler or regent.

* * *

The annals of pre-1066 England are sparse, and references to women in them even sparser. Where fuller narratives blossom, Emma and Edith did appear, though often fleetingly, Edith an even rarer bird of passage than Emma. The everyday workings of power and politics were largely ignored and detailed narratives were usually provoked by crises. It is only in relation to these that either woman was mentioned. Reference to them was sometimes to heighten narrative effect, and the appearances of both are determined by stories to which they are rarely central. Such sources invite us to fill the gaps, to recast the stories with women's own priorities. Already, however, these chronicles indicate that Emma if not Edith played a part in the crises of eleventh-century politics, which often centred on family and succession. To contemporaries their marriages appeared significant, and the links and alliances they embodied important. They were described through identities as daughter, wife, mother and widow which require further consideration. Even when used for dramatic effect, their dignity and standing is revealed; to run out a Queen into the bleak winter or send a consecrated woman from court was a drama not merely because of woman's vulnerability, but because of royal women's status. And by the last stages of her life Emma was of sufficient

---

[84] On which see e.g. Lawson 1993, pp 96–9, Sawyer 1994, pp 18–19.

[85] *Knytlinga Saga*, which may be based in part on it, belongs to the second half of the thirteenth century, Kristjánsson p 164. It has also been argued that the appendix to the Jomsviking saga in the fourteenth-century Icelandic Flateyjarbók and printed by A. Campbell as an Appendix to the *Encomium*, pp 92–3, may contain stories which descend from this lost saga, Poole 1987, p 291.

moment for the crises of *her* career to count as the crises of eleventh-century English politics, grave enough to move even the laconic annalists to detailed comment.

The Norman sources presented a simpler picture. Emma left Normandy to marry and Edith crossed into Norman sights only briefly in 1066; neither woman was central to Norman writers. Emma was important only for the dynastic links and glory she brought, though those links took on a new significance in and after 1066. Oddly, some Norman sources present both women more actively than the early English chronicles. In neither case was this female activity described for its own sake or in its own context, but to justify or criticize male actors. When women are used as part of male-centred narratives the actions they are allotted require careful scrutiny. Nonetheless female action, even independence, was thinkable, and we are encouraged to test its possibility, nature and purposes in a narrative constructed around these women themselves.

The Scandinavian sources often echo the Norman in placing Emma within their concern with marriage and dynastic glorification. Both shared the eleventh-century appreciation of marriage politics. For Northern writers Emma was a remote English queen whose Scandinavian line died with Harthacnut and had little other call on their attention. They do, however, offer a brief glimpse of another Emma of 1016, the embattled woman in the city. Along with the wilful Norman Semiramis, and the Anglo-Saxon Chronicler's English queen, this was a third face of Emma in 1016–17. Whether there were more, and how they come together, remains to be seen.

After 1066 Emma and Edith were developed in different directions as later writers lamented, justified or explained 1066, repositioning the generations before that great event in relation to it. An English queen, an evil earl's daughter, a saint's wife, a hero's sister, a greedy predator, a prophetic woman, Edith appeared in many guises. Emma lost her English name and much of her English identity, though not as a great patroness; she did not always attract greater affection in the process. The Scandinavian dynasty of which she had been a part sank into relative insignificance in the eleventh-century story, and her bids for regency and power became irrelevant. Distance permitted rather more recognition of the dilemmas of motherhood and revealed more of the ambiguities of a wife's position, but little was added to the detailed political lives of either woman. The perennial interest in the personal dramas of royalty, the sex-lives of the great and the special vulnerability of women combined to produce a final romanticized picture. Significantly in it Emma and Edith have merged and drawn in elements of ninth- and eleventh-century empresses to become a composite, half fairy-tale 'Queen'.

At the end of the eleventh century Godfrey, prior of Winchester, wrote celebratory poems on Emma and Edith. He wrote within living memory of both and at Winchester, the place where they were most likely to have been remembered, a church closely connected with them and the Old English dynasty, their own dower borough.[86] His assessents of both are adulatory, yet significantly different. Emma is a resplendent gem, a mother of kings, a wife of kings, illustrious in her royal offspring; as honourable in manners as her ancestors, virtuous in speech, pious in mind, generous of hand; she piled treasures above the stars, pursued justice, protected the church. She is, in fact, the Emma whom the stories have led us to recognize; identified through her marriages, her ancestry and her children, royal, rich and a great patroness, though her justice and speech hint at aspects of her activity the stories have obscured. Edith too is made great by the nobility of her forefathers, though her royal marriage in turn magnifies them. Here again is an Edith for whom we are prepared, identified by paternity and marriage. But Edith is praised especially for her character and learning: she is beautiful, but also wise, of high reputation and prudent. If Emma piled riches to the stars, Edith has knowledge of them through astronomy; she is learned in measures, numbers, music, grammar and languages. Conspicuous by their absence are the speech, justice and protection of the church which hinted at Emma's activity. But in her learning this is an Edith whom we would not expect; unless we had paid particular attention to William of Malmesbury or gone on to consult the fourteenth-century chronicler Richard of Cirencester. Rather, unless, like them, we had read another story – Edith's own.

---

[86] Godfrey of Winchester, pp 148–9. He was prior of Winchester 1082–1107.

2

Emma's and Edith's Narratives

Emma and Edith have both left their own narratives of the eleventh century, or at least of parts of it. The so-called *Encomium Emmae Reginae* and the *Life of King Edward who Rests at Westminster* are works closely associated with these two queens. They were dedicated to them, they appear to have been commissioned by them, and in both cases the writers seem to have worked closely with the queen concerned. Neither work is in any sense an autobiography; neither places the queen herself centre stage, though Emma comes to dominate the *Encomium*'s later sections, and Edith as queen is one of the most important characters of the *Life*.[1] Both authors make it clear that they praise the queen through those connected with her. These two works speak with the voices of Emma and Edith, albeit through the mediation of their clerical authors. To understand them fully would require a study of eleventh-century historical writing which is beyond the scope of this work, but the stories constructed and the narrative choices made are nonetheless instructive. They offer rare opportunities to see the eleventh century through the eyes of politically active women.[2]

1 The *Encomium Emmae Reginae*: The Encomium of Queen Emma

The *Encomium* was written by a Flemish monk in 1041/2, during the reign of Harthacnut, and after Edward's recall to England. For Emma

---

[1] The section of the *Life* describing Edith has been lost. Barlow's edition reconstructs it from later writers, in his 2nd ed especially from Richard of Cirencester. There may have been more about Edith than appears from such reconstructions. But the lost section, even if entirely devoted to her, would not make her dominant in the work as a whole.

[2] Most commentators have been agreed on the closeness of e.g. the *Encomium* to Emma: A. Campbell, *Encomium*, pp xxi–xxiii, for whom Book 3 especially is 'entirely Emma's point of view', the characters of the *Encomium* reveal 'exactly how the persons in question appeared to Emma and her party'. The information the Flemish author had about English affairs and people must have been given to him by the queen herself, cf John 1980–1, p 65 where he is 'uncommonly well informed', the view of events even more so.

this was a point of triumph, if not a height of power as the mother of kings. The *Encomium* ends with a celebration of Emma, Harthacnut and Edward in a trinity of rule, united by fraternal and maternal love.[3] That image does not simply describe reality; it was designed to conjure it. The death of Cnut had ushered in a struggle for the throne, a rapid succession of regencies and brief reigns, and the death of a prince. The legacy by 1041 was a mood of suspicion and recrimination in which Emma was enmired. The relationship of the half brothers, Harthacnut and Edward, like Emma's own maternal history, was fraught with questions. She had been the mother of three of the claimants on the English throne, including the dead Alfred, and her erstwhile ally Earl Godwine was implicated in Alfred's death and openly accused of his murder. Emma's situation was precarious, threatened and difficult. By 1041 two of her sons were ruling jointly in England, but it was far from clear what the future would bring for them or their mother. The *Encomium* was meant to influence that future, through a version of the past which met the questions of the present. It was aimed at her sons, and more widely at the great men of the English. It was a political work, from a political woman in the thick of politics.[4]

The *Encomium* begins with an Argument which summarizes its story.[5] Swein, king of the Danes, subjected the kingdom of the English to his rule. As he was dying in 1014, he made his son Cnut his successor in that kingdom. But the English resisted Cnut, and there would perhaps have been no end to the fighting had it not been, with God's grace, for the marriage of this most noble queen. By her Cnut had a son, Harthacnut, to whom he gave during his own lifetime control of all he had. At Cnut's death Harthacnut was absent from England, securing the kingdom of the Danes. His absence allowed an unnamed and unjust invader (Harold) to enter his boundaries, take the kingdom and then kill the king's (Harthacnut's) brother (Alfred) in an act of unspeakable betrayal. Divine vengeance followed, striking down the impious, restoring the kingdom to its rightful owner. Harthacnut, obedient in all things to the counsels of

---

[3] *Encomium*, p 52.

[4] I agree with John 1980–1, Körner 1964 and M. Campbell 1979 that the work has some contemporary purpose, and a political nature, but unlike Körner and Campbell do not see it aimed against anyone, except Harold I, already dead; cf Lindquist 1967 against Körner on this same point. Searle 1989 sees it more as a praise poem, but makes Emma central to it. As will become clear I agree with John and Körner on the political nature of the work, but like Searle feel that Emma herself is the key. I would go further than any of them in seeing her as essential to the coherence and argument of the work, resolving the confusion which A. Campbell, p xxi saw in it. Lifshitz's view, 1989, that the work was written over a period from 1039 onwards and thus reflects several different aims takes due account of the different angles in the work, but introduces an unnecessary complication; those angles are united, I shall argue, in Emma herself.

[5] *Encomium*, pp 6–8.

his mother, then held it 'imperially' and increased its riches. And in his outstanding generosity, he shared its honour and wealth with his brother (Edward), as was fitting. The whole work is, the author states, in praise of Emma; but in order to give to posterity the memory of deeds touching on her honour, he will tell of 'you and yours'.[6] For him, as for Emma, this was how her story should be told.[7] Praise of the family (*genus*) is praise of the person. To Emma and her apologist her story and its justification was bound up with that of her family; her representation was through them and in association with them.

That family was her Danish family of marriage rather than her Norman one of birth. Emma's narrative began not at her birth in Normandy, nor in 1002, at her arrival in England, but in Denmark, in the 980s, and especially in 1013 with Swein's decision to bring a fleet against England in that year. It begins with Swein's ousting of his father Harold c. 987, his decision to invade England, prompted by Thorkell's failure to bring the spoils of his English victories to his lord Swein, and Swein's subsequent arrangements for his sons: Cnut is to accompany him to England while the younger son, Harold, is to remain as ruler of Denmark. Emma's story unfolds within that of the Danish conquest and rule of England. A wife's identity was with the family of her husband and son. Its opening section established that rule, without dwelling in detail on Swein's conquest; he is made to admit that he will not be loved by the English. Cnut is part of that conquest, though a less than whole-hearted supporter. He agrees to accompany his father in his attack, but out of fear of being accused of 'wily sloth' if he opposes. Emma was not merely a wife and mother but a queen, and her story is sympathetic to the English. The story pays apparently unnecessary attention to Swein's accession, to the succession dispute with his father, to Thorkell's actions, the arrangements for rule in Denmark in Swein's absence and to the passing of rule to Cnut in 1014. In fact these are two of Emma's central themes: succession to thrones, and the trustworthiness of should-be loyal king's men. The death of Swein is highlighted, literally, in the manuscript.[8] It is the death of a king, this is an essentially royal tale; and it inaugurates the rule of Cnut, a much more central character for the *Encomium* and for Emma.

Cnut's rule is not easily established. The English remember the unjust invasion of his father, and gather to expel him. He returns to his brother Harold in Denmark in 1014–15. Ensuing events and discussions in Denmark are another apparently extraneous section of Emma's story.[9] They centre on Cnut's claims to the Danish throne and his discusssions with his brother Harold over this. Cnut returns to Denmark in a dis-

[6] Ibid p 4.
[7] Ibid p 6.
[8] With an illuminated, coloured initial, BL Addit 33241 fo 19v.
[9] *Encomium*, 16–22.

tinctly unkingly way, with relatively few followers. Harold treats him well, sends his own followers to escort him so that he can arrive as befits a king, embraces him in a reunion, tearful with memories of their father. Cnut asks that Harold divide the kingdom of the Danes, Cnut's inheritance, with him; then, when they have acquired England, each will choose a kingdom for himself. Harold refuses. Denmark is his inheritance, given him by his father, with Cnut's agreement; he will not countenance division. Cnut listens in silence: God will decide the issue.

1035–42, and especially the recriminations and arguments of 1041, are the key to understanding the way these Danish events are told. The fitting feelings of brother for brother, the treatment of brother by brother were recounted with a view to how the meeting of Harthacnut and Edward in 1041 had been, or how, in Emma's view, it should have been. The division of kingdoms was a recurring, nagging theme in the family politics of Emma's career. Should Harthacnut have divided England with Edward in 1041? Or should they have had a kingdom each, Denmark and England? Should the division of 1016 between Edmund and Cnut have resulted in the rule of the whole by Cnut at Edmund's death in 1016, or should Edmund's brothers, including her own son Edward, have received his share? Should Cnut's death in 1035 have produced a division: between Harthacnut and Harold, between Harthacnut and Edward, and Alfred? Should Emma have worked, had Emma worked for any of these outcomes? Such were the potential questions in the acrimonious atmosphere of 1041–2. Cnut, to some extent the ideal ruler of the *Encomium*, raised the issue, asserted his rights, but left the outcome to God. God, as always, would speak on Emma's side.

Thorkell, the Scandinavian leader who had first attacked England then served as a mercenary for King Æthelred from 1012–15, is the other figure in Emma's Danish interlude. He returns to Denmark during Cnut's stay there. Cnut had lacked a kingly retinue because part of his army remained in England with Thorkell, who now held a half of a divided kingdom. In the *Encomium* divided kingdoms produce nothing but problems. Thorkell's motives were debatable. He had decided to remain in fertile England, rather than leave as if expelled. Some said he did this, not because he despised his lord, but to help Cnut when he came back. Others felt differently. The debates of the *Encomium*, like the tales told after 1066, encompass the recriminations and legacy of conquest. Thorkell returns to Denmark to make it absolutely clear that he is faithful to Cnut and offer his help and knowledge of England. Thorkell is the great man tainted with disloyalty, distrusted. Are he and his protestations of loyalty to be believed? In 1041–2 the actions and intentions of another great man and one whose name was often linked with Emma, Earl Godwine, were suspect and carefully scrutinized. The Danish interlude, raising questions of succession, division, family relations and the loyalty of the great is not a sideshow to the main story, but an integral part of Emma's tale. It even includes an example of proper filial duty to a mother. Before Cnut's departure for England in 1015 the brothers go together to the land of the Slavs to bring back their mother, Swein's discarded wife, who is staying there.

Cnut and Thorkell return to England, where Thorkell proves his loyalty at the battle of Sherston. Cnut stops the looting of his men. His attention is turned rather on the taking of London, the key to the kingdom since the great men are there. God now acts to reduce the likelihood of bloodshed. He took from life the prince who was in London, Æthelred (though not so identified), so that Cnut could enter freely. Peace is now made with Cnut and a day named for his entry into the city. But Edmund, the English prince's son, resists.[10] The *Encomium* makes no attempt to hide the resistance of the English to Danish rule. Cnut is a just king who restrains looting, concentrates on acquiring the kingdom itself, and presents a contrast to the youthful rashness of Edmund, though the two were probably little different in age. But there is no pretence that he was accepted readily by the English. The woman who was to make him acceptable is still to make her appearance. In her own narrative Emma's entrance will not be in association with London. She will not be the woman within the walls, the witness of valour, the loot of victory, the ransomer of cities. She is a negotiator, a player, on equal terms with Cnut. Her time has not yet come.

With Edmund in London is Eadric, ealdorman of Mercia, a great man on the English side, powerful, skilled in counsel but treacherous. At the battle of Ashingdon in 1016, he and Thorkell play matched parts. Thorkell rallies the Danes with the sight of the Raven banner predicting victory; Eadric calls for flight, hides his banner, and leads a section of Edmund's army from the field. After a hard-fought battle the English retreat, though Edmund does not give up hope. He does, however, receive back Eadric, who advises peace with the Danes, to be pursued in the only possible way, through a division of the kingdom between Edmund and Cnut. It is agreed; though Cnut insists on tribute from Edmund's share.[11]

Ashingdon and its outcome present the English as worthy enemies, as the Normans presented them in their descriptions of Hastings; an easy victory against ill-led cowards carried little warrior prestige. But Emma and her Encomiast never lose sight of their themes. Eadric and Thorkell raise again the problem of assessing the loyalty of the great. Once more the question is of division of the kingdom. The arguments for division

---

[10] Ibid pp 20–4.
[11] Ibid pp 24–30.

could not lightly be dismissed in the 1040s, since division had occurred in 1016; the English themselves had fought for it. Emma had not apparently worked for division between 1035 and 1041, and in her *Encomium* it had to be argued against. Division produced suspicion: when Thorkell had held half a kingdom he had been most suspect. It was proposed by traitors, in 1016 by Eadric. And it was no solution; in 1016 it did not prevent tribute being demanded. Division resulted from Ashingdon, and arguments about it festered for a quarter of a century. In the *Encomium* those arguments are about to be dealt their deathblow. God is about to save the English by disposing of Edmund, and Emma is to enter the story, to bring true peace.

The tale is half told before Emma makes her appearance, but her entry is carefully timed as part of the climax of the work. After the division of the kingdom in the wake of Ashingdon, God takes pity on the English. Remembering his own dictum, that no kingdom divided against itself can last, he relieves Edmund of the burden of the flesh. If both Cnut and Edmund survived, neither could rule securely and the kingdom would be brought to naught by renewed conflict. Edmund is given joy on a celestial throne, Cnut is now, in 1016, chosen by all. Division of kingdoms is not God's way. Cnut holds the kingdom peacefully, loves those who had fought faithfully for Edmund, but punishes those, like Eadric, who had not. When Eadric claims his reward, Cnut gives him one appropriate to a man who had been unfaithful to his lord. His head is struck off with a single blow: 'By this example may soldiers learn to be faithful, not unfaithful to their kings.'[12] In this royalist work, there was to be no doubt about the fate of traitors, and particularly traitors to kings.

All that Cnut now lacks is a most noble wife and sharer of his rule (*imperii sui consortem*). Such a royal bride is found in Gaul, in Normandy, a woman rich in wealth and lineage, beautiful, wise, the most outstanding woman of her day, a famous queen. She is especially sought after because she comes of a victorious people, one which had secured part of Gaul against the wishes of the Franks and their prince. Wooers, words and gifts are sent to the lady, but she refuses even to be betrothed[13] without a promise. 'It was said that the king had sons by another.'[14] So Emma, a mother wisely thinking of the future of her children, makes this stipulation. If a son is born by her the sons of no other would rule after him. Her word pleases the king, and after the oath was sworn, his will pleases her. By the grace of God she becomes Cnut's wife: Gaul and England rejoice, the army on both sides had long wished 'that by the

[12] Ibid p 32.
[13] To become Cnut's *sponsa*.
[14] Ibid p 32.

joining of such a woman to such a man, so worthy a woman, so worthy a man,' in the bond of marriage war would be stilled. The clash had been between equals; it is a union of equals which stills it.[15]

The description of the wooing and marriage asserted Emma's equality. No relatives were involved in the transactions. She was noble born, the pride in Norman ancestry echoes the Norman self-image of the early eleventh century, as found in Dudo of St Quentin. But it is she herself who negotiated, set terms and finally accepted. In *Semiramis* her independence was feminine wickedness and testimony to her brothers' weakness; in Emma's own tale it was celebrated. Emma was to be a sharer in rule. The idea was common in Europe at this date;[16] it was present in the rituals by which Emma was made queen (see below p 175), and by the 1040s it had entered deep into Emma's view of herself. It was through her, not through division of the kingdom, that warfare was ended, just as the coronation ritual makes the bringing of tranquil peace the queen's function. Emma was a wife, and a peace-maker, but especially a queen and peace-maker, and there is no hint of subordination. This is a triumphant celebration of her position, yet it too is overshadowed by the later events which shape the *Encomium* and Emma's narrative. Emma must remember the 'sons of another' who would later claim the throne. She might have preferred to forget them, to deny that another had sons. But the oath was central to her own arguments after 1035, central to the claim that she had always looked to the future of all her sons,[17] central to the prior claim of Harthacnut over Edward. She sowed seeds of doubt: 'it is said' that Cnut had sons by another. In 1035–6 she would deny that Harold, 'the unjust tyrant' was either a son of Cnut or of the 'other'. Yet she could not pass over the oath in silence, even though it lent credibility to Harold's birth. The tortuousness of her situation in 1035, and in 1041–2, begins to become apparent.

The joy experienced at the marriage of Emma and Cnut is magnified by the birth of their son, Harthacnut. They keep him with them, as the future heir of the kingdom, whilst other noble sons are sent to Normandy to be raised.[18] When he grew up, his father subjected all his kingdom to him with an oath, and sends him to Denmark with troops. Cnut himself, once he had become sole ruler of Denmark in 1018–19, is an emperor, ruler of Denmark and Norway, of England, Britain and Scotland. He is such a friend of churchmen that he seems a co-bishop to the bishops, a

---

[15] The choice of words here is critical: the clash was '*pares paribus*', the marital union is '*tanta . . . tanto, digna . . . digno*'.

[16] See Mor 1948, Vogelsang 1954, Delogu 1964 and especially Erkens 1991.

[17] The oath is first to a son of her and Cnut, but she wisely made the stipulation thinking of the future of her *sons – suis* and *ipsis* plural.

[18] *Encomium*, p 34. I have translated '*liberales filios*' as 'noble sons' in preference to Campbell's 'legitimate sons'.

monk to the monks. Italy, Gaul and Flanders bless him; his visit to St Omer illustrates his piety, where the author witnessed his actions 'with his own eyes'.[19] He is an example to other kings, and to his own posterity; all mourn his death, though there is great rejoicing in heaven. It was with this powerful, quasi-saintly king that Emma as queen shared rule.

Cnut's death opens the final act of the *Encomium*'s story, dealing with those very years 1035–41 whose events were the subject of suspicion, accusation and recrimination when the *Encomium* was written. Emma is now openly centre stage. The lady queen remains alone after the death of her husband, grieving for him and alarmed at her sons' absence in Denmark and Normandy. In that absence, the English, forgetful of the goodness of their king, desert the sons of the excellent queen, and choose as king a certain Harold, allegedly the son of Cnut by a concubine, though the rival assertion that he was a servant-girl's child taken to the bed of the indisposed concubine is, the *Encomium* insists, nearer the truth. Harold, fearing the future, sought to have his choice confirmed by the appropriate rites. He asks Archbishop Æthelnoth to bless him as king, to hand over the sceptre, kept in the archbishop's custody, and the crown, and to lead him, as it was right for no other to do, to the throne of the kingdom. The archbishop, a man of every virtue and endowed with wisdom, refuses, swearing that he would neither acclaim nor bless any other as long as a son of Emma lived; declaring his loyalty to them, he leaves the insignia of royalty on the altar, forbidding any other bishop to use them to inaugurate Harold. Neither threats nor gifts move him, and the despairing Harold leaves, spurning episcopal benediction and the Christian religion, hunting with his dogs whilst others were at mass, so that the English are ashamed of their choice. Yet their choice it had been, and they are equally ashamed to throw him out; he would be king to the end.[20]

Emma awaits that end silently and in prayer, but Harold lays traps for her. No one would allow him to harm her, so he plots to secure his rule by killing her children. He writes a letter, in Emma's name, to her sons in Normandy. In it the anguished mother, 'queen in name only', begs them to act; Harold is winning support day by day among the great. Those great men would prefer Edward or Alfred to rule, but one of them must come quickly and secretly, to receive their mother's counsel. This letter, sent by a tyrant, is received as a mother's gift. The sons reply that one will come, and a day and place is fixed. All is reported back to the enemies of God, and plots are laid. The younger son, Alfred, sets out. He refuses offers of aid from Baldwin of Flanders, and crosses from Boulogne with a few men. Getting wind of an ambush, he changes his

[19] Ibid p 36, this is one of the author's few personal asides in the work.
[20] Ibid pp 40–2.

plans; en route to his mother he is met by Earl Godwine. Godwine receives him into his faith, and in turn takes an oath to him and becomes his military follower. He diverts Alfred from London and lodges him at Guildford, dispersing the young man and his followers among different lodgings. After eating and drinking together, Godwine retires to his own lodging, to return in the morning to serve his lord with due honour. At this point Harold's accomplices appear. They deprive the men of arms, shackle them, and next morning lead them out to condemn them without a hearing. Delivered to executioners, they are put to death, only every tenth man spared by lot, not treated like the military followers that they were. The prince Alfred is martyred, a tragedy whose details the Encomiast will avoid to spare Emma's maternal grief, 'no sorrow is greater for a mother than to see or hear of the death of her much-loved son.'[21] He is taken to Ely, condemned by judges, his eyes put out and then slain. The monks of Ely bury him honourably. It is said that there are miracles at his grave; Queen Emma may rejoice in having such an intercessor in heaven.

These events are covered in great detail, the letter quoted in full, it and Harold's deception highlighted in the manuscript.[22] The responsibility of Emma and Godwine for the death of Alfred, and Emma's room for manoeuvre in the immediate succession to Cnut, were pressing questions after the accession of Harthacnut, and even more so after Edward's return from Normandy in 1041. There were those who had been utterly faithful to the memory of Cnut, or at least whose actions could be so presented, like Archbishop Æthelnoth. There were others whose actions had left more doubt about their unswerving loyalty, like Godwine. There was an incriminating letter to be dealt with, and the death of a prince. Emma made no attempt to mitigate the dastardliness of a deed which others might have seen as justifiable defence against invaders. Harold was a godless tyrant, a servant's son, who could not be the beneficiary of the promises of succession to Cnut's sons, but he was the choice of the English. Emma's efforts were concentrated on presenting herself as hemmed into inaction by the choice of the English, the unwitting victim of a terrible fraud, and as the sorrowing mother. Passivity not activity seemed her best defence.

The queen, smitten by the crime, uncertain and distressed, wonders what to do about the death of her son and for her own life and dignity. Some might ask, the author says, why she did not die; a strange question behind which surely lay others not openly acknowledged. Why had she

---

[21] Ibid p 44.
[22] The letter itself is separated in the manuscript, part of Alfred's name in the address is picked out in red, BL Addit 33241 fo 56r; Harold's fraud is marked out by a large and decorated capital, fo 57r and the description of the martyrdom is followed by a gap, fo 61r which editors of the manuscript have not chosen to make a break and end of a book, but which the scribe treats like the break in the story at the death of Cnut.

tried to save herself in these circumstances rather than working for her remaining sons? Why did she flee and save her own skin? She would willingly have died for the faith, but it is unfitting to die for the ambition for wordly rule. Rather she seeks to preserve the remnants of her dignity by seeking foreign shores. She sets sail to Bruges, where Baldwin of Flanders and his royally-born wife Adela receive her with honour and lodge her as befitted a queen. She accepts their generosity, whilst making it clear that she is not really in need. From here she sends messengers to summon Edward. Their discussions are protracted, but Edward, though sorry for her plight, tells her he cannot help, since the great men of England have sworn no oath to him. Help must be sought from his brother.[23] Emma now sends for Harthacnut. He is horror-stricken at her news, burns to avenge his brother and especially to obey his mother. To both ends he gathers troops, in case he should need to fight. But he comes to his mother with only ten ships, receiving en route a vision which foretells Harold's death and his own most just succession as the rightful heir. This will be God's final word on the English succession – delivering it to Emma's son. He sails on to Bruges; his meeting with his mother brings mingled grief and joy as she traces in his features those of her lost one, yet sees him, the survivor, safely before her. They await news of the death of Harold.

The English nobility, far from opposing him, rejoice at the prospective return of the lawful heir to the kingdom. When news of his and his mother's departure spreads, Bruges is torn with grief and weeping. Rich and poor alike bewail the loss on the one hand of Emma's company, on the other of her largesse. As they leave, the shore is alive with lamentation; all wish to go with her, this fellow citizen, never a burden, never an oppressor of the poor. None is dry-eyed as they finally depart. The English nobles come to meet them, to make amends to their king and queen, to place themselves under their dominion. With fraternal love, Harthacnut calls Edward back to hold the kingdom with him. And now mother and sons rule in a trinity united by maternal and fraternal love.

In these final pages Emma makes clear why, after working for all her sons, it was Harthacnut with whom she returned. It was he alone, to whom the oath had been sworn, who had the support necessary to avenge his brother, restore his mother and take his due inheritance. But the true heir was not forgetful of his brotherly duties; the family was reunited in rule, which was shared not divided. Emma's case turned on the strength of Harthacnut's position, the especial rightfulness of his claim, so that in the end it was as Harthacnut's brother, thus Emma's son that Edward was recalled. The argument was tailormade for the circum-

[23] Ibid p 48.

stances of 1041:[24] a tale of Danish rightful inheritance, whilst a Danish
king still ruled, yet one in which Emma could claim that she always and
still worked for the good of all her sons, that through working for the
claims of one son she worked for them all.

The *Encomium* demonstrates how central queenliness was to Emma's
own self-image. The whole work is royal and queenly. The manuscript
intended for Emma herself picked out royal names in half uncials, capitalized or highlighted them, and none more consistently than that of
Emma herself.[25] It opens with an illustration of her as a crowned, en-

Figure 1 Queen Emma and her sons, the frontispiece of the *Encomium Emmae*.
London, British Library, Additional MS 33241, fo 1 verso. Reproduced by
permission of the British Library

[24] Perhaps even to the extent of heading off any criticism of her involvement in
Harthacnut's invasion fleet and its costs; only ten ships come for her in Bruges, and
Harthacnut is promised in his vision the succession when Harold dies, obviating the need
to fight.
[25] Hers is the only name consistently so treated, including in the *argumentum*, BL Addit
33241 fo 7v. Royal names in general are so treated, including that of Alfred, fos 57r and
59v. It is significant that Edmund, son of Æthelred and briefly king in 1016, is never given
this treatment.

throned woman, with the author kneeling before her and her royal sons standing, slightly bowed, behind him (see figure 1). This is one of the earliest representations of a seated, majestic secular royal figure.[26] It is an image of authoritative maternity but especially of regality. It is as queen, *regina*, that she is most often described in the *Encomium*,[27] and her regal dignity is stressed at key points where it might be considered under-mined, as in her exile in Flanders.[28] For the *Encomium*'s author and scribe Emma was always and overwhelmingly a queen. It is a common presentation of the king's wife as patron, as in the chronicles which describe Emma and Edith in this role. It is the flattery of the commis-sioned author. But flattery works by playing to self-image. If this title summed up the author's perceptions of a middle-aged king's widow and mother who was his patron, his closeness to Emma suggests that it best reflected her preferred view of herself. In no other story is Emma as much the queen as in her own.

Her story is, however, no general praise poem. It is a specific justifica-tion and explanation of her actions geared to circumstances.[29] Like the eleventh-century English chroniclers, or Henry of Huntingdon later, Emma too saw herself as a Norman-born wife and mother of Danish kings. She basked in the glory they reflected on her. Yet whilst the chroniclers telescoped her life and understood it through these iden-tities, she used them to justify and explain it. Her apologia takes us closer to the problems which a woman's several identities could pose: the tensions between her loyalties as a mother and wife, particularly to her sons by a first marriage after she has married again; the inadequacy of maternal ideals to provide a script for a woman faced with several children, especially by different husbands. Her self-presentation used the same identities, but more selectively than the Chroniclers; from what it omits and elides as well as from what it includes and emphasizes we learn what being a wife and mother meant in practice for a powerful woman.

The story she tells is not a whole-life narrative but a highly political one, appropriate to a particular stage. She chooses to present herself as the wife of *a king*, Cnut, not *of kings*, Æthelred and Cnut, and as a mother of all her sons. Emma's is a Danish story, written in the reign of

---

[26] See Rezak 1986.

[27] 13 or so uses of *mater* or references to maternal feeling or action in the *Encomium*, clustered especially in Book 3's consideration of the death of Alfred, Emma's negotiations with Edward and Harthacnut in Flanders and her return to England. By contrast she is *regina* throughout the work, 25 or more instances.

[28] *Encomium*, pp 46–8; partly she accepts hospitality gratefully, but partly she always showed that she was not really in need.

[29] It may very soon have been overtaken by events. A version destined for Edward the Confessor makes some changes: its abbreviation of the reasons why Emma fled to Flanders suggests how central this was to her alone. This is Campbell's MS P, post medieval, but based on an early manuscript.

Harthacnut. It has no need to stress her first marriage,[30] but nor could it have done. Emma's story in 1041 had no place for Æthelred; it might have been different had it been written in 1043 during Edward's reign, though not appreciably so. Family politics determined the dramatic events of 1035–40 in which Emma was so deeply involved and of which she has given us the most detailed surviving account. The family structures which produced them and the ideals available to discuss them were too much at odds to allow her case to be presented in other ways. Specific to circumstances as it is, it is Emma's story as 1035–40 determined it should be told. This is not Emma's narrative recollected in tranquillity on the eve of death, weighed, assessed and revalued when the end was apparent, but it is not clear that she could have told these years very differently even had she commissioned it then. The years 1035–40 might have figured less prominently. We might have heard more about Emma's doings as queen, an identity of considerable importance to Emma herself. The set pieces about the much-loved queen, the hints of her sensitivity to queenly and royal dignity, and especially the equal share in rule which she stressed for herself as queen-wife of her husband and queen-mother of her sons might have been fleshed out with more details of the court politics and activities through which her queenship was exercised. That 'might' assumes an interest in and language to describe such exercise. The other eleventh-century stories, concerned with dramatic events rather than day-to-day politics, cast doubt on the existence of such a language. But Edith's story suggests that it was being forged and was particularly appropriate to a queen.

2 The Life of King Edward who Rests at Westminster

The *Life of King Edward who Rests at Westminster* has been seen as a strange work and has provoked much debate.[31] Its strangeness is no doubt due to the unusual circumstances in which it was written.[32] Although suggestions that it is a later forgery have been rebutted,[33] it has still been seen as lacking unity, beginning as a story of Godwine and his children, then shifting abruptly to a depiction of Edward's sanctity.[34] Yet the story has an essential unity suggested by internal parallels and con-

---

[30] See John 1980–1, esp pp 61–4 on the question of whether her first marriage was suppressed by the author.

[31] See M. Bloch 1923; Southern 1946; Barlow, *VitaEd* 1st and 2nd ed and 1970; Heningham 1946 and 1975.

[32] Barlow, *VitaEd* 1st ed, p xxx.

[33] Southern, Heningham 1946 and Barlow rebutting Bloch.

[34] Thus Barlow, *VitaEd* 1st and 2nd eds and 1970. He argues for composition across the years 1065–7. For contrary arguments see Heningham 1975 and Körner, pp 36–7.

trasts,[35] and coheres around the concerns, identities and arguments of Edith herself,[36] as a daughter of Godwine, as the wife and widow of a saintly king, Edward, and as an English queen. The work was produced for Edith in the immediate aftermath of the Norman Conquest.[37] It is another post-1066 English story, the most sustained and detailed of them all. Its argument is perhaps even more mediated through the eyes of the Flemish monk who wrote it than was that of the *Encomium*.[38] Nonetheless English voices can still be heard, and particularly that of an English queen. It is Edith's story, set within the memories of the survivors of the pre-1066 court, telling the recent English past in a form suited to the post-Conquest present. As with the *Encomium*, the key to the structure of an apparently incoherent work is its relationship to a powerful woman in the thick of events.

The story begins, once again, with the Danish invasions and Cnut's accession. For Edith the Danish conquest produced the rise of Godwine, her father, and the exile of Edward, her future husband. Cnut recognizes Godwine's great qualities: his skills as a counsellor, his utility in the rule of a new kingdom, and especially his trustworthiness.[39] Edward is the divinely protected heir, the hidden shoot of the old royal stock, which would blossom again. He had been designated future king by an oath sworn to him in his mother's womb (Emma's sole appearance in Edith's story is as the unnamed carrier of this royal infant). Bishop Brihtwold had been vouchsafed a vision of his return, of his chaste life, but also of the fate of the kingdom after his death, when God alone would dispose of it. 'The kingdom of the English belongs to God, after you he will provide for it a king pleasing

---

[35] See e.g. the designation of Edward by the people, which opens the work, 1st ed pp 7–8 and by God, which begins the section on the saintly Edward, pp 60–1; the similar descriptions of the king in life, pp 12–13 and in death, p 80; the contrast of the court as a place of display, and the court as a place for the care of the sick; the twofold causes of the fall of the English, in the political section, because of rebellion and division, in the saintly section, because of sin, and the importance of the Roman events both for the rebellion of 1065, and for the sins of church leaders etc. For argument for its literary unity see Heningham 1946 and especially 1975, where the unifying theme is seen as the kingdom of the English, not Edward. This unity obviates the need to argue for a split date of composition.

[36] As recognized by Barlow, *VitaEd* 2nd ed, pp xx–xxi.

[37] Heningham 1975, pp 33–4 dates it 1068–70, after the coming of Mathilda and before the 1070 purge of the English church. I consider that its concern with Edith and the succession may place it even earlier, perhaps 1066–7. Barlow also dates it early, to 1065–7, but whilst arguing for a split in the work and composition over a long period.

[38] Barlow, *VitaEd* 1st ed, pp xli–lix surveys arguments for Flemish authorship and for queenly patronage. Southern's arguments for Goscelin remain persuasive. M. Bloch recognized Edith as the heroine and identified the purpose of the Life as being 'to associate his (Edward's) wife with him', p 29. Heningham agrees on the centrality of Edith.

[39] *VitaEd*, pp 5–6.

to him.'[40] Edith's arguments are already apparent: the greatness of her natal family, the divine choice of her husband, and the English succession in 1066.

With God's will and Godwine's help, Edward returns, is consecrated as king and recognized by the surrounding rulers of Europe. An age of peace and prosperity is ushered in, a reign of Solomon after David. The king is decribed as he was, not in 1043, but in old age: tall with milky white hair and beard, full faced, rosy cheeked, with thin white hands and long translucent fingers, an unblemished and royal person; pleasant, but always dignified, terrible as a lion when roused yet so gracious in his giving and withholding of favour that his very refusals seemed greater generosity than his acquiescence; a king and lord in public, as one of his courtiers in private, but always saving his majesty; a king who delighted Britain with his concern for good law and justice.[41]

The next section of the work is unfortunately lost, but was concerned with Godwine's children, and particularly with Edith.[42] The section on Edith has been reconstructed from later authors who used the work; the comparable and comparative treatments of her brothers have disappeared.[43] Edith is the ideal bride for such a king: learned, chaste, beautiful, a Minerva to his Solomon.[44] Like him she is dignified, sparing in speech, never loud, speaking the tongues of Gauls, Danish and Irish as a native. She is generous, a keeper of her word, solicitous for the king's regal appearance, so that even Solomon in all his glory could not surpass him: in such activity a daughter and mother as much as a wife. And it is with maternal affection that she rears the boys of royal stock. Such a woman, raised by her parents to be without peer, is fitting to be blessed as Edward's wife, and consecrated as his Queen.

The story now moves from Edward's establishment on the throne to the events of 1051–2.[45] Godwine's fall and return and Archbishop Robert's part in it are recounted in detail.[46] Robert's domination of the

---

[40] Ibid pp 7–9.

[41] Ibid pp 12–13. NB the tense used throughout is the past 'erat'; this is Edward described not only as in old age but after his death.

[42] See the argument as set out in the initial poem, and internal references elsewhere.

[43] Barlow supplies the missing section from Richard of Cirencester, 2nd ed, pp 22–4, and argues the case for doing this, ibid pp xxxix–xl. Where he can be tested against surviving sources, John of Worcester, William of Malmesbury, Roger of Wendover and the VitaEd itself, Richard appears to have been a close follower of his texts. Barlow, 1st ed, p xxxviii, suggests the size of the missing section was c. 1,300 words. The section now supplied on Edith is about 500 words perhaps about a half of the lost section, Barlow, 2nd ed, p xxxix. In the original it may have been longer, but it nonetheless seems likely that Godwine's sons were also treated here.

[44] VitaEd, 2nd ed, p 22, both Osbert and Richard have the reference to Minerva.

[45] It is of course impossible to know whether the lost section dealt with the 1040s.

[46] Ibid pp 17–28. The emphasis on Godwine, and the stress on the domination of the king by Robert's council must make this a potential source, directly or more likely indirectly, for Richard of Devizes. Susannah features as the innocent in both, but this is a common topos.

king and his counsels, his scheming against Godwine, the accusation of
Godwine of plotting first against Alfred and now against Edward,
Godwine's offer to clear himself, the king's refusal and Godwine's reluctant flight, all culminate in Robert's attempt to separate the king and
queen. Edward mitigates Edith's fate. She is despatched to Wilton nunnery to await the outcome of events, grieving, but with royal honour and
an imperial retinue. There she spends a year in prayer and tears awaiting
the day of salvation.[47] That day is the return of her family, which the
author depicts as a triumph, but a carefully muted one. Last but not least
Edith is brought back by a royally-apparelled escort; like a calm sky and
smiling sun after the clouds and tempests, the daughter of the earl returns
to the king's bedchamber, to the joy of courtiers and kingdom alike. The
crisis which divided her father and husband and seemed her own undoing
was presented by Edith in such a way as to save Edward's honour, stress
Godwine's loyalty, finger Archbishop Robert and preserve her own dignity.[48]

The death of Godwine soon after makes way for his noble sons,
Harold and Tostig, on whom the king and his rule now relied. There
follows a digression on the visit of Tostig and Archbishop Ealdred of
York to Rome. The pope refuses to give Archbishop Ealdred a pallium
because of the irregularities of his appointment, and some of Tostig's
party are attacked by robbers not far from the Holy City. In this attack
the fate of the Northern noble Gospatric is highlighted. Apparently as
irrelevant as the Danish interlude in the *Encomium*, we shall see that
Rome played its own part in Edith's arguments. For the moment, however, the story resumes with the saintly Edward, rapt in prayer, concerned for correct monastic discipline, sparing of pomp, yet grateful for
the concern the queen showed for his royal array. Edith's picture parallels his. Far from restraining the king's generosity, she leads the way; she
is a queen so humble that she refused a seat at his side, though not in the
public display of church or royal feast. Even their patronage is matched,
his in the rebuilding of a monastery for men at Westminster, hers in the
reconstruction of Wilton, in stone, for women. Peace and prosperity
smile on the English, protected by such brothers, ruled by such a king,
and by such a queen.[49]

This tableau in fact separates the picture of a saintly king and queen
from their patronage of Westminster Abbey and Wilton nunnery. The
rebuilding of Westminster and Wilton has ominous undertones, looking
back to the golden age and forward to dire events to come. The devil
seems already to be at work to frustrate the queen in the fire in the city
of Wilton as preparations are made for the church's consecration. West-

---

[47] Ibid p 23.
[48] Heningham 1946, p 430–1 saw this presentation as Edith's.
[49] *VitaEd*, p 42.

minster is being rebuilt as Edward's mausoleum, and the story is turning towards thoughts of Edward's death, its circumstances and consequences.

The Northern rebellion of 1065 is covered in the same detail as 1051–2. For Edith the divisions of 1065–6 were as critical as the earlier crisis. Tostig's fierce attempts to restrain the lawlessness of the North had provoked murder, resistance and rebellion. At a great meeting at Britford near Wilton, the Northerners lay accusations against Tostig, and the testimony implicates Harold in the moves against his brother. Tostig believes it, though Harold clears himself with an oath. The division between the brothers is calamity enough, but it is compounded by the king's own failure to raise troops against the rebels; he falls ill, never to recover before his death. The queen is confounded, tearfully prophetic of the future ills of the kingdom; the whole palace descends into mourning with her. Tostig and his family, heaped with gifts by the sorrowing king, go into exile at St Omer in Flanders. Soon afterwards, at the Christmas feast of 1065–6, Edward dies, sick of soul.

The story has arrived at a critical transition. A long poem touches briefly on the dreadful events of the autumn of 1066, on the deaths of kings and earls and a Humber red with their blood, and dwells at greater length on the Welsh wars; none of this, the author feels, will please the queen. To achieve that end, he now switches his attention to the saintly Edward, to whom the last part of the work is devoted.[50] Chosen by God before his birth, Edward was a saint in life. He cured sickness, especially blindness and the king's sickness, through the water in which he had washed.[51] The story closes at his deathbed. The death of a king, passed over quickly before, is now elaborated as the death of a king-saint; the deathbed is another of the set-pieces of this tale. First the dying king wakes from a troubled sleep to tell a vision of two monks, who warned him of God's punishment about to fall on the English for the sins of their leaders; the kingdom will be delivered into the hands of the enemy for a year and a day. The king's vision includes a tree cut in mid trunk, separated, then miraculously rejoined without human hand, to leaf and fruit again from its own sap. Archbishop Stigand, standing with Harold and others at the bedside, whispers to the earl that the king is worn out by age and sickness, but others and especially the queen, sitting on the ground with his feet in her lap, ponder long.[52] The vision is interpreted as a sign of the obduracy of the English leaders, who will not repent; those who spurn it, and Stigand is surely one of them, will never do penance.

---

[50] The only surviving manuscript, BL Harley 526, is not divided into books, and there is no division here, fos 52r–54r, except through the insertion of the poem. Poems provide an articulation of and commentary on the work throughout.

[51] Another section has been lost here, which covered some of the miracles.

[52] VitaEd, pp 76–7.

Then the king utters his last words. He turns first to the queen, Edith: 'May God reward this my spouse for her great care in service of me. She served me devotedly, always stood by my side like a daughter, for which may she have eternal happiness.' Then stretching out his hand to Harold, he commends to his care the queen, the kingdom and the foreigners who had served Edward well. He commands his grave to be prepared and his passing to be made public, and then dies. His funeral, the prayers and alms after his death and the signs at his tomb draw Edith's story to its conclusion.

Edith and her author set down their story in the aftermath of 1066 as part of still unfolding events. William was king, but the fate of the English had not yet been sealed. English survival, especially that of an English queen, still seemed possible. Edith's story was told in part as personal panegyric, but her own importance and that of her family was always stressed with an eye on survival. It was told in an English context of explanation and recrimination after 1066, as exculpation, yet also as a claim to a role in the new regime, though not exactly that which Emma had played across 1016–17.

It was concerned to explain the Norman Conquest in ways which flattered rather than blamed Edith. On the one hand the Norman Conquest was presented as a result of the divisions of the English first manifest in the Northern rebellion and the train of events which it began. The division between her brothers and the powerlessness of her husband brought to naught the queen's counsel, normally so efficacious. What that counsel was or might have been in 1065 we are left to wonder; but we can be in little doubt that it would have been for the good of a kingdom for whose future ills she now weeps tears, not of female weakness but of prophecy. On the other hand, England's calamities were the punishment of the flock for the sins of its shepherds. The king had always known this, so too had the queen; both had often warned of it.[53] When Edward's deathbed vision spelt out the future, Stigand might scoff at the ramblings of a sick old man, but the queen pondered his words. Sins bringing down conquest and disaster was an age-old analysis articulated by Gildas in the sixth century, Alfred in the ninth and Archbishop Wulfstan in 1013–17. Sin and division both smack of the recriminations which turn back internally to seek the causes of defeat. When voiced by a queen such analyses can bring female prescience and good counsel to the fore.

Edith, however, was not merely explaining the Norman Conquest. She stood accused of contributing to it. It was alleged she had helped instigate the Northern rebellion through engineering the murder of Gospatric at court, at Christmas 1064, acting on behalf of her brother Tostig. Though

[53] Ibid p 77.

the details of that death are lost, the Roman interlude in the *Life* may give some inkling of the suspicions and recriminations it engendered. The Gospatric in the Roman story was the nephew of his namesake murdered at court. In the *Life* he was presented as a faithful follower of Tostig, who impersonated his lord, was taken for ransom by robbers, then denied his mistaken identity and was released. As in the *Encomium* an apparently irrelevant interlude takes its significance from the queen's attempts to meet accusations. Behind it lie claims that Tostig had already shown his malice towards Northern nobles before 1064–5, betraying them into the hands of robbers. Edith presented Gospatric's capture as an instance not of Tostig's betrayal, but of his popularity with this Northern noble who tried to protect him. She rebutted a picture of longstanding tensions between Tostig and this Northern family which lent credibility to claims of her involvement in murder. The Roman story is angled at the debates among the English concerning their recent defeat. It connects with both the causes highlighted in the *Life*. The leaders of the English church were, according to the *Life of Edward*, guilty men, already denounced by the pope himself.[54] Stigand was the unworthy archbishop who disbelieved the king's ramblings, and Ealdred in 1061 was refused a pallium and deposed by the pope. Through the Gospatric incident the *Life* answers some of the arguments and recriminations surrounding the Northern rebellion and its contribution to the Conquest through English divisions. Edith's story is one of the tales the English told in defeat. In it she is already responding to others.

The narrative takes its coherence from the several identities which Edith combined. She was Godwine's daughter, and one of her prime concerns was to clear his name and show the glory of her family's past. The trustworthiness of the great was, as the *Encomium* showed, a burning issue in eleventh-century England, and few were as great or as suspect as Godwine. The *Life* addressed these suspicions. Godwine was loyal, always ready to prove his innocence, ever unwilling to act against his king. Harold and Tostig were celebrated, especially for their warrior prowess; they were bulwarks of the English kingdom and Edward's peaceful rule. Neither rash nor given to open discussion, their plans, their characterizations also addressed the tragic misunderstandings of motive and action in 1065. The Norman stories dissociated Edith from the Godwine clan: her own tale gloried in her father and brothers, but sought to explain and justify them. Edith, an English woman, could scarcely deny her family identity, and probably in the immediate aftermath of 1066 had no desire to do so.[55] She embraced and sought to burnish it.

[54] Ibid p 77. This argument would make this analysis not merely a Norman story, but also an English one after 1066.
[55] See Garnett 1986b for the suggestion that the anti-Harold story was not itself perfectly formed in these early stages of the Conquest.

She was also Edward's wife and widow, and his sanctity is not a shift in the story but central to its conception. Edith was presented as a wife, sharing her husband's rule, one in flesh with a saint. She was his daughter/wife.[56] The strange image presented the relationship of chastity and the stance of humility which befitted the wife of a saintly king, glossing over a barren union.[57] It incorporated a childless woman into her husband's family in a way which maternity would normally have done; paternity not maternity is the dominant parental relationship of the *Life*.[58] And perhaps through that, it made a daring bid for Edith's say in the inheritance, as did the *Life*'s association of Edith and the kingdom.[59] This daughter/wife, heiress, ward and widow, Queen of the English, was bound up with the future of England. She and the kingdom together were given into Harold's custody, entrusted to his regency.[60]

The portraits of Harold and Tostig also give insight into the courtier-politicians of Edward's last years and into the politics of the court, where the queen operated. The *Life* and its tale are unusual among eleventh-century English sources in the attention they pay to the royal court.[61] Those who lived in Edward's palace, frequented his presence and were his familiars run through it.[62] Speech, that central attribute of court life, is a recurrent theme. Closeness to the king is the key to success: Godwine and Robert were privy to Cnut's and Edward's secrets.[63] This awareness of the court and its politics makes the queen central. For Edith too, language and speech were crucial attributes. She was a good lady to her own people, true to her word, incomparably generous. Her solicitude for the king expressed itself in the proper presentation of his public, regal

---

[56] *VitaEd*, 2nd ed, p 24, 1st ed, pp 59–60, 79.

[57] Cf Barlow, *VitaEd*, p lxxviii.

[58] Edith is a mother, *VitaEd*, 2nd ed, p 24, as is Wilton, 1st ed, p 48–9, but fathers and children, the kingdom as a fatherland (*patria*), Edward as a father and the love of the English for Earl Godwine as a father recur far more frequently than maternal imagery see e.g. pp 6, 7, 9, 26, 30, 41, 59.

[59] Barlow 1970, pp 299–300 'It is possible that the special aim of the *Vita* was to justify the claim that Edith was Edward's heiress.'

[60] The words used to describe Harold at the deathbed directly recall those describing Baldwin's regency earlier in the work: Harold is *nutricius*, queen and kingdom are given to him, *tutandam*, *VitaEd*, p 79; Henry had left his *filii* to Baldwin, *nutriendum*, and the kingdom of the Franks into his *tutela* ibid, p 54. A Flemish monk must have known what he was suggesting here.

[61] For the wider European context for this presentation, already developing in the tenth century, see Jaeger 1985.

[62] *Frequentela*, *VitaEd*, p 54; *familiaribus*, pp 62 and 63, *palatini*, p 28, 53 etc.

[63] A *secretis* ibid pp 6 and 19; Robert was '*ordinarius . . . secretorum consilii sui*' always '*regi. . . . a secretis*', p 17; cf p 62. The term is a commonplace among those who describe tenth- and eleventh-century courts, see e.g. Dudo, pp 183, 195, 208, 220, 265 and cf Bishop Æthelwold at Edgar's court, Wulfstan, *Æthelwold*, p 42.

face.[64] The *Life*'s picture of Edith is of the perfect queen-at-court. As in the *Encomium*, queenliness is to the fore.[65] Like the *Encomium* it presents Edith as regal, and as a parallel if not an equal to the king: in patronage, in humility, in grave restraint. It is, as in the *Encomium*, an equal royalty which springs from marriage. Edward and Edith were two in body, but as one person.[66] But unlike the *Encomium*, the *Life* shows the queen in the palace, her centrality to it and its politics. When Edith was sent away in 1051 the inhabitants of the palace mourned, for she had been the guide and ruler of all royal counsels, the origin of all probity; her return was like that of the sun after storms, a joy to the courtiers and to the kingdom.[67] The flattery is obvious, but it should not obscure the author's awareness of where the queen's role was acted out: in the kingdom but through the court.[68]

The *Life of King Edward* is a very special story, of an English queen, presenting a version of the eleventh century with a view to her own survival after 1066. Its pressing contemporary concerns produce its picture of an ideal queen, almost a mirror of queenship. Like the *Encomium* it tells of the problems with which multiple identities faced women, in this case those of wife and daughter when a woman's natal family remained powerful. In the glory she took from her family of birth, Edith reminds us of the positive potential of such multiple identities. The loss or exclusion of the court dimension in most eleventh-century stories opens a hole at the very centre of our understanding of the queen. Edith the queen's story is a precious glimpse into that space.

* * *

Edith's story made a difference. It assured her place in the eleventh-century picture, literally so in the Bayeux Tapestry. This visual representation of the origins of the Norman Conquest combined English and Norman tales,[69] including Edith's own. It contains the only known contemporary portrait of Edith, shown as she would have wished in one of her own great set-pieces, Edward's deathbed scene (see figure 2). Edith's narrative joined the Norman and English ones in shaping later views of the eleventh century. William of Malmesbury was much influenced by it; Richard of Devizes' romanticization probably knew it, directly or indirectly; Richard of Cirencester copied it so extensively that

---

[64] VitaEd, p 24.
[65] *Regina* is once again the most common designation of Edith as of Emma.
[66] VitaEd, p 4.
[67] Ibid pp 24 and 28.
[68] There is almost an awareness of the relationship of court and kingdom: Godwine is loved by the kingdom not the court, ibid p 25, but Edith unites the two, p 28, and perhaps p 54.
[69] Brooks and Walker 1979, Bernstein 1986.

Figure 2 Edith at the deathbed of Edward the Confessor, Bayeux Tapestry – eleventh century. Reproduced by special permission of the City of Bayeux

he preserved Edith's own, now lost, portrait. She survived into later English history as a saint's wife. Edith herself portrayed Edward as saintly, and drew her own portrait to fit his. She thus avoided the fate of the French Queen Constance; saintly kings can have a devastating impact on the reputations of their worldly wives.[70] But if the resulting Edith is sympathetic, flattering, she was to become increasingly vapid.[71] By the thirteenth century she was eminently usable, presentable to the wives of Henry III or Edward I as a model, and particularly as a model of Englishness to foreign queens.[72] In the process, however, she had had to be separated completely from her vilified natal family, and especially from Godwine and Harold. The process is under way in Osbert of Clare's rewriting of the *Life of Edward* and complete in Aelred of Rievaulx's influential biography, where she is the rose sprung from the thorn bush.[73] The generations immediately after 1066 placed Edith sometimes along-

---

[70] On Constance see e.g. Dhondt 1964–5, largely perpetuating eleventh-century judgements. Edith, of course, also lacked the complications of Constance's life, namely, a female rival and sons.

[71] On the vapidity see e.g. Binski 1990, p 343; on the practical Edith of the Life, see Heningham 1946, pp 447–50.

[72] On this see Binski 1990, pp 343–4, Parsons 1992, p 61.

[73] Aelred, *Vita S Edwardi regis*, col 747 'sicut spina rosam, genuit Godwinus Edivam'. On the separation of Edith from her family cf Binski p 343.

side Godwine and Harold, sometimes in opposition to them. She herself was in no doubt that she was Godwine's daughter, Harold's sister and Edward's wife. But ultimately, and ironically largely as a result of her own efforts, it was as the latter alone that she would survive.

Emma's story had little or no impact on later ones. Cnut's sanctity did not take off as Edward's did. The Danish story as a whole was eclipsed by 1066, and with it Emma's tale, along with the Scandinavian versions of her. There is an irony here too, since the Danish conquest had already eclipsed Æthelred in *her* narrative. Women who enter history through the stories of recent dynastic intricacy are fated to be marginalized as dynasties become established, even more so if they change. Emma never became a 'mother of the dynasty' in England or Scandinavia.[74] The conquests of the eleventh century powerfully reshaped eleventh-century history. Edith's story, unlike Emma's, was preserved by the ultimately successful Conquest. It survived, though severely edited in line with that outcome; there was little use for Emma's.

Neither Emma nor Edith added any basic building blocks to those chosen by other chroniclers. Emma even omitted one in passing over her marriage to Æthelred. 1013–17, 1035–42, 1051–2, 1065–6 were the crises and dramas around which all the narratives were cast. But the choice and treatment of them varied from tale to tale, and Emma and Edith as political women saw them differently. The contrasts between their stories and the rest are not straightforward ones between on the one hand the confused, contradictory or fallacious,[75] and on the other the coherent and truthful. Nor are they simply differences between men's and women's stories. They do, however, call attention to the special features of married women's situations. The years 1051–2 had a particular meaning for Edith, dividing not just a king and earl but her husband and father. The details of the Danish conquest and English resistance signified one thing for English commentators c. 1016 and after, but something different for Emma in the 1040s; her sympathies had to encompass both sides as her marriage had joined them. Powerful women placed as links between victims and vanquished do not tell the same tale as either. Nor do they articulate, understand and interpret the narrative in the same way. Peace which is achieved through the exchange of passive women for an Adam of Bremen, is secured through the equality of marriage for Emma, and the activity of counsel for Edith. Marriage is a way of understanding dynastic history or justifying conquest for Adam, William of Jumièges and William of Poitiers, of negotiating conquest for

---

[74] Such women can continue to have a very important, often mythical role in later history, for royal women as well as men – see Empress Ma in the Ming dynasty, Soullière 1992, and to a lesser degree 'Good Queen Maud' in later English history.

[75] For such views see e.g. A. Campbell, *Encomium*, p xxi or M. Bloch 1923.

the English c. 1016, but for Emma and Edith it is the route to the king's side, to an equal share of royal power. Whilst all the stories use the same female identities of daughter, wife, mother and queen, queenliness, royalty and the court predominate for Emma and Edith as for no-one else, and Edith's story takes us closest to the area and type of politics in which women might have played a part.

Both Emma and Edith told their stories through men, father, sons and husbands. They themselves figure more than in the Chronicles' versions, but not as much as we might have hoped or expected. In this sense they do not challenge the story of the eleventh century as a story of men. There is certainly no sign of sisterhood: Emma gets no more than a passing mention in Edith's tale, and Ælfgifu of Northampton is more prominent in Scandinavian tales than in Emma's, and more sympathetically treated in manuscript E of the Anglo-Saxon Chronicle than by Emma. Their own narratives can be reused and infused with other meanings. When Edith is presented in the Bayeux Tapestry it is in relation to the claims of her brother not her own. It is easy to see Emma's and Edith's stories as those of victims, or at best of women co-opted by patriarchy into telling its own story, a co-option whose ultimate price will be their own reputations and especially their own strength and activity: Emma reduced to a conduit of Norman claims, Edith to an English rose.

Seeking to achieve their own ends through telling the story of their menfolk is, however, a debatable co-option. Both men and women can be used for another's narrative ends and with similar results. Cnut and Edward were used to argue Emma's and Edith's case; in Ottonian Germany the Saint-Queen Mathilda was deployed in the interests of men as well as women.[76] Mathilda became a bland wife and mother whose political role is obscured, but Cnut and Edward have also proved slippery to the historian's grasp, partly because of their wives' saintly characterizations of them.[77] It is easy to forget that the stories themselves are political activity. Telling them was part of Emma's and Edith's own strategies, of the very action we are now trying to recover. The question is not merely who is absent, and who is central, but who is telling the story and why. The ends which could be achieved, however, were different for men and women. Ottonian men could hope to bolster their own rule; Emma and Edith sought to survive. Emma certainly and Edith probably sought to survive as powerful women, to exploit the roles of

[76] The Lives of Mathilda are related to the Ottonian and Saxon succession struggles, though not directly commissioned as part of them. Lintzel 1961 a–c, for a political interpretation; Corbet 1986 muting the political significance; Althoff 1988 for the role among others of the nuns of Nordhausen and their interests and alignments.

[77] Witness e.g. the great debates over Edward's celibacy, and his rather passive character.

royal mother or widow. Neither woman, as we have seen, denied those identities. To understand them, and to pass final judgement on their victimhood or power, those identities will need to be fully explored.

Telling the various stories of Emma and Edith should not be a prelude to ignoring them as partial, dismissing them as biased or disarticulating elements of them to reassemble them in our own. It must be recognized that some are closer to events than others, some are constructed out of others, and especially that there was more than one, even at the time. Their perspectives and retrospectives must be noted; whether contemporary or late, all are selective narratives sparked by particular circumstances, shaped by their authors and rarely centred on Emma and Edith themselves. Later ones must be scrutinized for lost tales, and to uncover anachronistic judgements. The stories told by contemporaries had potential significance for the unfolding of Emma's and Edith's own lives: those told c. 1016, for example, had implications for Emma's place and power afterwards; those told in and after 1035 and 1066 passed judgements and made assessments which became part of politics, prompting new narratives, which were themselves political action, most notably Emma's and Edith's own. Ultimately the most successful narrative will be that which makes best sense of all the acceptable evidence, including that from the early stories.

That successful narrative will have to cope with the problems and omissions of the stories. Emma and Edith were rarely presented as active, and when they were became subject to the difficulty of describing active women. That activity must be sought, whilst recognizing that being an active woman may have been as difficult as describing one. The court and household, a major potential area of their activity, were normally omitted from the narratives, and must be restored. The identities through which the authors pigeonholed Emma and Edith must be investigated and their problems and strengths revealed. It is the looming figures of Wife, Mother, Widow and Queen who will fill some of the gaps in Emma's and Edith's stories and sharpen the understanding which will make best sense of the final narrative.

Part II

The Structures

3

The Faces of the Queen

Lady of the world, queen of heaven, bride of Christ and fruitful mother of the only son of God.

The eleventh-century titles of Mary mirror those of the eleventh-century English queen. The roles and identities they represent were used by the authors of the eleventh-century stories and underlay the careers of Emma and Edith. Like all roles they were dominant scripts which set the parameters of the parts which queens had to play. Such scripts are archetypes with great powers of survival and reassertion.[1] The powers and vulnerabilities of Emma and Edith as Lady, Wife, Mother and Queen were to a large extent already a part of the Great Play, or at least of its early medieval European version. But roles are social and context-governed. They have no single author, no passive audience and no final form. Queens play opposite kings, abbesses, reforming churchmen, lay nobles, and their parts vary in relation to each other and change over time. Emma and Edith were presented with the scripts as rewritten specifically for tenth- and eleventh-century English queens. But in life as opposed to art the scenes have not been predetermined; the characters must ad-lib. The actor is called on for a personal interpretation, and great ones can rewrite the part. Emma and Edith found themselves in circumstances which called for creative acting, as their predecessors had done before them. Emma's 'Wife', 'Queen' if not 'Mother', Edith's 'Widow' were surely among the great individual performances of the English early middle ages; Eadgifu and Ælfthryth, earlier English queens, loomed in the wings of the recent past. The final chapters of this book will be concerned with those individual performances; with the careers of two English queens as they were acted out. First the fundamental scripts and their tenth- and eleventh-century English rewrite must be examined.

*   *   *

[1] Stafford 1983, for more on these.

The titles of Mary are those used in the New Minster Missal's preface for the feast of the Conception.[2] What may seem the commonplace variations on the theme of Mary had special resonance in the eleventh century. The many faces of Mary were the many faces of the queen. *Domina/hlæfdige* (Lady), *regina* (Queen) *conlaterana regis* (she who was at the king's side) *regis mater* (king's mother): such were the queen's titles in tenth- and eleventh-century English documents. Mary as Lady, Queen, Bride and Mother paralleled these earthly queens. Her identities were their identities. She combined them just as Emma and Edith did. There were differences, and significant ones. Mary was the *sponsa Christi*, the ever-virgin bride of Christ; the queen was the king's wife, the one consecrated to the royal bed.[3] Mary's identities were linked in a ritual litany which slid over their contradictions and problems. Queens in the flesh added and accumulated, passed from one to another through their careers, experienced all the problems as well as the opportunities of the female lifecycle and its roles. The kingdom of heaven provided ideals but not straightforward role-models for earthly queens. Yet the eleventh-century Winchester scribe who described Mary under these titles had a living English queen before him of whom most of them were used. They and their meanings are the point of departure for a study of the structures of eleventh-century English queenship; the bone structure of the faces of Emma and Edith.[4]

'The Lady', or more correctly in Old English *seo hlæfdige*, was the title used to describe Emma on her arrival in England in 1002: 'the Lady Richard's daughter came hither', and at her death in 1052: 'In this year died Ælfgifu the Lady.'[5] It was the most common title of a king's wife in vernacular documents of the tenth and eleventh centuries;[6] so common that it could almost be translated as 'queen' to cover all the personae of the king's wife, mother and consecrated Queen. This portmanteau title was, however, sometimes used in a more discriminating way. Some Latin accounts based on vernacular documents translate it as *domina* not *regina*,[7] whilst the Old English *cwen*, from which modern English 'queen' derives, is frequently used to translate *regina* or to mean a king's wife.[8]

---

[2] 'Mundi domina, celi regina, sponsa Christi et unici filii Dei foeta mater', *The Missal of the New Minster*, p 190.

[3] As in S 909, 1004 'thoro consecrata regio' – a rare title of the queen in charters.

[4] For earlier general discussion see Harmer in *Writs*, p 448; Stevenson in *Asser*, pp 200–2, Campbell, *Encomium* in Appendix 1, pp 55–61

[5] *ASC*, MSS C, D and E s.a. 1002 and MS D s.a. 1052.

[6] See e.g. *Wills* 8, 11, 23, 26, 27, 29, 30 and the *Will of Æþelgifu*; R 49, 81, 86, 96, 98, 101, 114, 117; *Writs* 27, 70, 72, 94, 104, 112; *ASC*, MSS C, D and E s.a. 1002, 1003, 1013; MS C, 1035, MS D 1043; MS E s.a. 1048 (recte 1051) etc.

[7] *LE*, pp 157–8 the Latin version of the will of Leofflæd, and the metrical Calendar in BL Cotton Galba xvii and other MSS where Ealhswith is called '*veram* (or *caram*) *dominam Anglorum*', *Hampson*, p 110.

[8] See examples in the Old English *Concordance* where it appears, for example, as a translation of *regina* in the Old English translation of Bede, as Ælfric's preferred term for a king's wife, in Beowulf etc.

In 1051 manuscript E of the Anglo-Saxon Chronicle used the two words to suggest a hierarchical relationship between *hlæfdige* and *cwen* – Edith was not only the Lady but the consecrated Queen.[9] The highly charged political context should make us wary of reading from this to a universal eleventh-century distinction; but it also prompts investigation of the history and meanings of 'Lady'.

As a specialized title applied to the king's wife *hlæfdige* may be a term left over from ninth-century Wessex, originally denoting a lower, less queenly status. The ninth-century West Saxons, or more accurately the ninth-century West Saxons as reported by King Alfred, did not allow the king's wife to be called *regina*.[10] What title they did use we are not told; but the less regal *hlæfdige* is a candidate. Like so many claims about status and custom Alfred's statement was as strategic as it was descriptive; his insistence may be no simple reflection of ninth-century West Saxon usage. It was directed particularly against his own wife Ealhswith and the claims of her son Edward the Elder. Ealhswith was the first king's wife to whom the title 'Lady' was certainly applied,[11] though in a way which already shows how titles can change in meaning. The usage dates from the reign of her son Edward the Elder. Edward had every interest in stressing his mother's standing; what may have started as a title to demonstrate lesser status, was now reclaimed for a higher one. Whether she was or was not *regina* of the West Saxons, she was now the 'true (or dear) lady of the English' associated with the widest aspirations of tenth-century kingship to rule all the English. *Seo hlæfdige* would later be used of one of the most prominent of tenth-century queens, Eadgifu.[12] Applied to such women, used in such ways the term was filled with new meanings. The usage of titles so loaded with status implications changes over time and must be carefully historicized. The Chronicler's coupling of *cwen* rather than *hlæfdige* with 'consecrated' in the mid eleventh century might suggest that by that date what distinguished a Lady was that she was not anointed. But the title was used of women whose consecration is not in doubt.[13] The redefinition of queens through the practice of consecration sometimes called for distinctions to be made, and the shades of non-regality which *hlæfdige* trailed meant it was available when such a hierarchy needed to be expressed, as in the Chronicler's case. But that

[9] *ASC*, MS E 1948 recte 1051 calls Edith a *hlæfdige* who had been consecrated as *cwen* making an apparent distinction between a *hlæfdige* as a king's wife and *cwen* as a consecrated Queen.

[10] *Asser* cap 13; see Stafford 1981 and especially Nelson 1991b.

[11] See n 7. Note that *ASC*, MS A s.a. 672, 722, 737, 888 uses the term *cwen*, which was clearly a normal word for queen at the end of the ninth century in Wessex.

[12] *Wills* 11, the document, however, is later than Eadgifu's lifetime, referring back to a transaction involving her. It also uses the title of the contemporary queen, Ælfthryth, see next note.

[13] See *Wills* 11, dated after 973, using the title of Ælfthryth, and cf e.g. R 86 of Emma, *Writs* 70 of Edith etc.

does not mean that it generally denoted anything less than a Queen. By the time we encounter it used of Emma at her arrival in 1002 it had probably escaped most connotations of lower status which it may originally have had. By 1002 it could be applied to a king's wife, to his mother and to a consecrated Queen; the many identities of the queen had absorbed it into regality.

But 'lady' as opposed to 'the Lady' had a more general range of meanings. By the tenth and eleventh centuries it denoted a class status in relation to the land and its workers, to servants and followers. A full discussion of the idea of a 'lady' would have to begin from that of a 'lord', a task which would fill more than a book in itself.[14] All the uses of the word *dominus* and *hlaford* current by these central centuries of the middle ages fill *domina* and *hlæfdige* with their potential: lord of a people, an area, of land, of servants; used of kings, emperors, popes, bishops and abbots;[15] a master of servants, a male head of a household, a ruler, an owner or proprietor, and a husband.[16] In England a *hlæfdige* was one who commanded servants, ruled a household or a family; a house or household had a '*hlafedig*'.[17] It was a word which glossed *materfamilias*, and was equated with the 'mother of a community'.[18] The eyes of servants watched the hands of their lords, the eyes of serving maids those of their *hlæfdian*.[19] The origins of the word are linked with those of *hlaford*, lord, and *hlafeata*, a follower. All turn on the notion of the provision, making and acceptance of bread (*hlaf*/loaf), more broadly of the means of subsistence. Wherever else and however else the lord, lady and their followers were joined, their paradigmatic nexus was in the household itself. Whatever else she was or might be, a lady/*hlæfdige* was the mistress of a household.

By the tenth century 'lord' and 'lady' carried meanings of nobility and the exercise of power. So firmly was *domina* linked by now to high status, to the nobility, that it was widely used in Europe to describe queens, empresses, royally born abbesses and other women of the highest rank.[20] It is possible that its use for English queens is linked to this wider

---

[14] The literature is enormous: see e.g. Reuter 1979, Poly and Bournazel 1991. Reynolds 1994, p 36 warns about its interpretation.

[15] See Niermeyer.

[16] *Hlaford*'s many meanings in Old English are thus grouped together by Toller and Campbell 1972, p 549.

[17] Life of St Giles, ed from CCCC MS 303 for the Dictionary of Old English, line no 112. Cited in the *Concordance*.

[18] Ælfric, *Glossary*, p 301, domina/hlæfdige; materfamilias/hiredes modor oððe hlæfdige. See the *Concordance* for many instances of the term used in these ways.

[19] *Cambridge Psalter*, p 326, Psalm 122, verse 2.

[20] See e.g. *D O II* no 300 where Adelaide was '*dilectam matrem et nostram dominam*'; Gerbert d'Aurillac, letter no 50 to Mathilda, comitissa, wife of Godfrey of Verdun as '*domina*'; ibid no 66 referring to the *colloquium dominarum*, a meeting which included a

European usage; though more likely that in each case the connotations of the word made it appropriate to describe the queens who were in a sense the highest members of the nobility, just as lord described the king. If Alfred demoted queen to Lady he was too aware of the standing of royalty to allow the drop to be a large one. In 1086 a Domesday jury encountered the case of a Yorkshire woman who allegedly held her land freely and separately from the lordship of her husband, and then withdrew from him and and possessed it herself. Seeking to capture her full power and autonomy they could find no better way of describing her than holding 'as a lady'.[21] All the power of the noble, ruling class is contained in that description.

The Domesday jurors, or the recorder of their deliberations, using *domina* to describe a woman's power, even her independence of her husband, raise the first conundrum in a search for the powers, authority and position of the queen. *Domina* is the feminine, not necessarily the exact female equivalent of *dominus*. It shares the general public status of the class, but not necessarily all the meanings and connotations of a lord. One of the standard tenth- and eleventh-century uses of *dominus*, as of *hlaford*, was 'husband', to whom a woman as wife was subject; *domina/hlæfdige* never meant a wife. The class meanings of lord and lady filled them with power, which could cut across gender; the family meaning of lord established a hierarchy which confirmed gender distinctions. The implications of such contradictions for the power and authority of the queen will be a recurring theme. For the moment it is best to refine the definition of 'the Lady' as a queen's title: in the loosest sense 'queen', encompassing king's wife, mother and Queen, but most specifically the wife as mistress of the royal household and partaker in the king's status as the most noble of nobles.

Conlaterana regis/she who is at the king's side/wife, was the description most frequently used for Edith in the year following her marriage.[22] The title calls attention especially to the wife as a sharer in the king's status.[23] There is no precise Old English equivalent of it; its implications were perhaps covered by *hlæfdige*. The use of it for Edith at this date contrasts her with the still living Emma, the king's mother, who had lost her dominant position in the king's household. *Coniunx*/wife even

---

group of women including some or all of Duchess Beatrice, Empress Adelaide and Theophanu, Queens Emma, Mathilda, Abbess Mathilda of Quedlinburg, and possibly Adelaide, wife of Hugh Capet.

[21] *ut domina*, DB I, fo373r; discussed Stafford 1989b.

[22] S 1007, 1008, 1009, 1011, 1012, 1013, 1016. Only S 1010, for Thorth, a charter preserved at Wilton calls her *regina* at this date; see also the title used of her in S 1028 (1059), 1031 (1060), 1033 (1061), 1040 (1065).

[23] See Niermeyer, Latham and DuCange, for the meanings of *conlateranus/Collateralis* in a variety of circumstances suggesting if not always outright equality, a shared or substituted status.

legitima coniunx/legitimate wife was used of Ælfthryth, Emma's mother-in-law, at the time of the birth of her first son c. 966.[24] The concern was to stress the legitimacy of the marriage of a third wife, and thus the claims of her sons to inherit. These usages are very specific and highlight the relative rarity of 'King's wife' or some variant of it as a title. Even rarer are titles which call attention to the more sexually explicit idea of the wife as the king's bedfellow; found occasionally in Latin titles, and rather more often in Old English.[25] To those who wished to describe the queen through her titles, wifeliness, and especially the sexual relationship which we might feel made a woman a queen, was either the least important, the least powerful, or the least acceptable face of her power.

The explanation for this rarity may lie in the nature of the documentation and the public face of the queen it delineates. Most Latin titles are found in the witness lists of solemn diplomas; vernacular ones in such sources as literature and sermons, but also in the chronicling of public events and the records of land transactions and disputes. Many of these sources are concerned with the public world of the kingdom, of the royal or local courts. The witness lists of diplomas are in many ways 'official', in the sense that they record office-holders, bishops, ealdormen, abbots and members of the royal household. It is in her public functions that a queen is recorded. The status which is hers in the private world of the family is thus arguably unimportant.

This public/private, kingdom/family explanation is attractive but requires refinement. The family role of mother was happily acknowledged as a suitable description of the queen's public power, and a tenth-century king's mother, Eadgifu, mother of kings Edmund and Eadred, is one of the most regularly recorded witnesses of diplomas. Moreover some aspects of a wife's status could be recognized, as the meanings of *hlæfdige* showed: those in the household, and the power of the woman who stood at the king's side. It was wife as sexual partner which was least represented. The queen, of course, was far from the sole potential sexual partner of a king; sexual favour might be, but was not necessarily, a basis of her power. Insofar as it was, it was the most secret and the least legitimate. The sexual queen was a bad woman, not even acknowledged as queen. When the *Life of Dunstan* portrayed King Eadwig 'wallowing like a pig in a sty' with his wife, it omits to describe that wife as queen.[26] Titles are concerned with the public not the private faces of the queen;

[24] S 739 and 745; see also *Wills* 9, c. 970, for the 'cyninges wife'.
[25] In Latin charters see *thoro consecrata regio*, S 909 (St Frideswide charter, 1004) and S 955 (grant to Agemund, Shaftesbury cartulary, 1019); for the old English *gebedda/ibedda* see R 45 (of Ælfthryth); R 115, *Writs* 69 (of Edith).
[26] *Life of Dunstan*, Auctore B, pp 32–4; she is 'ignominiosa mulier . . . inpudens virago . . . Jezebel . . . furens femina'.

but they do not so much describe an obvious distinction as assert an ideology which labels public and private and assigns actions and individuals to one or the other. In the tenth and eleventh centuries the world of family was as much public as private, and a source of women's power. Yet it was precisely here that gender hierarchies had to be established and that power limited. The public/private distinction is one way of achieving this. It is not the family, but the sexual union at its centre which was here labelled as private. The labelling was never consistent; such an ideological distinction as public and private rarely is.[27] When Ælfthryth was consecrated Queen in 973, the lay nobility seem to have insisted that it was a royal bedfellow who was being consecrated, though their insistence was itself a statement about the limited status of a queen (see below p 164). Female powers could only be recognized in some of their forms. The lack of an acceptable public face made wife-as-bedfellow the least appropriate title to describe the queen. Such refusals provide the ammunition for attacks on queens, as in the *Life of Dunstan*. They make it more difficult for individual women to enact a role like Wife, which combines sexual partner and household mistress in a contradictory script.

There were few such problems surrounding the title of King's Mother. The King's Mother, *mater regis*, or some equivalent is a common title, the normal one for Eadgifu in the mid tenth century,[28] common for Ælfthryth after Edgar's death[29] and eclipsing *regina* for Emma herself between 1040 and 1044.[30] It is found in the vernacular as in the Latin documents.[31] There are no Lady Wives, but there are Lady Mothers.[32] Motherhood was the acceptable face of female power, even of authority. A widowed queen with a son who was king was more likely to be entitled the king's mother than queen. Those who felt uncertain of the desirability of the power of a man's wife were happier with that of his mother. Here was a publicly acceptable face of female power, even possibly a basis for

[27] See e.g. Rapp 1979.

[28] The only exceptions are the spurious S 477 – its use of the term *regina* to describe her should be added to other grounds for rejecting this charter, and the three so-called alliterative charters S 544, where she is '*felix*' and S 561 and 566 where she is '*evax*'. This charter type is creative in the titles it uses of many classes of witness.

[29] The four exceptions are S 835, 840, 843; in S 837 she is among the bishops which may be a result of a copiest's error.

[30] The exceptions here are S 998, Horton/Sherborne archive, grant to Ordgar, where she is *regina* and the spurious S 995, Bury charter in which she is *regina* and *mater* – and also *Ymma*, a name which she is never given in acceptable English sources before 1066. Cf Campbell, *Encomium*, pp 55–6 for discussion of her English and French names. All charter references to her by her French name or her double name, Ælfgifu/Imme, are either late copies or very dubious on other grounds. The *ASC* references to her French name are either insertions, over erasure, or in post 1066 manuscripts.

[31] For vernacular usage see e.g. *Wills* 15; R 69; 94; 96; *Writs* 104, and cf 9, 10, 16, 18, 24.

[32] R 96, of Emma.

regency itself; the world of family was not by definition a private one. That does not mean that expectations of motherhood were consistent nor that it was unproblematic for royal women as a foundation of power. And the preference of so many scribes for a family as opposed to an official role to describe her was prejudicial to the development of a notion of official queenship as a parallel to kingship.

That notion of an official status was most clearly recognized in the title *regina*/queen, the title charter scribes of Cnut's reign regularly gave to Emma,[33] and increasingly preferred for Edith in the latter years of Edward. *Cwen* is its closest Old English equivalent, the one Ælfric normally used for 'queen' in his writings of the late tenth and early eleventh centuries, including to gloss *regina*. Mary is heaven's *cwen*, and the queen of Sheba and Esther were *cwen*.[34] It was widely used to denote the king's wife or to couple queen with king.[35] If Lady was the class title of the queen, Mother if not Wife her family ones, Queen was perhaps her official one. It related her to the king and thus to ideas of office and the kingdom. *Regina* corresponded to *rex* in roughly the same way as *domina* to *dominus*. It might thus be expected to denote consecration or some similar formal inauguration, such as those which made a king. Few of its usages, however, are precise enough to be certain that this is what *regina* let alone *cwen* meant to contemporaries. No English queen was given that title formally in the tenth century before Ælfthryth,[36] and she was the first tenth-century English queen who was certainly consecrated, in 973. But if 973 were her first consecration, she was given the title before it.[37] The issue is complicated by the fact that Ælfthryth may have been consecrated twice, perhaps as early as 965.[38] Ælfthryth raises rather

---

[33] The only exceptions are S 955, 956, 964, 967.

[34] Ælfric, *Glossary*, p 300 and cf *imperatrix vel augusta, caseres cwen*; Ælfric, *Catholic Homilies II*, no 40 p 340, line 175ff; Homily on Esther, p 93, lines 36–8; Ælfric in his Grammar uses *regina*/*cwen* as his examples of the declension of the feminine gender in Latin and Old English, *Grammar*, p 24.

[35] See examples from Maxims, Riddles, the Old English Orosius and Bede etc. cited in the *Concordance*.

[36] At least in charter witness lists. An Eadgifu *regina* appears in a gospel book inscription in the reign of Athelstan: this may be Eadgifu, Edward the Elder's widow (thus Stafford 1981, p 17 and n 44), or perhaps more likely Eadgifu, wife of the West Frankish king Charles the Simple, in exile at her brother's court, as suggested by Keynes 1985, pp 190–3. West Frankish queens were certainly consecrated by the early tenth century. *Cwen* was used of Edmund's second wife by *ASC*, MS D 946, and in the same MS of Ælfthryth in 965. But both usages may be retrospective since this chronicle did not take its final form before the mid eleventh century or later.

[37] See S 731 (AD 964), 767 (968), 806 (968) etc.

[38] Arguments about her consecration and the claims of her sons to the throne were remembered at the end of the eleventh century. Unfortunately it is not clear whether they should be read as indicating that she was consecrated before or after the birth of her sons in the 960s. See Eadmer, *Vita Dunstani*, p 214 recalling that Edgar's first wife, Edward's

than allays doubts about whether *regina* implied consecration and office. The Latin *regina* if not the Old English *cwen* expresses the link between the *king* and the *queen*. It underlines how far many of her identities are connected to him and his regality, and transformed by that connection: she is the *king's* wife, the *king's* mother. The same title leaves unclear how far the connection necessarily extended to a share of his royal attributes and office, most fully expressed in his consecration. Such ambiguity bedevils the study of queenship, and the lives of individual queens.

Whatever *regina* meant, it did not transform a woman's status once and for all, as the acquisition of kingship did that of a man. Scribes vary between *regina* and occasionally some variant of wife, and it was normal for a *regina* to be called a *king's mother* after the death of her husband and accession of her son. More rarely titles could be combined for the queen, as Lady Mother, or Lady Queen, or Queen, King's Mother. A Queen always remained a Wife or Mother. In the Preface to the *Regularis Concordia* Ælfthryth was invoked both as a wife and as a queen

> And he (King Edgar) wisely ordered his wife, Ælfthryth, to defend the houses of nuns like a fearless guardian, so that a man might help the men, a woman the women without any breath of scandal.[39]

The Preface here makes a clear gender division, invoking 'woman' and 'wife'. But elsewhere king and queen were coupled together in a different hierarchy, that of power:

> The lordship (*dominium*) of the king and queen should ever be sought. . . . the fathers and mothers of monasteries shall come to do humble service/homage (*obsequium*) to the king and queen. . . .[40]

The queen was given supervision of women as a woman and wife, but her capacity to help and control them was rooted in a power she shared with the king; here she is Queen. Gender hierarchy and identity are to the fore in a context of sexual regulation and prescription; other status hierarchies when the question is of protection and patronage. Such combinations and changes indicate the possible accumulation of contradictions

mother, was legally wed, but not consecrated and cf Prior Nicholas' letter, *Memorials of St Dunstan*, p 423 with even more emphasis on Edward's mother's high status, but confirming that she had not been consecrated whereas Ælfthryth had. Nicholas and Eadmer both believed that Edgar was not himself crowned and anointed before 973. If these statements echo arguments about the succession in 975 they appear to have turned on whether respective candidates' mothers had been consecrated. Both Ælfthryth's sons were born before her recorded consecration in 973. For comment on this see Nelson 1977 (1986), pp 300 and notes, and 373.

[39] *Regularis Concordia*, cap 3 p 2. NB the translation 'Queen' on p 3 for *coniunx* is inaccurate.

[40] Ibid cap 10, p 7.

between the different roles of an individual woman, underline the multiple identities of women which have become a commonplace of women's history. Equally they signal the opportunities of multiple roles, one enhanced by another. It is perhaps no accident that all the surviving cases where queen is combined with other titles refer to Emma.[41]

The titles of the queen point in the directions a search for the structures of queenship should take. The public acknowledgement of titles suggests a need for further study of the royal court and household and its organization, of the queen as a landholder with followers, of the family and its roles, and of the idea of her regality: of Lady, of Wife, of Mother, of Queen. Although convenience dictates separation of these areas for study, the titles have indicated how far in practice they were combined. They grew out of each other, built one upon another, enhanced or sapped each other's powers. It was these roles or their combination which both linked the queen to other women yet separated her from them, which made her virtually the only tenth- or eleventh-century English woman judged fitting and important enough to be recorded in the witness lists of diplomas.

[41] Except for *ASC*, MS E 1048 recte 1051 – and this was a very special pleading.

4

Family: Structures and Ideals

When Emma crossed from Normandy to England to marry Æthelred in 1002, she became the second if not third wife of an older man, a young woman facing an existing royal brood numbering ten or more children. Within three years she had added a son of her own, and went on to produce another son and daughter. The relationships of such a complex family were not destined to be straightforward; her husband's recent family history was designed to exacerbate them. When she went on to marry Cnut in 1017, it was a second marriage for both of them; she was a widow, and he had previously entered a union with another woman. Both already had children, and were to produce two more together. Edith's marriage to Edward was a first marriage for both; its failure to produce children resulted in an attempt at her repudiation. The childless couple were surrounded by relatives, and attracted the attention of more. Family, its structures and its politics, was fundamental to the lives of both women.

Eleventh-century England was both a *regnum* and a *patria*; a kingdom and a patrimony, under a ruler who was also the head of a family.[1] The king was a *cyning*, a member of the kin, his claim to rule expressed as a genealogy in which the blood line of previous kings provided his legitimacy. Kings, at least in theory, were born; those who were not born kings hastily sought some alternative form of legitimacy. Queens, by contrast, acquired the part. The queen was queen by virtue of her family relationship to the king, through marriage as his wife, physically as his mother. As a wife she married in; whatever being a queen meant always derived from the relationship of husband and wife. Motherhood fully incorporated her, as the mother of a future king, in the fullness of time of the king himself. As a mother she was an integral part of the family; whatever being a queen meant sometimes derived from the relationship of mother and son. The scripts for relationships between mothers, fathers

[1] Nelson 1988.

and children and between husbands and wives were written by contemporary ideologies of marriage and motherhood, the nature and security of marriage itself, inheritance and claims on the family land, and by recent family practice and experience of all of these.

1 Wife and Marriage

Emma and Edith entered the eleventh-century stories as kings' wives, through marriage. Marriage was the most important transition in an eleventh-century woman's life. Old English terminology collapsed 'wife' and 'woman' together: to be an adult woman was to be a wife. Marriage was an essentially secular affair, made between families. It was made in stages: negotiations between families culminating in parental consent, leading to betrothal accompanied by gifts and the specification of dower and dowry, the gathering of a dowry, the leading to the husband's home, the final public rite and then the consummation in the marriage bed.[2] Marriage by stages is a lawyer's nightmare and a repudiator's charter. The omission of any stage can be an argument for a less than fully binding tie. Unequal or asymmetrical unions, even those intended at the time of making to be binding, were especially likely to be made without all the property exchanges. Tenth-century English kings had exploited this situation. They were often serial monogamists. Emma was Æthelred's second if not third wife.[3] Eadgifu had occupied the same place in Edward the Elder's tally, and Ælfthryth in Edgar's. Sometimes replacement decorously followed a previous wife's death, at others her repudiation and dismissal.[4] This marriage pattern left wives insecure during their husband's lifetime. It produced the tense step-relationships which fuelled family faction and succession struggles, in turn inhibiting the emergence of simple succession patterns in the tenth century.

Marriage was a source of power as well as insecurity. It joined a woman to her husband, gave her a place in the household and, if it were a full marriage, entailed a property settlement. Dower was provided for

[2] See e.g. Gaudemet, e.g. pp 185ff and for the steps in the making of an English marriage, Be Wifmannes Beweddung, *EHD I*, no 50.

[3] We cannot be certain whether Æthelred married twice or three times. His first wife was daughter of ealdorman Thored of York according to the twelfth-century Aelred, *Vita S Edwardi Regis*, col 741. Thored's prominence in the mid 980s and disgrace and disappearance c. 993 would date this marriage to the king's coming of age c. 985, coinciding with the temporary disappearance of Ælfthryth from court. The first wife's name is unrecorded. Worcester sources after 1066 made Æthelred's first wife Ælfgifu, daughter of the otherwise unknown *comes* Æthelberht; thus Fl Wig, ed Thorpe, I, p 275, Genealogia regum West Saxonum. This may simply be error, thus Keynes 1980, p 187 n 118, but the confusion may mask two marriages.

[4] Stafford 1981.

a wife and widow by the husband and his family.[5] Husband's kin retained claims on it, but the strongest claims were those of the children born of this new stage in the family, and of the widow herself. The size of her dower might be the result of the bargaining strength of the family of an in-marrying woman, but it also expressed the status of her husband within his own kin, and that family's perception of its own standing. A widow's claims on it were as a wife who continued in some respects the identity of her husband, and as a mother who held his inheritance for her children.[6] It was such claims which Cnut would have considered when he chose Emma, Æthelred's widow, as his wife in 1017. Emma herself could have seen them as a basis for regency in 1035.

The ideals of this institution gave power to a wife and protected her, but in neither case unambiguously. A man acquired a wife through negotiation with her family, but the resulting marriage was a partnership in which her counsel and her role in the household were accepted.

> A king shall buy a queen with goods, with beakers and bracelets; both shall be generous with gifts. Battle and warfare shall be strong in the noble man, and the woman shall thrive, beloved by her people, be cheerful of mind, keep counsel . . . know wise counsel for them both together, the householders.[7]

But the partnership of husband and wife brought problems.

> It is meet that a woman be at her table; a roving woman causes words to be uttered; often she defames man with her vices. Men speak of her with contempt; often her cheek fades.
>   A wife shall keep faith with her husband; often she dishonours him with her vices; many a one is steadfast in mind, many a one is prying.[8]

A wife's legitimate role, as sexual partner, counsellor and household manager, entailed a closeness and dependence which provoked fear. She

[5] Pollock and Maitland vol II, pp 420ff and Morelle 1988 for important general discussion.
[6] Scandinavian, including Danish inheritance practice, allowed a mother to be the heir of her children, Sawyer, B. 1988. This was possibly also an English notion, though there are no examples to prove it from these centuries. The *Leges Henrici Primi*, cap 70.20 makes a father or mother heir of one who died without children. The *Leges* are twelfth-century but deliberately archaic in some respects. Æthelberht's laws are the only early ones to deal in any detail with the question of marriage and inheritance. In caps 77 to 81 the emphasis on the bearing of children as the basis of a wife's claim on her husband's property has the same implications as reverse inheritance from children to mother, i.e. it gives the new conjugal unit priority in claims over the claims of wider kin on either father or mother's side, and effectively makes a wife who is a mother also her husband's heir. But these laws were already four hundred years old. Domesday Book has many examples of mothers and sons holding land together, but I know of no precise case of reverse inheritance in early England.
[7] *Anglo-Saxon Poetry*, p 311, translating *Maxims* I, ASPR, 3, The Exeter Book (1939), p 159.
[8] *Anglo-Saxon Poetry*, pp 310–311, translating *Maxims* I, ASPR, 3, The Exeter Book (1939), pp 159–60.

was an outsider with her own interests and connections, a potential threat to her husband's reputation through her own. These ideals view the role of wife from the husband's perspective. They allot her a powerful sphere of influence, but as part of a personal relationship which is shorn of all the complications of social context. The good wife and her legitimate powers are, for example, silently placed within an uncomplicated monogamous relationship to which the only threat is the woman's own behaviour, towards her husband or outsiders. Rival wives and their children do not exist. The ideal sanctioned a wife's influence and power, whilst turning a blind eye to the circumstances in which a woman might often be called upon to exercise them.

This age-old dichotomy, expressed in these gnomic utterances, existed in tenth-and eleventh-century England alongside Christian notions of marriage. These were articulated most clearly in the nuptial mass and its two long prayers blessing the bride and the newly married couple. They affirmed that marriage created a partnership and stressed that it was indissoluble. Woman had been created, formed from the flesh of her husband, so that they might be inseparable. It was a mystery in which the union of Christ and his church was prefigured. The injunction that man and woman should be joined had survived intact from the original state of Paradise, unaffected by original sin or the Flood. The ritual ended with a blessing of the couple;[9] or with a blessing of the marriage chamber and all who dwelt therein, that they might live in peace, according to God's will and grow old and multiply in length of days.[10] Such blessings hoped for peaceful life, health of mind and body and the joy of producing holy children, and after the end of the labours of this life, the society of the angels. The theology of marriage was a positive one. Marriage was a route to earthly and heavenly happiness. Children, especially holy children, were a gift, the stretching out of the generations was an earthly immortality which prefigured that of heaven. Procreation lay at the heart of marriage; so too did a society between the couple themselves, united as in one flesh. Consummation was not enjoined in the marriage prayers, but the ends they sought required it.

It was, however, the woman who was to be faithful, chaste, disciplined, modest, blameless. The chamber and bed where the couple would lie together might be blessed that it might be an abode of holiness, chastity, tenderness, the fullness of the law and obedience to God. But responsibility for achieving this fell especially on the wife. Blessing was called down upon *her*, that she might be loving and peaceful, faithful and chaste, an imitator of holy women, as loving to her husband as Rachel,

---

[9] See e.g. *The Claudius Pontificals*, Claudius I p 73, cf *The Pontifical of Egbert*, p 140.
[10] See e.g. *The Pontifical of Egbert*, pp 133–4, and the *Durham Collectar*, pp 220–5 (*The Durham Ritual* fos 51r–53v) where the blessings follow the mass.

as wise as Rebecca, as long-lived and faithful as Sarah. Joined in one marriage bed she was to flee illegal contact, strengthen her weakness with discipline, be shyly grave, worthy of respect in her modesty, knowledgeable in heavenly doctrines, fruitful in offspring, worthy and blameless. A common blessing of the couple could be matched by a blessing *of* the wife *for* the husband 'that you may see your children and your children's children to the third and fourth generation, and your seed be blessed by the God of Israel'. The equality of a shared flesh was negated by a hierarchy of the order of creation. The prayers recalled that Eve was created from Adam. Christian ideals of indissolubility underpinned the couple, enhancing the idea of the wife as partner and her security. But the stress on progeny as the fulfilment of marriage weakened, though never destroyed, these arguments in the face of childlessness. The equality of monogamy enjoined on both was limited by the onus still placed on the wife. Divorce was not endorsed, but the way was left open for accusations of adultery to threaten a wife rather than a husband. There was no script in this idealized world for the real-life complications of serial monogamy. Its silences or at least evasions officially implied that children were always a blessing never a problem. The potential for conflict between 'Wife' and 'Mother', and those within 'Mother' herself, went unacknowledged. The idealized worlds of the gnomic utterances and of the nuptial blessings overlapped.

Christian ideals in particular had implications for the making and unmaking of marriage, and thus for the security of wives and the claims of their sons. In tenth- and eleventh-century England marriage was caught up in the currents of church reform. Nowhere was this clearer than at the level of the royal family. Christian rites had long been involved in the making of marriage. The Roman nuptial mass, '*pro sponsis*', was known in England by the tenth century,[11] so too were the sets of marriage blessings, some of them independent of the mass and the church building, used for the blessing of the marriage chamber and bed.[12]

---

[11] It is the *Missa ad sponsam benedicendam* in Claudius I, the earliest of the four 'surviving true pontifical(s) of English origin', Banting, *Egbert Pontifical*, p xvi; it contains the basic prayers of that mass, pp 72–3. Leofric, in origin a Northern French pontifical, already had a fuller version of those prayers, *The Leofric Missal*, p 228.

[12] *The Egbert Pontifical* is the most important evidence of these blessings of the marriage chamber, ring, bed, and a general prayer for progeny apparently said over the husband, *Egbert*, pp 133–4 and see Vogel pp 427–8 and 452 . These blessings are also found in the *Durham Collectar*, ed Correa pp 220–5, though they are not complete since fo 53v was erased, see *The Durham Ritual*, ed T.J. Brown et al, Intro p 33. The original scribe of this manuscript worked in the first quarter of the tenth century in southern England, ibid p 38. Egbert is thus their second appearance in English MSS. Correa, *Durham Collectar*, p 224 n 626 notes that one of the blessings is 'common'. But this does not apply to the blessings as a whole, only to 'Benedic domine thalamum istum . . .' which begins and ends as in Egbert; Franz, p 181 cites its occurrence in an eleventh-century pontifical of the Benedictine

These rites were not necessary to the making of legitimate marriage. They were, however, undergoing development in tenth- and eleventh-century England,[13] suggesting considerable interest in them at this date.[14] Technically few tenth-century royal marriages may have qualified for nuptial mass or blessing. Both were forbidden for second marriages, though there was some hesitation over whether a marriage might be blessed if the woman at least were a virgin.[15] But reforming interest in marriage did not leave royal marriages untouched.

No descriptions of English royal marriages in the tenth and eleventh centuries have survived, though the author of the *Life of Dunstan* gave an account of a royal marriage in heaven. It was made with the witness of the king's great men, with dower (*dos*) for the bride and was accompanied by the singing of worthy praises.[16] Emma's father-in-law, Edgar, had provided dower for her mother-in-law, his third wife Ælfthryth. Soon after their marriage, Edgar granted land to Ælfthryth. The diploma which records it includes a quotation, unusual in English diplomas, of Christ's words that 'They shall be two in one flesh.'[17] At first sight Ælfthryth's diploma has the look of a dower document, designed to make a marriage especially binding by recording the property arrangements which accompanied it; a rare survival for contemporary Europe in

abbey of Lire in the diocese of Evreux – significantly where Egbert ended up. Blessings of the bed and chamber were known in Merovingian Gaul, see Ritzer and Vogel 1977, but by the tenth century evidence for them is confined to England. I hope to return to the marriage rituals in more detail at a later date.

[13] None of the Egbert blessings is listed in Moeller's collection from printed pontificals, the *Corpus Benedictionum Pontificalium*. The blessings from the Canterbury Benedictional, Moeller no 1020, have no analogues. That benedictional, dated to the early eleventh century, just after 1023, is the 'largest surviving pre-conquest English Benedictional . . . the climax of the tradition . . . begun under St Æthelwold', Prescott, p 132. Ibid p 155 n 314, citing the blessings for the bride and bridegroom in the *Canterbury Benedictional* as probably new English compositions.

[14] An interest which emanates perhaps from an affirmation of the role of bishops. They are part of a general proliferation of episcopal blessing formulae at this date, see Prescott, op cit. On bishops and reform see Darlington, Barlow 1963 and Stafford 1989a.

[15] See e.g. Vogel, p 424, and again, quoting Theodore, p 433, and for the reiteration of the prohibition in England at this date see for example Ælfric's letter to Wulfsige, Ælfric, *Pastoral Letters*, no 1 cap 26, p 7 – no priest must bless a second marriage; Wulfstan, *Institutes of Polity*, cap 17, the canons forbid the blessing of a second marriage. But Ælfric in his pastoral letter for Wulfstan implies that the marriage may be blessed if the woman is a virgin, *Pastoral Letters*, no IV, cap 156, pp 125–6. Perhaps this is why at least one English manuscript makes the mass one for the blessing of the bride rather than the couple. It is a mass for the blessing of the bride not, as is more usual, of the couple, in Claudius I, p 72 cf the *Benedictional of Archbishop Robert*, p 149, though in Robert it is a later addition to the MS; cf the *Durham Collectar* pp 220–5, the *Missal of Robert of Jumièges*, pp 269–70 and *Leofric*, p 228 where it is *Ad sponsas benedicendas*.

[16] 'condignas laudes' *Life of Dunstan*, Auctore B, p 41.

[17] S 725, AD 965.

general, let alone for late Saxon England.[18] Comparison with the un-doubted dower diploma which Richard II of Normandy, Emma's own brother, read out to his wife Judith is thus illuminating. Both quote the Christian theology of marriage, especially the emphasis on its binding nature. But in comparison with Richard's Norman diploma, Edgar's is perfunctory. Richard was made to recite a story of the relations of men and women starting in the Garden of Eden, one which likened the marriage of man and woman to the love of Christ for his church and insisted that those who were 'legally wed' (*legaliter nupti*) were joined by God and not to be separated: a single sentence was placed in Edgar's mouth. Richard makes pointed reference to all the stages of the making of a full marriage: Edgar merely refers in passing to the wife at his side, his '*laterana*'. Whilst Richard established both the land and household of his spouse, the Edgar charter does not cover all or most of the land involved in a queen's dower.[19]

Richard's is an exceptional document, and an insight into the meeting of Christian ideas and the politics of marriage. This match was impor-tant; Richard and Judith of equally high birth. The marital history of the Norman counts was chequered. This late tenth-century Norman count desired to be, and to be seen to be, a part of Christian Northern France. The result was pressure from bride's family and groom to specify that this was in every sense a full marriage, to hedge it around with all the secular and ecclesiastical rites available, and to preserve the documentary record in the family house at Fecamp. Edgar was a king and Ælfthryth a nobleman's daughter. Politics and equality did not press on Edgar as they pressed on Richard II.[20]

Reform, however, did. Edgar's grant to Ælfthryth may be a more accidental survival than Judith's dower document, but its sentiments echo a general affirmation of Christian marriage in England at this date, perhaps a particular affirmation of it for kings. There had been a special attempt to single out this marriage and stress its legitimacy, whether through blessing, insistence on the fulfilment of all the necessary stages or by other means.[21] Ælfthryth is the first tenth-century queen who was certainly given formal dower (see below, pp 127–8). The special emphasis extended to the sons of this marriage, and their names and claims (see below). The man behind all this was probably Bishop

---

[18] On them see Morelle. The Cluny series of dower documents is very unusual, see Stafford, 'La mutation familiale' forthcoming.

[19] For more discussion of the queen's dower, see below, 'The Queen's Lands'.

[20] The relative status of the spouses affected different forms of marriage settlement and marriage in the tenth and eleventh centuries as at other times and places; see Konecny for the so-called 'Friedelehe' of the Carolingians; Eames on Scandinavian marriages, and Musset 1959.

[21] Could there have been a blessing of *two* previously married people?

Æthelwold,[22] a known reformer, in the ascendant at court at the time. He would have been one of the great men who witnessed a royal marriage and was particularly concerned about queens. Edgar's third marriage was a special one.

What effect all this had on Æthelred's marriages, and on that to Emma in particular, has to be informed conjecture. No comparable dower diploma has survived for Emma or Edith. Doubt surrounds the number of Æthelred's previous marriages, their dates and the balance of pressures on them, making it difficult to assess their nature or likely impact either on his union with Emma or on his sons' claims on the throne. Æthelred's early marriage(s), like Edgar's, were to the daughters of nobles. His first, made in 984/5,[23] may have been less than full, and easily ended. By the 990s the same reforming influences as existed at his father's court in the mid 960s surrounded him.[24] If there was a second marriage c. 990, it was probably a fully legitimate union and its ending and the marriage to Emma a result of death rather than repudiation.

Emma's own marriage was surely legitimate and full. It sealed a politically important alliance. Her brother Richard's concern for marriage with all the formalities would have sensitized him to the proper treatment of his sister.[25] Christian blessings, if not a mass for the bride, could have been used. The 1002 marriage created a holy royal family. Emma was renamed for one of the dynasty's recent saints, Ælfgifu, Æthelred's grandmother,[26] and a son and daughter were named Edward, perhaps after a recently martyred king, and Godgifu, God's gift. Emma had what security full marriage could bring. Her sons would have been aware that their birth was fully legitimate, their claims on that score unassailable, an assurance her stepsons may have lacked.

Edith's marriage was far more vulnerable. As Godwine's daughter she, like Emma, is likely to have been given the benefit of all available marriage rites when she was consecrated queen in 1045; politics were at this point on her side. Yet in 1051 the king, supported by Archbishop Robert of Jumièges, tried to repudiate her. A marriage is not simply bound at the point of making. It is buffeted by subsequent events. The tightness of the initial knot matters, but it could still be undone. In this case changing political circumstances, but especially the failure of the union in its primary aim of producing sons, threatened Edith's security.

---

[22] The document survived at Abingdon, where Æthelwold had been abbot, and it recalls the emphasis on the legitimacy of this marriage in the 966 New Minster charter which he drafted, S 745. The land may have passed to Abingdon, but by 1066 it was held by a woman, Ælfgifu, and in 1086 by a royal servant, Regenbald of Cirencester, DB I, fo 63r.

[23] See above n 3.

[24] Keynes 1980, pp 189–93.

[25] The date of the marriage of Richard and Judith is uncertain, see below chapter 8 n 34.

[26] See below p 172 for details of her cult and its dating.

Only, apparently, her family's return in 1052 preserved her. Her repudiation and its outcome looks like a triumph of political necessity over principle; an Archbishop of Canterbury counselling a king to repudiate his wife, the strength of her family preventing it. If Edith was more secure than her tenth-century predecessors it was thanks to her father's ships not to Christian ideals.

The fate of a near-fifty-year-old king's barren marriage could not fail to be a political question, but it is a cynical and anachronistic view of mid eleventh-century churchmen to see it as nothing else. The argument was conducted in a Christian moral framework. Later stories of the king's celibacy and the queen's adultery are its survivals. Non-consummation and the wife's fidelity, even the fruitfulness of the marriage were all issues. Repudiation was still thinkable in the mid eleventh century, including by archbishops; the contradictions within Christian marriage ideas allowed it. But it required increasingly good excuses. It was Christian reform as well as politics which made Emma and Edith more secure than many earlier English royal wives, which ensured that both survived as wives to follow their husbands' coffins to the grave.

English and Christian marriage practices and ideals were not the only ones relevant to Emma. She faced Danish marriage practice in 1017, and its consequences after 1035. Danish marriage practice is often presented as distinct from that of Christian Europe. The Danes are alleged to have had a form of marriage by seizure, in which the forcible taking of a woman was then legitimized through a payment which is almost a ransom. The marriage of Cnut and Emma in 1017 has been interpreted in this way.[27] Danish marriage was monogamous, but concubinage was practised and the resulting situation was, it has been claimed, closer to polygamy than serial monogamy. The children of concubines could be recognized by the father for inheritance. Several Danish kings were sons of concubines.[28] All this has implications for the position of Ælfgifu of Northampton and the claims of her sons in 1035. Yet in these respects the distinctions between the recently pagan Danes and Christian Europe were not so sharp as they can be made to appear.

At issue here is the nature of concubinage and the claims of the children of mothers who could be so labelled. Throughout early medieval Europe there were unions which lacked some of the property exchanges by which a union's legitimacy could most readily be defended, particularly when the husband's status was considerably higher than that of the bride, and her family's bargaining power consequently reduced.[29] These

---

[27] See Colman and van Houts 1984, pp 87–8 and n 16. The evidence, however, is all late and its interpretation in much of the secondary literature affected by Germanism and ideas about barbarism and barbarian law which are suspect.

[28] Sawyer and Sawyer, pp 169–71, Eames, p 202.

[29] See Eames, Buchholz, Clunies Ross, Konecny.

unions were often undertaken by men in youth, when they either lacked the property to make a full marriage, or wished to keep options open, or both. Charlemagne, Lothar II, Edward the Elder, and the Norman counts Rollo and William all contracted unions of this sort. The status of a union was established to some extent at its inception, by the kind of exchanges which were then made, but was subject to redefinition. Some were later converted into full marriages, or more correctly, any doubt over the status of the children born of them was removed. Later fuller marriages could downgrade earlier ones, but this was far from an automatic deprivation of the woman and her children of all claims. So many sons born of these unions succeeded to inheritance that it is arguable that they were always seen as having strong expectations. These practices were far from confined to the northern fringes of Europe.

Concubine/wife is too stark a distinction to capture this shifting situation. But it was a distinction sharply drawn by Christian reformers. The claims of the women and children in these unions could be challenged, and Christian definitions provided another weapon in the armoury against them. The story of those challenges is that of the faltering triumph of Christian views of marriage. The last time the son of such a union had succeeded to the throne in England had been Athelstan in the 920s. The reformers of the late tenth and eleventh centuries represented an offensive in favour of Christian marriage, perhaps particularly at royal level. To that extent Cnut's conquest marked a shift, and the situation of Emma vis-à-vis Ælfgifu and her sons was a new one, or rather an older one revived. But the reformers had never completely triumphed, the claims of a woman like Ælfgifu and of her children were still arguable in England as in Denmark. The novelty of Emma's predicament should be recognized, but not overstressed.

Marriage made a Wife, and also a Widow. Widowhood was an important stage in the female lifecycle, and it was conceived as extending the married state beyond death. Confusingly, but instructively, Domesday scribes used *uxor* indiscriminately to describe wife and widow. A widow in some ways continued her husband's personality. The seal of a mid eleventh-century nobleman, Godwine, was recut for Godgyth, probably his widow.[30] For an eleventh-century churchman like Archbishop Wulfstan, consecrated chastity was the ideal of widowhood.[31] Widows should be chaste and not remarry, and their free choice should be respected.[32] These ideals grew out of a Christian veneration for chastity and the individual. But they also addressed a secular reality. A widow had a continued claim on her dead husband's lands; her remarriage was

---

[30] Heslop 1980. She may be his daughter, which would carry a different but significant message about female inheritance.
[31] See Wulfstan, *Institutes of Polity*, cap 18.
[32] Ibid and cf Liebermann, *Die Gesetze der Angelsachsen*, V Atr 21.1 and II Cnut 73.

a potential threat to his kin and to her own children. Almost all the women found exercising any power over land in tenth- and eleventh-century England, through, for example, the making of wills, were widows.[33] A widow was at one remove from her own family and its protection and control; she was both more vulnerable, but more likely to have and exercise freedom. The ideal of the chaste widow circumvented some of the problems; it offered protection to women, and to the property of husband's kin and children. A widow could represent her dead husband, incarnate her previous marriage, claim lands and power. She was both uniquely free and uniquely vulnerable – hence Emma's and Edith's hopes, plans, actions and predicaments in 1017, 1035 and 1066.

In an eleventh-century life of a saintly queen, Sexburga, the saint passed from an ideal marriage to an ideal widowhood via a period of regency.[34] She bridged the time from the death of her husband until the maturity of her son, via an extension of marriage and a fulfilment of maternal duty. The fruitful wife was also a mother, and widowhood drew its potential from both.

2 Mother and Motherhood

Mothers, or mother-widows, had been the most high profile women in the tenth-century English royal family. The tenth-century queens of whom we hear most are Ealhswith after the death of Alfred and during the rule of her son Edward the Elder, Ælfthryth after the death of Edgar and in the early years of the rule of her son Æthelred, but especially Eadgifu during the rule of her sons Edmund and Eadred. The power of these women derives from the combination of motherhood and widowhood, and especially from the first: Eadgifu had been an obscure royal widow for over fifteen years before the accession of her son Edmund brought her to prominence. Queen-mother was the role for which Emma struggled after 1035; any promises made to her sons by Æthelred or Cnut were concerned with her future as well as theirs. Childbirth offered a royal wife additional security, without making a queen unique and irreplaceable; the accession of a son made her both. Motherhood is a biological link which cannot be duplicated. Yet it is also a socially constructed role affected by child-rearing practices, the availability of adoption or other forms of substitute parenthood and by society's ideals.

[33] See, however, Stafford 1994 for warnings against over-interpreting these women.
[34] London, BL Cotton Caligula A viii fo 111v. Rollason 1982, p 30ff argues that this twelfth-century Ely life is closely based on an eleventh-century or earlier Life of the queen from Minster in Kent.

There is no evidence for procedures of adoption in England at this date. When Edward the Confessor named his great-nephew Edgar '*ætheling*', that is, throneworthy, it was a type of adoption, but one without known recent precedent. Yet the practice of fostering shows that parenting was not simply conceived of as a biological tie. Some tenth-century princes had been fostered. Æthelred's eldest son, Athelstan, had had a foster-mother, and his grandmother, Ælfthryth, had reared him.[35] The future King Edgar had as foster mother Ælfwyn, the wife of the most powerful noble of the mid century, Athelstan Half King.[36] It may be no accident that Athelstan is the nearest thing to a male regent tenth-century England produced.[37] Such substitute parenting merely underlines how far motherhood is a source of female power. The care of an infant or future king and the care of the kingdom went together. Edith's 'motherhood' of the royal boys[38] matched Edward's quasi-adoption.

Motherhood is a potent ideal, more so than wifeliness. As a result its own contradictions, like its historically specific nature, are even less acknowledged.

> If my son Robert were dead and buried seven feet in the earth . . . and I could bring him back to life with my own blood, I would shed my lifeblood for him.[39]

The words which Orderic Vitalis placed in the mouth of a later eleventh-century English queen, Mathilda, wife of William the Conqueror, speak the enduring script of motherhood, its 'normal', 'natural' feelings. A mother's care and concern for her children, and their biological basis, were an aspect of eleventh-century English motherhood. 'With what affection she is moved as she holds the infant in her arms, sees him hang on her breast, hears him cry as children do at the little hurts of his little body, and hastens to forestall all the evils which she fears may happen to him . . .'[40] Eadmer, writing c. 1115, is a late source. There is earlier evidence of such attitudes, though less lyrical. In the late tenth-century *Life of Æthelwold*, two miracles involved small children both brought to the saint's tomb by their mothers, one of whom was a household servant.[41] Compassion was seen as a maternal attribute;[42] God is as compassionate to his chosen as a mother to her children.[43] Ælfric often

---

[35] *Wills* 20.
[36] *Chron Ram* pp 1 and 53.
[37] Below p 187.
[38] *Vita Ed*, 2nd ed p 24.
[39] Orderic Vitalis, vol III, Bk 5, pp 102–4.
[40] Eadmer, *Concerning the Excellence of the Virgin Mary*, col 564.
[41] Wulfstan, *Æthelwold*, pp 66 and 68.
[42] Ælfric, *Catholic Homilies, 1*, no 17, appendix, printed in the *Concordance* from CCCC MS 188, p 179, line 4.
[43] Ælfric, *Lives of Saints*, vol I, p 502, line 251, legend of the Seven Sleepers.

Figure 3 The maternity of Mary, with the right hand of mother and child raised, perhaps in blessing – ivory panel, first half of the eleventh century. Reproduced by permission of the Ashmolean Museum, University of Oxford

speaks of a mother's sorrows. The emotional face of the nurturing mother was worn in mourning.[44] It was a mother's role to mourn her son's departing journey, 'the woman will wail who sees the flames engulf her son', [45] though she wailed with due restraint. In *Beowulf*, Hildeburh directed the cremation of her sons with dignity, rather than strongly expressed emotion.[46]

Tenth- and eleventh-century motherhood was dignified and authoritative as much as tender and emotional. Mary was represented both as a mourning mother beside the cross and as a witness to the world of her son's passion.[47] Mary as the nursing mother was not unknown in early English iconography, but the image was largely absent from the represen-

[44] See Hill, Kuefler and Smith, R.D.
[45] *Anglo-Saxon Poetry*, p 318, translating Fortunes of Man, *ASPR* 3, The Exeter Book, p 154.
[46] *Beowulf* lines 1114ff, cf Hill for her heroic sorrow and helplessness.
[47] See St Omer ivory, Backhouse et al, no 119 and cf ibid no 67, BL Arundel 60. Clayton, p 174 on her grief; on Mary like John as a witness, O'Reilly, p 171.

tations of her in the late Saxon period. Instead she is shown as a mother who presents her child to the world, an integral part of his mission of salvation[48] (see figure 3). Emotion was as likely to be presented as a feature of father/son relations as of mother/son. The most tender picture of late Saxon parenthood is paternal, of God the father and son, not of Mary and her infant.[49] In the *Life of Oswald*, Æthelwine's sons accompanied him on his last visit to Ramsey, prostrated themselves beside their weeping father, and suffered great grief at the sight of his tears. By contrast their unnamed mother was remembered for her contribution to her sons' birth and status.[50] A good mother began as a good wife, or at least a good noble wife; she contributed to her sons' futures but not necessarily through expressions of tender feeling. Wealhtheow, an ideal queen and mother in *Beowulf*, urges that the hero be given rich rewards so that he in turn will richly reward her children, be gracious in future to her son.[51] The abbess is a mother as much for her authority over her house as for her nurturance; *materfamilias* is glossed as *hlæfdige*, 'lady', and *hiredes modor*, mother of a community or household.[52] When Saints Eormenhild and Werburg, mother and daughter, entered the nunnery together they vied with each other; 'the mother ranks higher the virginity of her to whom she had given birth, but the virgin places higher the authority of her mother.'[53]

The Christian Bible which had Solomon prepare a throne for his mother beside him, and where Paul had woman saved through childbirth is one source of this high regard for motherhood.[54] In late Saxon England the two recurring maternal images in the clerically dominated literature were Mary and the Church. If the Church was a mother, it was less because of her care for her children, than because of the rebirth she gave them through baptism. 'The whole of Christ's church is Christ's mother, since she gives birth to Christ's own body through the holy gift of baptism.'[55] The more nurturing aspects of motherhood, equally apposite in their application to the Church's function, were not invoked. While the nurturance of motherhood is not always to the fore in this imagery, the respect due to it is. Reverence is due to Mary as a mother.[56] Since God

---

[48] Clayton, pp 168, 176–7.

[49] BL Harley 603, fo 1, discussed Kantorowicz 1947, p 84–5.

[50] *Vita Oswaldi*, pp 467 and 428.

[51] *Beowulf* lines 1162–1231.

[52] Ælfric, *Glossary*, ed Zupitza, p 301.

[53] *Life of Werburga*, PL 155, col 102. Rollason 1982, pp 26–7 for this twelfth-century life as a 'superficial adaptation of a more ancient Hanbury *vita*' of the late ninth or early tenth centuries; cf Ridyard, p 60.

[54] I Kings, 2.19 and I Timothy 2.15; cf I Kings 1.31 where Bathsheba *as a wife* bowed to David.

[55] Ælfric, *Homily for the Nativity of the Blessed Virgin Mary*, p 33, lines 219–22.

[56] Clayton, p 77, citing the Marian office in the portiforium of St Wulfstan, copied from a Winchester source.

is our heavenly father and the church our spiritual mother we should love and honour her.[57] The honour of father and mother are amongst the primary commandments for Ælfric.[58] Obedience and honour were due equally to mother as to father, and a mother's counsel was stressed.[59] The charter issued to Wherwell in 1002, places such sentiments in the mouth of Æthelred as a royal son, when confirming the possessions of a house founded by his own mother.[60] Like other charters it speaks of Christ's mother.[61] Unlike others, it includes in its proem not only the injunction to do penance, on account of which the king acts, but the commandment 'Honour thy father and thy mother that thou mayst live long upon the earth.' From such a world comes the mother of Ælfric's Maccabees, called in to counsel her recalcitrant son. In her speech to him she not only moves confidently from her own creation to that of God, but exhorts him to persevere so that she (not God himself) might afterwards receive him in blessedness.[62]

Motherhood was idealized. It was a mixed ideal, composed as much of authority as nurturance, emphasizing childbirth rather than child-rearing. It grew out of contemporary society. It was sensitive to age as well as gender. In tenth- and eleventh-century England the biological link of the young mother and child was overshadowed by the generational authority of parenthood, especially of noble parenthood. Where families passed on the means of subsistence and power to their children birth and nurturing were at best only the first stage of a long relationship.[63] It was particularly a picture of aristocratic motherhood, borrowing the strength of emotional authority from nurturing motherhood yet consistent with the physical separation of mother and child in fostering or nursing arrangements.[64] And it was crowned by its own heavenly parallel. Mary was *domina*, the equivalent of the wife as mistress of the heavenly court, even *sponsa Christi*, the virginal bride, but she never could be 'wife'. Christianity never had its Hera or Juno. Mary was, above all else, the

---

[57] Wulfstan, *Homilies* no 10c, pp 201–2; cf Ælfric, *Pastoral Letters*, Second letter to Wulfstan, cap 130, Fehr, p 198.

[58] See e.g. Ælfric, *Catholic Homilies*, II, no 25, p 233, line 89; Ælfric, *Pastoral Letters*, Second letter to Wulfstan, cap 129, Fehr, p 197.

[59] Wulfstan, *Æthelwold*, p 18.

[60] S 904, AD 1002.

[61] Shaftesbury S 899 and Burton S 906.

[62] Ælfric, *Lives of the Saints*, vol II p 78 lines 175–82.

[63] Some of the most emotional pictures of motherhood from these centuries, centring on the mother and young child, have been left by monks or other celibates, separated from their families and mothers at precisely this stage and unlikely to experience the more complicated and shifting relationships of parents and children, especially in connection with inheritance, at later stages of life.

[64] For Edward's fostermother Leofrun see *Writs* 93. She and her husband bequeathed land to Westminster, which also claimed various other gifts associated with Edward's family, namely, the lands given him by his mother at birth, the dower lands of Edith in Rutland.

mother; the Christ who had no earthly father took his human form from
a mother. It is no surprise that royal motherhood, the position of *regis
mater*, swallowed up queenship in the titles of even the most powerful
women, like Emma herself. Motherhood offered a more unequivocal
legitimation of women's power than the ideal of wife could ever do;
though it also provided the most potentially devastating arguments
against her.

Motherhood as an ideal, unlike marriage, or rather the image of the
wife, was overwhelmingly positive, but there are bad mothers in early
English literature. There was Mother as Procuress in the *Life of Dunstan*,
tempting King Eadwig from his coronation feast.[65] The sexual woman
overcomes the mother, but still in the interests of her daughter's advancement. She joins hands with that most horrific of early English mothers,
the monster, Grendel's mother, in *Beowulf*.[66] She comes by night to the
hall of Heorot to wreak revenge for the death of her son by slaying
Æschere. Her very monstrosity is indicative. She is not so much a 'bad'
mother, uncaring, unfeeling, unnurturing, as too good a one. Vengeful,
son-obsessed, her maternity makes her an anti-social being, murderous
and monstrous. Insofar as motherhood was nurturing and protective this
is its unacceptable expression. If Mary was its apotheosis, Grendel's
mother was its dark demonic face. The threats inherent in motherhood
itself were scarcely to be admitted in human guise.

Mother is a positive image but it hides as many contradictions and
problems as the more openly ambiguous ideal of wife. Orderic's
Mathilda stressed her self-sacrificing maternal feelings. The circumstances were crucial. She had just supported her son in rebellion against
his father. Her motherly love is invoked to justify the actions of a woman
who had just faced the difficulty of being both mother and wife in the
tortuous world of family politics. Orderic gives Mathilda her best argument, a cry of blood to blood, the mother's body to the son's which she
once bore. This is a partial voice of eleventh-century motherhood, the
best one to hear in the circumstances. In other situations the voice of
authority might be called on. Between them they had to cover all the
problems which could arise between children and mothers, over dower
and inheritance, in relation to younger and older children, among the
step-relationships created by serial monogamy. The ideals of motherhood provided a woman with no clear script for such clashes. Always
there lurked the contradictory loyalties of wife and mother, for which
neither ideal offered a resolution; and the fear of motherhood itself, of
the rebellion and murder which family politics could bring about, in

[65] *Life of Dunstan*, Auctore B, pp 32–4.
[66] I have drawn on the interpretation of Grendel's mother in Chance 1986 (1991) and
1990; it is not the only one possible or probable, but it is a socially very significant one.

which this powerful ideal was implicated, and which it could not be allowed to legitimate. It is small wonder that faced with the challenge of presenting her actions after 1035, when all the contradictions of wife and mother accumulated, Emma in the *Encomium* retreated into passivity.

These ideals of wife and mother had to stretch over a variety of family cycles and relationships. Emma was much younger than her first husband and possibly older than her second.[67] The partnership and unity of marriage could not mean the same in both situations. The age gap between husband and wife can have various implications for intra-family relationships. An older husband may be more indulgent or, as Herlihy suggests,[68] more dominant in a marriage, producing natural alliances of mothers and sons, with mothers as intercessors and protectors. A lesser age gap may make a partnership of husband and wife more likely, as Turner has argued.[69] But time and experience complicate such simple rules. Edith was at least 15 years Edward's junior, an age gap similar to that which separated Emma and Æthelred in 1002, but in this case joining an inexperienced king and English noble wife. Edith's marriage went through its own cycle of barrenness, accumulation of power and experience, and a husband's advancing age. The relationship is unlikely to have been the same at the end as at the beginning of the marriage. Age affected the relations of mothers and children. Emma for example was of a similar age to her older stepsons during her first marriage. Whether or not this made relations with them more difficult, a more maternal age-gap did not necessarily guarantee a bond with her own children Edward and Alfred. She was to be separated from them by second marriage and exile, and a pattern of childcare which involved fostering. The age gap between her and Harthacnut was greater, and he too was separated from her in early childhood and sent to rule Denmark.

Above all, these ideals had to cope with inheritance, and with the disputes and tensions it engendered. Marriage and motherhood defined the roles of Emma and Edith within the English royal family. The inheritance practices of that family were at the heart of the family politics within which they both operated.

---

[67] Emma by now was at least 27, probably well turned 30, see below p 211. If Cnut was born after his father's taking of power in 987 he was 30 or under. Cf the Empress Mathilda, who in 1114 married a man c. 30 years her senior, then, as a widow, was given as her second husband, Geoffrey of Anjou, a man ten years her junior. Emma's experience may have been similar.

[68] Herlihy, p 121.

[69] Turner, p 36, on the 'highly effective' husband and wife teams of the Anglo-Norman family.

3 The Inheritance Practices of the English Royal Family in the Tenth and Eleventh Centuries

The tenth-century English royal family could be represented as a descending tree with the significant ancestor as Alfred, or Alfred's father Æthelwulf. For inheritance purposes it appears as a narrowed family, which excluded daughters, and confined claim to the throne not only to sons but to the sons of a king who had reigned, giving priority to older over younger. A king's son did not pass on his claim to his own sons. Collateral branches were truncated, whether in the case of daughters or of younger sons who did not reign. The dynasty shed its branches.

Such a representation is distorting as a total picture of the family. It imposes a unilineal trunk on bilateral kinship's spreading bush. At any given time the significant relatives could appear much more or much less numerous than the tree suggests, widening, for instance, to include the relatives of an in-marrying woman or narrowing to a designated heir. Even as a picture of inheritance it is simplified. It is teleological, a map of significant roads to already known destinations. It is a reconstructed picture, based largely on an interpretation of outcomes rather than on the full range of contemporary possibilities. The branches which it presents as significant or insignificant are those which subsequent history showed to be so. In families which favour male heirs, and give preference to older males over younger, as this family did, the map has some accuracy. But family history as it happens is messier, as often the result of accident and struggle as of strict rules of inheritance. Claims subsequently extinguished could be eminently arguable at the time. Claims successfully made in one set of circumstances change the norms for the future, but never set them in stone. New situations revive old arguments, breathing life into other notions of family and inheritance.

Thus in the tenth-century English royal family the claims of all sons of a king opened the way to horizontal, fraternal succession, passing the throne from brother to brother, as well as vertical, filial succession, passing the throne from father to son. Strong arguments existed, dating back to the will of Æthelwulf, for the passing on of the throne without division of the kingdom. There is some indication that, in certain family circumstances, the fact of and preference for a unified kingdom may have led to recognition, if not designation, of an eldest son or brother during a king's lifetime. But the conquest of other English kingdoms by Wessex in the tenth century refuelled arguments for division. The position of daughters, and of remoter male kin, was more debatable than outcomes suggest. And the practice of serial monogamy produced step-relations, factions at court and succession struggles. The strength of respective wives and the struggles over the succession, both determined by the balances of contemporary politics, affected the way claims were argued and defined. A picture of the family based on outcomes is not irrelevant. The successful arguments of the tenth-century family were the most powerful legacy to the eleventh. But they were not the sole legacy. A range of snapshots of its recent history was also available. The scanty narratives can easily hide them from us, but they can still be discerned from a careful scrutiny of family naming practices or the choice of burial sites, of the witness lists and the changing meanings of a term like *ætheling*. The full recent family album needs to be reassembled.

a) Male inheritance and succession

For Emma as a mother and step-mother the claims of sons were critically important. They were not irrelevant to the sonless Edith. All sons of kings were *æthelings*, 'throneworthy', though grandsons of kings apparently were not.[70] From 900 until Edward the Confessor's declaration that his great-nephew Edgar was an 'ætheling',[71] the term was never used to describe any named individual who was not the son of a king.[72] Charter scribes described all Emma's six stepsons as *clito*, the Latin equivalent of ætheling. 'Throneworthy' is a highly charged political term, to be carefully scrutinized. It was a claim rather than a title, and those who used it and those who claimed it, throughout the tenth and eleventh centuries, were making political bids as much as statements of inheritance rules. Their success or failure affected subsequent meanings. All Æthelred's sons knew they had a claim on the throne; so did Emma. The strength of those claims, the extent to which they could be changed or defeated were questions which tenth-century practice had left open.

The naming of kings' sons is a guide to that practice. What may seem a trivial question of personal preference, the naming of a child, was fraught with significance in dynasties where rules of succession remained debatable and every hint of preference or precedence could be seized on by princes and supporters jockeying for position. Naming expresses a sense of family, how widely or narrowly it is defined, and the place of a child within that family and within its claims and inheritance. It is a rare guide to intentions before they were obscured by outcomes. Æthelred II

---

[70] Dumville 1979, pp 6 and 10, argued for claims passing to all the male descendants of a common grandfather. His examples are late eleventh and twelfth century, Edgar the ætheling and William Clito. The naming of Edgar as ætheling in the difficult circumstances of Edward the Confessor's reign is no guide to the connotations of the term earlier. William Clito built on changes which Edgar's designation helped create. Edgar is, however, a warning that the term was a highly political one with no fixed meaning.

[71] *Leges Edwardi Confessoris*, Liebermann, *Die Gesetze*, vol I, p 665, para 35 1c.

[72] The only possible exception is Beornoð æðeling ASC, MS A, s.a. 905. His father is unknown, though he may have been a Mercian or East Anglian king. The chronicle entry refers to his son, Byrhtsige, not as an ætheling, but the *son* of an ætheling.

was the most fertile king since his much-married great-grandfather, Edward the Elder. Both married two or three times, producing not just a numerous progeny but a set of step-relations. Edward's reaction to this had been to keep the options open. His children were given names which singled out none of his sons as the obvious heir. Only the eldest, Athelstan, was called for a previous ruler. He had been dandled on Alfred's knee, and his grandfather might have preferred him as the next king;[73] the choice of name was perhaps his. Edward apparently gave all his sons hope and expectation, but none too much. At this date indeterminacy hung over the inheritance prospects of royal males.

The mid tenth century saw some hints at a narrower view, with first Eadred then Edgar achieving prominence during their brothers' reigns, then succeeding those same brothers on the throne.[74] But Edgar's practice complicated any tentative shift towards designation. Edgar named his eldest son Edward, after his grandfather. The name of Edward, the military unifier of England, was a pointed choice in the late 950s when the kingdom was first divided by succession dispute, then brought together again in Edgar's hands;[75] it could be interpreted as a sign of a father's special favour. When Edgar married again for the third time, any such earlier plans were thrown into doubt. The two sons born of his third marriage were given unequivocally royal names: Edmund, after Edgar's father, and Æthelred himself, after King Æthelred I.[76] Such names indicated a growing historical and dynastic sense, but also underscored the legitimacy and throneworthiness of the sons of a third and debatably legitimate marriage.[77] The names of Edgar's sons laid stress on the elder over younger children of any union, but established no absolutely clear order of precedence among the sons of different marriages. About 970 AD a royal genealogy was compiled; it was of all the sons of Edgar: 'Edward and Edmund and Æthelred æthelings are the sons of King Edgar.'[78] After Edgar's death this even-handedness contributed to a struggle for the throne, whose outcome was the rule of his youngest son, Æthelred.

[73] Nelson 1991b for possible trouble between Alfred and his eldest son, and especially p 63 for the suggestion that Alfred may even have hoped to by-pass his son and pass the throne to his grandson.

[74] Thus Eadred in the reign of his brother Edmund, and Edgar in the first year of that of his brother Eadwig.

[75] Stafford 1989a, pp 47–51.

[76] Æthelred may have been Edgar and Ælfthryth's common ancestor. According to Gaimar, Ælfthryth's mother was of royal descent, line 3624, and Æthelred was named 'for his ancestor, King Æthelred', lines 3961–2. Edgar was a descendant of Æthelred I through his grandmother, Æfflæd; perhaps Ælfthryth was through her mother.

[77] S 745 for the same emphasis on the legitimacy of the marriage and the son, see above p 72.

[78] BL Cotton Tiberius B v, vol 1 fo 23r, and Dumville 1976, p 43.

Æthelred named his first six sons for previous tenth-century kings, virtually in the order of their succession.[79] The scribes of his charters maintained that order in the recording of their witnesses, at least until 1013.[80] A strict and unquestioned precedence is implied. But this symmetry is apparent only by omitting the second son, Ecgberht. Æthelred's sons born before 1000 AD in fact fall into two groups. The first two, Athelstan and Ecgberht, and the last four, named for the consecutive rulers of England since 940.[81] These two groups apparently mirror consecutive phases of the reign,[82] and lend some credence to the idea that Æthelred had married twice before 1002.[83] The first two choices, Athelstan and Ecgberht, had distinctly Northern resonances, recalling two earlier kings who had extended southern rule northward and in Athelstan one who was long remembered north of the Humber for his generosity.[84] These boys belonged to a marriage designed to cement Northern alliances in the mid 980s, and it was perhaps as a result that Athelstan retained North Midlands if not Northern attachments to the end of his life.[85] By the 990s the names suggest a strong sense of the dynasty's recent history, and perhaps a narrower view of that dynasty with Æthelred's grandfather Edmund as the significant ancestor. At the time of Emma's marriage, recent English royal family practice gave all sons a claim, ranked them by age, yet opened the possibility of argument for designation and for the mounting of claims by younger sons over older. The doubts and questions raised for sons by a father's second marriage may already have been felt once in Æthelred's family before 1000 AD. Athelstan as the eldest had taken precedence.[86] Yet Æthelred affirmed that all his sons shared common lands and household in the 990s,[87] whilst the naming practices of the 990s kept open if they did not reopen the claims of all sons. Politics and remarriage had constantly adjusted succession arguments, and the future precedents they created.

Whether or not Emma was aware of all this in 1002, she must soon

---

[79] Keynes 1980, p 187 n 116, following Barlow 1970, p 28.

[80] Keynes 1980, Table 1 'Subscription of the Athelings'.

[81] This emphasis on the recent history of the dynasty is echoed in e.g. S 876.

[82] On which see Stafford 1978, and Keynes 1980; the second phase would have to date from before 993 to accommodate the birth of Edmund and Eadred by this date.

[83] See however below n 116.

[84] For Athelstan's interest in St Cuthbert, Rollason, 1989b and cf Keynes 1985; S 451 for his association with Beverley, S 456 for Ripon.

[85] *Wills* 20.

[86] There is a hint of precedence when a woman making a will in the early 990s begs the queen that her relative may serve 'the ætheling'; *The Will of Æthelgifu.*

[87] Æthelred in a charter of the 990s is made to refer to the lands belonging to the king's sons, S 937, 'Terras ad regios pertinentes filios'; a man who witnesses a dispute of the 990s is the 'æþelings'' disthegn, R 66.

have become so; and in negotiations with her family, inheritance would have been an issue. Even if Æthelred's previous remarriages had not opened up the question of all sons' claims, 1002 did. Earlier practice suggests that promises would have been made that her sons would be throneworthy, though a designation of her firstborn as heir is less likely.[88] Her own sons were given the kingly names of Edward and Alfred. If Edward was given any special hope and expectation, it was quietly forgotten in the years immediately after his birth. Any hints of precedence or designation after 1004 point to Athelstan, the eldest son, not Edward. In the witness lists of these years sometimes he is the only one named;[89] sometimes he is specified as *'primogenitus'*, firstborn,[90] or as *'clito'*.[91] The tendency to single him out is especially marked at Burton abbey[92] in the North Midlands where he had connections. Whether this was a response to Edward's birth and hints made to Emma or to the military needs of Æthelred's last decade which recast relationships between a father and his adult sons,[93] it was a precedence which Athelstan's supporters if not others chose to stress. It provided a precedent on which his brother Edmund built after Athelstan's death.[94] The special attention paid to the ætheling by Archbishop Wulfstan may reflect this newly emphasized status.[95]

Whatever might have happened to Emma and her sons on the death of Æthelred in 1016, the conquest of Swein and Cnut changed the situation. After her remarriage to Cnut, Emma was once again faced by the sons of an earlier union, and after 1017 arguments about succession and inheritance involved not only recent English practice, but a Danish dimension. The names Cnut gave to his sons made no clear distinction among them. Cnut named all of his sons, whether by Emma or Ælfgifu of Northampton, for previous Danish rulers, recognizing all their claims; Swein,

---

[88] I would thus further refine remarks, Stafford 1983, pp 78 and 164.

[89] S 907, 909, 916.

[90] S 909, AD 1004.

[91] S 928, AD 1012. Sometimes he alone is given a verb and said to witness, whilst his brothers are merely listed, S 915, AD 1007, S 918, AD 1008: or one or other of his brothers, without a title, is specifically related to him, as 'frater predicti clitonis', S 922, AD 1009, S 929, AD 1012, or 'frater eiusdem', S 926, AD 1011. These variations may simply indicate the liking of scribes to vary the form of attestations, but their consistency in singling Athelstan out is notable.

[92] Where only he is *regis filius* or *clito* after 1009.

[93] Nelson 1991b, for similar suggestions re Alfred's later years.

[94] In 1015, S 934, after Athelstan's death, Edmund, his next brother in age, takes over a special designation, 'indolis subolis', hitherto used only of Edgar in 956, a time when Edgar's prominence in court politics was undoubted, and just before his bid for the Mercian throne. Dumville 1979, pp 8–9, sees the use of this title for Edgar in 956 as a 'brief deviation'.

[95] Dumville 1979, p 32. His emphasis may also reflect the revulsion felt after the murder of the ætheling Eadwig on Cnut's orders in or after 1017.

Harold, Harthacnut after his father, grandfather and great-grandfather.[96] He may even have felt that rule could be shared in England after his death, let alone in the wider collection of kingdoms which he assembled in the 1020s. As late as 1074 all sons of a Danish king could claim to rule, no age-order was established among them, and joint rule was still arguable if not necessarily always achieved.[97]

1016 and the coming of a rival dynasty arguably marked a turning point in tenth- and eleventh-century English dynastic politics. Cnut's death in 1035 opened a protracted succession dispute which dominated the mid and later eleventh century. Dynastic rivalries made the circumstances of 1035 especially complex, but in other respects they echo the long succession dispute which followed the death of Edward the Elder in 924, the last English king to die leaving several sons. Cnut's conquest brought heightened insecurities and the struggles of rival dynasties; but his empire revived arguments for division which had existed in the tenth century. Edward and his sons had acquired an ever larger empire over the kingdoms of the English. As with Cnut, rule of many kingdoms fuelled arguments, already strong, for the inheritance of many sons. Struggle over the succession had been the norm in tenth-century England. Of the eight kings who then ruled England, only two, Edmund and Eadred, had succeeded without dispute, and there are features of their reigns which point to a barely suppressed family tension.[98] Even without the complications of the Danish conquest there would have been trouble after Æthelred's death.

Tenth-century struggles had already produced royal murder and suspicious deaths long before that of Alfred in 1036. A remarkable number of Edward the Elder's sons and grandsons met a premature or violent end. There is something almost sinister about the silence which surrounds the male line of Æthelwulf in the tenth century,[99] a silence broken only by the sound of sudden and fortuitous royal death. Three if not four successive succession disputes were resolved by the premature death of a young king, though only one is recorded as royal murder;[100] history

---

[96] Lawson 1993, p 115.

[97] Sawyer and Sawyer 1993, pp 62–3.

[98] Stafford 1989a, pp 37–44.

[99] Even as assiduous a researcher as William of Malmesbury could find few records of the tenth-century male descendants of Æthelwulf after 924: the exiled Edwin, *DGRA*, Bk II cap 139, pp 155–7 – Symeon of Durham has Edwin drowned at sea on Athelstan's orders, *Historia Regum* s.a 933; Malmesbury also mentions Alfred's grandsons, safely dead and buried after the battle of Brunanburh, Bk II cap 135, p 151 and Edmund, who predeceased his father Edgar and lay at Romsey, Bk II cap 159, p 180. cf Gillingham 1994, p 39 on murder in the English royal family pre-1066.

[100] 924, 955–9, 975–8. The debatable one is 946, when Edmund was murdered at Pucklechurch. Only the Northern D version of the *ASC* gives any detail of the murder. The West Saxon sources are, as usual, silent.

would pin that deed on a woman, Queen Ælfthryth.[101] Were this a tale of a Turkish sultanate rather than the story that made England suspicion might be aroused. It may not simply be loss of sources which has deprived us of the tender Ottonian family scenes which adorn the German Lives of Mathilda. Being a male descendant of Æthelwulf was a risky business; male branches often fell from the family tree. Perhaps it was a case of genetic weakness, perhaps a tendency to strong girls, but by 1002 Æthelred's six sons had cause to ponder uneasily on their recent family history. Circumstances ensured that the death of Alfred in 1036, like that of Edward the Martyr in 978, attracted outraged comment. It was the comment rather than the deaths which was unprecedented.

Tenth- and eleventh-century practice and precedent allowed arguments for designation and indeterminacy, and suggested that no plan or favour was immutable. That flexibility was stretched to its limits by the failure of Edward's and Edith's marriage to produce a son. Divorce and remarriage, one way to cope with this, proved impossible. There was no recent precedent for the eligibility of a male other than the son of a king. When Edward the Confessor named his great-nephew Edgar 'ætheling', he was going against established custom, making the grandson of an English king throneworthy. In choosing to designate, however, he may have had some English arguments on his side,[102] as well as being influenced by the French practice he had witnessed in exile. His lack of direct male heirs recalled the situation of Athelstan, Eadred and Eadwig, who had been succeeded by step-brother, nephew and brother, perhaps with prior designation. Deaths natural, suspicious and murderous had deprived Edward of all of but great-step-nephews. His family circumstances required him to name an heir. If the choice lacked exact precedent, its contestable nature did not. The English succession was nothing if not arguable in the tenth and eleventh centuries. This was both a strength and a weakness for Emma and Edith. Neither could ever be certain of the future which succession to the throne had in store for them; that very uncertainty stirred the troubled political pool in which they fished.

In the 1050s Edgar was not Edward's only great-nephew, though he was the only one descended through the male line of the English royal family. There were other male descendants of Edward's father, King

---

[101] Active on behalf of her own sons before and after her husband's death, she stood accused of complicity in her stepson Edward the Martyr's death. The deed had taken place whilst the young king was visiting her and those who had been staying with her were its known perpetrators; *Vita Oswaldi*, p 449, written between 995 and 1005. The rabid attack on her in the *Passion of Edward the Martyr* comes from Shaftesbury nunnery perhaps as early as Cnut's reign or before, ed Fell, Intro.

[102] Dumville 1979, p 18ff is less inclined to allow for the precedents of designation.

Æthelred: Harold, son of Earl Ralph and grandson of Edward's sister Godgifu; another unnamed grandson of Godgifu and Eustace of Boulogne; Gospatric, grandson of Edward's half sister Ælfgifu, and possibly Siward and Ealdred, perhaps grandsons of Eadric Streona and Æthelred's daughter Edith. All were royal men whose grandmothers had been the daughters of a king. Edgar's grandfather, Edmund, had been not only the son of a king, but briefly king himself. Edgar was the obvious choice in a family where the male line had precedence. But the female line was far from irrelevant. Edith had the young Harold as her ward; he was probably one of those royal boys to whom she was a mother.[103] If the claims of sons were always uppermost in Emma's calculations, those of daughters and their descendants were central to the family situation in which Edith found herself, doubly so if she claimed a type of surrogate daughterhood of Edward in 1066. The claims of wives, widows and mothers mattered to both queens.

b) Female inheritance and claims

From 918 onwards there was no precedent for a claim on the throne by a woman or through a woman. Women shared in the inheritance: dower for wives and widows, royal nunneries for daughters, wives and widows, grants and bequests of royal land to wives and mothers,[104] even some recognition of a married daughter's claims.[105] But 911–18 apart, the tenth and early eleventh centuries did not throw up a failure of the direct male line which would have tested whether women's shares in inheritance could extend to claims on the throne itself. A successful test strengthens any claim: untested claims are weak, but not yet shown to be indefensible. To decide how far a recognition of women's family membership through provision from family lands could support wider claims involving all a family's possessions, including the crown, a deeper consideration of women's place within the family is necessary.

Naming and burial practices again provide the first clues, particularly when they are compared with those of sons. There is a greater variety of women's names among tenth-century royal daughters than among royal sons, especially sons from the latter part of the tenth century. Ælfthryth, Æthelgifu, Æthelhild, Eadhild, Wulfgifu: Emma and Æthelred were following an already adventurous tradition when they named a daughter Godgifu. Sons were increasingly given kingly names, daughters were more likely to be named for their mother's, grandmother's or great-grandmother's families. Thus Eadburh, daughter of Edward the Elder,

---

[103] DB I, fo 129v, *VitaEd*, 2nd ed, p 24.

[104] For latter see S 489, Edmund's grant to Eadgifu and *SEHD* 21, Will of Eadred leaving extensive lands to his mother.

[105] See land left to Æthelflæd in the will of her father Alfred, *SEHD* 11.

was called after her grandmother's Mercian mother.[106] Ælfgifu, Æthelred's grandmother, provided not only a name for her granddaughter-in-law, Æthelred's wife Emma, but also for her great-granddaughter, his child. Both Æthelred and Edgar called a daughter after their great ancestress Eadgifu.[107] An inheritance of names could extend to more material legacies. Eadburh was given her grandmother's mother's name; she also joined the nunnery of Nunnaminster, Winchester, founded on her grandmother's own land.[108] Sons' names suggest increasing attention to a patrilineal trunk, daughters' tend to remember patrilineal female ancestors, but retain memories of the wider bush and of inheritances other than the patrimony.

This more marginal place in relation to a family increasingly defined by inheritance in the male line, was epitomized in death. Those daughters who entered nunneries were buried there: Eadflæd and Æthelhild alongside their mother at Wilton[109] where Edgar's daughter Eadgyth/Edith would also be buried.[110] Remoter male relatives were also buried in nunneries. Thus Ælfgar king's mæg (kinsman) was buried at Wilton in 962,[111] as were royal men in the male line who never ruled like Æthelwine and Ælfwine, grandsons of Alfred. Wilton was later believed to have been founded by Athelstan for their souls.[112] It was

[106] For Ealhswith's mother, see Asser, p 24, cap 29; for Eadburh/Eadburga daughter of Edward, William of Malmesbury, DGRA, Bk II, cap 126, p 137. For a tendency to name daughters for paternal grandmothers in the Carolingian dynasty, see Bouchard 1988. The problem of identifying maternal kin makes the shift she notes to naming for maternal grandmothers in tenth-century France and Germany difficult to test for England, though on balance England looks more like the Carolingian patrilineal pattern.

[107] Both were already royal family names among Edward the Elder's daughters, and Æthelred's daughter may have also been called after her unnamed mother. There is debate about Edgar's daughter Eadgifu, abbess of Nunnaminster: R 49 and Robertson's comment p 348 argued that Edgar could not have had a daughter old enough to be abbess of Nunnaminster at this date, but R 49 is otherwise acceptable, and we know little about the age of tenth-century abbesses. Was she named for the grandmother already in retirement at Nunnaminster?

[108] See An Ancient Manuscript, ed Birch, p 96, where the site of the nunnery and its boundaries is described as 'þæs hagan gemære þe Ealhswith hæfd æt Wintanceastre'; cf Æthelweard, Chronicle, p 52. and LVH, p 5, where Ealhswith is 'the builder of the Nuns' Minster'. Dumville, 1992a, p 84 argues that the boundary may be a sort of title deed. For Nunnaminster's royal connections through Eadburh, Ridyard, esp pp 96–102.

[109] William of Malmsbury, DGRA, Bk II, cap 126, p 137.

[110] Goscelin, Life of Edith p 96. The burial of a daughter of Edward the Elder at Romsey is more debatable. Meyer 1981 pp 349–50 has Edward Elder found Romsey for his daughter Æthelflæd, whose feast on 29 October distinguishes her from St Æthelflæd daughter of Æthelwold, feast 23 October. Edward the Elder and Ælfflæd had a daughter Ælfflæd according to Liber Monasterii de Hyda, p 172. William of Malmesbury, DGP, p 175 has an Ælfflæd buried there, though he knows nothing of her. The problem is exacerbated by possible confusions between 'Æthelflæd' and 'Ælfflæd'.

[111] ASC, MS A s.a. 962. It is not clear whether he was kin on the father or mother's side.

[112] William of Malmesbury, DGP p 186, and DGRA, Bk II, cap 135, p 151.

not.[113] The choice of a nunnery for their burials indicated the royalty of such men whilst safely denying their or their descendants' throneworthiness: acknowledged their kinship, but not their claims to the throne. Burial in a nunnery aligned royal men with royal women, feminized them, cut them off from the trunk. Edmund the ætheling, Æthelred's older brother who died in 971, was buried at Romsey. His burial in a nunnery associated him with the women of the family, and with the non-ruling males. Someone later tried to destroy that memory. The entry recording it was erased from the Winchester Chronicle, though when, why and in whose interests remains unclear.[114]

The messages which naming and burial site sent out were not lost on contemporaries. Athelstan, Æthelred's oldest son, Emma's eldest step-son, was buried in 1014 in the Old Minster, Winchester, the first non-king to be buried at Winchester since Edward the Elder's brother, Æthelweard.[115] However much succession plans fluctuated between 990 and 1014, Athelstan's claims were carefully recognized in death. His brother Edmund would have been especially anxious to see that they were.[116] When Edmund Ironside went on during his brief marriage to choose the names of Edmund and Edward for his sons he selected the two most popular recent dynastic names, asserting his own and his sons' claims. One of those sons, Edward the Exile, later called his son Edgar, keeping alive the boy's identification with the ruling dynasty. He was happy to let his daughters' more exotic names, Margaret and Christina, reflect their foreign birth and dynastic marginality.

Accident ensured that no woman's claims on the throne after 918 were tested, but names and burials suggest that those claims were seen as different from those of their brothers. The difference is underlined by the witness lists of charters. In the tenth century no princesses, even princess-abbesses, were ever listed here alongside the æthelings.

[113] See Ridyard 1988, p 140, founded c. 830 by Alburga sister of King Egbert and widow of Weohstan, ealdorman of Wiltshire, cf VCH Wilts vol 3, p 231, both citing the fifteenth-century Chronicon Vilodunense. Yorke 1989, p 113 n 19 rejects this evidence as late, preferring William of Malmesbury. The detail, however, is surpisingly circumstantial for a fifteenth-century forger.

[114] ASC, MS A s.a. 971. The erasure would have been in the interests of his brother Æthelred, in the struggle for the throne after 975, but is unlikely to have been as early as this. The entry survived in MS G, BL Cotton Otto B xi, fo 47v, a copy of MS A. This MS was produced 1001 × 1012/13, see ASC, MS A, ed Bately, p xiii, at which date the entry should still have been in MS A. The erasure may be connected with the claims of Æthelred's sons, but the circumstances are unclear.

[115] In his will, Wills 20, he left Adderbury, Oxfordshire, to Christ and St Peter at the place where he was to be buried. In 1066 the Old Minster, Winchester, held 14 and a half hides here, DB I, fo 155r; for Æthelweard's burial at New Minster, LVH p 6.

[116] This may strengthen the case for seeing these two as full brothers, and thus not associating the two groups of sons' names with two marriages; cf above p 85.

A gendered separation in naming or burial makes a distinction, but does not determine all the meanings of that distinction. The nunneries were *royal* as well as *female*, housing royal daughters and occasionally widows or repudiated wives, linked with royal lands and royal servants. Burial there sent one message about throneworthiness, but another about family membership. Æthelred had been his father's youngest son. He named all his male offspring to affirm his own and their place in the dynasty and the succession. The names of his daughters were chosen from a wider pool, but usually still a family one. Daughters were of royal blood, members of the royal family; paradoxically this is never clearer than when they married out of it. Women who married joined a new family, and simultaneously extended their own. Æthelflæd was buried in the Mercian town of Gloucester; but it was in the east porticus of a New Minster founded on the model of her brother's foundation at Winchester.[117] Æthelflæd became a Mercian queen, but never lost her identity as a West Saxon princess.

The marriage patterns of royal princesses are incomprehensible without the identity and claims which a daughter took with her. Five of Edward the Elder's daughters made splendid marriages in France and Germany, taking their old royal blood to new dynasties, and their West Saxon claims to a safe distance. The other five ended their days in English nunneries; before 1002 all subsequent known royal English daughters similarly buried their claims in consecrated celibacy. Almost all Emma's daughters and stepdaughters, by contrast, married. Her three stepdaughters were married to Æthelred's nobles. Royal daughters were now used to cement noble loyalties; Æthelred's sons-in-law remained loyal to the king almost to the end.[118] Emma's own eldest daughter's marriage was made in Northern France, the younger was sent to Germany as a bride. Invasion, conquest and exile produced new circumstances. They were still handled through the dual identities of the daughter/wife, but now in marriages which left English royal blood in many eleventh-century veins. Edward and Edith attempted to gather some of it back to the royal court.

Daughters' claims and their capacity to transmit them were in abeyance only as long as fathers produced sons. Failure in the male line revealed facts which marriage had always acknowledged, that daughters were an integral part of the dynasty. Their claims may have differed from men's, being postponed or ranked lower, but as long as

---

[117] ASC, MS C s.a. 918 and cf Hare 1993.

[118] Eadgyth/Edith to Eadric Streona, *Fl Wig*, s.a. 1009; Ælfgifu to Uhtred of Northumbria, Symeon of Durham, ed Arnold, vol I p 216; Wulfhild to Ulfcytel according to the Jomsviking saga. A fourth daughter married into the nobility is suggested by the king's son-in-law Athelstan killed at the battle of Ringmere, *ASC*, MSS C, D, E s.a. 1010; this may be Wulfhild who would thus have married Ulfcytel as a widow.

the throne passed by blood within a family of which they were members it was difficult to extinguish them. Blood can be sexless as well as gendered, carrying claims in the right circumstances to women as well as men.

Widows also had claims on their husbands' lands, as did mothers on those of their children. When royal daughters were named for grandmothers, female and maternal ancestors were drawn more tightly into the family traditions. A name could be a reminder that both maternal and paternal blood passed to sons and daughters.[119] Female family names were *family* as well as *female*, and many of them were the names of the mothers of kings. When Emma married Æthelred her name was changed to the English 'Ælfgifu', that of her husband's grandmother. The step was an unusual one, a response to the first non-English royal marriage in a century and a witness to the dynasty's strong sense of its recent history. There was to be no doubt of the incorporation of this foreign bride into it. The name change signals both how far a wife was seen as an outsider to her husband's kin, but also her absorption into her new family. Her incorporation became complete in the next generation. Children are in no doubt that their mother is part of the family. Mothers had claims on the family land.[120]

The years 911 to 918 demonstrated the potential of women's claims. In 911 Æthelflæd had become queen of Mercia, ruling that kingdom on her husband's death. In 918 she died, and her daughter, Ælfwyn, was chosen to succeed her by a section of the Mercian nobility.[121] The political and family context was crucial. Æthelflæd was the daughter of Alfred and the sister of Edward the Elder; she became ruler of Mercia whilst her brother ruled in Wessex, and during a period when independence, equality or dominance were the issues between the two kingdoms. These issues were negotiated through two female successions. Æthelflæd as sister and daughter of a West Saxon king and widow of a Mercian one could express the aspirations of both kingdoms. This was only possible for a woman whose marriage placed her as a link between families, identifying her with both; as blood daughter of the first and partner and sharer of her husband's identity in the second. The succession of such a woman postponed trouble by satisfying both sides. Her own daughter incarnated some of that dual identity. To choose her was less an act of simple rebellion, than an attempt to keep alive that balance between

---

[119] The precise views on conception and the male and female role in it current in early England are unclear. The ancient world bequeathed two rival theories and the position of authorities such as Isidore of Seville is often uncertain, see Cadden 1993, cap 1 esp pp 52–3. A mother's contribution to her son's status was certainly acknowledged in e.g. the *Vita Oswaldi*, above p 78.

[120] See above p 67 and n 6.

[121] On these two women see Wainwright 1975.

Mercia and Wessex which her mother's rule had meant.[122] These choices of female rulers simultaneously satisfied the desire for a separate ruler of Mercia, and for one acceptable to, that is related to, the West Saxon house. They encompassed a Mercian separatism so strong that *even* a woman, provided that she was a Mercian king's widow or daughter, was acceptable. They indicate a West Saxon power which could back the rule elsewhere of its women. But especially they express a West Saxon/ Mercian balance so fine that *only* two women so placed by marriage and birth as to link them could satisfy both sides. They demonstrate the capacity of women, as daughters and widows, to negotiate links between kingdoms through the claims and identities they carry, as Emma did in 1017 and Edith might have hoped to do in 1066.

The events of 911 to 918 are not an exact parallel of 1066 let alone 1017 or 1035, and they are remote in time from Emma and Edith in the mid eleventh century. They might be dismissed as irrelevant, even as Mercian practice as opposed to West Saxon. There is certainly no indication that either Æthelflæd or Ælfwyn became role models or set precedents. To expect them to is to miss the real significance of their rule. Neither would have been chosen had women and their marriages not linked families together; that pattern was not Mercian or West Saxon but North West European and wider. Women occupied a different position in families from that of men; a different conception of family itself. Neither woman could have been chosen had women as daughters and widows had no claims to inherit. In the right circumstances those claims could be argued even to the rule of a kingdom.[123] As mother, widow, and most creatively as daughter-wife, Emma and Edith could have hoped for at least regency.

* * *

In 1052, Emma's son Edward buried his mother in the Old Minster, Winchester. Thirteen years later Edith was laid to rest by William the Conqueror in Westminster Abbey beside that same Edward. The first message of both burials is the unity of these women with the dynasties

---

[122] It has been assumed, including by me, Stafford 1989a, p 33, that Ælfwyn was Æthelflæd and Æthelred's only child. Since the choice of a son as king by Mercian nobles in 918 would have had very different implications from the choice of a daughter, this should perhaps be reconsidered. In 957 the Mercian choice of a West Saxon prince Edgar met some of the same needs. By now, however, the balance had tipped towards Wessex; the choice of a man indicated the strength of desire for a ruler in Mercia itself, that of a West Saxon male, the recognition of West Saxon power.

[123] Barlow 1970, p 299, invoked Roman law to explain Edith's claims as a daughter/wife. Such influence is possible, but the claims of tenth- and eleventh-century English women had the capacity to expand in this way.

into which they had married. For late Saxon England the burials were unusual. Emma was the first queen certainly buried in the Old Minster, one of the great mausolea of the dynasty.[124] She was also the first queen since Ealhswith certainly to be buried with her husband;[125] and Ealhswith had ended up with Alfred thanks to the body swapping of her son Edward the Elder.[126] Nunneries were the normal place of retirement of queens and the normal place of their burial. Ælfgifu wife of Edmund was buried at Shaftesbury,[127] Ælfthryth at Wherwell,[128] Ælfflæd and her daughters Eadflæd and Æthelhild at Wilton where later they would be joined by the body of Abbess Wulfthryth second wife of Edgar.[129] The decision to bury Emma alongside Cnut and Harthacnut at Old Minster and Edith at Westminster alongside Edward was not a simple adherence to custom.

It would have been difficult for the serial monogamist kings of tenth-century England to have established a royal mausoleum in which they and their wives could be buried; there were too many wives, too much family tension for that. If tenth-century royal husbands and wives were not often united in death, the problem would have been deciding which ones to rejoin in the grave. The burial of Emma and Edith with their husbands might thus be read in the context of the long struggle for Christian marriage and indissolubility; a recognition of a unity which was, if not new, certainly recently reaffirmed in England. Edith joined in

---

[124] Ælfgifu, widow and separated wife of King Eadwig was possibly buried there, see *Wills* 8, where she leaves Risborough to 'ealdan mynstre' where she is to be buried. This is normally assumed to be Old Minster, Winchester, an assumption borne out by the fact that the will goes on to make gifts to New Minster and Nunnaminster, i.e. covering the three Winchester houses. But Old Minster has no recorded association with Risborough. Archbishop Lanfranc held Monk's Risborough in 1086, DB I, fo 143v, as a result of a transaction with the bishop of Dorchester in Æthelred's reign. Is it conceivable that Ælfgifu was arranging to be buried at Dorchester? A bequest to New Minster would seem in order for the wife of Eadwig, but a burial at Old Minster, not next to her husband, seems unlikely. Eadgifu, a woman who survived her husband to pursue an active career for over forty years is another possibility for burial in the Old Minster, but we have no clear indication where she was buried.

[125] Æthelflæd, widow of King Edmund and his survivor by many years, may have been buried with hers. Her burial place ought to be indicated by the gifts she makes for her soul in her will, *Wills* 14. She leaves land for her soul and for that of her husband Edmund to Glastonbury, where he was buried, but also to Canterbury. The will probably dates after Edgar's death, since its bequests to Glastonbury include his soul, and he too was buried there. Was she called Æthelflæd 'æt Domerhame' because she lived there in retirement, was buried there, or because she gave it to Glastonbury? Once again we are ignorant concerning Eadgifu.

[126] Edward had his mother buried in the New Minster, and moved his father's body from the Old, *LVH*, p 5.

[127] Æthelweard, *Chronicle*, p 54.

[128] Gaimar, lines 4082ff; see her obit, BL Egerton, 2104A, fo 43r, a Wherwell book.

[129] William of Malmesbury, *DGRA*, Bk II, cap 126, p 137; Goscelin, *Life of St Edith*, p 275.

the long quiet of death a husband who had tried but failed to repudiate her in the heated politics of life. Like all burials, Edith's made as many statements about the living as about the dead. It was William I who placed Edward and Edith together at Westminster. On her deathbed Edith had vindicated her chastity against accusations of adultery, or so it was later claimed.[130] For William the royal couple entombed together spoke of the legitimacy both of marriage and of his kingship. They celebrated Christian marriage; William's own union with Mathilda had been debatable and a chance to stress his pious concern for the institution was not to be forgone. They allayed any final doubts about the wife and marriage of the saint who had designated William as king. Christian burial gave an opportunity to reassert Christian notions of marriage, to make two in one flesh in the grave, whatever the problems had been in life. Edith's burial with Edward may be a sign of her greater security as wife and widow than some of her tenth-century forebears. It was appropriate that the burial like the security should stem from contemporary politics as well as from Christian ideals.

Unity in death did not, however, mean that the tenth-century insecurities and bitter step-relationships of serial monogamy had disappeared; if anything they had been exacerbated by Danish conquest. Emma's son laid her to rest not beside Æthelred, her first husband and his father, but beside her second husband, son of the conqueror of that father. It was a strange choice and perhaps a final indication of the divisions between mother and son which serial monogamy brings, the estrangements and tensions over which the ideal of motherhood cannot paper. Perhaps it should be seen as an intervention in current succession questions, asserting that Emma was Cnut's wife, aimed against Ælfgifu of Northampton and her descendants.[131] It may have been seen as burying the Danish dynasty and all its connections, including the recently exiled Godwine, whilst Edward planned a new dynasty and a new mausoleum to house it at Westminster. Alternatively it may have been a gesture of reconciliation with Danish interests, in England and Denmark when the king was seeking support after Godwine's fall. The beauty of such a burial may precisely be its capacity to mean many things to many people. The questions it raises are appropriate ones for a woman whose life had been lived within the complexities of family politics. Perhaps, however, the burial should be understood in relation mainly to Emma's own life, particularly her strong connections with Winchester, where Cnut and Harthacnut were buried, the dynastic mausoleum a final recognition of her great power. That power had derived from her family position but also from her roles as mistress of the household, patroness and queen.

[130] William of Malmesbury, *DGRA*, Bk II cap 197, p 239.
[131] Her sons possibly had their own descendants relevant to the English succession mid century, Stevenson 1913.

5

Household, Land and Patronage

Between c. 980 and 988 a six-storey tower was added to the church of New Minster, Winchester, at Æthelred's expense.[1] Each of its levels was carved on the outside, and the first was devoted to Mary.[2] She was depicted surrounded by the lords and citizens (*principes* and *cives*) of the heavenly Jerusalem, 'the most excellent Mary, mother of God'. Perhaps the image was of a mother with her child; it was certainly of a great queen within the court. The image, situated only yards from the late Saxon royal palace in Winchester (see figure 9), would have become a familiar one to Emma and to Edith in their frequent visits to the city. They would have seen it as they came and went to take their own place in the royal household, court and palace. Heaven too, they were reminded, was a court, with a queen who was (if not a wife) a mother and Lady.

1 Household, Court and Kingdom

To understand the eleventh-century queen's place in the royal court, that court itself must first be investigated. As long as kings rule in person, the household which surrounds them is the centre of the kingdom. Hincmar, the theorist of ninth-century Carolingian government, knew this. 'Those things which are relevant to the strength of the king and his kingdom' centred on 'the administration of the royal household'; government of the kingdom rested equally on the 'constant and unfailing governance of the palace' and on the government of the entire realm. The right organization of rule as a whole depended on the right organization of the rule

[1] Account of the tower and its building and decoration in *LVH*, pp 12–13; discussion in Biddle 1975, p 135–6 and 1976 p 315.
[2] This difficult passage of the *LVH* and its architectural implications are discussed by Quirk 1961.

of the palace. It was both a centre and microcosm of the kingdom; its members should be chosen from different regions, so that those who sought to approach the king would find access easier when they discovered him surrounded by those linked to them by family and local affiliation.[3] Hincmar's statements echoed throughout the middle ages and beyond,[4] not least in late Saxon England.[5] Asser portrayed Alfred as the ideal king, firmly placed in his household. It was his *familia*, where blood relatives, servants and followers lived together: Alfred kept his eldest son and youngest daughter always at court, where they were raised, along with the sons of nobles, by tutors and nurses.[6] Nobles came in rotation to serve him in the manifold duties of the court. They were rewarded each according to rank and office, as were craftsmen and foreigners. Half of his revenues went to secular purposes, and the bulk of that to the upkeep of his household and its servants.[7] He instructed and provided for goldsmiths, who made treasures in precious metal at his command,[8] and falconers, hawk-trainers and dog-keepers, who were essential to his hunting.[9] Royal halls and chambers were built, residences moved and reconstructed to house the king and his following.[10] When Alfred sought a metaphor for wisdom, available to all yet unequally grasped, he turned to the royal residence; to the varied routes people took, all to the one lord, to arrive at his service where 'some men will be in the chamber, some in the hall, some on the threshing floor and some in prison'.[11] The royal household was a group of people which took its unity from the king and its hierarchy from his service.

The tenth- and eleventh-century English royal household encompassed churchmen and warriors, military and administrative functions and attracted men of great wealth and standing.[12] Its military element, by the

---

[3] Hincmar, *De Ordine palatii*, caps 11–13, 18.

[4] See Fortescue in the fifteenth century where the royal household is the 'supreme academy of nobles of the realm', to which all nobles' sons were called, whose esquires should be chosen 'of sundry shires by whom it may be known the disposition of the counties', quoted Morgan 1987, pp 34 and 36.

[5] Campbell, J. 1987, p 217 on the functions of the royal household. Larson 1904, Darlington in *VCH Wiltshire* vol II, Barlow 1963, esp pp 15ff, Keynes 1980, pp 159–60 and 1988, and especially Campbell are essential reading on the royal household in the late Old English period.

[6] *Asser*, cap 75, pp 57–9.

[7] *Asser*, caps 99–101, pp 85–8.

[8] *Asser*, cap 91, p 77.

[9] *Asser*, cap 76, p 59.

[10] *Asser*, cap 91, p 77.

[11] Alfred's translation of St Augustine's Soliloquies, *Alfred*, pp 143–4.

[12] Prestwich 1981 warns against separating these functions from the household as a centre of royal upkeep in the twelfth century. This warning applies in the preceding centuries.

eleventh century known as the housecarls, could provide the nucleus of a royal army.[13] When Edward wished to apprehend Godwine in 1051 he sent out men from his own palace.[14] Its chapel was served by royal priests, some of whom went on to be bishops, some of whom continued in court service even after becoming bishops.[15] The chapel housed the royal relics, provided for religious service and for some of the king's secretarial needs.[16]

The household also contained the royal treasure, with the palace at Winchester serving as almost a permanent treasury by the eleventh century.[17] Later stories told of a great chest in Edward the Confessor's private rooms containing his money; when a poor servant tried to rob it the saintly king warned him of the approach of Hugolin the chamberlain.[18] Hugolin was remembered elsewhere as responsible for the royal treasure. He allegedly kept copies of the king's documents in the *gazophilacium*, along with the treasures.[19] A *gazophilacium* c. 1000 AD was translated as a *madmehus*, or treasure house,[20] and by the end of the eleventh century there was an especially important one at Winchester. In 1087 William Rufus went after his coronation to Winchester to inspect the *madmehus* and the gold, silver, vessels, costly robes, jewels and many other precious things his father had gathered there.[21] Whether travelling in boxes with the king[22] or amassed at Winchester, the treasure was one of the responsibilities of the king's officials, especially his chamberlain, Hugolin.[23]

[13] The function and nature of the housecarls is disputed, see Campbell 1987 and Hooper 1994; Hooper 1994 makes clear how little difference of substance there is between them on this issue of a military household.

[14] *VitaEd*, p 23.

[15] Barlow 1963; Keynes 1988, p 191 n 63 on the preferment of royal priests in Wessex in the tenth century; Life of Swithun, Ælfric, *Lives of Saints*, vol I, p 457, for Æthelwold's continued regular attendance at court as a bishop.

[16] Keynes 1988.

[17] Hollister 1978 (1986), p 210.

[18] Aelred, *Vita S Edwardi Regis*, col 746.

[19] *Chron Ram*, pp 170–2.

[20] Ælfric, *Glossary*, p 321.

[21] ASC, MS E 1086, recte 1087.

[22] Metcalf, 1980, p 24 argued that royal income by the eleventh century had outstripped the capacity of any box under the royal bed.

[23] The question of a permanent staff allocated to this role alone has sometimes dominated debate, see Barlow 1963, pp 121–3. Hugolin was a high-ranking royal official/noble whose service is likely to have been wide-ranging, cf Prestwich's remarks on the twelfth-century *familia*. He, like many of his twelfth-century counterparts, was probably not dedicated to a single area of household service, though this does not mean that he did not have others under him who were. Hollister 1978 (1986), pp 221–2 warns against placing too much emphasis on officials, when as late as the 1130s Robert of Gloucester could still control the treasury. A member of the royal family in such a role is an interesting parallel to the queen and Hollister's remarks 'that (this) tells us a great deal about the actual functioning of the Anglo-Norman government' could equally be applied pre-1066.

Hugh/Hugolin was a permanent court official. Such men might travel from the court at the king's command to give judgement or order arbitrations, or sometimes on more grisly business, as when Styr was sent to exhume King Harold in 1040.[24] The royal household included many others. It consisted of all those who personally served the king in whatever capacity, in daily attendance on him or attached to one of his many residences,[25] coming to court in rotation or serving when the king was in their area. A 'king's thegn' in Domesday was often literally a 'king's servant', though not necessarily engaged constantly in his service.[26] He or she often held land later formally associated with such occasional royal service, what were later known as 'serjeanties'. Indeed some of the occasional household and other services of the tenth and eleventh may be fossilized and revealed in thirteenth-century serjeanties. The duties of Særic, a king's thegn in Wiltshire, are not specified in Domesday Book. By the thirteenth century, whoever held his land acted as usher in the king's hall.[27] The king's servants could be relatively humble people, but the royal household also numbered among its officials the greatest men in the kingdom. King Alfred's mother was the daughter of his father's butler/*pincerna*;[28] his horsethegn/marshall one of the best thegns lost in the battles of the 890s;[29] Æthelmær, son of Æthelweard, descendant of King Æthelred I and one of the leaders of South West England c. 1000 AD, was Æthelred II's discthegn.[30] In the reign of Edward the Confessor, Ralph and Esgar the stallers ranked among the richest men in England,[31] and Robert son of Wymarc was both the king's kinsman and his steward of the royal palace.[32]

The landholdings of Edward's leading household officials were widely scattered.[33] Edward, like Hincmar, may have felt that men should be

---

[24] *SEHD* 18, the Fonthill case, where Ælfric the king's Hrælthegn, keeper of his clothes or wardrobe, was one of those ordered to arrange the reconciliation and arbitration. For Styr, *Fl Wig*, s.a. 1040, p 530.

[25] For this distinction recognized in the Will of Eadred see Whitelock, *EHD I*, p 556 disputing Harmer, *SEHD*, pp 121–2.

[26] 'Tainus' clearly has no single meaning in Domesday Book, but there are strong arguments for seeing it as often denoting royal service, see Campbell 1987, p 212 and references there.

[27] Appendix 2; essential discussion and references on this question of serjeanty in Campbell 1987, p 211ff. Strict continuity of type of service is debatable.

[28] *Asser*, cap 2, p 4.

[29] See *ASC*, MS A, s.a. 897.

[30] S 914 vernacular version.

[31] Clark 1994, p 14, on Stallers, Mack 1986.

[32] *VitaEd*, p 76, *regalis palatii stabilator*.

[33] Mack 1986, pp 128–9; Clarke 1994, p 127 argues for geographical concentrations in different parts of the country though his listing of the lands of individual stallers shows a wide scattering.

recruited to the household from all regions, but royal service was also profitable and provided opportunities to acquire land. Edward gave the church of Huntingdon to two of his priests, who in turn sold it to the royal chamberlain, Hugh/Hugolin, who sold it on to two Huntingdon priests.[34] The long arm of the court reached out into 'minor provincial centres' where a royal chamberlain could acquire and trade in property.[35] Edward's household had close contact with the wider kingdom. Great courts, like those at Christmas and Easter, saw people summoned from all the kingdom to attend,[36] but service to the king in his household, already involving a surprisingly large proportion of the population,[37] also bound the kingdom together. The royal household was both a model for the unity of the kingdom, and an integral part of the working of that unity.[38]

In the household the king's dignity was maintained and displayed. In his twelfth-century reworking of the *Life* of Edward the Confessor, Osbert described him as a king 'rich in rule, glorious in the palace, terrible in the kingdom'.[39] If this passage was not in the eleventh-century *Life* it should have been. 'A worldly king has many thegns and stewards. He cannot be glorious unless he has the dignity which befits him and many serving men who wait on him in obedience.'[40] A king must have *noble* servants who minister to him in many ways.[41] On great occasions he had to look the part. King Edgar had a cloak of *purpura*, of costly purple, or perhaps shot-silk taffeta.[42] Amongst the king's thegns or royal servants in Wiltshire in 1086 was a woman Leofgeat 'who made and makes orfrey (gold fringe) for the king and queen'.[43] A king must have suitable places for the enactment of royal dignity. Alfred built and rebuilt residences. Edward the Confessor built a new church at Westminster, attached to a new palace complex.[44] At his table, wherever it might be, he must be kingly among his followers. When the royal overseers came from

---

[34] DB I, fo 208r.

[35] Campbell 1987, p 209.

[36] *Vita Oswaldi*, pp 425, 427 and cf p 436 for summoning to the coronation.

[37] Campbell 1987, pp 215–16.

[38] On the similar functions of the royal households of the fifteenth and sixteenth centuries see Morgan and Starkey 1987, and Starkey 1977. It will be difficult to test Starkey's suggestion that the 'agent symbol' was a 'specific contribution' of early modern miracle working monarchs to the art of government (1977 p 222) until more work has been done on medieval courts and households.

[39] *VitaEd*, p 67, supplying the lost portions.

[40] Ælfric, *Lives of Saints*, vol I, p 6 writing to ealdorman Æthelweard.

[41] *Asser*, cap 100, p 86.

[42] He gave it to Ely, see *LE*, p 117 and cf Dodwell pp 145–9 for the suggestion that this was shot-silk taffeta.

[43] DB I, fo 74r.

[44] Vince 1990, 32–3.

the household to inspect preparations for Athelstan's visit to Glastonbury, they came to ensure there would be sufficient of the right sort of
food and drink. Æthelflæd rushed to church to pray that there would be
enough for the 'royal dignity'. The king and his household must be, and
be seen to be, fed well.

Dignity came at a price. Royal estates, particularly in southern England, were organized for the upkeep of the household, for its provision
whether in kind or cash.[45] Behind some of the shire customs or
consuetudines of Domesday Book lie the demands of a semi-itinerant
court. Markets and mints grew up or were developed on royal estates, to
service the buying and selling essential to provide for the varied needs of
the royal court. Reeves and sheriffs were called on to meet its demands.
In Wiltshire the royal estates were organized to support the household. In
addition Edward of Salisbury, the sheriff, had yearly '130 porkers, 32
bacon hogs, 2 pecks and 8 sextars of wheat and as much of barley, 5
pecks and 4 sextars of oats, 16 sextars of honey or 16s, 480 hens, 1,600
eggs, 100 cheeses, 52 lambs, 420 fleeces and 162 acres of unreaped corn
and £80', so that 'when the reeves do not have enough for the *firma* (i.e.
for the royal provision)[46] Edward could make it up from his own.'[47]

The household was the centre of a major economic enterprise and of
its costs. The early twelfth-century chronicler Eadmer has left a devastating critique of the evils and oppressions of the late eleventh-century royal
household. Those who attended the court of William Rufus plundered
and destroyed, laying waste the territory through which the king passed.
What they could not eat they burnt or forced people to sell for their
benefit. They washed their horses feet in the drink which they could not
consume. 'When it became known that the king was coming, all the
inhabitants would flee from their homes, anxious to do the best for
themselves and their families by taking refuge in woods and other
places.'[48] Norman kings may have been particularly oppressive, but
earlier households had to be paid for too.[49] The miracle stories associated

---

[45] Stafford 1980.

[46] The *firma* or *feorm* which occurs over and over again on the royal lands seems to refer
to the rents and renders due, but also to the specific organization for royal provision; in
some shires certain royal lands are specified as being *de firma*. *Feorm* in vernacular
manorial documents can refer to food provided for workers at certain times of the agrarian
year see e.g. *winterfeorm* and *Easterfeorm*, Rectitudines Singularum Personarum, Liebermann, *Die Gesetze*, cap 21.4, *midwintres feorm*, ibid cap 9.1.

[47] DB I, fo 69r.

[48] Eadmer, *Historia Novorum*, pp 192ff.

[49] Asser, for example, describes the household from the king's viewpoint. Henry I has left
the first precise recording of the royal household and its permitted demands; this does not
mean that either its organization or the problems of providing for it were new at that date.
See Green 1986 p 27 on Henry I's Constitutio Domus Regis as part of his reform of abuses
of the royal household.

with tenth-century saints display a recurring concern with the problem of feeding royal visitors. Æthelwold provided an unfailing draft of beer and mead for Eadred and his followers, who on this occasion included some proverbially hard-drinking Northern nobles.[50] The king's relative Æthelflæd was concerned about the provision of Athelstan's court when the king came to visit her in Glastonbury. Those who had charge of the royal provisioning came the day before to see whether all was ready and fitting, and warned her that the mead might run out. Thanks to her prayers to Mary, the mead never fell below a hand's measure, even though the king's *pincernae*, as was usual in royal feasts, hurried about the whole day serving people from horns and other vessels.[51] When Athelstan was told of all this he was made to respond as a good king. He left, saying 'We have sinned in greatly oppressing this handmaid of God with our unnecessary multitude.'

Royal and other high ranking households were a strain on those who had to support them at all stages of the middle ages. In charters of the eighth and ninth centuries churches had tried to limit the extent to which the king and his officials could call upon their lands for the upkeep of their households and hunting.[52] If we hear little of this by the tenth and eleventh centuries it is not because royal provisioning was not a burden, but because the articulate holders of great estates no longer paid it, at least not as an imposition on their land as opposed to their hospitality.[53] The shire customs of Domesday Book, like the earlier charters, were still concerned with the limitation of royal provisioning; sheriffs and shire communities had been left to compound for the remnants of older dues. Eadmer, an English monk reacting to the Norman Conquest, allows us to hear the rare voice of the peasantry on whom these burdens ultimately fell. Tenth-century saints' lives do not speak with Eadmer's bitterness, and are concerned with the price paid, not by the poor, but by religious houses or nobles. The later Welsh tractate restricted the scale of an itinerant royal household to 36 persons on horseback, but allowed also for a king's bodyguard, his goodmen, his servants, his musicians and his poor.[54] The saintly Edward the Confessor daily dispensed the necessities of life to the poor at his court. They, like the foreigners he received, had

[50] Wulfstan, *Æthelwold* pp 22–4.

[51] *Life of Dunstan*, Auctore B, pp 17–18.

[52] For some comment on this see Wormald 1982, p 97; Brooks 1971, p 71.

[53] If bookland gave exemption from such payments by now all noble land was considered bookland, see Reynolds 1994, pp 333ff, and cf Brooks 1971, p 71.

[54] *The Law of Hywel Dda*, p 6, part of the tractate known as 'The Laws of Court'. On the tractates, of which the Laws of Court is one, see *Welsh History Review*, Special Number, 1963, 'The Welsh Laws' especially Goronwy Edwards. Jenkins, ibid p 54, notes that the Laws of Court were obsolete by the thirteenth century; Edwards 1956, pp 170–1, argues that such dues were taken and rights exercised by the Norman kings. They may give some insight into late Saxon practice in some areas.

to be provided for. The milky white translucent hands of the king dispensed but did not create royal largesse. Royal generosity and sanctity as much as the dirty feet of courtiers' horses had a price someone else had to pay.

The English royal household seems to have undergone organization or reorganization c. 1060.[55] Household reorganization may be a response to criticism of costs, or an attempt at reform of the kingdom and its administration. It may also mark or underline a court style, in this case a formal one. The royal household brought together the powerful and the would-be powerful, the talented and the ambitious around the source of patronage and advancement, the king. The resulting political tensions are managed through different court styles.[56] The military style of Charlemagne or William Rufus was comradely, familiar, bringing the camaraderie of the battlefield into the court itself. The Imperial formality of Louis the Pious was, by contrast, distant, sober and grave. The styles of the late Saxon court are difficult to recover from the surviving evidence. The military households of the king and the royal princes late in Æthelred's reign may have bred a warrior style; that of Cnut, experienced in battle, even more so. Only the skaldic verse[57] and small fragments of what may once have been a stone frieze at Winchester celebrating warrior-kingship survive to give a hint of it. The frieze is not precisely datable,[58] and neither it nor the poet's battle-praises tell of the way relations at Cnut's court were managed. Descriptions of Edgar's coronation at Bath, or the portrait of Edward in the *Life* suggest a formal, distant style with the emphasis on royal dignity and gravity. These sources are clerical and monastic, and the ideal possibly remote from reality, though clerics, especially clerics of a monastic training,

---

[55] That formalization is suggested by the titles given to witnesses in the diplomas of Edward's reign. Even before 1060 some witness lists make divisions among the witnesses, separating *nobiles* from *ministri*, for example, see S 1002, 1003, 1019. c. 1060 a new group of household servants comes together at the top of the non-earlish lay witnesses, Esgar, Robert, Ralf, Bundi and Wigod (though this date does not mark the first appearance of all of them). The emergence of a new household group like this is no new phenomenon; see the discussion of such changes in Æthelred's reign in Keynes 1980 and Stafford 1979. What is new is the fact that several witness lists after 1060 make some attempt to distinguish these men and others, S 1030, 1033, 1036, 1041, 1042. Scant as it is, this evidence points to some reorganization or more formal development which the witness lists are registering. For more discussion of these witness lists and the titles in them see Keynes 1988.

[56] Cf Gillingham 1995a, Elias, Starkey 1977 and 1987a.

[57] E.g. Hallvarðr's eulogy of Cnut, printed and translated, Frank 1994, pp 119–21.

[58] Biddle 1966, pp 329–32 and plate LXII. A narrative frieze, perhaps 80 or more feet long and four and a half feet (1.37 m) high, set either around the interior or exterior of the Old Minster, it probably celebrated the Volsungs, the common ancestors of Danes and English. It may have been a structural part of the late tenth-century rebuilding, or, as Biddle suggests, set up by Cnut to depict the traditional, common history of England and Denmark.

formed a large component of the late tenth- and eleventh-century English court. A Carolingian-style movement for moral regeneration of the kingdom, close to and part of the royal household itself, lasted for several reigns. Edgar by the 970s, and Æthelred in the 990s, presided over courts which probably had some of the tone of that of Louis the Pious. Edward's court may deliberately have recalled this heyday of his dynastic forebears.

The palace complexes which were built and remodelled in the tenth and eleventh centuries appear to have been a stage for such formality (see figure 9). The secular buildings constructed at Winchester or by Edward the Confessor at Westminster sadly remain unexcavated. Both palace complexes were close to great churches. At Winchester, the Old Minster's westworks were extensively redeveloped in the later part of the tenth century to house the tombs of former kings. The redevelopment included a balcony on which the king could appear to his people and brought the church and the palace into the closest possible physical proximity.[59] Edward's building of Westminster Abbey as a royal mausoleum was attached to new palace buildings.[60] At Gloucester Archbishop Ealdred undertook a remodelling of the minster church during Edward's reign which would have provided an 'appropriate setting for royal ceremonial'.[61] Such a determined phase of reconstruction points to a concern with the ritual presentation of kingship.

The formality of royal rituals in church need not extend to the style and tone of court, certainly not to all occasions when a king was surrounded by his household or to all stages of his life. Styles of court life vary according to the king's personality and age and according to circumstances. A coronation meeting at Bath and a hunting household lodged at Cheddar call for a different tone; a military style may be specific to a king's youth and maturity, or deliberately recollect it in advancing age. But the late Saxon evidence as a whole signals a general formalization of the style of kingship. It was expressed in the portrait of the gravely joyful Edward, dignified, walking with eyes downcast, in public a true king, in private with his courtiers acting as one of them, but with his royal dignity never impaired.[62]

'Warrior' or 'formal', many eleventh-century courts were already inhabited by courtiers, were already 'courtly'. The subtle code of courtliness would eventually entail an aestheticizing of manners, refinement of emotion and expression of sentiment through minute gestures,

---

[59] Biddle 1975, esp p 138 for the royal connections and 1986, pp 62–3 for the possible continuity of the west front balcony in the later cathedral at Winchester from a similar one on the Old Minster's westwork.

[60] Gem 1986 and Vince 1990.

[61] Hare 1993, pp 22 and 17–26 on Ealdred's work there.

[62] *VitaEd*, p 12.

and above all controlled and restrained speech. Some aspects of this are already discernible in the eleventh century and before.[63] Speech and gesture already played an important part in the court worlds of *Beowulf* or Hincmar. The formal greetings, the peace-making speeches, the grim jokings, the verbal status challenges of *Beowulf* are all ritualized tools and expressions of household relationships and management.[64] Hincmar was well aware of the significance of speech at court. The right things must be discussed by the right people. There were subjects appropriate to General Assemblies and others fitting for permanent household servants, though maintaining that distinction was a problem, as was the way such discussions were conducted. Discussion was the way minor and major affairs were discriminated and politics managed.[65] Discussion of the general good easily turned to particular persons, who in despair might be driven to treason.[66] Speech needed to be controlled. It excluded and included. The king's speech should discriminate ranks and statuses yet make all feel welcome; he should greet the important, sympathize with the aged, rejoice with the young and chat with those rarely seen.[67] He should use such opportunities to gather information, to hear the grumbles of the people, to enquire into potential rebellion, on all of which those who spoke to him would already have spoken to others in the kingdom at large.[68]

By the eleventh century in England controlled speech was both the mark of the courtier and of regality. The court was a place where talking was a tool of government, a means of advance and a constant source of friction.[69] Cnut favoured Edith's father Godwine because of his eloquence, he was 'profound in speech'.[70] He and his sons were slow to anger, tolerating wrongs. Harold knew when to keep his counsels to himself and when to speak out, was guarded and controlled. Tostig was even more so, and chaste of tongue; he never too readily communicated his plans with anyone.[71] The courtier's wary speech easily tips over into the vice of failure to take counsel. Edward the Confessor could be gravely joyful, approachable, at times terrible in his anger, yet so gracious in the granting or refusing of petitions that even his denial seemed like generos-

---

[63] Jaeger 1985 passim and p 13, Gillingham 1995, pp 148–9 for late Saxon England.

[64] Clover 1980 and Enright 1988, pp 182–3 on the importance on Unferth's speeches in *Beowulf*.

[65] Hincmar, *De Ordine Palatii*, cap 33.

[66] Ibid caps 29–31.

[67] Ibid cap 35.

[68] Ibid cap 36.

[69] Speech is an essential element in the treatise on courtly love, Andreas Capellanus, *De Amore*. Duby 1991, pp 274–5 for its role in the regulation of the Capetian court.

[70] *VitaEd*, p 6.

[71] Ibid pp 31–2.

ity, his affability making refusal seem like a favour.[72] Edward's speech
and demeanour were kingly. When he burst suddenly into laughter at the
feast table no one around him joined in; they listened in silence to an
inversion of his normal behaviour which they rightly interpreted not as
merriment but as a sign.[73]

2 Mistress of the Household: Queen, Household, Court and Kingdom

In Hincmar's ideal Carolingian palace, the queen had a central role. She
was responsible 'for good order . . . for the presentation of the king in
dignified splendour, for annual gifts to the men of the household'; she
and the chamberlain saw to preparations for the household's activities,
making gifts to legations, freeing the king of concern for the household
and palace.[74] She was the organizer of the palace and of the royal dignity,
a giver of gifts and provider for its magnificence.[75] According to the
capitulary on the running of the royal estates the Carolingian queen
shared with the king responsibility for the royal estates and for issuing
orders to the stewards, for giving permission for stays in the royal
residences.[76] The Welsh tractate later described the one-third share of
royal dues and booty the queen could command, the annual tribute of
food and drink the king's clients/villeins paid to honour her, the protection she could extend over the royal hall, the gifts she, like the king, made
to household servants, the organization of her own household and its
relationship to that of the king.[77] Tenth- and eleventh-century England
has left no tract on the palace, no capitulary on the running of the royal
estates, no 'Laws of Court' to regulate the internal and external relations
of the royal household. The gnomic poetry, however, left no doubt of a
noble or royal wife's role in the household, as a counsellor and gift-giver,
responsible for its hierarchy and order: 'being liberal with horses and
treasures, everywhere and at all times before the band of comrades
greeting first the protector of nobles with mead . . . knowing wise counsel
for them both together.'[78] And Domesday Book provides a unique

[72] Ibid p 12.

[73] Ibid p 67, a section supplied from the twelfth-century work of Osbert of Clare, but
whose consonance with the description of the king in the surviving eleventh-century
sections of the life inspires confidence that it may have been taken from the original.

[74] Hincmar, *De Ordine Palatii*, cap 22. I have translated 'milites' as 'men of the household',
it has a wider meaning than 'fighting men'.

[75] Ward 1990, pp 207, 216–17 and 219 on *honestas* and translating *honesta domina* as
'munificent gift-giver'.

[76] *De Villis*, cap 16, 27.

[77] *The Laws of Hywel Dda*, 'The Laws of Court', pp 6, 8ff, 17, 28–31, 124.

[78] *Anglo-Saxon Poetry*, p 311, translating *Maxims* I, ASPR, 3, The Exeter Book (1939),
p 159.

source to go beyond the theory to the practice, particularly in the case of Edith.

In Domesday Book the royal households and the role of the queen in them can be glimpsed, though not fully reconstructed. Domesday Book's compilers were not primarily concerned to delineate the royal households. However, their interest in royal rights, dues and lands ensured the inclusion of much information about royal servants and followers and their holdings. This fleshes out the picture revealed in diplomas and their witness lists, in turn reinforced and supplemented by later evidence of land-holding in return for royal service.[79] The evidence is often fragmentary and tantalizing, but it suggests that the queen had a household of her own; that it shared characteristics of the royal household in its relationship to the kingdom; that it was on occasion separate, on occasion part of the larger royal one, so that her own household did not exclude her from a role in the royal household itself.[80]

Edith's household was identified in the witness list of the Waltham charter which recorded the meeting on the occasion of her brother Harold's foundation of Waltham abbey in 1062.[81] As usual the king was surrounded by an array of bishops, abbots, earls and great nobles. Unusually those nobles were described not simply as *ministri*, thegns, but precisely. The result is a rare view of a meeting of a great court which was also an expanded royal household:[82] Esgar, overseer of the royal hall (*procurator regis aulae*), Ralph and Bundi, officials of the hall and the palace (*aulicus* and *palatinus regis*), Baldwin and Peter the king's chap-

---

[79] The continuity between the later serjeanties and eleventh-century royal service has been made clear in the work of Darlington, *VCH Wilts*, II and Campbell 1987. To exploit this potential fully for the reconstruction of late Saxon royal service and household is beyond the scope of this book, though, like a full study of the royal lands, it is urgently needed.

[80] Appendix II lists the servants and followers of the queen and gives details of the principles used to identify them. Reference should be made to it for detail concerning what follows.

[81] S 1036.

[82] The Waltham charter and its witness list has been much debated. Round 1904, p 81 accepted it; Barlow 1963, 120–1 and 1970 p 164 was sceptical; Keynes 1988, p 197 notes 66 and 69 brings together the range of earlier opinion. Keynes' own detailed discussion is inclined to acceptance, but Clarke 1994, p 128 has renewed scepticism of what he sees as a 'conflated list', an 'interesting forgery' reflecting the twelfth- not the mid eleventh-century household, whilst the editors of the *Waltham Chronicle*, pp xxxviii–xliii are inclined to accept it as a charter of Edward the Confessor, as am I. Most of those whom the Waltham charter identifies as members of the household can be verified as such from other sources, Keynes 1988, p 206; the only exceptions are Yfing and perhaps Wigod. The agreement of the list with other evidence on the queen's household has some bearing on wider questions of its acceptability. Its allocations of 'job descriptions', which are the major bone of contention, are in most respects consistent with earlier English terminology and household structure and far from unique in the charters of Edward's reign. If the list is a post-Conquest forgery it is a remarkably well-informed one.

lains, Robert and Osbern his relatives, Regenbald his chancellor, Wigod, his butler (*pincerna*), Azor and Yfing his stewards (*dapifer*). Each of the last had a queen's equivalent: Harding the queen's butler followed Wigod, Godwine, her steward, Yfing. At this great meeting the lay nobility were distinguished according to their intimacy with and service to the king and queen. In 1072 another group of men gathered, in the upper room of the westworks of Wilton abbey; this time it was around Edith alone and to witness the sale of land at Combe by Azor to Giso, bishop of Wells.[83] They included Æthelsige the steward, Ælfwold the burthegn or chamberlain, Godwine *hos*,[84] two cooks, Æthelric and Rabel, two goldsmiths, Theoderic and Æthelsige, and a number of clerics. Several of those present were named but given no title, including Harding and Wulfweard the White. Harding was the queen's butler, and Godwine may be the queen's steward of the Waltham list. The failure to identify Harding with the queen's service may be nothing more than a scribal quirk. Yet it prompts questions about the nature and formality of the queen's household in the mid eleventh century, about changes in it over time and about its relationship to the royal household, a relationship which, for the dowager Edith in 1072, had been severed.

Edith had many servants and followers. She had chaplains such as Ælfgar and Walter, later bishop of Hereford; perhaps Walter the deacon served in this capacity on her East Anglian estates, or Sigar when she was in Kent. Ælfwold, present at Wilton in 1072, was probably her chamberlain; land of hers was held by a chamberlain of that name in 1086. She had stewards, like Godwine and Alfred, who may have managed her household and/or her estates; a Godwine continued to hold queen's lands at farm in 1086. Her local estate managers included Colwine, the reeve who administered her extensive revenues in Exeter and farmed important royal lands in Cornwall, Eadric who held her manor of Dorking in Surrey, and perhaps Lank in Berkshire and Bedfordshire or Wulfweard the White whose underlings included reeves in Dorset from whom he held pledges. The scale of the queen's lands (see below) means that these men must be merely the tip of the iceberg; many of those associated with her service in 1066 would have had similar local responsibilities. Some of those responsibilities were very specific. Ælfwine the huntsman held land from her in Hertfordshire; Wudumann had been entrusted with the care of her horses; Ælfric, if not Ælfbold, Rabel and Æthelric, were her cooks. Her service could be intimate – she had a lady of the bedchamber, Mathilda – or it could be intermittent; in Wiltshire a widow, Leofgeat held land from Edith and Edward in exchange for producing orfrey, gold fringing, for them. It could include the deployment of the craftworker's

---

[83] Dickinson 1876.
[84] Perhaps *hostiarius*, usher.

skills, whether in the embroidering of gold textiles or in goldsmithery itself: the father of Ælfweard the goldsmith, himself probably a goldsmith, held of her, and two goldsmiths were with her at Wilton in 1072.

Edith's service had the capacity to attract or create people of considerable wealth. Judging by the value of their lands recorded in Domesday, her identifiable followers ranked high among the nobility. Excluding the earls, Brictric ranked thirty-fifth, Harding sixteenth, and Wulfweard the White eighth. If women like Wulfgifu Beteslau and Wulfwyn of Cresslow were her servants or their widows, they ranked 39th, probably higher, and 23rd respectively.[85] The queen's service could consolidate if not found a fortune. Ælfric, Wihtgar's son, had administered the eight and a half Thingoe hundreds for Emma in Suffolk; Wihtgar his son may have continued in Edith's service, though by 1066 Bury claimed these lucrative jurisdictions. Wihtgar son of Ælfric was one of the richest men in East Anglia in 1066, and in the kingdom at large held an estate as valuable as that of Bundi the staller, one of the king's high-ranking household servants. The queen's service appeared desirable to the sons of well-placed royal servants, and could prove the solid foundation of a dynasty. Harding was the son of Eadnoth the staller. In the pursuit of the queen's interests he developed that skill in litigation for which he was later remembered, and which laid the basis for his family's continued prosperity in the twelfth century. Foreigners were among those who benefited from her. Walter her chaplain was a Lotharingian, as perhaps was the deacon she rewarded in East Anglia. Mathilda, her woman of the bedchamber, sounds like a Norman who entered the queen's service either before or after 1066. Theoderic the German goldsmith may have served her as much as the king. On the whole her servants were members of the English nobility; some like Sigar in Kent from venerable old families, the majority of them men and women of more humble background.[86] Some of their estates have all the appearance of recent accumulations of geographically diverse lands, or at least the recent inflation of an ancestral heritage by the profits of queen's service: witness those of Wulfweard the White and Wulfwyn of Cresslow, and of Wulfgifu Beteslau if those held by a woman of that name on the queen's fee in East Anglia are included.

The total size of Edith's household is difficult to estimate. Seventy to eighty people can be associated with her with varying degrees of certainty. This number includes many who served on her estates and thus were not regularly with her, yet excludes others close to her but whom Domesday Book as a record of certain types of landholding ignores. It is

---

[85] Clarke 1994 pp 38–9.
[86] At least if the size of their estates is any indicator.

probable, for example, that the female element in Edith's household is underrepresented. The costs of the queen's household are even more imponderable. The scale of her landholding is some indication of her expected needs, though this was also related to the queen's function in the government of the kingdom and to her more general responsibilities for patronage and the royal household. Domesday is of little direct help. On the royal estate of Eardisland in Herefordshire it was customary that when the *domina* or lady came to the manor the reeve gave her 18 ora 'so that she might be happy', whilst he gave 10s to the steward and other officers.[87] The Lady in question was almost certainly Edith,[88] and the steward and officers perhaps hers. But the payment is too small to have provided for her needs; it simply recognizes her status and dignity and those of her servants. Rarely does the survey hint so strongly at the sort of royal or queenly wrath which officials might face if that dignity were affronted. But that does not tell us how much it cost to keep her. The queen almost certainly on occasion travelled alone with her household, and not merely when she was despatched to Wilton with royal pomp in 1051. What such travel involved, how it was organized and what it cost are questions which can be asked but not answered.

Edith's household and following was illuminated by Domesday Book; it was unlikely to have been a new phenomenon though it would be unwise to assume that its scale and nature had been uniform in the past. In the absence of a Domesday survey, Emma's known servants are inevitably fewer, but the identifiable ones fit a pattern very like Edith's. Orderic Vitalis compared the hopeful followers who accompanied Mathilda to Germany in the twelfth century with those who had come with Emma, suggesting that Emma brought a French contingent in 1002.[89] When she arrived she brought with her at least one French servant, Hugh, who was given charge of Exeter. The Bretons Wymarc and the father of Ralph the staller may also have been among her followers.[90] But if others came, they have left no trace in the surviving sources.[91] All

---

[87] DB I, fo 179v. An ora = 16d–20d.

[88] Campbell 1987, p 207 makes her the wife of Earl Morcar. Morcar is said to have held the estate in 1066, though in view of his youth he was probably unmarried. Eardisland has all the appearance of an estate which has been royal in the recent past. It follows directly after Edward's lands, and before those of Harold. Most importantly it is closely linked with Edward's own estate here. Although now identified as Kingsland and Eardisland, these two consecutive estates are both named 'Lene' in Domesday Book; each rendered £6, each was 15 hides, and the churches of the two linked together. 'Lene' looks like a royal estate divided into two, half given to Earl Morcar, or perhaps his predecessor Tostig, but the payments still royal ones.

[89] Orderic Vitalis, vol VI, Bk 11, cap 38, pp 166–8.

[90] Larson 1904, p 195 on Emma's possible Normanization of the court.

[91] Orderic may have exaggerated, or attached to Emma, blame for later arrivals, even including 1066 Normans in her extended baggage train.

her other known servants were English. The unnamed goldsmith who had responsibility for her relics had a brother who was a monk at Malmesbury. Wulfweard the White began his long career in lucrative royal service with Emma; his ability to move smoothly from mother-in-law to daughter-in-law betokens the flexibility of the successful servant. Ælfric son of Wihtgar administered the Thingoe hundreds for Emma; judging from the wealth of his son he became as prosperous through doing so as a Wulfweard or a Harding. His relative, Leofgifu, was also in the queen's service; her will is the only one addressed solely to the queen in Saxon England.

Service of the queen could be a family affair. Ælfric may have entered the queen's service via Leofgifu rather than vice versa. Women were instrumental in gaining patronage in household office for their male relatives. In the 990s Leofsige secured a place in the ætheling's household through the request of his relative Æthelgifu to the then dowager queen.[92] Wulfweard's wife and daughter remained under Edith's patronage, and may themselves have been linked to her through service. Ælfric's family, unlike Wulfweard's, did not apparently make the shift from Emma's service to Edith's, though our exiguous information about eleventh-century noble relationships makes this a hazardous statement. If correct the question may be less of character than of the vagaries of the queen's service itself. In some circumstances serving the queen could be a means of survival. English people like Harding, Ælfsige, son-in-law of Wulfweard the White, and perhaps Wulfgifu Beteslau and Ælfweard the Goldsmith survived the Norman Conquest. Service to Edith and associa-tion with her may have proved a factor in their relatively safe route through the difficult years following 1066. But when a queen fell, her servants suffered. The Thingoe hundreds passed to Bury St Edmunds after Emma's fall in 1043; queen's service in East Anglia was curtailed. It was perhaps now that the family of Ælfric son of Wihtgar ceased to be queen's servants. The lack of a West Saxon base distanced Ælfric's family from that contact with the court which could have diverted other spoils in their direction. The queen's service shared many of the characteristics of her own position, both lucrative and insecure.

Emma's best-known servant was Stigand. If not a native East Anglian he and his family acquired extensive lands there, sometimes lands con-nected with the queen. Stigand was close to Emma: he may have been the queen's own chaplain, or enjoyed a high rank in the royal household with which she had been associated. The careers of servant and mistress went hand in hand. In 1043 Stigand and Emma rose and fell together. In April, or soon after the coronation then, Stigand was appointed bishop of Elmham. In November the queen lost lands and treasures, and Stigand was deprived of his bishopric. If the queen's service had already raised this queen's priest to a bishopric, it soon restored him to office. Emma after 1043, as after 1035, was firmly ensconced in Winchester. Winchester was her dower borough, the heart of the royal administration, formerly a scene of activity for Emma's mother-in-law Ælfthryth in dowagerhood. The queen and the royal administration were centred on the household in the great palace of Winchester. Stigand went on to become bishop of Winchester in 1047. In the tenth century Ælfthryth had been the ally of an already established bishop of Winchester. In the 1040s the relationship was reversed; a dowager now ensured the advance of her own former household official. Even more glittering prizes awaited him; the Archbishopric of Canterbury in 1052, perhaps even the running of the whole late Saxon administrative machine by 1066.[93] In his case, association with the queen, or a role in the royal chapel close to her, proved the route to the highest eleventh-century offices, though at one point it was almost his undoing. If the cases of Wulfweard and Harding suggested that the queen's service paid, Stigand's career shows how rewarding service to a woman still closely involved in the royal household could be, but also, on occasion, how dangerous.

Emma and Edith acted as much within the royal household as in their own. An attempt to identify the queen's household and followers stresses its separation. A corrective emphasis on the parallels, shared features and close links with that of the king is required. People of similar kind and status are found in both households. Of the twenty richest laypeople in England in 1066 after the earls, one was a woman, Eadgifu the Fair, probably an earl's widow, and of the remaining nineteen, twelve were or had been royal servants in the household.[94] Three of them had served the queen. Royal service, whether of king or queen, brought similar rewards and attracted similar people, in Eadnoth and Harding's case, father and son. The estates of both king's and queen's servants exhibit the same scattering of lands, the same dubious relationships with ecclesiastical lands.[95] Both chose foreigners as well as English servants. In some cases it is not even easy to tell whether a person is a servant of king or queen.[96] If the queen's household and followers sometimes seem close and personal, sometimes to stretch out into the kingdom at large, so too do those

---

[93] Campbell 1987, p 218.

[94] Clarke 1994, p 38. Brictric Ælfgar's son, Esgar, Robert, Ralph, Eadnoth and his son Harding, Wulfweard the White, Bundi, Azur and perhaps Æthelnoth of Kent were all men recently identifiable as great household/royal servants, Karl, Ælfstan, from earlier in Edward's reign – all on the basis of regular appearance at the top of the lay witnesses and/or specific designation as such. Ælfric, father of Wihtgar Ælfric's son, had been in Emma's service.

[95] On which see more below pp 153–5.

[96] See Gode and Leofgeat who served both king and queen.

of the king. Similarities in life extended into the grave, when servants of king and queen found their way into royal mausolea. Hugolin was buried in Edward's own foundation of Westminster. Whether by Edward's wishes, or William's duty to Edward's memory, or both, burial with his master seemed the most appropriate end for this man, 'of all the great nobles of the kingdom the most faithful to the king'.[97] Emma made special arrangements between Old Minster, Winchester, and Wulfweard regarding Hayling Island. These were partly aimed at securing the burial of Wulfweard in the church so closely associated with his royal mistress and the dynasty.[98]

These parallels could betoken separation of the king's and queen's households, as parallel but distinct; but the crises of Emma's career between 1035 and 1043 indicate her power in the royal household itself. In 1035–6 Emma stayed at Winchester 'with the housecarls of her son the king'.[99] These may have been men possibly attached to Emma as queen and mistress of that household.[100] Hincmar's ninth-century Carolingian queen had been responsible for the payment of such men. At Wallingford Edward's housecarls lived on land connected with a previous queen.[101] The housecarls' support of Emma in 1035 may, however, be no more than a calculation members of the household made. The military household were at Winchester, where their former royal master had just been buried, and Emma's dominant position there could have swung them in her favour. No one could be quite certain which turn events would take after 1035, and Emma and her son were as good a gamble as any. The housecarls' loyalty to her need not argue any general queenly responsibility for them. Her possession of the royal treasure, on the other hand, must have weighed in their calculations of her strength to survive, if it does not indicate her role in their maintenance.

[97] Flete, *Westminster*, p 83.

[98] DB I, fo 43v.

[99] *ASC*, MS E s.a. 1036.

[100] On the basis of the wording 'the housecarls of her son the king' it has been suggested that in 1035–6 Emma was supported by housecarls sent by her son Harthacnut, and thus not part of the English royal household, Hooper 1994, p 93. In view of the dispute over the succession the wording may be emphasizing that her son Harthacnut was king, rather than that the housecarls were his.

[101] DB I, fo 56r: 15 acres on which Edward's housecarls had lived were held in 1086 by Miles Crispin; his twenty tenements in the town were linked to the manor of Newnham Murren in Oxfordshire, which he also held. That manor had been in the hands of the dowager queen Ælfgifu in the mid tenth century; she had left it in her will to the ætheling, *Wills* no 8. This does not prove a longstanding link between queens and housecarls. Wallingford in 1066 was in the hands of Edward's kinsman Wigod. The holding of land by a royal kinsman which had previously been in the hands of a queen and an ætheling confirms the general arguments about the use of royal estates as family provision, with constant adjustments depending on the structure of and relations whithin that family, see below 'The Queen's Lands'.

The eleventh-century queen's control of royal treasure is in less doubt. In 1035 Emma kept the royal treasure of which her stepson Harold later deprived her. There is no doubt that it was royal treasure, Cnut's treasure, which she possessed.[102] The issue in the attack on Emma in 1043 was again her possession of treasure and land. She held land, gold, silver and other treasures which the king felt were rightfully his. Edward left her with what he considered sufficient for her needs.[103] The question was of the transition from a queen's role to that of a dowager, from responsibility for the needs of the household and kingdom to that of a retired widow, a transition deferred for Emma by the events of 1035 to 1042.[104] A dowager queen, at least one who was replaced by a new queen/wife, lost these responsibilities; so too did a repudiated wife. When Edith was sent from court in 1051 she was dispossessed of all she had, in lands, but also in gold, silver and all other things.[105] Edith's fall in 1051 involved the loss of her wifely status, of her control of royal treasure and of her management of the royal household. It was felt most keenly by the *palatini*, the courtiers or household members.

That part of the treasure located at Winchester was the particular concern of the queen, and contained the basis of the royal dignity for which she was also responsible.[106] Edith if not Emma was concerned with the visual presentation of royal dignity and majesty. According to the *Life* of Edward she arrayed Edward in garments of great splendour, adorned his throne with gold-embroidered coverings, provided him with a staff encrusted with gold and gems for his everyday use and directed the smiths to hang his saddle and horse-trappings with golden birds and beasts.[107] One of the goldsmiths who was attached to Edith held land which was later specifically connected to the forging of the king's crown and regalia.[108] The foreign nature of Edward's adornment struck the author of the *Life*. One foreign craftsman working for the court, and still with Edith in 1072, was Theoderic the German goldsmith. He has been associated with the cutting of Edward's great seal as well as the coin type

---

[102] *ASC*, MS C 1035, Harold took from her all the best *gærsuma* which she was keeping and which Cnut had had.

[103] For the latter detail see *Fl Wig*, s.a.1043; the *ASC*, MSS C and D stress the taking from her of lands, gold, silver and other treasures.

[104] For similar troubles in Germany between Otto I and his mother Mathilda and Adelaide and her son Otto II see Lintzel 1937, Schmid 1971; Uhlirz 1957 and Althoff 1993.

[105] *ASC*, MS E 1048 (recte 1051).

[106] *Fl Wig*, s.a. 1035 has Harold acquire the *regia dignitas* and then take the treasures from Emma, as if one required or entailed the other.

[107] *VitaEd*, 2nd ed, p 25, restored from Richard of Cirencester. Cirencester's Spanish carpets may be an anachronism – see Parsons 1995, p 18 on Eleanor of Castile's introduction of foreign luxury, including carpets on the floor.

[108] See Appendix 2, Ælfweard the Goldsmith and his father.

in which the king appears enthroned in majesty,[109] both modelled on German Imperial images, and a significant enhancement of the royal image.[110] Theoderic may have executed the design, even suggested the models, but no mere goldsmith could have controlled the decision to change the most public image of the king in this way.[111] Such a decision, with all its political implications, must have emanated from higher authority, from the king and his counsellors, but perhaps especially from the queen. If Edward's image was remade in line with that of a German emperor, who more likely to have masterminded the makeover than his wife, in whose company after 1066 we still find the craftsman responsible for its execution.

Edith's household had a recognizable identity, but was also part of the wider royal one. The two could come together, and frequently enough for this to leave its mark on the fixing of royal dues. In the Waltham charter the two households appeared side by side, as they were to do again in 1065.[112] By 1066, if not before, provision had been made at Eardisland, Herefordshire, for a queen's household which would be travelling with the king's and which required only token recognition rather than full-scale supplies.[113] Women's households later in the middle ages existed separately from those of their husbands in some situations, but were absorbed into them in others. The Welsh tractate, with its payments for a queen's steward and officials and concern for the relations between them and the king's servants, dealt with precisely such a situation. The royal household probably underwent special organization or reorganization c. 1060, of which the more formal development of a queen's household was possibly a part.[114] This may have created a new

[109] Dolley and Elmore Jones 1961, p 220ff; Keynes 1988, pp 216–17 for Regenbald's possible association.

[110] See Rezak, pp 61–2 and 65, dating it to 1057 and also suggesting Byzantine inspiration; no English coin bore the figure of a seated king again until Henry III, Dolley and Jones p 215; the only earlier English parallel was the seated emperors coinage issued by Alfred and Ceolwulf jointly, itself a very significant part of late ninth-century royal image building.

[111] The same argument must apply to Regenbald, who, although a more important man than Theoderic, was surely not in a position to mastermind such a change.

[112] See S 1042 a charter for Giso of Wells, a man associated with Edith. This is the only other charter witnessed by Harding, and he is here called *pincerna*, to distinguish him from the five *procuratores/* stallers, that is, royal household officials. The connections of Waltham and Wells with the queen may suggest that her household servants were either only present in such circumstances, or, more likely, only recognized in them.

[113] Above n 88. The token payments to her in the shire customs, like Norwich's *gærsuma* rendered to the queen, or the cash and gold given to her from Northamptonshire, or the royal manors of Bedfordshire, similarly acknowledge status as much as contributing to household provision. Some of these may also represent the fossils of older payments to king and queen.

[114] See above n 55.

household, or more likely formalized an existing one.[115] If this separated the queen and her household more sharply from that of the king, it was a step in that demarcation which many have seen as leading ultimately to the queen's side-tracking in the development of administrative kingship.[116] On balance, if this development had begun before 1066, it had not progressed far.

Hincmar's queen, controlling the revenues and personnel of the household, is also *Beowulf*'s Lady with the Mead Cup, or the gnomic poet's queen who was 'everywhere at all times before the band of comrades greeting first the protector of nobles with mead, present(ing) straightway the first goblets to the prince's hand . . . know(ing) wise counsel for them both together'.[117] These are not different women; each is a partial picture of the queen in the household. *Beowulf*'s is the Lady who smooths the relationships of the war band, agent of her husband as reinforcer of its coherence, order and hierarchy,[118] operating through the speech and gesture which are the medium of court action. Verbal politics are as open to women as to men; the formal speeches of *Beowulf* are made by queens as well as kings and courtiers.

Edith's queenly style was the essence of her portrait in the *Life* of Edward, and speech was at its core. She was a skilled linguist, a counsellor, 'grave and reserved, sparing and discriminating among those to whom she addressed her speech, speaking quietly . . . never with shouts of laughter or raised voice', yet capable of capturing any sight, however distressful or squalid, in fitting words.[119] It is a description of her as a courtier, like her brothers; of her ability to smooth or handle any situation by some appropriate utterance. It is also a description of her as a queen, the female counterpart of her husband's formal kingship.[120] The

[115] A queen's household had certainly existed in English kingdoms before the eleventh century, see Charles Edwards 1989, p 32. The translations which emanated from Alfred's circle suggest that a queen's household existed then and perhaps that it was responsible for the upbringing of at least female royal children. The Old English translation of Bede has Edwin's daughter Eanflæd baptized along with eleven members of the queen's household, *thære cwene hirede*, Old English Bede, Bk II, cap 9, p 124, cf the Latin *familia eius*. The *eius* could be construed as referring to that of the queen who has just given birth, but most logically it would denote Edwin's, as it does to modern translators. It is surely unlikely that a translator unfamiliar with a queen's household would make this mistake.

[116] On which see e.g. Facinger 1968, for France, and in general McNamara and Wemple 1974.

[117] Above, n 78.

[118] Enright 1988.

[119] *VitaEd*, 2nd ed, pp 22 and 23, cf Dudo, pp 185, 289 for skill in speech as an attribute of an ideal noble wife.

[120] The phrases 'cum quovis . . . interdum communicare', 'cum quovis non facile communicare' and 'eloquio cum quovis non facilis' are used respectively of Harold, Tostig and Edith, *VitaEd*, 1st ed, pp 30 and 32, 2nd ed, p 22. Not only does this show how far the author saw Edith as a parallel to her brother-courtiers as well as to her husband, it

formal, controlled, remote style of an Edward the Confessor is a regal rather than a gendered one. Edith could readily be presented as his parallel. As a way of managing court relationships this style may be especially accessible to women.[121] One reason is the distance it sets, a barrier against imputations of sexual impropriety. The formality which sets the queen apart as royal does not, however, annihilate her femininity, nor totally protect her from accusations of sexual misbehaviour. By stressing the moral tone of the court it can increase her vulnerability. Courts are courts, however formal. An almost Carolingian concern with a godly state underlay the formal style identified as dominant in the late Saxon court. That concern emphasized moral regeneration, and it is surely no accident that stories of queenly sexual misconduct date from this period, encompassing Edith if not Emma.[122] Edith cleared herself on her deathbed of the lingering charges of adultery.

If the style of Cnut's court was more military, we have been left with no picture of Emma's place within it. The skaldic verse produced at Cnut's court largely ignores Emma, but this may be a function of the genre. Military values are not, by definition, inaccessible or unattractive to women, especially to those raised among them. The *Encomium* written for Emma contains one of the most detailed surviving descriptions of a Viking fleet in full array; the author did not feel that his patroness's predilections required a tactful silence on such matters. If the military frieze at Winchester was produced in Cnut's reign, there is no need to distance Emma from its commissioning.[123] The warrior band had a role for the Lady with the Mead Cup, idealized in *Beowulf*. It is even possible that the poet had Emma in mind when *Beowulf's* Lady with the Mead Cup took her final shape.[124] The chivalric ethos of the court of knights had its Lady on a pedestal. A queen can operate in a more military court, and the skalds are far from giving us a complete picture of its workings. Lacking sources to illuminate how Emma did so, it is futile to speculate further.

The style of the court is an important issue for the queen's participation in political life, though it should not be divorced from the court's composition, and the questions that composition thrusts to the centre of royal and court politics. Concerns of a court where warrior-nobles

underlines the likelihood that Richard of Cirencester was quoting verbatim from the eleventh-century *Life* in at least some of his description of Edith.

[121] See Wright, P. 1987, on Elizabeth I's adoption of it. Wright argues that in this case it was a particularly feminine adaptation, and involved a largely female personnel. It was, however, also the style of Elizabeth's grandfather, Henry VII.

[122] Depending on which one or both lies behind the Richard of Devizes story.

[123] The 'military' Emma, and the Norman ethos from which she came are argued by Searle 1989.

[124] Damico, p 197 n 26 and pp 60 and 206 n 10 has argued for a late date for *Beowulf* and the association of Queen Wealhtheow, Wealhland (?Normandy) and Emma.

predominated at a time dominated by war and battle, as in the latter stages of Æthelred's reign, might exclude her, though the part her lands played in the defence of the kingdom (see below) urges caution about such a generalization in the eleventh century. But even in such a court, as long as the openness of succession forefronted family politics she had a legitimate role. As long as churchmen were there as active participants, ensuring that ecclesiastical questions were also political ones, the queen was given a voice. Above all it is the household nature of the personal rule of kings which ensures the participation in it of his queen and wife. As long as she remained involved in the supply and running of the household, and with access to the gifts it produced, she could operate there.[125] As long as she was attached to the king's body as his wife and mother it was difficult to exclude her from it.

The question of the queen's role in the household takes us to the heart of questions about her power, its nature and extent, epitomized in questions about the physical or administrative separation of her own household and its relationship to the king's. Are the queen's power and her household separate, different and possibly lesser as female; separate, parallel, and possibly equal as regal? Are they confounded with that of the king in a common regality, or was there a gendered distinction of functions even within a common household? Is the very association of her power with the household a sign that it is feminine?

There was some evidence for a separate existence of queen's and royal households, some for a hierarchical relationship between them, but also much to point to common functions and patterns and the confounding of the two. The queen's household is best seen as crystallizing out of the royal one; reabsorbed on occasions, separate in its concern for her lands and revenues, but never totally detached from it. If it is difficult to apportion an eleventh-century queen's functions and responsibilities between these two households, that is merely another sign of the queen's integral place in the kingdom. It was often necessary to speak of 'household and followers', because the line between them was not always easy to draw; the eleventh-century evidence makes it difficult to distinguish a Household, a Council and Administrative Servants, distinctions which have allowed historians to clarify later developments and to argue for a demotion of queens as these specialized forms developed. That clarification has, however, sometimes meant an obscuring of the flexibility which households, always rooted in personal service, long retained.[126] In the

---

[125] Facinger argues that the loss of control of treasure was a key loss for later French queens, and cf Parsons 1995, cap 2 for important discussion of the loss of English queens' control of e.g. their dower lands during their own lifetimes. As he makes clear, such a loss could result in readjustments to compensate her and make different provision for her patronage.

[126] cf warnings of Starkey 1977 and 1987, Morgan 1987 and especially Prestwich 1981.

king's presence all royal households were his household, and geographically remote followers became part of it when he was in their area. To be a late Saxon king's thegn was to have a seat and special responsibility in the king's hall, even though that seat might only be taken in a local hall during a local progress.[127] The households of other members of the royal family long functioned as part of the government of the kingdom because of their identification with that of the king, and of both with the extension of the royal presence itself.[128] The king's wife in particular, united with him in marriage, could not be divorced from it, however separate her own followers might be in many circumstances. To that extent her household and power through the household were inevitably gendered, as those of the king's wife, though it was a gendering which meant power and opportunity for the woman who occupied that position. It was also familial and regal. The households of male princes existed and functioned as a result of *their* membership of the royal family.

Within the royal households some of Emma's and Edith's household activity has a feminine air. Edith undertook the upbringing of royal children at court. Her husband's great-nephew if not nieces were there by the late 1050s. Queen Ælfthryth had been responsible for the upbringing of her grandsons in the 990s; the younger princes may have been with Emma rather than in the military court of their father Æthelred after 1007.[129] Although she had no children of her own, Edith had the responsibilities of queen for the children of the royal blood. There are tantalizing hints that she arranged marriages for members of her own and the king's household, as later queens would do: certainly those of her chamber lady Mathilda and of Wulfweard the White's daughter, possibly that of Ælfweard the Goldsmith.[130] The queen's responsibility, even the nature of her household itself, changed over her female lifecycle. A queen, whether wife or widow, who lived alongside adult sons or grandsons with a household of their own, or alongside a dowager, may have found her household and following curtailed.[131] A dowager, especially after her

[127] Geðyncðo cap 2, *EHD* Vol I no 51.

[128] Starkey 1987.

[129] The appearance of the younger children after 1008 is rare: in S 923 they appear along with Emma, though in S 920, 931 and 933 and 934 without her. S 931–3 date from 1013–15, when it is not clear whether Emma was in England, and which were, in any event extraordinary years when the unity of father and sons could well have been stressed.

[130] See Appendix II – Mathilda, Ælfweard, Wulfweard and his son-in-law; perhaps Eadric who had married his daughters and used some of her land at Dorking acted with her permission. Dowries of royal servants provided from ecclesiastical lands, as perhaps for Mathilda, must have been made with royal permission, and help produce the sorts of confusions of royal, ecclesiastical and royal servants' lands we see after 1066, see below pp 153–5, 138–9 and p 151 on Bromfield. See also Cooke 1990.

[131] During the 990s when the ætheling's household was formed, Ælfthryth lost lands, and thus presumably some of the followers attached to her through them. Their household was formed in some way under her aegis, perhaps even out of her own, which gave her an

son's marriage, unless she eclipsed his wife, lost her roles, and with them not only the lands, but also the servants necessary to them. However many servants Edith had had in 1066, they may be underrepresented in Domesday Book. By 1086 there had been a new queen with new servants: Mathilda's servants, like Humphrey or Aubrey, are more readily identifiable than Edith's.[132] Emma's fall in 1043 was a relegation to widowhood, and encompassed the fortunes of her servants. To this extent a queen, whether in her own household or in the king's, remained a woman, a prisoner of the inexorable shifts of the female lifecycle, even more so than a king whose own court changed in composition if not style over his reign.[133] A cycle of households, the upbringing of children, the arraying of the king, the arrangement of marriage, show a queen's role in the household as a development of the gendered ones of wife and mother.

Few if any of these activities, however, are apolitical, some of them are scarcely feminine and the queen's roles stretched beyond them to the undoubtedly royal. The public/private distinction can obscure a proper appreciation of what counts as politics and political action. Running the household and managing the court are politics. The queen's household functions extended to control of servants scattered through the kingdom and of treasure if not housecarls at court. She provided for the public face of kingship. She reared heirs to the throne and arranged marriages which might bind the disparate household together or ensure the survival of loyal servants' children. Such a woman was not a pot and bottle washer. These functions are royal. Most are extensions of a wife's household activities, but in a household far from private and extra-political. Some are concerned with the female members of the household, others with the male.[134] Some, especially those concerned with the military household, come close to the masculine.

additional source of patronage, but in the long run probably diminished her personal influence.
[132] See e.g. DB I, fo 63v for Aubrey the queen's chamberlain, probably Mathilda's; for Humphrey see e.g. fos 163r, 170r for Mathilda giving him lands, fo 30v for his collection of the queen's wool from Kingston, fo 36v for his holding in Surrey 'de feuo reginae' etc.
[133] For changes in composition see e.g. Keynes 1980 on Æthelred. Nelson 1993a on the dominance of Charlemagne's daughters at his court; this may be especially a description of the court of the later years, when age and perhaps accumulated tensions prompted a new style of court rule.
[134] Responsibility for the female members of the household was not purely a woman's concern. It is interesting for example that one of the later serjeanties associated with a group of women at court shows only a tenuous connection with the queen in 1066 and 1086. Catteshall in Godalming, DB I, fo 30v has a longstanding connection to the royal household and especially to its female members. It was held from the reign of Henry I if not before by service in the royal household. By the time of Henry II it was held by service of 'keeping the linen', or rather by being 'usher of the laundresses'. The service due from this land was described in an Inquisition post-mortem of the reign of Edward I as that of 'marshal of the

Shifts in the queen's household occurred and followed a feminine norm. Those shifts, however, occur in specific circumstances, allowing the normal to be contested, as Emma tried to do in 1043, and more successfully between 1035 and 1042. In such a contesting an eleventh-century queen demonstrated the reality of her power, and the means at her disposal to do so were a result of her royal position as a Lady. Men attached to her through her household, allies formed at court, the loyalty, knowledge, and tangible wealth which were a legacy of her household activity gave a royal widow, in the right circumstances, a potential for independent action of which the independence of other widows was but a pale reflection. Such attachments might be shaken, but did not necessarily die with the old king. A queen's circumstances were always those of the kingdom as well as the family. The households of such women underwent a cycle, but it was a political as much as a female one; a queen's not merely a wife's. Edith's household and following in 1066 were those of a childless woman whose mother-in-law was long dead. The household gathered around her in 1072 was a dowager one, but very special; a household of English survivors, preserved by their attachment to a queen who had also survived grouped round a last representative of an English past.[135]

Through the royal household and her own servants, the queen was placed in the centre of a kingdom whose unity and unification were not only symbolized but created there. This central position throws light on the choice of Emma to be Cnut's queen in 1017, on her own capacity to act after 1035, and on the basis of Edith's hopes for survival after 1066, as well as on the day-to-day power of both women in which the narrative sources had little interest. It was a queen's position, and a wife's. The same centrality, the same problematic combination of the regal and the feminine become even clearer when we turn to examine the queen's lands.

common women following the king's household,' *Inq post Mortem*, old ref 29 Edward I no 58, now Edward I, 98 (31). Is Painter 1957, p 101 correct in defining this office as 'marshall of the court prostitutes'? In 1066 and 1086 Godalming was royal land. Like many tenth- and eleventh-century royal service lands it passed from royal servant, to religious house, in this case Reading abbey, and then back into royal control and service use, see *VCH Surrey*, vol 3 p 32. Reading abbey was founded using largely former queen's estates – see my forthcoming 'Cherchez la femme . . .' – which provides the only possible connection with the queen. In view of Painter's definition and his own subsequent reputation it may be of interest to note that Ranulf Flambard held the church there in 1086, DB I, fo 30v.

[135] It was larger than any previous dowager household of which we have evidence in England, though since that evidence derives from the wills of Æthelflæd, widowed for 40 or more years, and probably faced by another dowager, Ælfthryth, and of Ælfgifu, a disgraced and restored queen, neither may be in any sense a typical dowager queen's household, if there is such a thing.

3 The Queen's Lands

On the day King Edward died his wife Edith was the richest woman in England; after the king, Archbishop Stigand and Earl Harold, the richest person.[136] The lands assigned to Edith in Domesday were worth between £1570 and c. £2000 per annum.[137] They were not scattered uniformly throughout England. Like Edward's a large proportion of her land was concentrated within Old Wessex, in the ancestral heartland of Devon, Somerset, Wiltshire, Berkshire and to a lesser extent Dorset and Hampshire: her lands here were worth between c. £790 and £870. Surprisingly, a larger proportion of her estate lay outside the old West Saxon shires: this part was worth between c. £900 and £1200 a year. Her estates included towns and their revenues, as well as churches and religious communities. The pattern of her estate was like the king's in its wide geographical spread and the variety of elements which went into its making, but unlike his in that proportionately more of it, judged by value, lay east of Wessex and north of the Thames.[138] In some areas Edith's lands fill gaps in the royal pattern, most notably in the North East Midlands; in others they reinforce the royal concentrations in Somerset or Wiltshire. This unique picture of the landholding of an early English queen is derived from Domesday Book. Its reliability is subject to all the caveats and problems which surround the interpretation of that record.[139] The pattern of Edith's lands, both before and after 1066, raises questions about Edith's identities as the widow of Edward or the daughter of Godwine, and for the disentangling of those of wife, widow and queen. These problems arise first in the interpretation of the Domesday evidence for her landholding.

Studying women's landholding in the Domesday record poses particular difficulties since there are circumstances in which Domesday Book is

---

[136] Clarke 1994, p 14 for comparative figures for the largest lay holdings. The richest monastic estate was that of Glastonbury, valued at £827 18s 8d, see Knowles 1966, p 702. The estate of the Archbishop of Canterbury, by far the richest English bishopric, was valued in 1066 at £868, Brooks 1984, pp 311–13; cf Smith 1994, p 219 for a figure of £1,145 and £1,040 for Winchester. Stigand's holding of Canterbury, Winchester and a personal fortune estimated at £755 meant that he outstripped everyone except Harold and the king.

[137] See Appendix I for the basis of these figures and some of the problems in arriving at them. The upper and lower limits are on the one hand lands definitely held by Edith, and on the other, these plus lands more debatably hers and those of her tenants. Meyer 1993, p 81 estimates Edith's estates at c. £1550 p.a.; Fleming 1991, p 65 n 51 at just over £400; Barlow 1970, p 153 n 1 at £900.

[138] Cf the map of Edward's lands in Hill 1981, p 101 – note, however, the problem of disentangling the estates of the earls and especially of Earl Harold and the royal lands in 1066. Hill mapped lands by hidage; I have used money values since the hidage of royal estates is not always given.

[139] See Appendix I for further discussion.

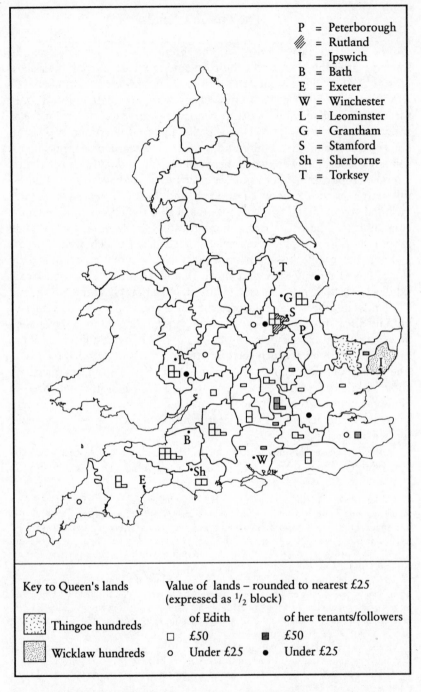

P = Peterborough
= Rutland
I = Ipswich
B = Bath
E = Exeter
W = Winchester
L = Leominster
G = Grantham
S = Stamford
Sh = Sherborne
T = Torksey

Key to Queen's lands

Thingoe hundreds

Wicklaw hundreds

Value of lands – rounded to nearest £25
(expressed as $^1/_2$ block)

	of Edith		of her tenants/followers
□	£50	■	£50
o	Under £25	•	Under £25

Figure 4 Queen's lands showing the value of Edith's lands in Domesday and major towns and places associated with her and Emma

likely to obscure women's landholding, others in which it may unduly highlight it.[140] Since Domesday constituted in some respects the recording of a claim and title for 1086 land holders,[141] the naming of 1066 predecessors was of considerable moment. Women, whose claims on land might be debatable or temporary, were not desirable predecessors and Domesday may underestimate women's landholding in 1066 as a result. Dower and other temporary family provisions of land are cases in point. Edith's dower might thus be underrecorded, a royal widow's lands listed silently as part of the royal estate; she held less land in Hampshire and Dorset than might be expected.[142] In general, however, there is no apparent reticence over listing Edith's lands. In Devon and Somerset Edith's lands are separated from the rest of the king's lands by a subheading 'Queen Edith held the lands written below'.[143] Edith's very survival after 1066 highlighted her estates, ensuring that any tendency to lose them in the royal lands was counteracted by an awareness of their separate identity and administration. Edith enjoyed considerable status after 1066, and 1086 landholders would have felt little inhibition in claiming her as a predecessor; in her case the converse may have applied, especially where surviving Englishmen wished to stress their legitimacy by pointing to the fact that she had given them land.[144] The scale of Edith's landholding in 1066 does not suggest that her gender led Domesday Book greatly to underestimate her landholding. Whatever identities ensured her survival also ensured the recording of her enormous wealth.

It was not as a daughter of Godwine or sister of Harold that Edith survived but as the wife and widow of Edward and as an English queen.[145] Harold's forfeit lands went to form the earldom of Hereford; Edith's strategic Leominster did not.[146] In Sussex some of her lands, like those of

---

[140] Stafford 1989b.

[141] Holt 1987.

[142] A very recent reorganization of the royal lands in Dorset may have occurred after Edith's death thus obscuring her landholding here by its reabsorption into the royal lands, see Stafford 1980.

[143] DB I, fos 100v and 87r. In Somerset Edith alone is separated in this way. Devon Domesday also separates the lands of other members of the Godwine family, and of Brictric, whose lands had passed to Queen Mathilda. This may be a separate listing of any group of lands which were considered royal lands, but had been temporarily in other hands in 1066, which has interesting implications for Brictric.

[144] Possible in the case of Wulfweard the White's son-in-law, for example.

[145] For the view of her as Godwine's daughter, see Cutler 1973. Fleming 1991, p 65, n 51 prefers not to allocate her to the Godwine family or Edward 'since her resources and loyalty are so difficult to determine'. Meyer 1993 sees the lands of Edith, as of most English queens of the tenth and eleventh centuries, as coming from her natal family. Hill 1981, p 100 hedges, listing Edith separately, but then noting that she was a member of the widespread Godwine family.

[146] The only one of her lands which went into the early settlements in Herefordshire was Frome, which had been held of her by her brother Tostig. For the chronology of the Norman settlement here see Lewis 1985.

her natal family, went into the construction of the defensive lordships of the south coast. These may have been lands inherited from her father, lost by Edith as Godwine's daughter. But King Edward's own lands had been incorporated into the reorganization of this shire after 1066.[147] Nothing indicates that her losses here were those of a Godwine family member rather than a queen. In Devon her lands were singled out within the royal estates, as were those of her mother and brothers. Here she seems to be treated as a Godwine family member. But in fact all are highlighted as holders of former royal land. The Godwine family had been the successful royal servants *par excellence*. Much of the land they held was royal land; like a queen's holding it was singled out in Domesday. The Domesday scribes need not have been making any particular link between Edith and her family. The perspectives of some of the chroniclers led them to see Edith primarily as Godwine's daughter. Her landholding suggests that identity was quickly absorbed into that of an English queen. Edith's lands did not, on the whole, share the fate of those of her natal family after 1066. Unlike them she remained in possession until her death.

How much she retained after 1066 is debatable. Most of the land listed as Edith's in 1066 was royal land by 1086. Since Domesday Book lists only 1066 and 1086 holders, it is possible that it had either passed straight to the king in the early years after the Conquest, or had passed through the hands of William's wife and queen, Mathilda, and back to the king after Mathilda's death in 1083, i.e. that Edith had retained little of it after 1066. But there is not much to indicate that this happened. Some of her lands were probably lost early; those in Sussex and Kent which passed to the count of Mortain and Odo of Bayeux, for example, probably belong to the reorganisation of the south coast relatively soon after 1066.[148] Others she certainly held after 1066, perhaps until her death in 1075.[149] Chesham, Shortley and Shipton in Buckinghamshire, for example, were given by Edith after 1066 to Ælfsige as dowry with Wulfweard the White's daughter.[150] She gave land at Wix in Essex to Walter the deacon after William's arrival.[151] Ixworth Thorpe and Baylham in Suffolk may not have changed hands until after Edith's death.[152] All these details have

---

[147] See e.g. Lewes which had passed to William of Warenne, DB I, fo 26r, Pevensey and Eastbourne which had passed to the count of Mortain, fo 20v, both men who had also succeeded to Edith's lands.

[148] Mason 1966 and Fleming 1991, pp 146–8.

[149] Cf Fleming 1991, chap 5 for some chronology of dispossession and esp p 179 for the suggestion that it was largely disloyal nobles who lost lands, 1066–c. 1073, with new and wider dispossessions beginning 1073–5.

[150] DB I, fo 153r.

[151] DB II, fo 87r.

[152] DB II, fo 421r and 448v; at Ixworth it is a question of whether the *eius* in the entry refers to Edith or to Sparrowhawk; at Baylham of whether we read *regina Edeva* as a mistake for Edith.

been recorded because of special circumstances: the survival of an English royal servant's son-in-law as a tenant-in-chief, or the peculiar detail of Little Domesday. The absence of references to Edith's landholding after 1066 elsewhere in Domesday Book is more in keeping with the laconic nature of the text. Some of her lands were used to consolidate the holdings of Norman lords in the Midlands and elsewhere, but this development may have been as late as the mid 1070s, after her death.[153] Except in the South East, Edith's lands do not seem to have been involved in the initial forfeitures and allocations of the first years after the Conquest, such as those in the Welsh Marches.

William's provision for his wife and queen, Mathilda, points to Edith's continued holding of an English queen's estate after 1066. Domesday Book gives no indication that Mathilda took over any or much of Edith's former land, either in the immediate aftermath of 1066, or even after Edith's own death in 1075. Provision for Mathilda should have been made soon after the Conquest, and certainly by the time she arrived to be crowned in the early summer of 1068. At this stage the bulk of Edith's lands were apparently unavailable for her endowment; Brictric's lands had to be used to form an estate for the new queen. Nor does it appear that Mathilda received Edith's lands after the latter's death in 1075. In 1086 Mathilda's lands in Devon were separately listed, in Gloucestershire they were separately farmed by her chamberlain Humphrey; in neither shire were Mathilda's lands confounded with those of Edith, in neither case are there any grounds for arguing that Edith's lands went to Mathilda. Rather than passing to Mathilda, Edith's lands often went back to the royal estates, or to sheriffs and other royal servants.[154] The balance of probability is that Edith kept the bulk of the lands listed as hers in 1066 for several years afterwards, and possibly until her death.

In this respect she was a far from typical late Saxon dowager queen or royal widow. Dower lands provided for a widow when the bulk of the lands she and her husband had held passed to her children and to her son's wife. Two tenth-century dowager queens left wills, Æthelflæd, widow of Edmund, and Ælfgifu, widow of Eadwig.[155] Both left land to the king, which perhaps involved the return of dower, and in Ælfgifu's case the bequests were substantial. Neither, however, approaches Edith's holdings in scale. How much Emma retained as dower land after 1043 is unclear. Emma, like Ælfthryth before her, is said to have received

---

[153] Fleming 1991, p 179.
[154] In Buckinghamshire, Bedfordshire, Middlesex and Hertfordshire e.g. to the sheriffs Geoffrey de Mandeville, Robert d'Oilly, Hugh of Beauchamp and Edward of Salisbury; in Leicestershire to the sheriff Hugh of Grandmesnil. For the identification of English sheriffs, Green 1990.
[155] *Wills* nos 14 and 8.

Rutland, and lands in Rockingham Forest, Northamptonshire, and Winchester, as her dower.[156] In Winchester it was Emma not Edith who was remembered as a landholder in the twelfth century,[157] though how large a stake a dowager like Emma retained in such a central royal town, or in the strategically important North East Midlands must be questionable.[158] Edward's dispossessions of her in 1043 were a reduction to dowager status, and may also have entailed dispute over the extent of her dower land.[159] If Edith retained a large proportion of her 1066 lands, no recorded tenth- or eleventh-century dowager, apart possibly from Emma between 1035 and 1043, was comparable.

Edith in 1066 was a peculiarly well-placed dowager. Her family situation meant that she faced no earlier dowager queen with whom she shared dower land. At the time of her marriage Æthelflæd faced a powerful and wealthy dowager, Eadgifu; by the time she made her will, two if not three queens had been provided for from the royal lands, and she herself may have remarried. Ælfgifu was the exiled wife of Eadwig; her will was made with the permission of his brother and supplanter, Edgar; her marriage had involved the dispossession of Eadgifu, subsequently reinstated, taking place whilst Æthelflæd was still alive. What each received or retained is not necessarily comparable to the situation of Edith, whose mother-in-law was dispossessed before her marriage, and, more importantly, was long dead by 1066. Dowager lands were not and could not be a fixed quantity. They were determined by family structures at the time of marriage and subsequently, and by the circumstances of widowhood. Edith in 1066 held a maximum dower estate, protected by William I's desire to appear as a legitimate king and guardian of widows. But the scale of her holding points beyond even the most generous dower provision; in 1066 if not in 1075 Edith held the lands of Edward's wife and of a late Saxon queen.[160]

The queen's estate in late Saxon England was not fixed, for the royal estates themselves fluctuated; it was, however, a queen's estate formed largely from the royal lands. The history of late Saxon queens' lands

---

[156] Gaimar, lines 4132ff; Gaimar, though a twelfth-century source, had access to information from Wherwell, Ælfthryth's foundation, which lends credibility to his statement. Note, however, that Rutland was the dower of twelfth-century queens.

[157] First Winchester Survey, c. 1110, Biddle 1976, p 46. This survey used an earlier one of Edward the Confessor's time. Barlow, ibid, pp 9–10 dates it c. 1047 or c. 1057 on the basis of moneyers; the fact that Emma is remembered as a landholder may be an argument in favour of 1047.

[158] S 1014, AD 1046, a grant in Rutland could indicate a reorganization following the transmission of Rutland to a new queen, Edith.

[159] Above p 115 n 104 for Ottonian parallels.

[160] Meyer 1993 argues that there was no such thing as a queen's demesne at this date and that queens' lands came largely from their natal families. It will be apparent that I do not agree with this interpretation.

cannot finally be written apart from that of the royal lands of which they form a part; lacking that, all conclusions must be provisional. The need of any family to provide on occasion for more than one wife and widow means that there must be fluctuation in the queen's estates; losses and grants on the one hand, and acquisitions through dowry and the extension of the kingdom on the other produce changes, and the lack of any earlier source as complete as Domesday makes comparisons over time fraught with difficulty. Allowing for all this Edith's estates appear to have been substantially made up of older royal lands, however acquired, not Godwine family lands, and there is considerable continuity, if not always with earlier queens, then with lands used to provide for royal family members.

Some lands occur in the hands of several queens over the course of the tenth and eleventh centuries: Wantage,[161] Lambourn,[162] Cholsey,[163] Damerham,[164] Amesbury,[165] Exeter,[166] Rutland,[167] Rockingham,[168] Win-

---

[161] Wantage was left to Ealhswith in Alfred's will, *SEHD* 11. It was Alfred's birth place, already perhaps associated with his mother, Asser cap 1, p 1. Eadred's will in the mid tenth century, *SEHD* 21, left the estate to his mother, Eadgifu. By 1066 it was in the hands of the king and the bishop of Lichfield, DB I, fo 57r.

[162] Lambourn was left to Ealhswith by Alfred, *SEHD* 11; Æthelflæd of Damerham left it in her will to the king, as if she had held it as dower, *Wills* 14. The land seems to be attached to Bedwyn, see Dumville 1992a, p 110 n 263. Bedwyn was a great royal estate, which apparently housed a female community in the early to mid tenth century, Meritt 1934; it was left to Edward the Elder in the will of Alfred – if Nelson 1991b is right about the links between Ealhswith and her son in Alfred's reign, the grant of land to her here may be no accident. By the second half of the tenth century Bedwyn was associated with the æthelings and their upkeep, S 937. In 1066 it was part of the organization of the 'farm of one night' manors on the royal estates; Lambourn was in royal hands, DB I, fo 57v, with two holdings, one in the hands of Wulfweard (?the White), fos 61v and 68v.

[163] Held by Æthelflæd of Damerham, *Wills* 14; Ælfthryth exchanged land here with her son King Æthelred in the 990s, S 887; by 1066 in royal hands with a detached portion still part of its *firma*, DB I, fos 56v, 57r and 62rv.

[164] Will of Alfred, *SEHD* 11. Damerham was the site of a religious community, possibly of women; Alfred associates it and its fate with Ælfflæd, who is probably to be identified with his niece of that name who married Edward the Elder after Alfred's death. King Edmund granted land here to his wife Æthelflæd, with reversion to Glastonbury, S 513, who held it in 1066. Yet King Eadred in his will, *SEHD* 21, left the *ham* at Damerham to Old Minster, Winchester, suggesting that the history of this huge royal estate may be more complicated than the simple transmission Ælfflæd – Edmund – Æthelflæd – Glastonbury, though see Keynes and Lapidge, *Alfred*, p 326 for the suggestion that Eadred left a different estate at Damerham to Old Minster.

[165] Alfred in his will left it to his son Æthelweard, *SEHD* 11; granted to Eadgifu his mother by Eadred in his will, *SEHD* 21, then in the hands of Ælfthryth, who apparently founded, or in some way endowed, a nunnery there, Finberg 1964, no 331, p 103 and *Liber Monasterii de Hyda*, p 207.

[166] *ASC*, MS C s.a. 1003; Edith held in Domesday.

[167] Gaimar, above n 156.

[168] Gaimar, above n 156.

chester.[169] The continuities survived 1066. Exeter, held by Emma's reeve in 1003, was in the hands of Edith in 1066 and later of Edith/Maud, wife of Henry I, who granted £25, two-thirds of the revenues of Exeter, to Holy Trinity priory, London.[170] Rutland had even longer associations with the queen. From a possible dower of Mercian queens in the early tenth century and before, its farm was still paid to Eleanor, wife of Henry II, appears to have been part of the dower of Berengaria, wife of Richard I, and was granted, along with Rockingham, to Isabella as dower by King John in 1204.[171] Edith did not hold all these lands, but these obvious continuities are the tip of a deeper iceberg which only appears when the queen's lands are fully integrated into those of the royal lands more generally and into the patterns of its family provision. Edith in 1066 held land which Alfred had left to his sons at the end of the ninth century.[172] Land which Æthelweard, Alfred's youngest son, was left in his father's will is later found in the hands of various queens long before much of it turns up in royal and queen's hands in 1066.[173] One of Æthelweard's lands was Meon, Hampshire. In the mid tenth century Meon was in Eadgifu's hands; she gave the charter for it to Edgar when he was an ætheling.[174] Edgar returned some of it to her, his paternal grandmother, some of it to Wynflæd, his maternal grandmother.[175] The history of the

---

[169] Many queens held land here: Ealhswith, who held the land on which Nunnaminster was founded, *An Ancient Manuscript*, ed Birch, p 96, where the site of the nunnery and its boundaries is described as 'þæs hagan gemære þe Ealhswith hæfd æt Wintancastre'; see also above p 90 n 108; Ælfthryth, Gaimar lines 4132ff; Emma, Gaimar op cit, S 925, Winchester Survey, c. 1110, Biddle 1976 p 37 no 23 and note and p 46.

[170] BL Lansdowne 114, fo 55, cited Round 1899, p 85.

[171] Ramsey 1908, p 170; below for more discussion of Rutland.

[172] eg. Lifton, Devon; Candover, Hants; Crewkerne and Chewton Mendip, Somerset.

[173] See e.g. Amesbury; Dean perhaps the *Æthelingadene* of S 904 – Keynes 1980, p 187, n 117 suggests the estate was so named because Ælfthryth raised the æthelings there. In 1066 lands which Æthelweard had held were held by Edith: Crewkerne, Som, fo 86v; Milborne, Som, fo 86v, though Keynes and Lapidge, *Alfred*, p 320 n 53 prefer to identify the land of Æthelweard with Silverton, Devon, DB I, fos 117r and 100r; Lifton, Devon fo 100v. For a possible move of land in the opposite direction, from queen to ætheling, see the will of the ætheling Athelstan, *Wills* 20, for *Eadburgebyrig* (Adderbury, Oxon), which he purchased from his father and left to the Old Minster, Winchester. Eadburh was the name of the early ninth-century Mercian queen who married Beorhtric of Wessex, and also of Ealhswith's mother, who was a member of the Mercian royal line. Is this an example of an estate which came to the West Saxon kings as dowry with a Mercian bride, but then later came into the hands of æthelings: see below on queens' dowries.

[174] See S 811 'tempore quo clitonis fungebar officio mea michi ad custodiendum commisit ava'.

[175] S 811, AD 959–963, Edgar to Eadgifu 'matrona ava mea' 65 hides; S 754 grants 8 hides at Meon to Wynflæd; see also S 417, Athelstan to Æthelweard minister, AD 932, 12 h W Meon, and S 619 Eadwig to Eadric minister, 50 hides – bounds are of East Meon – and cf S 283. There was a religious community here, see S 718, to St Andrew's church, Meon, 963, Ambersham in Steep (then in Hants), Sussex – *ad usus servorum dei inibi degentium*. There are, of course, several different estates carved out here and the detailed history of the estate requires careful reconstruction.

estate calls for careful elucidation, but Edgar certainly felt it was appropriate land with which to endow royal women. By 1066 most of this huge estate was in the hands of the bishop of Winchester, Emma's associate, Stigand. By 1086 it had come full circle back into the hands of King William himself.[176]

Tracing the fate of lands left by Queen Ælfgifu in the later tenth century emphasizes the continuity of the queen's lands within royal family lands. The bulk of estates left by Ælfgifu were in Buckinghamshire, where she made bequests or restorations to the king and to royally-connected churches. Edith's lands in Buckinghamshire were in the same area, some had been among Ælfgifu's bequests, and not merely those to the king. Few of Ælfgifu's ecclesiastical bequests had any long-term effect. Chesham, Whaddon, Marsworth, Wing and Linslade were all left to the king or to royal churches; all were in the hands of Edith, tenants of Edith or men closely connected with her by 1066. Chesham was in the hands of Edith's man Brictric in 1066; she used land here to provide for the son-in-law of her servant Wulfweard the White. Whaddon was held by a royal servant, Edward Cild,[177] who was one of a group of men, mostly Edith's, whose holdings clustered around her great estate at Milton Keynes. Haversham belonged to Countess Gytha by 1066, the widow of Edward's nephew. It too was close to Milton Keynes. Gytha's son and heir, Harold, was in Edith's own hand as a royal ward,[178] and his mother held the land once in the hands of a queen. The history of Ælfgifu's lands is a royal and royal family one. Berkhamstead, which Ælfgifu left to three people, two men and a woman, with reversion to Old Minster, was held in Domesday, not by the Old Minster, but by three people, a priest, a warden and a widow 'almsland (*de elemosina*) of King Edward and of all the kings who preceded him'.[179] One of those 'kings' who preceded him had been a royal widow who seems to have used the land, as Edward had, to provide for servants and perhaps their widows. Amongst those who succeeded her were not only the king himself, but his wife and her tenants and his nephew's widow.

The concentration of Ælfgifu's lands lay in Buckinghamshire, where Edith later held a substantial estate. These are not the ancestral, patrimonial lands of the West Saxon royal family, but those of the wives of English kings, whose estates along with their kingdom had grown during the tenth century. The geography of Edith's lands is that of an English queen's estate. It holds clues to the unification of tenth- and

[176] DB I, fo 38r and 40v; Stigand held 72 hides *ad opus* of the monks of Old Minster and 20+ *in episcopatu*.
[177] DB I, fo 147v where Edward is 'teignus regis Edwardi' though cf fo 146r where he is a man of Earl Harold.
[178] DB I, fo 148r and for Harold fo 129v.
[179] DB I, fo 142v.

eleven-century England, and to the role in it of marriage, family and the queen.

The English kingdom brought together the earlier kingdoms of Mercia, Northumbria and East Anglia and with them what remained of their royal lands. Edith's lands outside Wessex fossilize some of those remnants. The core of Edith's holdings in the North East Midlands was a survival of earlier dower provision for Mercian queens. Her most valuable cluster of lands lay in what would later become Rutland. Rutland exhibits many peculiar characteristics. It straddled the eleventh-century Nottinghamshire/Northamptonshire borders,[180] yet it retained some identity of its own, most notably in the name, *Roteland*, under which part of it is surveyed in 1086. It was later a shire in its own right.[181] The name recalls the older names of *regiones* or *provinciae*, the great estates even mini-kingdoms of the seventh and eighth centuries, anomalous in the eleventh-century world of shires.[182] The association of the area with the queen and her dower goes back long before 1066, to Mercian queens of the ninth century at least. In 894, after the death of Alfred's sister, the Mercian queen, in Rome and the marriage of his daughter to the new Mercian king, Alfred sent an embassy to the Vikings of York to negotiate about possession of an area to the west of Stamford, between the woods of Kesteven and the Welland,[183] roughly speaking Rutland, an area peculiar in its virtual absence of Scandinavian place-names.[184] Alfred was negotiating the control of old Mercian dower land, which had passed from his sister to his daughter. Rutland is the fossilized remains of Mercian dower provisions, its peculiar structure preserved in the hands of the queens of the enlarged West Saxon kingdom which became England.

Nor does it stand alone. In 1043–4 Edward the Confessor granted the eight and a half hundreds of Thingoe to Bury St Edmunds.[185] His mother Emma had held them previously, either as dower or some other form of

---

[180] See e.g. Stenton 1908, Phythian Adams 1977 and 1980, Hart 1992b and 1992e.

[181] The name *Roteland* in 1086 covers only part of the later shire, and excludes Witchley wapentake, then in Northamptonshire, which is clearly connected in various ways with the queen's holdings in Roteland itself, see e.g. the place-name links between the various 'Hwicce' place names in all three wapentakes of Martinsley, Alstoe and Witchley, and, incidentally, in Northamptonshire itself, Cox 1994, pp xlv, 55–6, 221–2, and cf the cross 'border' links suggested by Luffenham and Luffwick. Edith Weston in Martinsley wapentake is not west but east of its manorial caput in 1086, Hambleton, but it does lie to the west of Edith's manor of Ketton in Witchley, with which it shares common land, Phythian Adams 1977, pp 69–70.

[182] See Stenton 1908, p 136 n 30 noting the parallels with Holland, Framland, Aveland in Lincolnshire and Cleveland further north; see below for other possible units of this type associated with the queen.

[183] Æthelweard, *Chronicle*, pp 50–2.

[184] Phythian Adams 1980, p 9.

[185] *Writs* nos 9, 10, 18 and cf the confirmation *Writs* 24, AD 1065–6.

landed settlement on the queen;[186] she lost them in her fall and partial deprivation in 1043. The eight and a half hundreds comprised the whole of West Suffolk, bounded to north and south by the little Ouse and Stour, a 'miniature' shire and a unit likely to be considerably older than the gift of it to Emma.[187] Its almost unique status as a virtual shire court[188] parallels the late development of Rutland as a shire. Its survival after 1043 owes much to its ecclesiastical lordship; its survival up to 1043 may well be linked to its use as queen's land or dower.[189] Another group of hundreds in East Suffolk was also associated with the queen. The five and a half hundreds of Wicklaw or Sudbourne were allegedly bought from Edgar by bishop Æthelwold for his Ely foundation,[190] yet the queen played a key part in their acquisition. Sudbourne was given to Æthelwold by Edgar and Ælfthryth for his translation of the Rule of St Benedict into English;[191] Stoke was secured for Æthelwold by Ælfthryth.[192] These two places are associated with the possession of the Sudbourne hundreds.[193] Eadgifu, Ælfthryth's grandmother-in-law, had also had an interest in the area.[194] The Wicklaw hundreds may have been in Ælfthryth's hands if not Eadgifu's. The land and extensive commendation which Edith and her followers held in Suffolk were but a pale remnant of once extensive

[186] Hurnard 1949, p 320 and Cam 1963a, p 100 make them her dower; Harmer, *Writs*, p 145 her dowry (?recte dower); Davis 1909, pp 418–19 her morning-gift; Hart 1992e, p 198, dowry.

[187] Harmer, *Writs* p 437, Davis 1909, pp 418–19, Lobel 1935, p 7. Hurnard 1949, p 319–20 refers to the holding of a court here in the tenth century, though the case, *Memorials of St Edmund's Abbey*, p 31, may be early eleventh.

[188] Hurnard 1949, p 324 and Cam 1963b, p 190 and cf Douglas 1932, pp clv and 9 for the wide definition of jurisdiction here.

[189] It is worth noting in relation to this series of hundredal groups and franchises which are associated with the queen in Eastern England, that in twelfth-century Ely traditions the Island of Ely over which the abbey claimed franchisal rights was seen as the *dos*, dower of Æthelthryth, see *LE*, bk 1 cap 4, p 15 etc. There are obvious reasons to claim this given the importance of the saint to the monastery's claim and the dower claims of twelfth-century women. But it is possible that another motive was the association of so many other franchises and groupings of this type with queenly dower land.

[190] *LE*, Bk II cap 5, p 77.

[191] Ibid cap 37, p 111.

[192] Ibid cap 39, p 111–12, if, as seems likely, the *matrona Ælftreth* is the queen, a likelihood increased by the fact that Stoke was the southern settlement of Ipswich, see Hart 1992f, p 46, itself a borough in the queen's hands in 1066. Hart p 71 suggests that Ipswich may have been the 'wic' of the Wicklaw hundreds with its meeting place at Thingstead to the north of Ipswich; cf Lobel 1935, p 7 for the suggestion that Thingoe, the meeting place of the West Suffolk hundreds, was the tumulus just NW of Bury, a likelihood increased by the fact that a woman in flight from a court here took sanctuary with St Edmund, *Memorials of St Edmund I*, p 31.

[193] *LE*, Bk II cap 41, p 114.

[194] Eadgifu may have been the original refounder of Ely, to which she gave lands before Æthelwold's activities in this area see S 572; she and Wulfstan of Dalham actively acquired land in East Anglia which passed to Ely, *LE*, Bk II cap 43, 114–15. She gave land in

queenly holdings and jurisdiction here which had passed during the late tenth and eleventh centuries into the hands of royally-connected churches.

These Suffolk lands could have passed into the hands of Edward the Elder at the time of his conquests. But conquest was not the only mechanism by which the English kingdom was united. Women and marriage, as was clear in the case of Æthelflæd of Mercia, are unifiers and means of negotiating the problems of unification. Marriage settlements are a potential source of the extended estates of kings and queens. The dowries of tenth-century royal brides make for interesting speculation. Eadgifu, daughter of a Kentish ealdorman, may have brought useful dowry in Kent. Her son Eadred recognized her importance in the South East by trying to grant her all his booklands there, as Alfred had earlier left them to his son and heir Edward.[195] Ælfthryth, Emma's mother-in-law, was daughter of a great noble from the South West;[196] some of the extensive royal lands in Devon, if not in Dorset or even Somerset, could have come with her. A series of brides from north and east of the Thames demonstrate the importance of Mercia and Eastern England to West Saxon kings between the mid ninth and mid tenth centuries and the possibilities for land acquisitions here through marriage. From the marriage of Alfred to Ealhswith to the mid tenth-century unions between Eadwig and Ælfgifu,[197] Edgar and Æthelflæd,[198] perhaps Edmund and Ælfgifu[199] and later Æthelflæd,[200] all these women should have brought dowries north of the Thames.[201] After 1002 Edmund Ironside's Eadgyth

Essex to *matrona Ælftreth*, probably again Ælfthryth, which that woman went on to give to Æthelwold who then exchanged it with St Paul's, *LE*, Bk II cap 31, p 105. Was Wulfstan Eadgifu's reeve, a queen's servant in East Anglia? – see his activity also at Winchester.

[195] *SEHD* nos 21 and 11.

[196] Gaimar, line 3604ff.

[197] She had some links with the family of Athelstan Half King and her grandfather may have been ealdorman Æthelfrith, a Mercian ealdorman, see Hart 1992c; I would thus correct my identification of her as a sister of Æthelweard the Chronicler, Stafford 1981.

[198] William of Malmesbury, *DGRA*, Bk II cap 159, p 180 and cf *LE*, p 79 n 6.

[199] Ælfgifu cannot be identified with any certainty. Edgar's maternal grandmother was Wynflæd, S 744, who should thus be her mother, perhaps the Wynflæd of Wills no 3; both women's associations are with Wessex.

[200] Daughter of Ælfgar, ealdorman of Essex, *Wills* nos 2 and 14, but also a widow of a Mercian ealdorman, *LE*, Bk II cap 64, p 136. There is no reason to assume that her marriage to Edmund preceded her marriage to the ealdorman; in fact the remarriage of a royal widow in England at this date would be unusual. It seems likely that she retired to her estates, including the great royal manor of Damerham, with which estate the late eleventh-century D MS of the *ASC* associated her, after Edmund's death. At the time of her marriage to Edmund she may thus have been not merely a daughter of the ealdorman of Essex, but the widow of a Mercian one.

[201] The surviving wills of Ælfgifu and Æthelflæd are poor sources for such dowries; wills are difficult to interpret and rarely tell us of all the lands associated with any particular individual.

if not Cnut's Ælfgifu of Northampton could both have reinforced holdings in the North East Midlands.[202] A married woman was a link in the process of unification and the dowry she brought or dower she was given a way of smoothing its progress. Rutland held by Æthelflæd a sister of a West Saxon king who was also queen of Mercia could be an outpost of West Saxon control without undue offence to Mercian sensibilities. In 946 Æthelflæd of Damerham, daughter of an ealdorman of Essex, married King Edmund. This marriage may have been as important as Edward the Elder's conquests in the acquisition of land in Suffolk.[203] If the Suffolk hundreds and Ipswich formed part of former East Anglian royal land or even the dower of earlier East Anglian queens, a grant of them to an East Anglian woman by a West Saxon husband would have recognized local feeling.

The queen's lands were a crucial element of the defence and organization of the kingdom, by 1066 especially in the North Midlands and the Welsh Marches. In the North Midlands the queen's holdings were matched by those of the recently revitalized Peterborough abbey. The parallel concerns of queen and church brought them into co-operation and conflict which underscore the importance of the queen in the kingdom. In the Welsh Marches the queen's lands *were* church lands, held through the claims of royalty and family. They underline the significance of the woman who, as both queen and wife, could legitimate the acquisition and control of key ecclesiastical estates.

In the North East Midlands Edith's possessions stretched from Northamptonshire at Finedon with its various attached lands, in what would eventually be known as the eight hundreds of Oundle,[204] north through Rutland to a series of huge estates in Lincolnshire at Nettleham, Gayton, Horncastle and Grantham, including her urban holdings in Torksey and Stamford. Control of this area north, south and west of the Fens was essential to anyone who aspired to extend rule into England north of the Trent and Humber, or east into northern East Anglia. Important routes passed through it, particularly through the stretch of land between Leicester and Stamford, much of which Rutland straddles; the route north west to Nottingham and York, or the route north to Lincoln and

---

[202] Is the problematic split of Rutland in 1066 into Roteland and land lying in Northamptonshire attributable to the difficult situation between 1015 and 1017 when potentially three royal women, Emma, Eadgyth and Ælfgifu of Northampton, two of whom originated in this area, had to be provided for?

[203] *Wills* 14 for her land here. She too was interested in religious houses here, most notably Stoke, perhaps Stoke by Nayland though conceivably Stoke outside Ipswich, which would thus be associated with her and before her with her father; the foundation at Stoke has never been satisfactorily identified. Ælfgar was ealdorman of Essex, but the conquest of East Anglia from Essex could well have brought former East Anglian royal land into the hands of ealdormen here, see Dumville 1992a for the critical Danish/Wessex border here in the late ninth and early tenth century.

[204] Although not so named pre-1066, the grouping certainly existed, see Hart 1992b.

thence to York, whether via the Trent and its crossings or the Humber ferries.[205]

In the 960s Æthelwold, himself virtually a 'palace-bishop', associated with Queen Ælfthryth, holder of Rockingham Forest and Rutland, planned a monastery in this area. His original plan was not for Peterborough, where the abbey was eventually to be placed, but Oundle. According to Peterborough tradition, Queen Ælfthryth persuaded him to move it to *Medeshamstede*, the later Peterborough.[206] The histories of the queen and of Peterborough were entwined for the next hundred years. The first abbot, Ealdulf, was appointed from the royal household.[207] In 1006 Peterborough provided, briefly, a bishop of Winchester, a bishopric with a virtually household role in late Saxon England,[208] and closely connected to the queen. An abbot of Peterborough, Ælfsige, accompanied Emma and her young children into safety and exile in Normandy in 1013, taking advantage of the famine there to acquire a hoard of cut-price relics for Peterborough.[209] Emma apparently tried to secure a second abbacy at Ramsey for him in Cnut's reign.[210] Both Emma and Cnut made use of the Peterborough scriptorium and its renowned illuminator, Earnwig, in the production of those splendid manuscripts which they used to such good effect as gifts (see below). Between Edith and Peterborough these relations appeared to turn sour, in quarrels over lands, bequests and her servants' holdings.[211] The longstanding links of queen and abbey demand a careful scrutiny of these tensions (see below).

[205] It is possible that an earlier queen, Eadgifu, had been granted land at Howden and Drax at the far side of these Humber ferries, see S 681, AD 959, a grant to the *matrona Quen*, preserved at Peterborough. Peterson 1995, pp 223–4 has plausibly argued that the *matrona* in question was Eadgifu, and the *Quen* glosses *matrona* as 'Queen'. This would confirm the involvement of queens in this area from at least the late ninth century and the deliberate extension of queens' lands here for strategic reasons.

[206] Hugh Candidus, pp 28–9 and cf Hart 1992b, pp 161–3. Oundle, like Rutland, was an ancient *provincia* or *regio*. Judging from the amount of royal and queenly land within its eight hundreds it had once been royal land. Edith's holdings here have already been noted; Cnut had a royal residence here at Nassington and half of Willybrook hundred was still in royal hands immediately after 1066. Hart ibid, p 160ff suggests recent royal acquisitions, though remnants of an old royal estate are equally likely.

[207] Hugh Candidus, pp 29–30 makes him a *cancellarius* of King Edgar, though the precise allocation of office may be untrustworthy. Hugh makes no effort to hide the lay origins of Ealdulf, who had been a married man before his appointment. Is it only coincidence that this same man was raised to the bishopric of Worcester and after that to York precisely at the time of Ælfthryth's re-emergence in the 990s?

[208] Hugh Candidus, p 47. Cenwulf held the bishopric only very briefly in 1006. ASC, MSS C, D and E record his death in 1006; his successor, Æthelwold II, was in place by 1007.

[209] ASC, MS E 1013 and Hugh Candidus, p 48.

[210] The story in Hugh Candidus, p 50 of Ramsey saved from destruction by the king at Emma's entreaty and then offered to Ælfsige involves Fenland abbey rivalries, but an attempt by Emma to get a second abbacy for her friend is a possibility.

[211] See accounts in Hugh Candidus, pp 40 and 67 and S 1029.

Peterborough was in many ways the royal monastery of the Fenlands, a nursery of northern bishops and, in the eleventh century as earlier, the head of a monastic empire.[212] It and the queen's lands were the keys to the North. Peterborough's significance in the newly unified kingdom can be in little doubt; nor should that of the queen and her vast holding with which Peterborough's lands marched. At Peterborough the queen's partnership was with a reformed house increasingly anxious to establish its autonomy. In spite of the close association of the abbey and its foundation with her and the royal household, there were bound to be problems. At Leominster on the Welsh Marches Edith did not so much work with a religious house, as control one. Here reform worked, paradoxically, in her favour.

Leominster on the Marches of Wales was another of Edith's strategic estates. At a time when the cross-border attacks of the Welsh king were the most pressing royal problem, at Leominster and Hereford Edith and Bishop Walter, her former chaplain, controlled the routes north and south along the Marches and along the Wye valley deep into mid and south Wales. Leominster is one of that series of huge manors along the Marches of Wales which by 1066 were in the hands of people like Brictric son of Ælfgar, Edith's mother Gytha, Robert FitzWymarc and Edith herself.[213] The thread which joins them is not a Godwine connection, but a combination of royal service and royal family membership. This critical area had been placed by Edward the Confessor in the hands of members of his own family, including his queen. The nature of much of the property here highlights another element in the queen's resources, namely church and especially nunnery land.

Leominster was a nunnery before and after its takeover by Edith. The continuous history of a religious community can be traced from the seventh to the mid eleventh century.[214] Its huge *parochia* and estates, which can still largely be reconstructed in Domesday and in the *parochia* described in 1123, indicate an old-established and important house. Its collection of relics was that of a community rich in associations with early saints, linked to Wessex from the reign of Athelstan.[215] It ranked

[212] For the earlier history of Peterborough see Stenton 1933, Peterson 1995 and Stafford 1986.
[213] Maitland's 'gigantic manors', p 145 and cf Round, *VCH Herefords* vol I, Intro to DB Survey, pp 284–6; Deerhurst held by Edward's relative Odda and then by Westminster Abbey should be added to these, see on this Wormald 1993.
[214] See esp J. Hillaby 1987 and more briefly Kemp 1968; for the *parochia* at the time of the foundation of Reading abbey, to which Leominster was assigned, see *Reading Abbey Cartularies*, no 354. There is little to commend a view of a disappearance in the early tenth century as suggested by Fleming 1985, pp 248–9 nor a refoundation by a tenth-century Mercian ealdorman, as Meyer 1981, p 336 n 5. A community existed there, for instance in 958, when the boundaries of its lands were noted in an adjoining charter, S 677.
[215] Discussed in Hillaby and Bethell 1972.

high among the West Midlands houses to which a man like Wulfgeat of Donnington made bequests in his will.[216] The scandal of Swein's abduction of its abbess in 1046 has been taken as its deathknell.[217] But Domesday Book refers to an abbess and to provision for feeding the nuns in 1086; the *victus monialium* points to a division of revenues between queen and community, possibly like that between Wherwell and Ælfthryth before 1002.[218]

Edith's holding of Leominster cannot be precisely dated. She may have been given it as dower.[219] She may have acquired it after 1057, when her brother Harold took over the area. Her presence may be no earlier than the appointment of her chaplain, Walter, to Hereford in 1060. But 1046/7, after the abduction of the abbess, Swein's disgrace and Edward's appointment of his nephew Ralph as earl in West Mercia[220] is the likeliest date. A queen had general claims on nunneries, but anything more than overladyship required specific pretexts and circumstances, and allegations of the abbess's misconduct provided them.

Other West Midlands minsters came into lay control in Edward's reign, often in suspicious circumstances. Godwine allegedly brought about Berkeley's destruction by procuring the seduction of the nuns and then complaining to the king.[221] The story may be a garbling of the Leominster abbess's case,[222] and the anti-Godwine bias of later chroniclers is evident, but it may preserve some memory of a pretext for the taking of the community and its lands into Godwine's control. In 1051 Godwine gathered his troops against the king at Beverstone, one of the minster's dependencies.[223] Bromfield's fate is clearer. This minster lay to the north of Leominster between Ludlow and Shrewsbury. It had lost half its lands by 1086 to the son-in-law of Robert FitzWymarc, another of the king's relatives, just as Edith held half of Leominster's endowment. In this case Domesday is more explicit about how those revenues had come into Robert's hands. The Canon Spirites had held them until he was

---

[216] *Wills* 19.

[217] Thus still Hillaby pp 656–60 though with due appreciation of its strategic importance, cf statements in Henry I's foundation charter of Reading which speaks of Leominster's destruction owing to its sins, and the alienation of its lands into lay hands, *Reading Abbey Cartularies*, no 1 'peccatis exigentibus olim destructae sunt . . . quas manus laica diu possedit earumque terras et possessiones alienando distraxit'. I have discussed this in more detail in 'Cherchez la femme . . .' forthcoming.

[218] Lennard 1959, pp 400–1 and n 5, on its survival, cf DB I, fo 180rv; for Wherwell S 904.

[219] For similar gifts of nunneries to queens as dower and other gifts see Æthelflæd of Damerham returning Damerham, Reading and Cholsey, at least two of them with religious communities, in her will, *Wills* 14 and cf Edmund's gift of the nunnery site at Minster to his mother Eadgifu, S 489.

[220] For the dating of this see Barlow 1970, p 93.

[221] Walter Map, Dist V, cap 3, pp 209–10.

[222] Freeman, vol II note E, 2nd ed, p 545 thought it was a garbling of the Leominster story.

[223] Taylor 1894–5, p 80.

exiled, on unspecified grounds. Robert had then gained them. The king had been about to act against Robert at the Christmas court at which he died in 1065–6. The grounds for action were not Robert's holding of ecclesiastical land, but his use of it as dowry to endow his son-in-law, with the danger of more permanent loss. Bromfield had earlier reacted to the imminent arrival of Walter, the queen's chaplain, as bishop of Hereford by securing a writ guaranteeing the minster its rights.[224] A new bishop, perhaps especially a former queen's chaplain, at a time when the king and royal household were tightening control of the Marches, appeared as a threat. Beside Berkeley and Bromfield, the abbess of Leominster's abduction takes on a more sinister signficance. Was Swein acting to gain the nunnery and its land; was he set up in some intrafamily quarrel; were his actions used, even engineered, by Edith and the king as an excuse to take over Leominster?

At Leominster Edith controlled a still existing community, not a defunct one, one of a series in the West Midlands at Berkeley, Tewkesbury, Much Wenlock, Pershore and Deerhurst, many of which were in lay hands. The queen's holding of nunneries was not unusual. Tenth- and eleventh-century English queens often held land on which communities of men and women were established. The king's wife was provided for in this way, but the royal family as a whole were involved in the holding of religious communities and their lands. Damerham was held by Ælfflæd and Æthelflæd,[225] Reading by Æthelflæd, Minster in Kent by Eadgifu. There may still have been communities at Tisbury, which passed from Ælfgifu to Shaftesbury,[226] and already at Amesbury when first Eadgifu then Ælfthryth held it.[227] Some of these communities were of women, but not necessarily all. Princes too held land on which female as well as mixed communities existed. Alfred left the lordship of the community at Cheddar to his eldest son, Edward, and the lands claimed as belonging to the æthelings in the 990s included Bedwyn, which had a community of nuns linked to Winchester.[228] In the case of Cheddar, the community was to choose Edward as its lord. The nature of the relationships between the communities and these lay holders is not always clear and need not always have been the same. Queens may have been lay abbesses, and may have held all or only part of the lands and revenues attached to the communities. In 1002 Wherwell took the oppor-

---

[224] The writ dates to 1060/61, and was probably issued whilst Hereford was awaiting the arrival of its new bishop in early 1061; for the writ and its dating see Harmer 1959.
[225] Will of Alfred, SEHD 11; Æthelflæd, Wills 14.
[226] See S 1256 and 850 for its complex history.
[227] Ælfthryth allegedly founded a nunnery there, but it was an old monastic site, see Barker 1982, p 105, possibly in continuous existence.
[228] See S 937 for the æthelings' lands; Parkes 1983, passim and p 137 n 51 and Dumville 1992a, pp 79–81 discuss the entries made in a gospel book here relating to a female community in the tenth century.

tunity of Queen Ælfthryth's death to clarify its relationship to her.[229] It claimed that she had appropriated 60 hides at *Æthelingadene* for her own uses, which were now to be restored and allocated to the feeding and clothing of the nuns, and sought confirmation to the nunnery of the 70 hides at Wherwell whch Ælfthryth had possessed as long as she lived. Here the queen appears to have held all the nunnery's lands, though Wherwell may not be typical. Its anxiety to face a new queen armed with an unambiguous freedom may have led it to include all the lands on which Ælfthryth could possibly have had a call. Edith's half of Leominster's endowment was not unusual or excessive.

The queen's claim on nunneries, unlike those of other laypeople, had been blessed by none other than tenth-century reformers themselves.

> And he (King Edgar) wisely ordered his wife Ælfthryth to defend the houses of nuns like a fearless guardian, so that a man might help the men a woman the women without a breath of scandal.[230]

The *Regularis Concordia*, issued from a royally sponsored synod c. 970, incorporated the queen within the supervision of the English church, specifically in relation to nunneries. It gave queens, who already founded nunneries, patronized them, retired to them as widows, even held them as dower, general oversight and protection of them. Edith's acquisition of Leominster may have been dubious, but it was sanctioned. The Ælfgifu who had control of the monastery of Evesham earlier in the century[231] was presumably none other than Queen Emma herself.

If Peterborough and Rutland were the keys to the North, these churches mattered to anyone who aspired to rule in and control the West Midlands, or to organize their defence against incursions from the West. After 1066 Normans were as aware as their English predecessors of the strategic significance of these concentrations of church land; a Norman earl like William FitzOsbern would farm them as part of his continuation of the defences which Earl Harold had set up against the Welsh.[232] Norman high-handed, and foreign, handling of them drew down heavy criticism.[233] Mercian earls had been active here before, and left a sweeter memory: Earl Leofric of Mercia was remembered for his benefactions not only to Coventry, which he founded, but also to Worcester, Evesham, Chester, Wenlock and Leominster and in Lincolnshire to Stow.[234] Although West Saxon kings had had an interest in the area since Athelstan if not before, their rights or claims to control these houses were tenuous.

[229] S 904.
[230] *Regularis Concordia*, cap 3 p 2.
[231] R 81.
[232] Lewis 1985, esp 199–201.
[233] See in particular Green 1983, on Norman sheriffs and on Urse d'Abetot in particular.
[234] *Fl Wig* obituary of Leofric, s.a. 1057.

The queen's claims to protect nunneries were a bonus. Edith's interests in the west and north east of the Midlands parallel Leofric's. His patronage of houses along the western edges of his ealdormanry, and also on its north eastern flank at Stow was matched by her role in the North East Midlands in tandem with Peterborough, and in the west at Leominster. In the former she held family dower land, in the latter exploited the gender-specific potential of a queen's relationship with nunneries; in both her presence mirrors that of a Mercian earl ruling the Midlands in the king's name.

Edith and her predecessors held church lands as the wives and widows of lay patrons had done since the days of Bede; those holdings were often now deployed to key strategic effect in the defence and rule of the wider kingdom. In all this they were the wives of kings, and queens. 'Church', 'Kingdom', 'Family' were still not watertight categories; the 'public' and the 'private' still flowed together as often as they separated. The queen's lands place her across all these boundaries, questioning them in the process. The *Regularis Concordia* justified a queen's activities in relation to nunneries by invoking both gender and regality. As a woman and the king's wife it was especially appropriate that the queen be responsible for nunneries; but it was as a Queen that her lordship (*dominium*), along with that of the king, should be sought by abbots and abbesses.[235] If ambiguity dogged the queen's identity, in this case her different personalities reinforced each other.

Edith's holdings in the North East Midlands included *soke*, i.e., the profits of justice, in her lands in Lincolnshire. In the Thingoe hundreds Emma's officials administered a virtual shire court. The queen's control of these lands went beyond agrarian revenues. It extended to the growing towns which were such a feature of late Saxon England. Leominster was an urban as well as an ecclesiastical holding, and far from Edith's sole urban possession. She held about half the tenements in Stamford, the whole of Torksey and Grantham, in addition to Bath, Sherborne, a stake in Exeter (which her reeve Colwine administered for her) and in Ipswich (where the reeve Brun was in her commendation) as well as houses in Canterbury, Lewes, Worcester and a *burg* in Leicestershire. The association of English queens, or king's wives, with towns and fortified places was a longstanding one. Ealhswith had lands in Winchester on which she founded Nunnaminster; it may already have been a queen's dower borough.[236] Ælfthryth, Emma and Edith herself were all closely linked to it. Women and queens regularly held and defended fortified places in the early middle ages.[237] Viewing the fortification/palace/town as a royal

---

[235] *Regularis Concordia*, cap 10, p 7.
[236] Above n 169. For Ipswich as a dower borough see Martin 1985, p 159.
[237] Stafford 1983, pp 117–20.

residence this is a household activity. Seeing the palace/town/church as sometimes a royal mausoleum, as at Winchester, it is the royal woman's family duty to pray for its dead. Town revenues, with their long-term reliability, were an ideal dower arrangement.[238] The West Saxon kings, however, were responsible for the foundation and even creation of boroughs as fortified places and trading centres. Almost half of the dwellings in the Alfredian burh of Wallingford in 1066/86,[239] linked into the defences of Wessex, were attached to nearby Newnham Murren, which a mid tenth-century dowager queen, Ælfgifu, left to the ætheling in her will. The queen's urban holdings match the king's interest in town development; they are royal and queenly. Through them she, like him, participated in the kingdom's growing wealth. Through them she and her servants played yet another role in its defence and administration, of which the towns were a part.

Edith's lands were both the patrimonial lands of a ruling family, and the extended inheritance of a century and a half of kingdom building. They have their roots in the ninth-century Wessex of Alfred, in ninth-century Mercia if not East Anglia; in the patrimonies of earlier kingdoms, if not the dowries of in-marrying brides. Their geographical concentrations were in Old Wessex, and on the borders and flashpoints of tenth- and eleventh-century English royal power. They were affected by current family structures and developed through the politics of marriage, but those politics were also those of the wider kingdom. They are the lands of a wife and widow, their geography and scale charting the rise of the West Saxon family to power as the English kingdom was built. That dramatic rise transformed the kings of Wessex into kings of England, and their wives into its queens. They included ancestral West Saxon holdings, alongside the revenues of jurisdictions and towns which had grown, or been acquired and developed, as kings of Wessex became kings of all England. Edith's lands suggest how important the king's wife had been in that process. She was both an extension of the king and a part of other families. The horizontal spread of a family through its women can embody, express and satisfy loyalties and sentiments which the vertical patrilineal stem necessarily excludes. At the same time the binding of husband and wife, mother and son, made the queen an ideal agent of royal power, more fully a part of that power than any other. Close to the king, but separate from him, capable of accommodating local feeling and traditions, yet drawing them into unity with the king, the queen in her lands, as in her household and servants, had an important potential in the new kingdom of England. The queen was a central and eminently adaptable part of the process of rule, defence and unification.

---

[238] For such considerations in the choice of dower see Morelle 1988.
[239] *Wills* 8 and DB I, fo 56r.

4 Patronage

Edith and especially Emma were remembered as patrons, as givers of textiles, relics, manuscripts, offices, lands and less tangibly of influence and protection. Edith was also remembered as a despoiler, a taker of treasure, a rival claimant for land, a queen whose favour had to be purchased and her interests bought out. As givers or takers both women participated in politics where clientage and patronage were methods of operation. Their activity must be seen in the context of eleventh-century giving and notions of property. The actions of both queens were part of the normal exercise of power in eleventh-century England, a fact which many representations, whether adulatory or critical, too easily obscure or distort. The queen as pious patron or predatory despoiler was also the queen as politician.

The memory of Emma was of a generous patron. At Ely an inventory made in 1134 listed her gifts of precious textiles to the church. They included an altar frontal worked in gold and silver with an image of Christ in majesty, seven cloths with gold worked fringes (orfrey) and one of rich purple fabric, perhaps shot silk taffeta (*purpura*), adorned all round with orfrey work and precious stones, a *purpura* pall for each saint and each altar, and four woollen dorsals.[240] The twelfth-century Ely monks also recalled a blood red altar cloth with a gold border a foot wide, and the magnificent *purpura* one worked with orfrey and adorned in a chequer pattern with gold and gems which she made for them, as well as the gold and gem-worked silk cloths for each saint,[241] and, richest of all, the cloth she gave to cover the tomb of St Æthelthryth. The twelfth-century Abingdon Chronicler told of the gold and silver shrine she and Cnut had given to the church. It bore an inscription recording the two hundred and ten mancuses of gold and twenty-two pounds of silver which had gone into its construction.[242] At Winchester they remembered her striving with Bishop Ælfwine to adorn the church of St Swithun, a contest which she won.[243] Canterbury tradition recorded the cup of gold worth 13 marks, two altar cloths, two copes with gold tassels, and a golden ornamented text which Emma had given.[244]

Canterbury was not the only church to which Emma gave books. She sent an English psalter to her brother Robert, Archbishop of Rouen.[245] She and Cnut have been associated with a lively production of de luxe manuscripts in the third decade of the eleventh century, most of which

[240] *LE*, Bk 3 cap 50, p 288–94.
[241] *LE*, Bk 2 cap 79, p 149.
[242] *Chron Abing*, I p 433.
[243] *Annals of Winchester*, p 25.
[244] Gervase of Canterbury, *Gesta Regum*, p 56.
[245] Orderic Vitalis, Vol II, Bk 3, p 42.

were intended as gifts for English and foreign churches or individuals.[246] Gifts of manuscripts linked Emma and Cnut with such English churches as York, Canterbury, London, New Minster and Bury, and with cross-Channel recipients in Germany, Scandinavia and France. Peterborough, with its strong ties to queens in general and Emma in particular, was a major centre of this production. Wulfstan of Worcester remembered how a skilled scribe and painter of manuscripts who had taught him there as a boy gave Emma and Cnut a psalter, which eventually ended up in Germany.[247] Ervenius was the scribe who taught Wulfstan. He is the same Earnwig who followed Emma's close associate Ælfsige as abbot of Peterborough.

Emma was an acquirer of relics, and her acquisitions were almost invariably followed by their distribution. When the bishop of Benevento visited England in Cnut's reign, Emma bought from him the body of St Bartholomew, which he happened to have with him; she gave most of it to Christ Church Canterbury, though retaining the arm for herself.[248] Whilst staying in Rouen after the death of Æthelred she bought the body of St Ouen, which she again split on her return to England, this time keeping the head for herself and giving the body to Canterbury.[249] New Minster was thus particularly favoured by her gift of the head of St Valentinus.[250] A queen's gifts were much sought after, and sometimes the process of giving was shortcircuited. Emma kept the head of St Ouen; after her disgrace, her goldsmith purloined it from her reliquary and gave it to Malmesbury where his brother was a monk.[251]

Sherborne attracted her largesse in a more standard way. According to Goscelin writing c. 1100, she and Cnut came to visit St Wulfsige's shrine at Sherborne. There the king pointed out to her the poor state of the church; the poverty of the angelic citizen Wulfsige was an accusation of them, weighed down as they were by gold and jewelled ornament.[252] It was up to her to repair it. She gave twenty pounds' worth of silver for the repair of the roof. Sherborne is a rare instance of Emma as a patron of buildings. She may have contributed more than general support and intercession to the development of Bury and St Benet Holme.[253] But according to the surviving sources her most generous building patronage

[246] Heslop 1990.
[247] Coleman, Life of St Wulfstan, p 5.
[248] Eadmer, Historia Novorum, pp 107–10.
[249] William of Malmesbury, DGP, p 419.
[250] ASC, MS F s.a.1041, see Plummer's remarks, vol II p 223 that she had a fancy for saints' heads.
[251] William of Malmesbury, DGP, p 419.
[252] Goscelin, Life of St Wulfsige, p 81.
[253] Gransden 1992, pp 91–2 for a careful assessment of Emma and Cnut's role at Bury. Bury certainly should have been a queenly borough, having the same relationship to her hundreds in West Suffolk as Ipswich did to those in the east.

was far away in western France where the rebuilding of St Hilaire at Poitiers was in 'large part paid for by the queen of the English'.[254]

Edith as a patron is a pale reflection of her mother-in-law. She was certainly a builder, rebuilding Wilton in stone and providing it with a westwork, presumably to house relics.[255] Like Emma she gave textiles, and like Emma made gifts to at least one French church, a precious amice wondrously decorated with gold and precious stones to the abbot of St Riquier.[256] Some of Edith's patronage has certainly gone unsung. The ring which she gave to embellish an image, perhaps of Queen Bertha at Canterbury, is recorded only because the goldsmith in charge of it, Spearhavoc, lost it and found it again thanks to his prayers to St Letard.[257] Her misappropriations and greed, by contrast, were much harped upon. At twelfth-century Abingdon they recalled how she came after 1066 to Abingdon to take treasure.[258] She ordered the most precious things to be brought. Spurning the monks first offerings she called for objects yet more ornate. At the command of the imperious lady, they brought a chasuble with gold edging, a choir cope of the very best, and a white stole and text of the Gospels, adorned with gold and gems of the most admirable work. Peterborough monks remembered her taking the gold Gospel and 300 pounds' worth of ornaments which Archbishop Cynesige had left to Peterborough with his body.[259] Evesham told of her order that all the relics of the monasteries of England be gathered at Glastonbury so that she could take the best for herself. The shrines were opened by a goldsmith, so that she could satisfy her desire with their contents, until Evesham's St Odulph checked her cupidity by striking her blind.[260] It was as a taker and a would-be taker that Edith's memory lived on.

The contrast extends to the role of both women in appointments and in gifts made to them. Both had extensive patronage in office at their command; the running of their estates and local interests required officials, as did the royal households. Their patronage here passed almost entirely without mention, apart from the implied criticism when the Anglo-Saxon Chronicler singled out Emma's reeve and his role in the

[254] *Chronicle of St Maixent*, p 126, discussion in Oursel 1984, pp 175–84 and Camus 1982. Camus, pp 108–9 assesses the case for the queen in question being Emma.
[255] *VitaEd*, p 47 and cf Ridyard 1988, p 109 for suggestion of the westwork's use for relics.
[256] Hariulf, p 238.
[257] Goscelin, *Translation of St Augustine*, col 46. In the story a ring of Queen Edith's is lost, prayers are said to St Letard for its recovery, and images of Bertha and Letard are made in gratitude. But this account makes no sense of the making of an image of Bertha. It is more probable that Spearhavoc had been commissioned to do this, and that Edith's ring was part of the commission.
[258] *Chron Abing*, I p 485.
[259] Hugh Candidus, p 71.
[260] *Chronicon Abbatiae de Evesham*, pp 317–18.

betrayal of Exeter in 1003;[261] only Domesday Book and charters permit its fragmentary reconstruction. Payments made to both queens by laypeople must have been common; again only stray references to money paid to the Lady in a couple of wills attests to these.[262] Inevitably it is payments made to them by churchmen, and their role in ecclesiastical appointments which attracted comment; and again it is Edith whose finger has been detected in the simoniacal pie and on whose head the opprobrium has been heaped. Emma's voice was surely heard in the appointment of Earnwig to Peterborough if not of Stigand to Elmham; but Peterborough remembered only her intercession with a drunken Cnut to save Ramsey at Abbot Ælfsige's request and to give the abbey to him.[263] Emma's aid cannot always have been freely given,[264] and saving an abbey to give it to a friend is an action capable of less flattering interpretation. But it is of Edith's not Emma's rapacity that we hear. Payments from Ramsey, Peterborough, Evesham;[265] a role in the appointment of bishops Hermann of Sherborne and Giso of Wells[266] add to the portrait of her greed.

Edith's alleged hunger for church treasures is a reminder of the value of the textiles, manuscripts, relics and ornaments which queens gave. The spiritual value of a gospel book, a church ornament, a relic is imponderable, their sumptuous form was an attempt to give it fitting physical expression; the result was a gift of the greatest spiritual and secular worth. The manuscripts which Emma and Cnut gave were beautifully produced and illuminated, often in gold. Their bindings have all been lost, but would have been sumptuous, like the gold cover of the Echternach Codex which Empress Theophanu commissioned.[267] The great cross and images of Mary and John, which Emma and Cnut gave to New Minster rendered 500 pounds of silver and 30 marks of gold when destroyed by Henry of Blois in 1141. The abbot of St Riquier deposited Edith's amice in the abbey treasure, but later two churches were acquired in exchange for it. The gold recovered from an Old English cope incinerated at Canterbury in the late fourteenth century produced a cash value comparable to the contemporary cost of building a new cloister at Buxley abbey.[268] Eadmer at the end of the eleventh century could still be moved by the splendour of the vestment Æthelnoth had

---

[261] ASC, MSS C, D, E s.a.1003.

[262] In both cases Emma, *Wills* nos 27 and 29.

[263] Hugh Candidus, p 50.

[264] Coleman, *Life of Wulfstan*, p 5 tells the story of Earnwig producing manuscripts in return for preferment, but implied criticism is of Earnwig rather than Emma and Cnut.

[265] *Chron Ram*, pp 169–70; Hugh Candidus, p 67; S 1026.

[266] William of Malmesbury, *DGP*, p 183; *Ecclesiastical Documents*, p 17.

[267] See Westermann-Angerhausen, 1991 (1995) for Theophanu, and Heslop 1990, pp 179–81 on the likelihood that Emma's and Cnut's manuscripts had rich bindings.

[268] Dodwell 1982, p 181.

given to the bishop of Benevento.[269] Such objects were so precious that stories gathered around them, as well as their givers. When Nigel of Ely bought Ely from the king for his son Richard in the mid twelfth century, he took its treasures to finance the transaction, among them the cloth Emma gave to cover the shrine of St Æthelthryth. He sold the cloth to the bishop of Lincoln, who in turn offered it as a gift to the pope. The latter, recognizing that a cloth of such value must be from 'an old and famous church', ordered its return. The bishop tried to realize some of its value on his way back to England by having the gold prized off it. But the orfrey was such fine and solid work that it was like stone; it could not be moved.[270] Such were a queen's gifts. Their value is a necessary corrective to a story of patronage too often told simply as a record of land grants.

The patronage of both Emma and Edith did, however, include land. Emma gave Newington to Christ Church, acquiring it from Cnut after Ælfric forfeited it;[271] she bequeathed land at Kirby to Bury,[272] and together with Harthacnut gave land to Ramsey for the soul of Cnut.[273] Edith was remembered as a benefactor of Wells, granting Milverton and Mark to bishop Giso.[274] Emma almost certainly made gifts of land to the Old Minster, Winchester, where she and Cnut were buried: her son Edward confirmed her grant of the urban property of Godebegot in Winchester to the Old Minster,[275] and after 1066 the Old Minster claimed that she had left them land at Hayling Island in reversion, after the death of her servant Wulfweard the White.[276]

Such claims indicate the more contested and complicated nature of patronage in land as opposed to movable wealth. Sometimes there are straightforward allegations of dispossessions, as at Peterborough where Edith and Edward are claimed to have taken lands by force which they later restored.[277] More often it is a case of land grants, or land grants in which they were involved, apparently failing to take effect or being the subject of later dispute. Winchester tradition claimed a gift of nine 'ploughshare' manors from Emma after she cleared herself of charges of adultery: one was Wargrave, still held by Edith in 1066;[278] another was

[269] Eadmer, *Historia Novorum*, p 110.
[270] *LE*, Bk 3 cap 122, pp 371–3.
[271] R 96, cf S 1638; S 950 for a gift of land at her instigation.
[272] *Writs* 17.
[273] *Writs* 57.
[274] *Writs* 70 and 72.
[275] *Writs* 111.
[276] DB I, fo 43v, and also R 114.
[277] Hugh Candidus, p 40 on the restorations she and Edward made here, and compare p 67 and London, Society of Antiquaries, MS 60, the Liber Niger, fo lxv for them taking lands from Peterborough by force; cf S 1029 in which she is made to claim a bequest to Peterborough as her own.
[278] DB I, fo 57r.

Hayling Island, on which claims remained unresolved as late as the mid twelfth century.[279] Marston and Islip were the site of Edward the Confessor's birth, and Emma allegedly left them to her son to commemorate it. Westminster claimed that Edward completed the circle of his life by giving the place of his birth to the church of his burial. Yet Wrodis the chamberlain held Marston later and was apparently Westminster's benefactor.[280] Westminster also claimed that Edward gave land in Rutland, reserving only a life-holding for Edith; in the event this produced no more than Westminster's claim to the tithes of Rutland churches, which took over a century and a half to realize.[281] Of Edith's own gifts to Wells, Milverton may have passed at least in part and temporarily to Bishop Giso, but some or all of it remained in Edith's hands, and the whole was in King William's by 1086.[282] These patterns were not new; few of the bequests in the dowager queen Ælfgifu's will made in the 960s remained long in the hands of their beneficiaries, if they ever reached them. Many were, as already shown, back in Edith's hands by 1066.

The pictures of Emma and Edith are of women involved in patronage, particularly ecclesiastical patronage; of givers of highly prized gifts of textiles and precious metalwork, and of more contested grants of land. The pictures set up a contrast between a munificent Emma and a more predatory Edith. Some real contrast is likely. But a closer scrutiny of the nature and purposes of the portrayals, and of the gift-giving which they depict, not only serves to correct the balance, but reveals more of the active politics in which both women engaged and on which our sources are so often reticent.

Emma was certainly a generous giver. The English church in the reign of Cnut was recovering from the impact of the Viking invasions under Æthelred. It had a great need for patronage, to finance rebuilding which had been neglected, especially to replace church ornaments, books and vestments lost as a result of taxation to pay *heregeld*. If that patronage was provided on an unprecedented scale by Cnut, it was partly in response to an unprecedented need. It was also by way of restitution on the part of the Viking conqueror, perhaps even an attempt by him to erase his uncomfortably recent pagan origins.[283] Emma, Æthelred's widow, the English queen, the symbol of reconciliation, was inevitably at the side of Cnut the patron as of Cnut the king. Emma and Cnut, a foreign queen and a foreign conqueror, both with wider European connections, and Cnut with pressing European needs, had many stimuli to and opportunities for foreign patronage; more than Edward and Edith,

[279] R 114, DB I, fo 43v and *Writs* 111 and see Harmer's comments, pp 384–5.
[280] *Writs* 104, and Harmer's comments, p 522.
[281] See *Writs* 94, and Harvey 1977, pp 27, 47, 356–7, 404.
[282] DB I, fo 87 and 89v.
[283] Gem 1975 and Heslop 1990, p 178; Cnut was not a pagan at the time of his conquest.

so often associated with foreign hospitality and patronage by historians. Cnut's journey to Rome was a specific opportunity for largesse, and it may have been now that the author of the *Encomium* witnessed his generosity to St Omer.[284] Emma's ramifying French family were a constant occasion of giving. Cnut's patronage of Chartres may be connected to Emma's uncle Arfast, who was a monk there. The link between England and Aquitaine, recognized in the rebuilding of St Hilaire in Poitiers, is likely to have been through her family ties.[285] William of Aquitaine was her second cousin once removed.

Emma's opportunities for ecclesiastical patronage ensured the rosy glow which surrounded her memory in many later monastic chronicles. The predatory Edith raises more difficult issues. Personality contrasts, between a pious Emma and hard-faced ambitious Edith, are possible, but suspect without consideration of the problems of interpretation they raise.[286] The sources call for careful handling. Many of them are post 1066, and all are ecclesiastical; the late eleventh- and twelfth-century sources for Emma and Edith's patronage are mainly monastic.[287] In some cases this made them more misogynistic, and by the twelfth century more critical of wealth and power itself. They often enshrine unacknowledged stereotypes of female action, alternatively pious or greedy, and split the complex motivation and nature of patronage into rival black and white faces. Beyond such obvious source questions lie deeper ones surrounding longer-term church/lay relations in their English royal context, concerning the nature of patronage and the power exercised through giving and taking.

By the twelfth century, from which many of the records of their actions date, time and the replacement of the dynasty had placed a distance between the writers and these two women. Images of both were now constructed and deployed in the current interests of abbeys, not to flatter living women; a continued relationship with a patron was no longer primary. No writer, monastic or other, wished to offend a living patron, but that inhibition was now removed. The result was not always critical, but it was more susceptible to certain stereotyped pictures of lay ecclesiastical relations and of femininity. Disappropriations lent them-

---

[284] Heslop 1990, p 180 suggests that the pilgrimage provided the occasion.

[285] Rather than simply via Fulbert of Chartres, as suggested by Gem 1975, p 40. Fulbert was in contact with Cnut's court and was treasurer of St Hilaire, but Gem notes the chonological problems, which do not apply to Emma. Emma's own uncle Arfast, Gunnor's brother, was a monk of Chartres; documents place him there at least during the years 1029 × 1033, Bautier 1975, p 68.

[286] Heslop 1990, p 180 on Emma, political in her patronage during Cnut's lifetime, pious after his death; an analysis which would require a more accurate dating of Emma's patronage than is possible. And Barlow 1963, p 52 on Edith as 'an ambitious intriguer, hard on occasion and always tenacious, well able to look after herself.'

[287] Stafford 1993 for fuller discussion.

selves readily to the stereotypes of predatory laity and greedy women. Edith as the imperious lady ordering the disgorging of Abingdon's treasures is Woman decked out in the Church's wealth. The polarity the image enshrines was well established; Archbishop Wulfstan had warned that married priests adorned their wives rather than their altars.[288] She was the Laity commandeering the Church's property, exercising that secular control which the *Regularis Concordia* had defined as the direst threat to the survival of monastic observance itself.[289] And as Woman and Laity her power was delegitimized into imperiousness.

There are more flattering but equally partial representations. Thus the twelfth-century Ramsey chronicle tells how five marks of gold were given by the abbot to Queen Edith so that she would intercede with the king concerning a dispute between Ramsey and Ælfric son of Wihtgar.[290] As a result Ælfric was forced to give up his plea, and the king took judgement into his own hands and made it in favour of the abbey. What the chronicler had forgotten or deliberately ignored was the fact that Ælfric had been one of Emma's servants in East Anglia. Ælfric, like Emma, had apparently lost favour in the new regime and with the new queen. Edith's interest may have required special recognition in a case involving a former queen's servant. All such considerations are obscured behind an image of pious wifely intercession. Intercession is itself reduced in such interpretations. It is taken out of the exercise of power and placed at a safe moral distance, feminized as a womanly virtue. Hugh Candidus has Emma intercede with a drunken Cnut to save Ramsey at Ælfsige of Peterborough's request. Not only is the political context and significance of Emma's patronage lost in this image, so too is the reciprocity of which intercession is part. The gifts, service and loyalty which it commands are elided. The intercessor as powerful, essential to petitioner and petitioned alike, is masked. Any unease surrounding a queen's involvement in the powers of patronage is allayed. In such sources queens appear as domineering viragoes or saccharine patronesses. By taking queenly actions out of political context, these chroniclers have taken politics out of queenly action.

Little that Edith did was new, though much of it was presented in distinctly unsympathetic sources, or in different types of sources which provide a new perspective on well-established activities. Payments had long changed hands between kings, queens and churchmen. The judgemental detail of twelfth-century monastic chronicles makes them appear different from those laconically recorded as gifts and heriots (a form of death-duty, or inheritance payment) in tenth-century wills. Queen Eadgifu was shown in the tenth-century Lives of Dunstan and Æthelwold

---

[288] Wulfstan, *Institutes of Polity*, cap 12.
[289] *Regularis Concordia*, cap 10 p 7.
[290] *Chron Ram*, pp 169–70.

attempting to gain preferment for both men. The portrayal is a flattering one. Queens who advance saints are not corrupt dabblers in simony. And sanctity's clear lineaments hide any earlier blemishes in the form of gifts or payments by holy men to queens. Unhappily for many patrons, sanctity is as often a retrospective and interested judgement as an innate quality instantly recognizable to the discerning. The late Saxon church with which Edith had dealings provided few likely candidates for sanctity after 1066. Views of that church after the Norman Conquest did nothing to hide the warts, but rather focused a low and searching beam to highlight them and to cast a harsh light on the lay patrons with whom they were involved. Though not necessarily on all. Whilst 1066 did little to enhance Edith's reputation *vis-à-vis* churchmen, it helped silence any criticism of Emma. Stigand became a personification of corruption after 1070; but any role Emma his erstwhile patron had in his rise was unlikely to be stressed when that same patron was the one blood link between the Norman conquerors and their English conquest. Hagiography, demonization, the need for heroes and villains and the rewriting of the past by contemporary politics all contributed to the images of Edith and Emma as patrons.

Twelfth-century chroniclers drew on their house memories. Those had been shaped by 1066, and by the disputes over ecclesiastical land which it spawned. The Norman Conquest and its land disputes, and Domesday in particular, shed peculiar illumination on the mid and late eleventh century. Lay holders of land in 1066, like Edith, often appear predatory towards churches in the evidence presented to the Domesday commissioners. The seizure of control of West Midlands minsters by exile and forfeiture have already shown the relationships between the court and churches in an unsavoury light, much of it cast by the evidence of Domesday. Domesday Book provided opportunities for partial and partisan evidence, allowing churches to simplify the issues of ownership in black and white terms, and to make capital out of the discredited status of many members of the old regime. The sorry story of Bromfield and Robert FitzWymarc was no doubt told by Bromfield clerks to Bromfield's advantage. But Domesday evidence was not alone in making such accusations. Tenth-century founders and reformers had already expressed fears about the use of crimes of abbots and abbesses as an excuse for depriving the church of God.[291] Behind both lie the long-running tensions between lay and ecclesiastical claims on land, which recur throughout the early middle ages, and which were passing through an acute phase in the tenth and eleventh centuries. Behind accusations of deprivation may lie predatory laity and manipulated justice, but also contested conceptions of property. Powerful lay people were especially able to abuse their

---

[291] An Old English account of King Edgar's establishment of monasteries, *EHD I*, no 238.

position to deprive the church. It would be unwise to seek to whitewash them in the eleventh century or in the tenth. It is, however, necessary to understand them, to ask whether the ecclesiastical notions of claims and property by which the laity stand judged and convicted were theirs, and the only defensible ones. It is necessary to ask whether in a predatory Edith we are dealing with a new villain, a new face on old sins, or a redefinition of sin itself, and one which she herself might not have accepted.

The clerical perspective has a tendency to freeze one stage in the reciprocities of gift-giving. It is the nature of gifts to create and sustain a long-term relationship between donor and recipient.[292] They do so because they never lose their link with both sides or their connection to the reciprocal benefits they are designed to ensure. Neither giver nor receiver has them completely; they continue to symbolize the mutual benefits of the relationship. When those benefits cease to be mutual, when the situation of one side or other changes dramatically, when one or the other fails to perform, questions arise. Can the gift be retrieved, or redirected? Are there points at which it should be handed back? Gifts to churches are especially fraught. The laying up of treasure in heaven renders the tests of earthly reciprocity more difficult to apply. It could be argued that no gift to a church could ever be recovered or reused. But for donors all gifts were also deposits on earth; their repossession was arguably defensible when need was great. The donors of the Abingdon treasures which Edith demanded are not specified, perhaps through ignorance, perhaps deliberately.[293] There must be a suspicion that the donor was, if not Edith herself, then Edward or a previous king or queen; that her act was a family repossession. Edith may have been showing her greed, may have been acting indefensibly in her raiding of the Abingdon treasure. But it is at least worth speculating that she was reclaiming gifts in the particular circumstances after 1066 with more legitimacy in terms of contemporary eleventh-century notions than the Abingdon Chronicler allows.

Disputes over church land, reclamations and dispossessions involving church land, gifts to churches which then remain in royal family or royal servants' control, even whole communities and their lands in royal hands

---

[292] A vast literature, see e.g. White 1988, Rosenwein 1989, and for anthropological perspectives Mauss 1954 and Strathern 1988.

[293] References by name to donors of gifts may itself be strategic, designed to stress the relationship, or to further vilify those who took them away – see the careful listing of donors in Ely's twelfth-century lists of lost treasures, and in the specific story of the theft by Richard Fitz Nigel. The naming of donors in these cases not only shows the identity retained by the gift with its donor, but the particularly unjustifiable nature of the disappropriation by someone in no way connected with that owner, half admitting the residual claim by the donor and his or her heirs.

raise similar questions about property and the extent of agreement about its nature, permanence and exclusivity. Late tenth-century reformers condemned lay control of monasteries and their lands, a condemnation which would encompass Edith's control of Leominster. Their strictures were used at the time by communities seeking to escape queenly control; they provided, for example, a language within which Wherwell sought a redefinition of its links with queens in 1002.[294] The condemnation was, however, ambiguous, and the use of it often specific in time and place. The strictures applied to monasteries, and many communities were still of debatable monastic status. And they specifically excluded the king and queen. The *Regularis Concordia* blessed and encouraged a special relationship between queens and nunneries, a protection not easy to distinguish from control. Individual houses like Wherwell used these condemnations to redefine specific relationships; in Wherwell's case with a new queen in 1002. Such a redefinition did not extend to Wherwell's relations with all queens and family members; by 1051 the nunnery was in the hands of Ælfthryth's own granddaughter, Edward the Confessor's sister. And it certainly did not redraw relations between all queens and all churches. Holding or claiming a monastic community or part of its lands was an established part of the organization of the royal family and its lands and remained so. It was seen even by those who were becoming critical of lay control as protection not as abuse. And the freedoms sought from ties to patrons' families, especially the royal family, were limited and specific. Edith's holding of Leominster, for example, must be judged from such a murky mid eleventh-century perspective and not from that of the twelfth century when the divisions had become much sharper.

Edith's servants held land claimed by nunneries. This is part of a larger phenomenon. In 1066 many royal servants held land which had apparently been given to churches in the past, or which churches were claiming as theirs. It was in Wessex, where royal servants, royal land and royally connected churches were most thickly clustered, where close geographical proximity made the royal family the neighbour of saints, that the phenomenon is most common, though it is found elsewhere. Wulfweard the White held land claimed by Old Minster, Winchester[295], and Salisbury.[296] Harding held Cranmore claimed by Glastonbury,[297] whose lands were also in the hands of Hugolin, Edward the Confessor's chamberlain,[298] and Gotshelm the cook.[299] Former English royal servants were important benefactors of Shaftesbury after the Norman Conquest, often

---

[294] See pp 218–19.
[295] DB I, fo 43v.
[296] DB I, fo 66r.
[297] DB I, fo 98v.
[298] DB I, fo 66v.
[299] DB I, fo 77v.

restoring lands claimed in Domesday Book.[300] Claims by churches on lands in the hands of royal servants complicate any simple picture of Emma or Edith as donors of land, just as they caused problems between Edith and Peterborough.

These claims, restorations and disputes need to be seen against a history in which church land and royal servants were intertwined and entangled. In 1001 Æthelred made a grant of Bradford to Shaftesbury. The land was cheek by jowl with the holdings of royal servants: on one flank lay Leofwine's land, the huntsman of that name who received a grant there from Æthelred in 987,[301] on another the land of Ælfwine the hoarder/treasurer. The entanglement went far beyond geographical contiguity. When Edgar granted the huge estate at Taunton to Winchester, it was occupied by royal servants, who were to come to an accommodation with their new ecclesiastical lord.[302] In 997 Æthelred restored Downton and Ebbesborne to Old Minster, Winchester.[303] He referred specifically to the charters he and previous kings had granted for this land in return 'for the various services of their servants' (pro variis ministrorum meritis). A string of such charters made to these servants survive in the Old Minster cartulary.[304] In the cartularies of Wilton or Shaftesbury grants directly to the nunneries themselves are outweighed by grants to vassals, ministri, chamberlains and other royal servants: in 1066 the land was recorded as church land.[305] Various scenarios can be reconstructed on the basis of such evidence. Kings' servants gave land to churches, and churches leased land to them. Churches were undoubtedly dispossessed by kings and royal officials; all due allowance for pressure exerted by the powerful must be made. Conversely churches claimed back land which they had lost, or perhaps even never had. But when Winchester claimed to have been given Ebbesborne and Downton by Egbert and Eadred as well as Æthelred,[306] yet tenth-century kings continued to give land here to their servants, we must allow either for continual cycles of disappropriation and restitution, or blatant forgery, or (what is just as likely) changing

[300] Cooke 1990.

[301] S 867.

[302] *Writs* 108, Queen Ælfthryth's testimony concerning the grant of Taunton to Winchester is explicit on the point. After Taunton was granted, Edgar bade all his thegns/servants who held any land there to hold it in accordance with the bishop's wishes or give it up, and claimed that he had no land there now to give, and no longer dared be its head. The need to make such statements suggests how often a king might remain head of land given to churches, and how often those established on it might retain their primary allegiances to him.

[303] S 891.

[304] See e.g. S 522, 635, 640, 696, 861.

[305] E.g. S S 478, 666, 719, 789. Meyer 1981 noted the disproportions in these cartularies, and remarked how little of the land held by e.g. Nunnaminster in 1066 appeared to have been directly granted to the nunnery.

[306] S 275 and 540.

notions of ecclesiastical property and the rival tenacity of claims from lay patrons' kin.[307]

The *Regularis Concordia* re-emphasized the queen's claims to nunneries, unwittingly providing welcome legitimation in the very language of reform itself. It concentrated in the persons of king and queen the claims of all lay patrons, and of the wider royal family. It aspired to invoke what reformers saw as the benevolent meanings of protection and patronage, but it could not suppress their exploitative face, not least because that face did not necessarily appear to the laity as evil. The claims on old royal and family land to provide for the family's and kingdom's needs were as defensible to the laity as the goals of the separation and protection of church endowment were to reformers.

Clear divisions between church land and royal land may have existed more in the ideologies of late tenth-century reformers and their twelfth-century successors than in tenth- and eleventh-century lay minds. Tenth- and eleventh-century English churches held land surrounded by royal servants' holdings and land on which royal servants were established. Members of the royal family held churches and their lands. The arrangements clearly differed from church to church. Much must have depended on the size, strength and organization of the community, its former history, its geographical situation and relationship to the royal lands. The relations between individual kings and individual houses must have varied. Exploitation and abuse must have occurred. But we must be wary of accepting the language of tenth- and eleventh-century reform as an adequate description of contemporary notions of property, especially lay notions. Reform does not simply tackle abuses; it redefines accepted practice as abuse. Edgar's and Æthelred's gifts of Taunton, Downton and Ebbesborne belong to periods when reform was dominant at court. They accept that redefinition. But in the process they reveal an established practice of supporting royal servants on what was in some respects church land. It would be long before the injunctions of reform clearly separated once and for all the lands of churches and those of their royal patrons. All conclusions must be tentative, and a proper interpretation of this situation must await full study of the royal lands, royal servants and West Saxon churches. But it would be unwise to label every lay holder of ecclesiastical land as an exploiter, or to accept at face value every claim by a church after 1066.[308]

The reputation of Edith has been affected by the turmoil and dispute over landholding after 1066, by the issues concerning gift-giving it raised

---

[307] Cf on the latter Wormald 1993, pp 2–7.

[308] Cf Reynolds 1994. Much of our picture of the tenurial arrangements and complexities of the early middle ages comes from ecclesiastical documents and perspectives trying to cover, explain, allow for or clarify the relationship of ecclesiastical and lay claims on land.

and by the redefinitions of lay–ecclesisatical relations between the tenth and twelfth centuries.[309] Although unlikely to have been as pure as the driven snow, she should not be caricatured as a selfish predator. Edith's, and presumably Emma's, resources included claims on land which churches could assert was theirs. There may be differences between them depending on the relative strength of reforming ideas at various stages of the eleventh century. Emma was married in 1002 at the height of reforming influence. She may have received less nunnery and church lands in her dower than earlier queens, though the evidence either way is scanty; Edith's holding of Leominster or her servants disputing land with churches after 1066 are not necessarily signs that she was more hard-faced or rapacious than her mother-in-law. A declining tolerance of lay control of ecclesiastical resources by the mid eleventh century may in fact have left Edith less room for manoeuvre than earlier queens; her reputation ironically perhaps the result of less of the sort of action later defined as exploitation. 1066 saw many English laity branded as villains. A major revolution of landholding called on churches to explain the holding by laypeople of lands they claimed, and provided opportunities to maximize those claims against laity now badly placed to defend themselves. A similar revolution at any time over the previous two centuries and before would have left a similar wreckage of reputations in its wake. Throughout that period, as before, lay families had their own views about their relations with churches and about the lands which joined them. Edith's holding of Sherborne, the seat of a bishopric, smells of abuse; Edith's holding of Sherborne, a West Saxon royal family mausoleum, has the odour of wifely piety. The apparently contrasting pictures of Edith and Emma as patrons must be read with an eye to these problems of interpretation.

Whether vilifying or praising, the later pictures of Emma and Edith as givers or takers are at their most misleading when they take the politics out of their actions. Patronage was a way of self-presentation and image building. Archbishop Sigeric gave Glastonbury seven altar cloths worked with white lions; the church was hung with them on his anniversary.[310] Gifts were a constant reminder of the patron, in life as in death. The reminder was sometimes graphic. The book bindings from the manuscripts which Emma commissioned have been lost, but they may have pictured her; the surviving binding of a late tenth-century Echternach manuscript still shows its female donor, the Empress Theophanu. Both Emma and Edith patronized the cults and tombs of holy queens, part of the development of a concept of queenship itself. Ely is well served with

---

[309] The same is true of Ælfthryth, much affected by reform and her relations with nunneries. I hope to return to this topic at a future date.

[310] William of Malmesbury, *De Antiquitate Glastonie*, p 136. The church was hung with Sigeric's seven *pallia* 'in anniversario eius'. Scott translates as the *church*'s anniversary; Sigeric's is equally if not more likely.

twelfth-century inventories, and Emma may have been equally generous elsewhere. It may have attracted her as the burial place of her dead son, Alfred. But Ely, the cult centre of Æthelthryth, England's most famous saintly queen, would have had a special appeal to Emma. One of Edith's few recorded instances of giving was connected to the fashioning of a huge image of Queen Bertha at Canterbury.

The reciprocal links between patron and client were one of the most important ways power was built, sustained and exercised in the eleventh century. No queenly action in the North East Midlands could be apolitical or disinterested, just as no Peterborough judgement on it could be entirely impartial. Emma helping Abbot Ælfsige acquire Ramsey was not a simple act of piety but a queen advancing a close ally in an area where queens had a strong landed interest. Her patronage was active participation in the area and its rule. Edith securing office for her chaplain as bishop of Hereford was also securing her own and her husband's control of the Welsh Marches. A careful reading of patronage is necessary in order to show the queen making the links of clientage politics. The nature of eleventh-century sources meant that she was rarely seen deploying those links; those sources thereby denied insight into the political activity of queens, as they obscured that of kings. The danger in such a rereading is the importation of twentieth-century cynicism and *realpolitik* into judgements on the past. Eleventh-century pious donations were not a smokescreen to cover politics. Piety and politics were inseparable in such a thoroughly Christian environment. Ironically it is church sources themselves which can invite anachronistic reading with their one-dimensional view of patrons and their partial view of property. They hide the extent to which contemporary lay ideals combined pious and political motivation. They present as evil villains people whose motivation might be mixed, but was defensible on their own terms. Careful rereading of these sources restores something of the politically active Emma and Edith. It is eleventh-century powerful women who stand revealed, not plaster saints nor acquisitive Jezebels.

The queen's patronage was integral to her power, and raises once again the question of how far that power and the resources from which it derived was gendered. Twelfth-century chroniclers used gender stereotypes to describe both women; in some respects the patronage they record appears gendered. Emma was a great giver of textiles, and textiles had the strongest feminine gender connotations.[311] Among the renders which the royal lands made were wool to the queen from Cirencester and from other royal estates; Queen Mathilda gave Ste Trinité Caen 'a tithe of the queen's wool'.[312] The disputes which arose over Emma's and Edith's gifts of land suggest the inhibitions surrounding the disposal of

[311] See e.g. the distinction of maternal and paternal kin in the ninth century in Alfred's will, SEHD 11, 'spindle side and spear side'.
[312] *Actes de Ste Trinité*, no 12.

temporary female family endowments of dower. There is even a pattern of feminine patronage and protection of nuns and widows. Edith gave permission for a nun to leave land to Westminster.[313] The queen appears twice at the end of the tenth century giving testimony or acting as oath helper in cases involving widows,[314] and on another occasion was called in as a *forespreca*, a sort of advocate, in a joint will of husband and wife, which specifically concerned land held by a widow.[315] Two widows' wills were declared jointly to king and queen,[316] and one to the queen alone.[317] Some general protection of and claim over widows as well as a specific bequest may lie behind Edith's dispute with Peterborough over a London widow's will. And when after 1066 another London widow, Eadgifu, remarried Otto the Goldsmith, Edith's concern with widows and gold-smiths raises the possibility of her hand in the match.[318] The queen's link with widows may grow out of her responsibility for nunneries, since consecrated widows were a feature of the eleventh-century church.[319] Conversely a queen who was a recognized patron of widows may have appeared a suitable protector of nuns. Kings were especially responsible for widows. Hincmar had called for special access to court for them, for special mercy and pity which officials should show them.[320] The evidence is too scant for anything but tentative suggestions, but a formal English development in queenship of a specific aspect of the king's office is possible; and with it, as in the queen's responsibility for nunneries, a gendered split of royal power.

It was, however, the fact that Otto was a goldsmith as well as that Eadgifu was a widow which permits speculation about Edith's involvement. Edith employed the goldsmiths' arts to adorn her husband, a wifely duty; but the adornment was royal and its purpose the enhancement of his regality. A queen's patronage was far from being confined to textiles. Manuscripts and work in precious metals carry no feminine connotations. The queen's patronage is often difficult to differentiate from that of the king; Emma and Cnut are usually considered as joint patrons. She and Edith were concerned for the cult of holy queens, but that was part of a wider cult of royal sanctity in which kings and queens participated. The royal saints Edmund, Wigstan, Edith and Edward all received aid

---

[313] *Writs* 79, Datchworth and Watton left to Westminster by the nun Ælfwynn 'at(foren)' Edith the Lady.

[314] R 69 and *Writs* 108.

[315] *Wills* 11.

[316] *The Will of Æthelgifu* and that of Leofflæd, *LE*, Bk 2 cap 88, pp 157–8.

[317] *Wills* 29; this woman is closely connected with men who were queen's servants and with the royal land at Bramford. She was herself almost certainly one of the queen's female servants.

[318] On Eadgifu see *St Paul's*, Gibbs pp 136 n 1 and 280.

[319] Wulfstan, *Institutes of Polity*, cap 18.

[320] Hincmar, *De Ordine Palatii*, cap 25.

and encouragement from Cnut and/or Emma.[321] And if dispute surrounds the lands given by queens, hinting at doubts about how far women could give, dispute also surrounded the gifts of kings. The tenacity of royal family claims extended to both. Once again 'state' and 'family', 'public' and 'private' fail adequately to describe this world. Once again the identities of the queen are confused if not inseparable.

* * *

Household and court were unquestionably sources of a queen's power: as mistress of lands, resources and servants, dispenser of patronage and as participant in a politics which turned on the management of human relationships through the mechanisms of speech and favour. It is entirely appropriate that the clearest picture of a king and queen in a late Saxon household and of the court which surrounded them is in the *Life* of Edward the Confessor commissioned by his queen. The ideal it presents was not, however, the only one. As with 'Mother' and 'Wife', there were other idealizations of 'Lady'. Some, like all idealizations, stripped action of context and magnified certain aspects at the expense of other more problematic ones. Thus Hincmar's queen upholding the moral tone of the palace was the woman who had to deal with its male courtiers, only a hair's breadth away from suspicion and accusation, the slippery slope which led to burning ploughshares. When Emma was presented as a patron, the queen-in-the-household as giver, the New Minster artist paralleled her directly with Mary standing above her (see figure 5). But the heavenly parallel, like the black and white pictures of benefactors and despoilers, masked a more difficult sublunary world of gifts and reciprocities, and a less than clear demarcation between Family, Church and Kingdom within which gifts had to be made and resources controlled. Others acknowledged the legitimate power of the Lady of the household, but spoke also of the fears the exercize of power by women could evoke. *Beowulf*'s Lady with the Mead Cup and Grendel's mother delineate the acceptable and unacceptable faces of the queen-in-the-household. As a holder of treasure, a maker of gifts, counselling and speaking, she was the necessary cup-bearing lady. But when engaging in such activity for her own ends, she was monstrous, Grendel's mother fighting the hero alone in her hall beneath the mere. These idealizations inform both the positive and negative judgements on Emma and Edith. They must have hampered their own exercise of these roles. In their own presentations of themselves neither woman ever chose to wear the face of female ambition.

Emma and Edith were variously exposed to the opportunities the idealizations offered a queen. They lived in an eleventh-century English

---

[321] For a full discussion see Ridyard 1988 and Rollason 1989a.

Figure 5 King Cnut and Queen Emma (Ælfgifu) – from the *Liber Vitae of Hyde Abbey*. London, British Library, Stowe MS 944, folio 6. Reproduced by permission of the British Library

household which was administratively as well as ideally the centre of the kingdom. Its resources by 1066 were carefully organized, its dues maximized. It reached out through its servants and through payments to it into the kingdom as a whole, incurring costs, and criticism – of kings and thus potentially of queens. They lived not in one uniform royal household, but in different ones which changed from king to king and through their respective husband's lifetimes as well as their own; sometimes in a military ethos, more often against a background of formalized, ritual court behaviour. The queen stood near the centre of the household in eleventh-century England, and thus near the centre of administration, rule and politics. This world of the household was always one where women could act, did act, were expected to act – but where their action could cause unease. If Wife and Mother in relation to the king's body were difficult roles, Wife, Mother and Lady in relation to his household were equally fraught.

Effective participation in political action depends on what are defined as the political questions, aims and issues of the day, and its participants are those who are acknowledged as having an interest in these or who can impose themselves as being so interested. Effective participation rests on authority and on power. Power is the ability or chance to realize our own will, if necessary against the resistance of others. It is efficacy, that is, the ability to act effectively, perhaps though not necessarily through coercion, threat and force. It is the ability to have and follow a strategy, to be a social actor, to have long- and short-term aims and to be able to follow them. Power may be both competitive, i.e. involved in a situation where our own desires come up against those of others, but also relational, i.e. the power of one person over another may be the result of a permanent or semi-permanent relationship between them. It may be conceived economically; power is the ability to convert the labour of others into our own prestige or status. Power may be legitimate or illegitimate; there are ways of exercising it which are or are not acceptable. Fully legitimate power is close to authority. Power stresses the *ability* to act, authority the *right* to act. Authority is a short circuit around the system of power. It induces obedience without the need for force, payment or argument. A person with authority can command simply by the position he or she is in. Authority is 'socially sanctioned power'; power sanctioned by the gods, by age, by gender, by status, wealth or military prowess.

In eleventh-century England political questions, aims and issues included succession to the throne, relationships with British and European neighbours, ecclesiastical reform, more widely the realization of a Christian state and the continued unification of the kingdom – and most basically the continuation of royal rule. The means of action were the exercise of preferment and patronage, the exercise of justice (which could itself become a means of patronage), and the command of force. Emma and Edith were well placed to be effective participants in much of this. With their recognized place in household and family, through their wealth, their lands and followers and the patronage they could exercise both Emma and Edith had power. They had the power, and the authority, of Wife, in Emma's case of Mother, and of Lady. Power and especially authority can also reside in office. It remains to discover whether either woman went beyond some powerful combination of Wife, Mother and Lady to participate in the royal office itself, as Queen.

6

Queen and Queenship

In 973, some thirty years before Emma's arrival, her mother-in-law
Ælfthryth was crowned and anointed at Bath as part of the Imperial
second coronation of her husband Edgar. The order of service used on
that occasion was the traditional *ordo* for the consecration of an English
queen, prefaced by an explanatory and justificatory rubric:[1]

> The king's coronation ends. Which the queen's consecration follows. For
> her honour the oil of sacred unction is to be poured by the bishop on the
> crown of her head, as is shown on the following page, in church and in the
> presence of the great men she is blessed and consecrated to consortship of
> the royal bed with honour fitting to high royal status, and we also decree
> that she be adorned with a ring for the integrity of the faith and with a
> crown for the glory of eternity.[2]

The impressive occasion was chronicled by a near contemporary of
Emma's, the Ramsey monk Byrhtferth. After describing the rituals of
Edgar's consecration, but not Ælfthryth's,[3] Byrhtferth gave a rare early
description of the ensuing coronation feast. Whilst the king sat crowned
with the bishops, ealdormen and all the dignity of the English, the Queen
ate with the abbots and abbesses. She was clothed in fine linen with an
overgarment embroidered with many different precious stones and
pearls.[4]

[1] Nelson 1986 p 372 and n 55, and 373–4 argues convincingly that this rubric is to be
associated with Ælfthryth's consecration.

[2] Nelson, 1986 p 372. It is thus in the Sherborne and Sampson Pontificals, Claudius II, *The
Claudius Pontificals*, p 95 and with the omission of several phrases in BL Addit 57337 fo
63r, the Anderson Pontifical. In what appears to be the earliest form of the Second King's
ordo, that in the *Benedictional of Archbishop Robert*, the consecration of the Queen simply
follows that of the king: 'finit consecratio regis. Incipit consecratio reginae ab episcopo
dicenda', pp 147–8.

[3] Perhaps because the author was anxious to highlight Oswald's role.

[4] I have thus translated 'circumamicta varietate lapillorum et margaritarum'. It is possible
that the fine linen garment was clothed with such stones, but amicta would normally signify
some sort of overgarment.

Borne aloft above the other matrons, she whom royal dignity arrayed, since after the death of the great ealdorman to whom she had previously been married she was worthy to enter the royal bed, was an emblem of richness. . . . When these royal nuptials were completed, all went home, blessing the king and queen, desiring for them that peace and tranquility of which kings of old had been worthy.[5]

It was perhaps to celebrate the Imperial coronations of 973, even specifically that of Queen Ælfthryth, that the *Benedictional of Æthelwold* (see figure 7), that masterpiece of late Saxon illumination, was produced.[6] The manuscript is remarkable for its emphasis on royalty, and especially for its queenly image of Mary; no earlier representation of the coronation of Mary in a Western manuscript is known.[7] This Winchester book was produced for the use of Bishop Æthelwold, the man associated with the composition of the Preface to the *Regularis Concordia*, the Rule of Life for English monks and nuns produced c. 970, and with the account of King Edgar's establishment of monasteries attached to the translation of the *Regularis* which Æthelwold made at Edgar and Ælfthryth's behest.[8] Like the Preface to the *Regularis Concordia*, the account gave king and queen a shared, even equal role in relation to the reformed religious houses.

He (Edgar) established monks . . . in some places also he established nuns and entrusted them to his wife, Ælfthryth, that she might help them in every necessity. He was himself ever enquiring about the welfare of the monks, and he kindly exhorted her to take thought for the nuns in the same way, following his example.[9]

In 1002 Emma arrived in an England where the Queen had recently been exalted, particularly by church reformers. Queens may have been consecrated before 973; a ritual for the consecration of an English Queen dates back to the late ninth or early tenth century. But either it was rarely used, or, more probably, there was no context in which the rite could assume larger significance.[10] The unification of England and the growing power

---

[5] *Vita Oswaldi*, pp 436–8.

[6] Clayton, p 159 citing R. Deshmann's unpublished thesis.

[7] Clayton, p 162.

[8] *EHD I*, no 238 for the account, which follows the Rule in BL Cotton Faustus A x. *LE*, Bk II cap 37, p 111 for Edgar and Ælfthryth granting land at Sudbourne, Sk in return for the translation. The fact that Sudbourne was given seems to associate this especially with the queen and her patronage, since Sudbourne is the centre of the five and a half hundreds of Wicklaw, on which see above, 'The Queen's Lands'.

[9] *EHD I*, no 238, above p 140 for the quotation from the *Regularis Concordia*.

[10] The earliest English coronation *ordo* does not appear to have had a Queen's *ordo* attached to it. *The Lanalet Pontifical*, which contains the First Ordo, also has a Queen's *ordo* on fo 56, without a rubric/heading and in the original hand of the MS. This is not, however, associated in the MS with the coronation *ordo* for a king, which is found at fo 88. Lanalet's Queen's *ordo* was probably copied from that elsewhere associated with the

of its kings expressed in an ideology shaped by religious reformers provided that context. The queen's witness in charters, beginning in the 940s, signified her inclusion in the hierarchy of the new expanded kingdom. Ælfthryth, if not Eadgifu, heralded a new dawn in the history of English queens, of which Emma was the immediate heir.

A new dawn, but a clouded one. The rubric which prefaces the coronation *ordo* used for Ælfthryth states that aspects of that consecration, if not the entire event, required a royal decree. It points to opposition to her consecration in 973. There were many reasons why it might have caused concern; objections to the elevation of this Queen in particular, or to that of Queens in general.[11] If some wished to stress Ælfthryth as a Queen, others saw her status differently. For them a 'king's wife' or 'bedfellow' was an adequate description. The discussions which lie behind the 973 rubric emphasized both.[12] Even Æthelwold saw her sometimes as a Queen, sharing royal lordship, sometimes as a wife and woman; the Preface to the *Regularis Concordia* alternates between both. The notion of a Queen or Queenship as distinct from a king's wife was elusive and contestable in late tenth-century England. King's Wife, King's Mother, Lady were all clear, if overlapping identities. Queen was more blurred. Rather, as the use of the title *regina* showed, it sometimes appears as no more than a crown on the head of motherhood, a consecration of wifedom.[13] But when crowns and consecrations provoke debate in the royal councils, they are not to be dismissed as trifles. The search for late tenth- and eleventh-century English Queenship is a quest for the elusive; but it is a necessary one if the power of Emma and Edith is to be understood.

Second English *ordo*. For the date of the Second Ordo and the associated Queen's *ordo*, see Bouman 1957, rebutting Schramm 1968, but now Nelson 1986; and the latter for the suggestion that the *ordo* may have been used for Edward the Elder's wife, Ælfflæd. All the continental manuscripts of the earlier version of the Second English *ordo* are accompanied by this Queen's *ordo*. The variants of this earliest version of the Second Ordo seem to have crossed to the continent in the early to mid tenth century, see Turner, *The Claudius Pontificals*, p xxxiii and discussion by Nelson 1986 pp 367–9. A Queen's *ordo* for use in England must thus itself date from the early to mid tenth century. For the lack of queenly titles in England before Ælfthryth, see Stafford 1981, p 17 and nn 42 and 44, and above.

[11] It may well be that the controversy was due to a decision to consecrate a Queen after a long gap, since 900 or 918; or to the circumstances of 973 in general, when arguments about a second consecration for a king, let alone a consecration for a Queen already married to that king for over eight years and possibly herself already consecrated, must have arisen. The objection might have been to Ælfthryth herself, whose marriage to Edgar was a second marriage.

[12] In most respects the rubric is a gloss on the rite which is to follow; that rite includes no mention of marriage, consecration to the royal bed or similar. This suggests that the stress on marriage in the rubric comes from the arguments surrounding the decree.

[13] Cf Erkens 1993 on Carolingian queenly consecration strengthening marriage and queenship.

1 Queenship in Tenth- and Eleventh-Century England

The Queen's consecration was a status-changing rite: once consecrated she was no longer solely a woman or wife, but a Queen. At the beginning of the ceremonies she was led into the church and prostrated before the altar in prayer, before being raised by the bishops and then prayed over.[14] Prostration symbolizes an annihilation of the previous personality, a preparation for rebirth in a new one.[15] It opens the consecration rites of monks, kings, bishops and others whose status was being emphatically changed; the king's own prostration begins the English Second Ordo.[16] The King was to be a New Man, the Queen a New Woman. Next she was anointed with oil on the head.[17] Her anointing paralleled her with the king, and perhaps differentiated her from him. Like him she was anointed on the head, though possibly not, like him, with chrism.[18] The Queen's consecration was nonetheless truly a 'sacring'.[19] Anointing in these status-changing rituals 'focused attention . . . (on the) gulf separating the office from its incumbent'.[20] It signified a particularly rich outpouring of divine grace intended to provide help in the performance of that office: the prayer which accompanied it spoke of the 'abundant pouring out of the spirit of God's blessing' upon her, chosen and made worthy by divine sanctification. The anointing of the Queen indicated not merely that her status was changed, but that she had taken on a 'public' office or specialized role.

The rubric of 973 emphasizes that role was consortship of the royal bed, wifely fertility. But the symbolism and meanings of the rite itself carried other messages. The Queen was given a ring. A ring was part of marriage ceremonies. In the earliest known consecration of an English Queen, that of Judith in 856, it was a wedding ring. 'Receive this ring, a sign of faith and love and a bond of conjugal joining.'[21] Hincmar, who produced the order of service for this occasion, embedded the consecration of Judith as Queen in a marriage rite, complete with marital gifts.

[14] See the rubric to the earliest version of the Queen's ordo, Ward 1942, p 358. Later versions lack this rubric; all those attached to the second version of the Second Ordo have the rubric which stresses why the Queen is crowned and anointed.

[15] See esp Nelson 1975 (1986) at p 334.

[16] As in Claudius II, *The Claudius Pontificals*, p 89.

[17] Ward 1942, p 358 and the rubric at the beginning of the second version of the Second Ordo as in Claudius II, p 95.

[18] Nelson 1982 (1986), pp 383–4 arguing, against Schramm, that in the Second and First English ordines chrism was already used for the king's anointing. If it was not used for the Queen the distinction between king and Queen here is thus older than the Third Ordo, but J. Nelson, personal communication, raises the possibility that it was used for both.

[19] Lanoë 1993, p 51.

[20] Nelson 1977 (1986), p 296.

[21] *Coronatio Iudithae Karoli II Filiae.*

Figure 6 The so-called Quinity, from the prayer book of Ælfwine, abbot of the New Minster. London, British Library, Cotton Titus D xxvi and xxvii, folio 75 verso. Reproduced by permission of the British Library

But the Queen's rite as used in England in the tenth and eleventh centuries shows no sign of derivation from the marriage rite.[22] The prayer which accompanies the giving of the ring calls it a sign of the Holy Trinity, by which the Queen may shun all heretical depravities, bring barbarian peoples to the heavenly power of God and call them to the knowledge of truth.[23] The public role of the Queen, as in the *Regularis Concordia*, was defined as a Christian one. The New Minster miniature showing Mary as Queen of heaven and part of the Trinity (figure 6) is almost an illustration of this prayer; Mary like the Queen is the enemy of

[22] This does not mean, of course, that a queenly consecration and a marriage could not be associated together, rather that a Queen was not simply or primarily a consecrated wife.
[23] Claudius II, *The Claudius Pontificals*, p 95; cf Nelson 1997 (forthcoming) on the significance of the ring in the ninth-century Erdmann *ordo*.

heresy, treading Arius beneath her feet.[24] And in England c. 1000 AD the danger of heresy was being stressed, and the cleansing of the church demanded.[25] This was no simple ring of marital bonding; it joined the Queen to the Kingdom and to the King in his public duties. When the king received his ring it was 'a sign of holy faith, of the unity of the kingdom, of the increase of power, by which you may triumphantly repel your enemies, destroy heresies, unite those subject to you and be joined for ever to the catholic faith'. The union here is between king and church. The Queen was part of this. She too is concerned with heresies, with the bringing of people to true knowledge.[26]

Finally the Queen was crowned. 'Receive the crown of glory, the public honour of delight, so that you may shine out in your splendour and be crowned with eternal joy.'[27] The crowns of king and Queen signified health, prosperity, the good things of this life and the next: glory, delight, splendour for her; overbounding health, prosperous joy and the riches not only of grace but of all good things for him.[28] When Byrhtferth remembered the Queen magnificently arrayed, he was not relegating her to a feminine function of display. Both king and Queen were regal in their splendour, set apart, incarnating the prosperity and wealth of the kingdom. But the king's prayers added that the crown was for him the public honour of justice and strength, that he was crowned in compassion and mercy. The Queen was associated with him in actions against barbarous nations and enemies, but not in the justice which is the king's alone. There were symbols which she did not receive: the sword of warrior kingship and the rod of justice. Nor was there apparently any ritual for her enthronement. A throne was normally prepared for Edith on public occasions; her rejection of it in private was a sign of the special

---

[24] On this miniature see Kantorowicz 1947, Kidd 1981–2, and O'Reilly 1992, pp 174–9. None makes the link with the Queen's ordo which seems to be called for in the full interpretation of this image. The recent linking of Queen Constance with the Orleans heretics gave the issue pressing contemporary relevance, see Bautier 1975 (1991). The question of the Trinity as an image which can be used to incorporate a more feminine element into the godhead is a very interesting one – see its use in this way in the late middle ages and in the Sister Books of late medieval Germany – where the Trinity becomes a Quaternity.

[25] See e.g. Ælfric's Letter for Wulfstan, *Pastoral Letters*, ed Fehr, no IV.

[26] The prayer which follows for king and Queen underlines the parallels and differences in the meanings of the ring for both of them; see the king's prayer Ward, p 354 '*Deus cuius est omnis potestas et dignitas da famulo tuo* pro spiritu *suae dignitatis effectum*, in qua te remunerante permaneat. semperque timeat. *tibique iugiter placere contendat*' . . . and cf that in Claudius II p 96 for the queen '*Deus cuius est omnis potestas et dignitas da famulae tuae* signo tuae fidei prosperum, *suae dignitatis effectum*. in qua tibi semper firma maneat, *tibique iugiter placere contendat* . . .' The Queen's prayer adds that the ring is a sign of faith, something already stressed in the prayer for the tradition of the ring in the king's *ordo*.

[27] Claudius II, *The Claudius Pontificals*, p 96.

[28] Ward 1942, p 355.

humility appropriate to a queen.[29] The queen's throne signified her status. But it did not symbolize her place in the rule of the kingdom as the king's did. The Queen's *ordo* ended with a prayer which is adapted from that said after the king received the sceptre. Both prayers begin alike "Lord fount of all good things and giver of all increase, grant to your servant to rule well in the dignity which s/he has received, and strengthen the glory shown by you to her/him . . .' Both had received some sort of office; both were to rule. The king's prayer went on to call for his honour and blessing among the kings of the earth, the stability of his rule, his justice, joy and happiness, but also for his fecundity in offspring. The Queen's omitted the justice and rule, but also all reference to her fertility. If the *ordo* enshrines the common ecclesiastical vocabulary of tenth- and eleventh-century English Queenship,[30] its messages were mixed. The Queen was a New Woman, and more than a consecrated wife and mother; wifely fertility was conspicuous by its absence from the lexicon, and presented with an opportunity to stress it, the ritual maintained silence. She was anointed as regal, paralleling the King in some but not all of his functions.

The late tenth- and early eleventh-century consecrated English Queen on earth was given role models in heaven. Cults of holy queens and particularly that of Mary Queen of Heaven grew up and flourished. The most famous group of saintly queens in early England were those who formed part of the so-called 'Kentish Royal Legend', which gained a new popularity in this period.[31] Its subjects were not recent rulers, but the kings and queens, princes and princesses of the age of conversion, women being prominent among them. These holy men and women had come to be grouped in a genealogy of royal sanctity long before the eleventh century, with sanctity, royalty and blood reinforcing each other.[32] In its origins such an approach may have been a Christian alternative to pagan genealogy,[33] and its beginnings lie in Kent, East Anglia and Mercia long before this time. Although the grouping contained no West Saxon saints, it remained popular at a time when the West Saxon kings had come to dominate England.[34] The promotion of these cults was in the interests of the religious houses which held the relics, but they were not the chief

---

[29] *VitaEd*, p 42.

[30] Nelson 1982 (1986), p 383 on such a vocabulary as 'general, uncontentious and normative'; and Reuter 1993, p 209 for a vocabulary 'transcending time and place. (producing rites) resembling each other much more than did the polities in which they were used'.

[31] On which see esp Rollason 1982, but also Ridyard 1988 and Rollason 1989a.

[32] For an overview of recent views, including his own, on royal sanctity see Klaniczay 1990, pp 79–94 though without reference to this English royal legend.

[33] Rollason 1982, p 41.

[34] Though if Scharer, forthcoming is right about the Kentish origins of Ecgberht, it may have had a special meaning for his descendants.

architects of its late Saxon popularity.[35] The cults could express regional resistance to West Saxon rule, but they were also adopted in Wessex itself. The key to the legend's popularity now lies in its royal nature and political utility. In its tenth- and early eleventh-century forms the legend was still primarily royal. As an accumulation of royal sanctity it had potential for all kings – and queens. In the tenth and eleventh centuries it had a particular relevance as a union of English sanctity to reinforce a new political unity.[36] The legend was strong on female holiness; its major saints, judging from surviving lives, were women, Mildrith, Domna (Lady) Eafa, Werburga and Seaxburh, several of them being queens. The gender balance of this amalgamation of royal sanctity had obvious relevance for queens of the unified kingdom.

The picture of queens given in the *Lives* is a flattering one.[37] Far from emphasizing otherwordly self-abnegation, royal and noble attributes were accepted and sanctified. Domna Eafa is a model for noble female sanctity, lacking the vices of the nobility but strong on the potential for virtue which wealth and status created. Thus she was 'not filled with arrogance, nor with worldly pride, nor with malice, nor with insulting words; she was not quarrelsome or contentious. She was not treacherous to any of those who trusted her. She was the benefactor of widows and orphans and the comforter of the wretched and afflicted, and in all respects humble and gentle.'[38] She was, in other words, the ideal *domina*, judged by the nature of her relationships with subordinates. She would be a patroness and have trusting followers. Operating in the day-to-day context of a great household, those relationships would turn on orders and the manner in which they are given, on speech and its ordered control. Domna Eafa did not divest herself of her wealth in an orgy of self-denial. Like the king, she was a benefactor of the poor, of widows and orphans. 'She was humble and gentle' with the humility and gentility, not of the self-effacing but of the great lady, of the queen, especially of the queen as the mistress of the household. Seaxburh is even more Queenly in her sanctity.[39] She held the kingdom for her son Hlothhere for thirty years,

---

[35] Where enough evidence has survived to see their development in the eleventh century, as in the Mildrith case, there is a shift towards a more institutional appropriation of the stories as the century went on, see Rollason 1982, pp 67–8.

[36] Rollason 1982, cap 4 and 1989a, cap 6 and compare the interest in other royal saints, both West Saxon and Northumbrian at this date.

[37] The contrast with the life of Æthelthryth, produced by Ælfric, which lays no emphasis on her status as queen or even on the fact that she was once a queen is an interesting one; *Lives of Saints*, I, pp 432–61.

[38] Swanton, 'A fragmentary life', 1976, pp 22–3 and 26. The negative definition of virtue, as an absence of the typical vices of the class, should be compared with Fulbert of Chartres' famous letter to William of Aquitaine on the subject of fidelity, also early eleventh century, see Fulbert of Chartres, *Letters*, no 51.

[39] See the fragments of her life, Swanton 1976, pp 23–4 and 27.

bought territory from him to endow the minster she was building at Sheppey, and obtained a blessing from Rome to protect its estates. In the midst of such activities the author records her angelic vision of the future Viking attacks. The vision is a royal one, and it is associated not with fasts and mortifications, but with the exercise of royal duties by a woman who was acting as a regent, and the beneficial expenditure of royal wealth.[40] It is a suitably Queenly vision at a time when a Queen's consecration emphasized that she shared with the king the duty of protecting the people.

These lives held up a Christian mirror to queens, and the reflection it gave back was didactic but unashamedly royal. The picture persisted in English royal hagiography throughout the eleventh century,[41] though challenged by rival definitions of sanctity. The mid eleventh-century anonymous *Life* of Mildrith, for example, sanctified a queen's marriage. Mildrith's mother, Domna Eafa, was 'given to Merewalh son of Penda king of the Mercians in legitimate marriage (*in consortium legitimae copulationis*), and with the consent of God's mercy they had delightful children'. When Goscelin reworked the *Life* for Canterbury he omitted all reference to the marriage, preferring to stress Domna Eafa's three precious gems, three holy brides of Christ.[42] The nature, purpose and patronage of the life in question was critical. Some authors working for some patrons highlighted royalty and royal marriage, others quietly ignored them. The most flattering pictures of saintly queens are found in the fragmentary, anonymous lives. It is tempting to associate them not merely with the Kentish nunneries, but with houses closely connected to and patronized by tenth- and eleventh-century queens themselves.

The evidence for that connection is often circumstantial, but cumulatively convincing. Emma was alleged to have been devoted to St Mildrith's intercession; her return to favour early in Edward the Confessor's reign was attributed to it.[43] Mildrith was a Kentish *princess*, Edith preferred a Kentish *queen*. She was involved in commissioning a statue of Queen Bertha, wife of Æthelberht of Kent, the first English Christian king. Bertha, the archetypal English queen-as-missionary, was especially appropriate to a Queen entrusted at her consecration with the duty of calling barbarian peoples to the knowledge of the truth. Bertha featured in the Kentish Royal Legend, though not as one of its saints.[44] That

[40] The life exists only as a mere fragment, so the full characterization is unavailable, though the context of the vision is clear. However, the complete early twelfth-century life contained in BL Cotton Caligula A viii, which appears to be based on the lost vernacular life, lacks emphasis on ascetic practice.

[41] As witness Goscelin's lives of Edgar's daughter Edith and her mother Wulfthryth, discussed Stafford 1993.

[42] The eleventh-century Life is in Oxford MS Bodley 285; for dating and extracts compared with Goscelin see Rollason 1982, pp 60–1.

[43] Goscelin, *Translation*, cap 18, pp 176–8.

[44] Was there an attempt to develop a cult around her from Emma's days or before? Bertha is invoked in the early eleventh-century Litany in BL Galba A xiv, which Lapidge locates at

legend must have been of interest to an earlier English queen, Eadgifu in the mid tenth century. Eadgifu's father was an ealdorman in Kent, she retained extensive landholdings there, and held Minster in Thanet if not Ely, both associated with the saintly royal women of the legend.[45] She may even be a lost link in the transmission of the legend to Wessex. If English unity on earth was mirrored in a celestial unity of its saints in heaven, English queens had an interest in promoting both. Living queens could utilize their dead forebears and their powers to bolster themselves. During the tenth and eleventh centuries Balthild, the English slave who had become a Frankish queen, was recovered as an English royal saint, and the cult of the most famous Frankish saintly queen, Radegund of Poitiers, developed in England. Balthild's relics came to the royal nunnery of Romsey.[46] Radegund was known in England from the beginning of the tenth century, but her cult flourished around Winchester and in the West Country in the eleventh.[47] Her relics were at New Minster before the end of the eleventh century.[48] No English queen can be firmly associated with either cult, though Emma's connections with Poitiers, New

a nunnery in the Winchester orbit, possibly Shaftesbury, *Anglo-Saxon Litanies*, no XVI.ii. My thanks to Janet Nelson for drawing my attention to 'missionary queens'.

[45] Eadgifu had possession of one if not more of the Kentish minsters with which the legend is often associated, namely Minster in Thanet, S 489; she also had strong links with Ely before its tenth-century reform – when it may have still been a female house. Many of the royal women in the legend are connected with Ely, and Seaxburh, of whom lives were certainly produced in the tenth or eleventh centuries, linked the two. For the dating of the lives of Seaxburh, see Rollason 1982, p 30, who dates the vernacular fragment between the late ninth and the late eleventh century and suggests Minster in Sheppey as its origin. This or some other vernacular life closely related to it was available to the Ely author of the early twelfth-century Vita Sexburge found in Cambridge, Trinity College, O 2.1 and BL Cotton Caligula A viii – see Ridyard 1988, pp 56–8. Minster in Sheppey, which is not listed in Domesday, probably formed part of the great royal manor of Milton or of nearby Newington, which together with Milton formed the later hundred, Tatton Brown 1988, pp 107–8. Sigar had held Newington of Queen Edith; it received dues from Milton, DB I, fo 14v, and from Minster in Sheppey (*Sexburgamynster*) according to the Domesday Monachorum, p 78; there is an interesting later story garbling the links between Sheppey, Milton and Newington which parallels the stories of Leominster and Berkeley and would repay further investigation, Douglas, *Domesday Monachorum*, p 13 n 7. The queenly connection of the late eleventh century may extend back into the tenth.

[46] She was there by 1013 × c. 1030, when the List of Saints Resting Places was compiled, see Rollason 1978 passim and p 68 on dating, and was already invoked in a litany, perhaps associated with Shaftesbury or another West Saxon nunnery, of the second half of the tenth century, see Salisbury Cathedral MS 150, printed *Anglo-Saxon Litanies*, Lapidge, no XLIII.

[47] She is invoked in eight Litanies, two of them in continental manuscripts of late ninth-century date, including the Leofric Missal, *Anglo-Saxon Litanies*, nos V and XXIX.ii, and five associated with Winchester or West Saxon nunneries, ibid nos XII, XVI.ii, XXIV, XXVII, XLIII. She is in three Kalendars: the Glastonbury one of c. 979 × 87 in the Leofric Missal, and two from Evesham/Worcester, from the second half of the eleventh century, Oxford Hatton MS 113 and CCCC MS 391, printed, *Kalendars*.

[48] *LVH*, p 149, a relic of the clothes of St Radegund.

Minster and the West Country coincided with Radegund's popularity.[49]
Lives of saintly queens could be a mirror and their cults a sacralization of
contemporary queenship.

In Saint Ælfgifu, Emma's grandmother-in-law, eleventh-century
English queens had a recent model. Ælfgifu was the only near-contemporary English saintly queen.[50] Her cult was established at Shaftesbury by
the last decade or so of the tenth century,[51] and flourished, again especially around Winchester, by the early eleventh. When Emma married
Æthelred she was given the name of this, his sainted grandmother. The
late tenth and eleventh centuries saw a growing cult of royal saints in
England, including of the half-brother, half-sister and grandmother of
Æthelred. Individual religious houses were responsible, but this was also
a cult of the dynasty, and of royalty itself.[52] Along with the Kentish
legend it peopled heaven with holy kings, holy princes and princesses,
and holy queens. If heaven were the ideal society, queens were there *as
queens*. And that ideal hierarchy had at its head its own Queen, Mary. As
the cults of former queens grew, as the power of current Queens was
more formally acknowledged, Mary, and especially Mary *Regina*, came
to prominence.

The cult of Mary was strong in England in the late Saxon period.[53] It
was expressed in church dedications, visual representations and sermons,
in new offices and private prayers. In sources produced overwhelmingly
in a monastic environment, the cult of Mary was often a Benedictine and
private devotion.[54] But it had a public face in Mary as Queen of Heaven.
Although running as a leitmotif through all expressions of her cult, her
Queenship was especially prominent in the visual arts.[55] Earlier Mary had

---

[49] For the Poitiers/West Country connections see Beech 1990.

[50] Cf the closely contemporary queenly saints of Ottonian Germany, see Corbet 1986, Folz
1992.

[51] The mention in Æthelweard's *Chronicle* is critical to the dating of the cult, making it no
later than his death c. 1000 AD. The kalendar in the Bosworth psalter in its present form is
no earlier than 988, though based on a possibly Canterbury exemplar of c. 969, see
Korhammer 1973 and cf Dumville 1992b, p 50. Ælfgifu's feast may have been in the
original exemplar, or added at the same time as the reference to Dunstan, thus 988 × 1008.
It may be an argument in favour of a later date that the probably Shaftesbury Litany of the
second half of the tenth century in Salisbury *Cathedral* MS 150 does not contain an
invocation of her, although it does feature other saintly queens, Balthild and Radegund. By
the time the nun's prayer book, BL Cotton Galba A xiv, from Shaftesbury or some other
Winchester-connected nunnery was written in the early eleventh century, the cult was
flourishing. The prayerbook contains not only a Litany which includes her, but a special
prayer for which there is no medieval analogue, see *A Pre-Conquest English Prayerbook*,
pp 189 and n 102.

[52] For the various interpretations of this cult see Rollason 1989a and Ridyard 1988.

[53] Clayton 1990.

[54] Ibid especially pp 133 and 274.

[55] Ibid p 273.

Figure 7 Mary as Queen – the death and coronation of Mary from the *Benedictional of Æthelwold*. London, British Library, Additional MS 49598, fo 102 verso. Reproduced by permission of the British Library

often been represented carrying a child, as a mother; now, as Queen or as a symbol of the Church, she carried symbols of power. In the Bury Psalter, she holds palm branch and sceptre and is enthroned.[56] Even when accompanied by her child she is often a *theotokos*, a bearer of God,

---

[56] Clayton, p 169; Temple, *Anglo-Saxon Manuscripts*, plate 262.

showing her child for the salvation of the world, not a loving mother.[57] Winchester and particularly the New Minster were centres of this cult.[58] Bishop Æthelwold was an enthusiastic supporter; witness the novel representation of the Coronation of Mary in his Benedictional (figure 7), and her prominence in the illustration of his New Minster charter, where she appears carrying the symbols of the passion and Christ's victory.[59] It was at New Minster that Abbot Æthelgar raised the tower whose sculptured decoration gave pride of place to Mary Queen of Heaven surrounded by the heavenly court. At New Minster in the first half of the eleventh century two new Marian feasts were introduced, her Conception and Presentation, not celebrated anywhere else in Europe at this date;[60] in their prayers and offices she was an autonomous Queen, saving the world and bringing good to it.[61] It was at the New Minster, at the time when Emma was Queen, that the image of Mary as part of the Trinity in the prayer book of Ælfwine was produced. Here her child included her in the image of the Godhead itself, and Mary was equated with the Queen as she trod the heresy of Arius beneath her feet.[62] In the personal prayer book of the abbot of a house closely connected to Emma herself, the Mary of private Benedictine devotion merged with the crowned Queen of Heaven.

Emma and Edith were both consecrated Queens. Emma was consecrated at the time of her marriage in 1002; a charter of 1004 speaks of her 'consecrated to the royal bed'.[63] Edith was the first English queen whose consecration was mentioned by a contemporary chronicler.[64] The rites used for Ælfthryth, already known in England for two generations and more, remained basic to those used for the making of an English queen until the end of the eleventh century,[65] but not unaltered. At some date between 973 and 1044 significant changes were made to the rite for the making of a king.[66] Such changes may have no political signifi-

---

[57] Clayton, pp 165–7, especially at Canterbury; cf Backhouse, *Golden Age of Anglo-Saxon Art*, no 122 for Mary as a mother, but presented as queen of the angels. In general on Mary *Regina*, Warner 1976.

[58] See e.g. Clayton, pp 50–1; 74–5, 110ff.

[59] BL Cotton Vespasian A viii fo 2v.

[60] Clayton, pp 50–1.

[61] Clayton, pp 78–81, 83, 87.

[62] See above n 24.

[63] S 909. This is the first occurrence of this uncommon title.

[64] Retrospectively by *ASC*, MS E, s.a. 1048, recte 1051.

[65] Garnett, forthcoming. Nelson 1982 (1986) dated the Third Ordo to 1066 or just before; Garnett argues, on the basis of manuscript and political grounds, that the Second Ordo was used in 1066. If the king's Third Ordo is to be dated later, there is no argument for seeing the associated changes to the Queen's *ordo* as any earlier.

[66] The so-called third recension of the Second Ordo is found in CCCC 44, printed *Three Coronation Orders*, pp 53–64, with the Queen's *ordo* at pp 61–3, and apparently in the badly damaged BL Cotton Vitellius A vii, fos 3rv and possibly 2v–3v, where only fragments of the Queen's *ordo* are legible. Dumville has recently suggested a date after about 1020,

cance.[67] Liturgical texts cannot be treated like chronicles or charters. Their authors and revisers worked in a tradition where text spoke to text, on a time-scale which partook of the nature of the eternity towards which they aspired rather than of the fevered sublunary world they inhabited. Rites were revised, if at all, as much because new forms became available to their authors as because contemporary events demanded it. But in this case the changes were so significant as to prompt the suspicion that contemporary politics produced them. It was not only the king's rite, but the hitherto extremely stable Queen's *ordo* which were altered. The changes in the prayer for the giving of the Queen's ring were minor;[68] the antiphons which the manuscripts of this *ordo* alone include may simply have been omitted from those earlier manuscripts. But the addition of a series of benedictions over the queen is a major alteration. The antiphons invoke her role as Queen of the English people, and refer to her as the glory of the Anglo-Saxons.[69] The blessings bring her consecration more into line with that of the king.[70] These blessings and their remarkable content parallel those of the king. They speak of the Queen as *consors imperii*, a sharer of rule, of her institution as Queen over a people and the peace and prosperity to be wished for in her days. They seem too dramatic for a liturgical exercise without political content. The manuscript evidence suggests that the change occurred between 973 and 1044 and the most likely occasion is the consecration of Cnut and Emma in 1017.[71]

'broadly ... the middle quarters of the eleventh century' for CCCC 44, and the production of Vitellius A vii for Ælfweard of Ramsey, who was bishop of London 1035 × 44, 1992b, pp 71 and 79. Michelle Brown, personal communication, dates both manuscripts to the second quarter of the eleventh century 'highly reminiscent of Eadui Basan/post Basan Canterbury, and orbit, materials, e.g. the Bury psalter of c. 1025–50'. These datings preclude Schramm's suggestion that the changes were made for William in 1066, 1968, pp 181–2. The changes must belong before the earliest datable manuscript, thus, in this case, before 1044 if not 1035.

[67] Nelson 1982 (1986), p 381.

[68] Whereas Lanalet, Robert, Claudius II, Anderson, Ratold etc. have the ring as the 'signaculum trinitatis', CCCC 44 has 'signaculum videlicet sanctae integritatis et innocentiae'. The prayer here echoes the rubric which speaks of the ring 'pro integritate fidei'; this sort of change fits Nelson's suggestion of a liturgist's reworking.

[69] 'Igitur gens anglica domini imperio regenda et regine virtutis prudentia gubernanda, quam rex regum subarravit fidei anulo ... hodie coronatur anglisaxonica divine virtutis gloria.' The latter may be translated 'Today the Anglo Saxon (feminine = Queen) is crowned with the glory of divine virtue' or 'Today the Anglo-Saxon glory of divine virtue is crowned.' In either case her association with the Anglo-Saxons is explicit.

[70] I have been unable to find any similar blessings of a queen in tenth- or eleventh-century English benedictionals, whether as free-standing episcopal blessings or as part of the consecration ordo. Nor are such blessings common elsewhere; the *Corpus Benedictionum Pontificalium* does not contain any blessings for queens in its Concordance of episcopal blessings taken from printed pontificals and benedictionals throughout Europe.

[71] Edward and Edith is less likely a) because the *ordo* seems on some grounds to belong to a consecration of king and queen on the same day – whereas Edward was consecrated

The years 1013–17 were equally if not more traumatic years than 1066. They included extensive ravaging, punitive tribute taking and a period of great internal strain and division. An invading army was still present in England in 1017. They saw the exile of a consecrated king, the rebellion of his son, and two Danish conquests in rapid succession. By 1017 the surviving members of the ancient dynasty had been exiled or murdered, and the horror which that elicited may still be witnessed in the pages of Wulfstan's own works, with their concern with the æthelings and their status. Although Cnut was a Christian king, the attacks, rule and settlement of recently converted Scandinavians evoked memories of the pagan Vikings of the ninth century. The years 1013–17 produced a retrospective on tenth-century rule as a whole, expressed particularly in criticism of Æthelred. If circumstances are sought sufficient to provoke a recasting even of the most traditional and conservative of forms, liturgical rites themselves, then here they are.

Potential recasters were to hand. The years 1013–23 were exceptionally rich in reflection on rule in England. Archbishop Wulfstan was responsible for the production of two if not three great lawcodes. Two if not all of these attempted to manage a transition of power across conquest;[72] one may have aimed to renew and make specific an exiled king's consecration oath, the other two extended that oath in legal form. Wulfstan's so-called *Institutes of Polity*, the only surviving work of political theory from early England, was probably composed and reworked now.[73] Lyfing, the Archbishop of Canterbury who spanned these years, was described in retrospect as 'an exceptionally wise man, whether in affairs of God or the world'.[74] Two such archbishops would have been capable of commissioning if not redacting a version of the coronation *ordo*, including the Queen's rite, to fit the extraordinary circumstances in which they found themselves in 1016–17; and if Cnut's consecration was delayed until his marriage to Emma in summer 1017, there was time to produce one. For Emma, if not for Edith,[75] we must seek the meanings of

almost two years before Edith; b) in spite of Godwine's influence the attribution of joint imperium to Edith seems unlikely and does not fit with the profile of the queen during the first half of the reign, whereas Emma's profile throughout Cnut's reign attests her political sigificance; c) if Dumville is right about Vitellius A vii it should have been made early rather than late in Ælfweard's pontificate, and in any case he would have been dead by the date of the coronation of Edith: he died on 25 or 27 July 1044 and Edith was married ten nights before Candlemas (i.e. 23 January) 1045.

[72] Stafford 1982 and 1989a.

[73] I am not counting here historical, biographical, hagiographical and other works which clearly partook of some of the qualities of mirrors of princes; on the date see Jost's edition 1959.

[74] *ASC*, MS D s.a. 1019 at his death. D's judgement may be later, but that would merely reinforce the significance of a man whose memory had lived on in this way.

[75] It is possible that this revised version was used for Edith, though the second version of the Second Ordo remained that seen as the traditional English one after 1066. It is a now

Queenship not merely in the traditional form of the Queen's rite, but in the specific changes of 1017; in hallowed ideas but also in their dynamic interpretation and application in dramatic circumstances. The fullest implications of the common vocabulary of Queenship were realized in the changes made to the Queen's rituals in 1017.

The king's ritual in 1017 was especially appropriate to a conqueror who was now to be King of the English. The rod which more than any other item of regalia symbolized the king as judge was no longer the rod by which the king brought back those who strayed on the path, put down the mighty and lifted up the humble. Rather it was the rod of mercy, by which the justice of God is to be promoted, the church of God peacefully ruled and its laws kept. It is not a rod of power and domination, but a rod of just judgement, clemency and the grace of God. It is the king's mercy and justice rather than his power which are emphasized.[76] It is specifically the rod of the Anglo-Saxon kingdom, by which the king is called to imitate Him who said that justice must be loved, iniquity hated. The emphasis throughout the king's and Queen's rites is on the 'English', on the rule of the English gens and people (*gens Anglica, populus Anglicus*), on the Anglo-Saxons (*Anglosaxonici*), on England (*Anglia*). This is more emphatically than ever before a consecration of an English king, a King and Queen for the English.[77]

There are no major changes to the prayers for the Queen; the king was to be consecrated in the traditional way as a symbol of continuity, the Queen even more so. But there is new emphasis: the partnership and association of the Queen in the king's rule, and the relationship for the Queen as well as the king to the English people is made explicit. The Queen consecrated using this rite is to be a peace-weaver, she is to bring tranquility in her days. But most of all she is to be an English Queen, and a consort in royal power. These ideas have their lineage in, for example, the Preface to the *Regularis Concordia*. But their full expression came in specific circumstances. If these revised rites reveal the thinking of some of those who tried to negotiate the troubles of 1013–17, their thoughts had a special place for the Queen. The interpreters of Queenship here shared the Anglo-Saxon Chronicler's views. He applied them to Emma, and it is difficult to avoid the conclusion that the authors of the *ordo* had the same woman in mind. As the widow of an English king she already was an

lost version of the second version of the Second Ordo, not the third, which lies behind the Third Ordo, see Garnett, forthcoming.

[76] The sceptre is no linger simply the 'sceptrum regiae potestatis' but the 'sceptrum regalis clementiae et regiae potestatis'.

[77] Cf Garnett 1986a on the concern for two peoples, *Dani et Angli*, in these early years. Wulfstan's great codifications made in these early years should be seen as a statement of the law of the English to which Cnut as a conqueror subscribed. Note also Wulfstan's 'Sermon to the *English*' dating to 1014.

English queen; her consecration could now serve as a symbol of continuity if not of unity. The fact that it was almost certainly a second consecration marked out its significance even further.[78] Emma's identities in 1016 made her attractive to Cnut and available to the English. Acceptable to both sides, she could carry their meanings. Her utility was her strength. Emma was stressed as a partner in royal power, but there is no sign that she is to express the more merciful 'feminine' aspects of that power. There was to be no doubt that the Queen of the English now married to their conqueror was to be a sharer in his power and rule. 1017 produced the theoretical apotheosis of English Queenship, ironically achieved in defeat and conquest.

The cult of Mary, and especially of the Queenship of Mary, found particular expression at Winchester, the dower borough of English queens. Here under the abbacy of that same Ælfwine whose prayer book included Mary as Queen in the Trinity, the *Liber Vitae* of New Minster was produced. Its frontispiece is a drawing of Cnut and Emma as donors to the abbey. It is the earliest surviving portrayal of an English queen and was probably penned by the same artist who drew Mary as a Queen and mother in the prayer book[79] (see figure 5). In one Emma bursts from the visual obscurity of earlier queens in an image which equates her in stature with Cnut, deliberately parallels her with Mary above her, and places her, along with Mary, on the superior, right-hand side of Christ.[80] In the other, Mary is portrayed as a crowned Queen, destroying the arch-heresiarch in a visual commentary on the consecration prayer of an English Queen. Each was modelled on the other, each enhanced the other; the cult of Mary Queen of Heaven went hand in hand with the growing prominence of the English Queen on earth.[81] It coincided with the growing recognition of queens in charter witness lists from the mid tenth century onwards (see below). Both were accompanied by a wider cult of holy queens which was in some senses a mirror of queenship, a commentary on its perceived duties and again on the prayers of the Queen's *ordo*. If the first adoption of Queenly consecration in England had occurred much earlier, it was the early eleventh century which saw a significant development of it, in the direction of Queenship as a share in royal rule. A general tenth-century growth of English royal power, of an ideology of kingship, of kingship as office was paralleled in

---

[78] S 955, 1019 is the second charter to refer to the queen as '*consecrated* to the royal bed'; both consecrations elicited some recognition in this way. A second consecration of a queen was very unusual, but the circumstances of 1017 may have justified it.

[79] *Ælfwine's Prayerbook*, p 12.

[80] For this latter point see Heslop 1990, p 157, n 16.

[81] Thus Clayton, p 165, though cf p 273 rejecting a connection between the cult of Mary Queen of Heaven and the position of English Queens on the grounds that the former was part of a private, devotional cult.

Queenship. In late Saxon England the queen was exalted, became the Queen. In the story of English Queenship, the mid tenth to mid eleventh centuries appear as a particularly glorious chapter. It is scarcely surprising that 'Queen' was the identity Emma and Edith preferred in the stories they themselves commissioned.

But . . . the story of Queenship is littered with 'buts', punctuated by doubt and contradiction. In the frontispiece to the New Minster *Liber Vitae*, the heavenly messengers bring a crown for Cnut but a marriage veil for Emma.[82] The unambiguous equality of the late tenth-century Cluny ivory, where Otto II and Theophanu are crowned simultaneously by Christ, is missing.[83] Mary, as the Church, and as Queen receiving regalia from heaven in the Benedictional of Æthelwold (see Figure 7), was brought a crown and sceptre, but the Queen's ritual contains no reference to a sceptre, the symbol of royal authority. Either the real Queen did not receive one, or she was given one, but without any formal prayer stressing its significance for her.[84] Either the earthly Queen was not in all ways the counterpart of her heavenly model, or for both of them 'royal power' given with the sceptre was not the same as that given to the king. The witness lists placed her formally in the hierarchy of the kingdom, but when Archbishop Wulfstan described the duties of the ranks of that hierarchy in his *Institutes of Polity*, she was absent. The eleventh-century Queen might be a sharer in royal empire, with duties to defend church and people, but unlike an eleventh-century king she took no oath to bind her to that people and to define the duties of a clearly differentiated office. The titles of an eleventh-century English queen called her sometimes *regina*, Queen, but also king's *conlaterana*, or, more often, king's mother; to become a Queen was not a once and for all change annihilating all other identities. The marital veil, the fluctuating titles, the silent sceptre, the omitted oath, all raise doubts about the nature of Queenship, and about the capacity of regality to eclipse gender. Whilst the triumphalist story of queenship traces a straightforward upward journey, much else points to persistent ambiguity.

The cult of holy queens is not clearly and straightforwardly a sacralization and glorification of Queenship, nor simply and primarily in the interests of Queens. Like the Ottonian saintly queens, English ones were dynastic, and as useful to men as to women. The cult of Ælfgifu rose alongside the high regard for her son Edgar, and combined in the

---

[82] For the interpretation of the veil see Owen 1979.

[83] Ehrens 1991, p 253 notes how far this Cluny ivory breaks with tradition in its representation of an equal coronation. Erin Barrett's forthcoming work on the iconography of the royal couple contains important comparative discussion of all these images.

[84] See Parsons 1992 pp 62–3 for discussion of the giving of the sceptre before and after its first mention in the Liber Regalis of the 1380s. Cf, however, the use of a prayer for the queen similar to that used for the tradition of the king's sceptre, see above p 168.

990s with a strong sense of the dynasty as a male lineage. That sense was not without benefits to queens, though it was more likely to venerate them as mothers. The women of the Kentish Royal Legend are mistresses of households and royal mothers as much as Queens. Only Seaxburh is given the responsibilities of a Queen. But she too is praised as a mother, her sons two kings, like two planets, her two daughters like two bright stars.[85] And her Queenly responsibilities are exercized during regency, when she is acting as king; their applicability to a notion of Queenship is debatable. Queenship and sanctity could have met as two mutually reinforcing degendering roles. But Queenship's inability to escape from the fertile female body limited that potential. That fertile body was not easily sanctifiable. Whilst the lives celebrated Queens, wives and mothers, the conservative liturgy indicated the problem established notions of Christian sanctity had in accommodating the sexual woman. Holy queens were treated differently from holy kings. In the New Minster Missal, the oldest true English missal,[86] there is no mass for St Ælfgifu *regina*; her sainthood, unlike that of King Edward the Martyr, never achieved that degree of recognition. It does, however, contain two masses for earlier saintly queens: one for St Æthelthryth, a favourite late Saxon saint, and another rather rarer one for St Seaxburh.[87] As usual Æthelthryth is celebrated as a virgin not as a queen; the Preface of the mass describes how she contemned worldly joys and spurned the beds of two kings, meriting the union of perpetual chastity with Christ. The mass of Seaxburh indicates the difficulty in finding liturgical expression for a married and fertile woman's sanctity. In the postcommunion she is Seaxburh *Virgo* (virgin), whilst the Preface reveals that parts at least of this mass were adapted from one meant for the virgin saint Edith.[88] The patterns of sanctity were flexible in saints' lives, and perhaps most so in miracles, but the deeper structures remained embedded in the conservatism of the liturgy. Virgin, martyr, confessor; these were the limited patterns of lay sanctity recognized in the proper of the saints. The *ordines* carried the common vocabulary of Queenship, the liturgy did the same for sanctity. Even here at New Minster, a house close to the heart of royal power and in other ways apparently sympathetic to queens and their representation, the only way the liturgy could commemorate a fertile married female royal saint was by turning her into a virgin.

The practice of Queenship is as elusive and ambiguous as the ideology. From Ælfthryth onwards, king and queen are found acting together. Sometimes payments or gifts are made to both of them, in the shire farms

---

[85] See the early twelfth-century Life in BL Cotton Caligula A viii, fo 110r.

[86] *The Missal of the New Minster*, ed Turner 1962, p vi.

[87] Ibid fos 105rv, p 108 and fos 116v–117r, p 121 respectively. Folz 1992, p 31 cites the mass for Æthelthryth in the Missal of Robert as one of the oldest. There were others, as the New Minster example shows.

[88] 'Cum esset Edita ex regali prosapia huius mundi pompam deserens transitoriam . . .'.

in Domesday Book, often in wills[89] and in other land transactions.[90] The Domesday payments are a general recognition of the queen's unique position alongside the king. If they relate specifically to any of her functions and identities, it is to that of mistress of the royal household, and of her own. Sometimes the payments are divided in such a way as to suggest a differentiation of roles. Heriot was the payment which acknowledged the lordship of the king, secured his permission to make a will and the inheritance arrangements in it and recognized the link between king and noble. It is paid to the king. Although the queen is often invoked in such wills, the payments to her are given no formal title and carried no such general meanings. They may be payments for her intercession, contrasted with his permission and guarantee. Occasionally the payment is explicitly stated to be in recognition of the queen's help, as with the 50 mancuses Bishop Æthelwold paid to Ælfthryth in the Taunton case, or the 30 which Brihtric and Ælfswith gave her so that she would be their advocate that the will might stand.[91] Records of the queen's intercession, especially in later twelfth-century sources, must be carefully interpreted (above p 150). Some contemporary sources make no distinction between the purpose of the payments made to king and queen. Evesham paid gold to both.[92] Intercession itself is part of the process of power, and could appear so to the petitioner and client. Mercy is a royal attribute and those associated with its exercise are associated with regality, none more so than the queen in her special position as intercessor throughout the middle ages. If an aspect of kingship is here becoming especially queenly, as was perhaps happening in the protection of widows (above p 158), it was a royal function. But where these payments recognize her help and advocacy, they link her as much to other powers in the kingdom as to the king himself.[93] In advocacy the queen joins ealdormen, bishops and archbishops, not the king; she speaks for others, he is the one spoken to. And in almost all payments, she is ranked below him. When the king gets 200 mancuses of gold, the queen gets 50; when Edward gets 6 marks, Edith gets one.[94] In only one case does the queen apparently get more; significantly a payment to Emma and by a woman.[95]

[89] See *Wills* 1, 8, 9, 11, 26, 27.

[90] E.g. R 45, S 1026.

[91] *Wills* 11 'to forespræce þæt se cwyde standan moste'. *Forespræce* denoted advocacy, speaking for and representing another, whether in a single case, or acting more generally as a patron, cf *Wills* 15, 16.ii, 17, R 59 and R Appendix 1 and cf laws of Edmund II cap 7 Liebermann, *Die Gesetze*.

[92] S 1026.

[93] Cf the queen's role as requester, parallel to other 'potentes' in Carolingian charters; I am grateful to Janet Nelson for pointing this out.

[94] R 45 and S 1026.

[95] *Wills* 29 the will of Leofgifu, leaving her an estate, and the king a cash payment of two marks of gold. The relative values are hard to assess, and the case is complicated by the fact

The joint action of king and queen cannot always be demarcated and differentiated in this way. Whilst most wills are declared to the king, and the queen is mentioned, if at all, only later, some were declared to king and queen together,[96] and some petitioners greeted king and queen in their requests.[97] The consent and permission to make a grant might be that of king and queen jointly,[98] or a grant or charter be so much a product of their joint action that their witnesses are combined, 'I Cnut king of the English with my queen Ælfgyfu confirm my own donation with royal security.'[99] In two cases Edith issued writs in her own name, granting land as a king might do, in the terms which would be used of a king, though with a hint still of shared authority.[100] Each case requires individual consideration of the context and the link of the grantee or petitioner to the queen. Allowance must be made for strategic or *parti pris* statements, emanating in Emma's case, for example, from her old friends at Winchester, or at the beginning of the reign of Cnut from Archbishop Wulfstan anxious to stress the continuities across Cnut's conquest. Requests made to king and queen jointly could be followed by action on the part of the king alone.[101] Some form of joint rule is suggested by these cases but it need not equate the role and power of the queen with that of the king.

These records begin with and are most numerous for Emma, and in the reign of Cnut not that of Æthelred.[102] They coincide with a peak of power, as indicated in the charter witness lists, and specifically of *Queenly* power, as indicated by the titles, and follow a coronation rite which laid a new emphasis on the Queen's share of the king's rule. They are found on the whole in writs, letters, wills and other vernacular records, more flexible forms than the solemn Latin diploma, more capable of registering changes in the status of the queen, though even a diploma witness list joins Cnut and Emma together by the 1030s. Even as strategic or *parti pris* statements, they could not go beyond the boundaries of the arguable and retain credibility. Such records may

that Belchamp, just outside Sudbury, the south borough of the Thingoe hundreds, may be a restitution of royal land held by Leofgifu as a queen's servant.

[96] *Wills* 23 and *LE*, Bk 2 cap 88, pp 157–8.

[97] *Writs* 27.

[98] S 1235 'cum consensu et licentia regis Edwardi atque reginae Eadgyðe'; R 86 'Here it is declared in this document how king Cnut and the Lady Ælfgifu granted permission (*geuþan*) to Eadsige, their priest . . .'.

[99] S 970 and 972, both from the Old Minster archive.

[100] *Writs* 70 and 72, both for Giso of Wells; in 70 she greets all 'our' thegns in Somerset, whereas Edward more usually greets all 'my' thegns.

[101] Cf *Writs* 27 and 28.

[102] The exception is S 1235, and here the fact that a husband and wife were jointly making a gift to St Albans may have influenced the record of the joint consent of king and queen, if indeed the queen's interest is not in some way involved.

signal no more than the scale of Emma's influence at this date, though it must be debatable how far influence can be distinguished from power. They underline Emma's exceptional position, though Edith's writs suggest it did not die with her. It is difficult not to conclude that Emma and later Edith shared some of the power of the king, and were perceived to do so. Yet still Queenship eludes us. Edith issued one of her writs as 'Edith, the Lady, the widow of King Edward'. Her share of his power was as his wife and widow rather than as his Queen.

When William the Conqueror was crowned late in 1066, he was crowned alone. His wife had not accompanied him on his expedition to England; she was not there to be made Queen at its culmination. In 1068, however, she crossed to England and was consecrated as an English queen, no doubt using a version of the Queen's *ordo* like that used for Edith, Emma and Ælfthryth, possibly the last English queen for whom this version was used.[103] She was to be as clearly a traditional Queen of the English as William was to be a King. The *Laudes Regiae*, the ritual praises of a ruler, were sung at her coronation, in a version produced, perhaps specially for the occasion, by Archbishop Ealdred of York.[104] These praises were unusual in the extent to which they paralleled King and Queen.[105] It is exactly where they seem to express the apotheosis of English Queenship in late Saxon England that Mathilda's *Laudes* departed from tradition.

The *Laudes* that were probably sung for Emma and Edith carried a more mixed message.[106] Long life and safety were called down upon the

---

[103] Garnett, forthcoming, on the use of the Second Ordo in 1066, and arguing that the Third Ordo had been put together by early in the reign of Henry I at the latest.

[104] Cowdrey 1981, and for Ealdred's composition, Nelson 1982 (1986), pp 398–9.

[105] Cowdrey 1981, p 58.

[106] I would identify these as the *Laudes* which survive in a late eleventh-century Canterbury manuscript, and became the basis of later English royal *laudes*. Cowdrey's arguments that they are post-Conquest, pp 64–5, are not entirely convincing. The arguments concerning the lack of a Pope's name, and the inclusion of Archbishop Ælfheah, are only relevant if it has already been decided that the *Laudes* are post-Conquest. Both would fit equally into an English context post c. 1016. The term *principes* is found in pre-Conquest descriptions of the lay nobility, occurring, for example, in charters of Edward the Confessor's reign, S 1036 and 1042. But Cowdrey's critical argument is the placing of the queen in the Canterbury *Laudes*, after the archbishops. He feels this must denote a period when there was no reigning queen, since this order 'can hardly have been permitted by any dynasty, whether English, Danish or Norman, while there was a reigning queen'. But this position was precisely the normal one for an English queen in the witness lists of charters from c. 1002– c. 1030, see e.g. S 902, 909, 923, 950, 951, 953, 955, 956, 962, 936, 963, 971; and S 916 and 952 where she is between the archbishops. Ælfthryth, before 1002, had normally been listed, especially during her husband's lifetime, after the archbishops and bishops. Far from suggesting that the *Laudes* are post-Conquest, this unusual order is a strong argument for placing them pre-Conquest, and dating them from the early decades of the eleventh century. It might be noted that the *Life of Dunstan*, Auctore B, p 41, describing a royal marriage in heaven, speaks of the singing of 'condignas laudes'.

king and Queen, who are King and Queen of the English. But only the king was 'crowned by God'. Like Cnut in the *Liber Vitae*, the king was crowned from heaven, the Queen was not. Christ, the redeemer of the world, was called upon to aid both of them. Then for the king, a trio of holy kings was invoked to help him, Edmund, Ermingild and Oswald. For the Queen, there was a trio of female sanctity, Mary, Felicitas and Perpetua, female saints, but only Mary being a queen.[107] The King is aided by saintly kings – kingship is holy – the Queen by martyrs, but martyrs who were also fertile mothers,[108] rather than saintly queens. If anything is holy here it is martyrdom and motherhood. The king is aided by men, the Queen by women; they are gendered as the *Regularis Concordia* gendered them when it called on the king to protect monks, the Queen nuns. The earlier English *laudes* were sung for king and Queen; in some ways they equate them, in others they differentiate, rank and gender them.

What is thus most striking in the revisions made for William and Mathilda is the equality. As in 1017 contemporary political circumstances found liturgical expression, and brought out the full potential meanings of Queenship. In the aftermath of 1066 William, an upstart duke and Conqueror, was anxious to stress his regality above all else, and his wife's along with him. When the primary issue was royalty, the Queen stood beside the king, as the *Regularis Concordia* had earlier recognized that she could: the lordship of king and Queen together was to be sought. What difference such ideological enhancement made to a queen is difficult to determine. Emma's high profile during and after Cnut's reign reflected the enhanced status 1017 gave her, though that high profile was arguably the product of the political circumstances which led to the adapting of the consecration rite, as much as the other way round. Queenship remained bound to family identities. Mathilda was Queen for the sake of her royal husband and for sons who would be kings rather than for herself. But its formalization made a mark on the women who exercised it. Emma herself never forgot the status spoken of in 1017. When her Encomiast treated the events at the beginning of Cnut's reign, he stressed her status as Queen, and her

---

[107] Cowdrey 1981, pp 72–3.

[108] Both Perpetua and Felicitas had small babies at the time of their martyrdom, see their passion, *Medieval Women's Visionary Literature*, pp 70 and 74–5. Some version of their passion was certainly known in England, see *Old English Martyrology*, vol 2 pp 29–30, though the picture of their motherhood is, to say the least, ambiguous: as in earlier versions Felicitas is miraculously delivered of her child before term so that she will be free to undergo martyrdom, but Perpetua is not specified as a mother in this brief text, and dreams of her restoration to virginity. The English martyrologies do, however, place rather more emphasis on Felicitas and childbirth than some others, see Kotzor, *Old English Martyrology*, vol 1, pp 281–2, and it is possible that the full passion with its concern with motherhood and babies was available in England at this date: there was a tenth-century manuscript of it, later at Compiègne, Paris BN fonds Latin 17626, see Armitage Robinson 1891, pp 10–11.

equality with Cnut. The equality was expressed in the context of the making of the marriage. Emma knew that what made her queen was marriage, but what brought out all the equality and partnership of marriage was Queenship.

There was no single, new, transcendent Queenly identity. The *ordines* provided a common vocabulary of Queenship, contestable yet full of potential. In 973 the debate turned on Queenship, marriage and motherhood. Its outcome was to defend the consecration of a Queen by referring to the honour due to the woman who would be the king's wife. She is to be raised to Queenly dignity, but it is his status which must raise her, and it is to his bed that she is to be raised. However specific to Ælfthryth and 973 the arguments and objections, their expression and resolution reveals shared assumptions and defensible sentiments. Some of those assumptions and sentiments saw the Queen as a parallel to the king, expressed in the old formulae of the *ordo*; others as his wife, the mother of his children, her glory and status a borrowed one on earth. These assumptions could both assert and contain the messages of power in the ritual. They could expand those messages to the shared rule of 1017, or contract them to the wifely emphasis of the twelfth-century Queen's *ordo*. For neither Emma nor Edith was the enhancement of Queenship irrelevant, but for neither did it replace her other identities.

2 Regency

The problem of distinguishing these indentities dogs understanding of the queen's fullest exercise of royal power, as regent. Regents exercise royal power temporarily, without being king. Regency is distinct from the passing on of royal orders or the capacity of bureaucratic institutions to function in a king's absence.[109] It is a form of delegation, especially during the lifetime of a king, but distinguished by its fullness and autonomy. An exercise of delegated power, like any share in royal power, can constitute a claim to regency, and its major claimants are often those who have a share in kingship, either through their relationship to the king's own physical body, his relatives, or through their relationship to the kingdom he rules. But especially after a king's death, those excluded from the succession or considered of particular neutrality may be deemed most appropriate.[110]

Regency in the early middle ages is not always easy to recognize. Before Agnes of Poitou was explicitly charged with regency in mid eleventh-century Germany any formal arrangements for regency, if they occurred, went unrecorded.[111] Regency often has to be inferred from

[109] See Bates 1982b, for a nuanced discussion.
[110] Goody 1966, pp 10–12 on 'stand-ins and stake holders'.
[111] Wolf 1991a, p 57.

events and actions after a king's death. Charters may tell one story, chronicles another, or several others.[112] People who apparently exercised the powers of regents are not always recognized as doing so in contemporary charters.[113] Descriptions of regency in the tenth and eleventh centuries variously speak of the nourishing and education of the young king, the keeping of king and kingdom, the rule and defence of the kingdom. Women who exercised or claimed such powers could be called 'kings' or 'dukes'; men could be described as exercising care of the royal household and as counts of the palace.[114] Claims by a family member to care for a child-king could be argued as claims to the care of a kingdom, and claims to caretake a kingdom involved wardship of the child-king. For contemporaries a gap in the active rule of a king raised questions about the king as a member of a family and also a ruler of a kingdom, about the person of the king and kingship as office, the answers to which were not cut and dried.[115] In the tenth and eleventh centuries the strongest claims on regency were still by family members, but regency forced to the surface issues about guardianship and rule, the safety of the heir and of the kingdom.[116] Regency raises many of the same problems as Queenship. How far could and should a family identity be separated from an official one? What was involved in kingship, what powers could and should a person substituting for a king have?

Regencies are of different types, depending on whether the king who is to be substituted for is a minor, and not recognized fully as a king; a minor, yet one who technically rules; a full-age king temporarily unable to rule through absence or incapacity; or whether the regency is necessitated by an interregnum, during which the identity of the next king may not always be clear.[117] Different claims to be regent may be more or less arguable in different situations. Succession disputes muddy the water by opening debate about the nature of the situation itself. What some might choose to see as an interregnum, during which the next king was still

[112] As in the case, for example, of Anne of Kiev and Baldwin of Flanders after 1060, where charters apparently tell of Anne's regency, and chronicles differ in the extent of power they give Baldwin, Olivier-Martin 1931, pp 25–6 and 16f.

[113] See Erkens 1991, p 256 on Theophanu. There are witnesses to her rule and power in chronicles etc., but the major signs of it in the charters are more interventions, differing from earlier queens only in the quantity not the type. English charters do not record interventions.

[114] The sources on Baldwin and Anne are especially instructive here. See e.g. those quoted by Olivier-Martin 1931 at e.g. pp 12, 16–17, 21, 25 etc.

[115] Among much stimulating work on this subject, see Kantorowicz 1957, Starkey 1977 and 1987 a and b; specifically for the tenth and eleventh centuries, Leyser 1994b, Olivier-Martin 1931, Erkens 1991 especially for women, Schneidmuller 1991, Laudage 1991.

[116] See e.g. Bates 1982, for Normandy, Schneidmuller 1991, especially p 356 removing the blinkers of later nationalist history from Lothar of France's claim to wardship of the young Otto III, Leyser 1994b, Laudage 1991.

[117] Olivier Martin 1931, pp 170–5 for distinctions.

unchosen and uncertain, others might call a minority or absence, during which the next king is known – though not accepted by all – but is either underage or absent. Debates and struggles over regency may thus also be debates and struggles over succession. Small wonder if the resulting sources can be contradictory and confusing.

It has been claimed that late Saxon England did not have female regents of the type seen in the Ottonian and Salian empires.[118] Female regency was certainly not inevitable; women did not normally rule and their capacity to substitute for a king was debatable.[119] But tenth- and eleventh-century England had all the prerequisites for early medieval female regency. The German female regents, it has been argued, derived their authority from consecration and sacralization and the family claims of women, all present in England in the tenth and eleventh centuries.[120] Late Saxon England faced the problems of minority, of royal absence through illness, exile and the rule of many kingdoms, and, in some eyes at least, of interregnum. The continued claims of all royal sons made uncles and brothers dangerous stand-ins, whilst the respect for motherhood laid a basis of female authority, and the age-old arguments that a woman, who cannot rule, is the best protector of an absent or minor king's interests retained its force. The sparse English evidence provides the merest hints of practice and argument in these cases. But in the life of Seaxburh written at this time a mother's regency required no special comment. The reign of Cnut, 1035 and 1066 all raised issues of regency as well as succession. Exiguous as it is the evidence demands detailed attention.

Tenth- and eleventh-century English kings were absent or incapacitated during at least three reigns. During Eadred's illness in the mid tenth century Athelstan Half King, ealdorman and member of a powerful noble family, may have acted in his stead. He was remembered as a 'half-King' 'who was of such power that he is said to have held rule and empire alongside the king in his own fashion'.[121] Æthelred's exile in 1013–14 left

---

[118] Dumville 1979, p 3 n 1.

[119] See Wolf 1991a, for a recent overview of the early middle ages, making it clear that it was never so common that it could be taken for granted.

[120] Leyser 1994a, p 158 suggests the coronation of Theophanu was constitutive and gave her rights on which her influence was built. Erkens 1991 sees the mid tenth to mid eleventh century as a great age for the rule and powerful roles of Ottonian and Salian queens, and one factor as the queen's raising to the sacral sphere, p 258; cf Olivier-Martin, pp 12–13 and 22 on the lack of need to appoint Anne of Kiev regent because she was already queen and had the resulting power. A much later regent, Louise of Savoy, not a consecrated queen, placed great emphasis on motherhood as the source of her authority, perhaps as compensation, McCartney 1993.

[121] 'Qui tantae potestatis exstitit, ut regnum et imperium cum rege tenere sua ratione dicitur', *Vita Oswaldi*, p 428. A pointed absence of the king's witness from many charters between 953 and 955 may argue for regency arrangements. Keynes 1994b interprets this as the setting up of an agency for the writing of charters, perhaps in the hands of Dunstan.

a gap for which no advance provision could be made. The English nobles and great churchmen met during his absence, perhaps at the instigation of the archbishops, in what might be seen as a kind of *ad hoc* regency council.[122] Cnut's rule of several kingdoms resulted in foreseeable absences in the 1020s which must have occasioned some arrangements. Different ones seem to have been made. His letter of 1020 distinguished the delegated duty of furthering God's law, shared by many, from the royal duty of dealing with those who defied the law, in which Earl Thorkell was to act 'with the power of us both'.[123] A council, differing little from that which would normally advise a king, and a regent who acted with royal power is indicated. Thorkell was perhaps succeeded as regent later in the reign by Godwine, who was allegedly made 'dux et baiulus', earl and guardian of almost all the kingdom,[124] though the persistence of a wider council under the control of the archbishops is suggested by Cnut's second letter from abroad, that of 1027, which was addressed to the archbishops and ordered all those 'to whom I have entrusted the counsels of the kingdom'.[125]

In none of these cases was a woman apparently regent, even though Eadred's mother Eadgifu was alive in the 950s, and Emma in the 1020s. All the contemporary evidence points to the regency of ealdormen or bishops in the case of royal absence. Yet the *Annals of Winchester* later claimed that Emma was regent during Cnut's absence, and quoted a letter sent to her and the archbishops, bishops and great men from Rome.[126] The *Annals* are late and to say the least confused, but they raise the possibility that the fragmentary contemporary sources may not tell the whole story. The Ramsey author of the *Vita Oswaldi* who recorded Athelstan's quasi-rule was boosting the image of the father of Æthelwine, Ramsey's benefactor; the 1020 letter may belong to the special circum-

---

[122] There was clearly a meeting or council to which Edward could be sent back in 1014 to negotiate his father's return, *ASC*, MSS C, D and E s.a. Archbishop Wulfstan, who preached a sermon to some such gathering of the English in 1014 admonishing them on their culpability for their recent fate, may have played a role in its assembly.

[123] *EHD I*, no 48.

[124] *VitaEd*, p 6. A charter of Baldwin of Flanders for St Peter of Lille, cited Olivier-Martin p 15 n 2 refers to Baldwin as 'procurator et bajulus' in 1066, whilst he exercised regency, and cf n 4 for a thirteenth-century use of *bajulus* for a regent, and pp 15–16 for its use to describe the Flemish founders of the kingdom of Jerusalem, under the emperor. The author of the Life of Edward came from Flanders, where, in the mid to late eleventh century, *bajulus* denoted quasi-regal power, though obviously the Life may flatter Godwine in attributing it to him.

[125] *EHD I*, no 53 cap 11. Mc Gurk, *Fl Wig*, p 516 translates 'quibus regni consilia credidi' as 'whose advice concerning the kingdom I have trusted'. I prefer Whitelock's translation.

[126] *Annals of Winchester*, p 16 'Rex Cnutus, regno Angliae Emmae reginae commendato, et regno Daciae Hardecnuto filio Emmae et suo.... (went to Rome, from where he addressed a letter)...Cnut dei gratia rex Dacorum et Anglorum, Emmae reginae archiepiscopis, episcopis et primatibus totius Angliae salutem.'

stances at the beginning of the reign; the 1027 letter may be addressed to the regency council not the regent. The importance of both Eadgifu and Emma in the witness lists during the reigns of Eadred and Cnut might reinforce the *Annals of Winchester's* late evidence. But the case for female regency during the absence of an adult king in late Saxon England is unproven and on the balance of evidence unlikely, unless, as is possible, 1040–2 was a period of regency.

Minority and interregnum regency were other matters. During a minority a mother's care for her underage son was one of a woman's strongest claims to regency. The pattern of Eadgifu's witnessing points, among other things, to a particular association with underage claimants (see below p 201). During an interregnum, a widow's extension of her dead husband's identity and a Queen's share of his rule made her a candidate for caretaker of his kingdom. There was precedent here from the late tenth century. The period 978–84 is unlike the beginning of most tenth-century reigns. The normal spate of grants to laymen and royal servants is missing, deferred until 984–90. A period of regency for the underage Æthelred is likely, with some role for his mother Ælfthryth and perhaps for Bishop Æthelwold of Winchester.[127] Her relatively high profile is consistent with this, though her failure to appear in all documents issued in the king's name at this date indicates that she was less than full or sole regent. The position was perhaps shared.[128] To some observers Emma was a regent for her son in 1035–7, at least in Wessex. She was described as holding all Wessex for him as regent.[129] The situation in 1035–6, however, was not at all straightforward. It could variously be seen as an interregnum whilst the succession was settled, where the need was for a caretaker regent, or the absence of a designated king

---

[127] It is impossible to be certain of Æthelred's age in 984. His birth c. 969 is suggested by his appearance in an unfortunately very suspect charter, S 774. Wormald 1978, p 63 saw 984 as the king's majority, but cf Keynes 1980, pp 174–6 opening the king's age wider and linking Ælfthryth's disappearance in that year with the death of Æthelwold. For doubt as to whether she really disappeared from court in 984 see below, pp 203–4.

[128] Though see above n 113 for the problem of assessing regency from charters in the case of Theophanu.

[129] *ASC*, MS E 'heoldan ealle West Seaxan him (Harthacnut) to handa'. Whitelock translates as 'they (Emma and the housecarls) should keep all Wessex in his possession', *EHD* 1, p 257. But the Lambeth Fragment of the Life of Seaxburh, dated to the mid eleventh century and to Kent, i.e. the same milieu as ASC MS E, suggests regency is the better meaning. It describes the thirty year (*sic*) holding of the kingdom by Seaxburh for her son, which can only be as a regent, in the following terms 'hæfde heo ða gehealdan þæt cynerice þrittig wintra, hyre suna Hloðhere to handa...'. Swanton, 'A fragmentary life', p 27. Swanton, p 16 places the Lambeth fragment at mid eleventh-century Canterbury, but Rollason suggests a late eleventh-century Exeter script, and a West Country preservation, though assigning its composition to Minster in Sheppey no later than the second half of the eleventh century, Rollason 1982, p 30–1. The plural form of the verb in MS E poses a problem, but may simply result from the mention of the housecarls.

who may also have been a minor. Emma as regent for a son who was obviously king may not have been how everyone saw the situation. In the case of an interregnum, her claims to be regent could be argued as Cnut's widow, a caretaker after his death. But in an interregnum which was also a succession dispute she would have been too *parti pris* to be acceptable to all. The relative novelty of female regency could only have exacerbated argument. The actions of the housecarls and the support of Earl Godwine are witness that Emma's claims, under whatever guise, were taken seriously.

Like Eadgifu alongside Eadred, Emma was dominant during the brief rule of her full-age son, Harthacnut. Whether either woman should be seen as a regent or a Queen is unclear; in either case motherhood was the grounds. It could be argued that Emma prolonged a minority regency after 1040. The end of regency is one of its problems; it can be prolonged especially when the age of majority is flexible.[130] There were English precedents for the prolongation of the power of a mother beyond her son's minority, Eadgifu in mid century and Ælfthryth in the 990s, but in neither case is there reason to see this as regency rather than prolonged influence. Harthacnut's reign was not a prolongation of Emma's regency, which, if it occurred, had ended at her exile in 1037. There were no arguments in 1040 for a minority regency for a man aged at least eighteen years who had already been ruling a kingdom in his own right. Emma's role after 1040 is difficult to interpret. It is more significant than that of Ælfthryth in the 990s, though like hers it may be linked to the fact that family issues, here the overwhelming question of succession to the throne, were at the forefront of politics. If it was a form of regency, it was a regency for a son whose dual kingdom made absence likely, just as Eadgifu's may have been for a sickly king. Each could have been argued on the basis of motherly care, not so much maternal care for an infant child, but rather from a unity of interest of mother and son. Emma's could also have been argued from Queenship, as a share in rule by a Queen not yet supplanted by a son's marriage and his new wife's conse-cration. Her Encomiast presented both arguments.

Harold's coronation hard on the heels of Edward's burial meant that 1066 saw neither a regency nor an interregnum. But after the fateful events of Hastings and its aftermath, some sought to present it as both, among them Edith herself.[131] The *Life* of Edward suggests that Edith's own argument was that Harold should have exercised regency in which she would have been involved, her own claim deriving from her position at the king's side, and her identification with the kingdom. The Normans preferred to present an interregnum in which Harold was an illegitimate

---

[130] Olivier-Martin, pp 77ff.

[131] Garnett 1986b for the complex and developing arguments about the nature of 1066.

usurper and Edith a caretaker widow, rather like Cunigund after the death of Henry II, whose major role was to transfer the kingdom to the legitimate successor.[132] Both arguments may have been deployed in 1035.

Regency raises questions of great moment about rule and Queenship; the sparse sources from tenth- and eleventh-century England allow them to be posed but scarcely answered. If Emma was excluded from regency during Cnut's absences, or acted as regent but not in such a way that the letters of 1020 or 1027 needed to be addressed to her, what does this show? Was her share confined to some areas of rule, excluding the punishment of transgression and the provision for the law of God and man with which Cnut was concerned in his letters, which were not and never could be hers? Did Queenship rest upon a distinction within royal rule which disqualified her as a woman from these areas of regency? Was it the case that the more formal and specialized Queenship became, the more it reinforced a gendered distinction within royalty? If the queen was rarely given regency for adult kings, does this indicate that her claims as Queen to share the rule of the kingdom were empty, her real claims deriving from her family identities of mother and wife/widow, the basis of minority or interregnum regency? Yet as long as kings ruled in person and their official bodies and physical bodies were so hard to separate, did those family roles still give her the widest claims, including to rule in the king's stead or alongside him, as Emma did after 1040? And in those claims, could the powers of Queenship not come together with those of wife and mother to provide at least an argument for a trinity of rule of Queen-mother and sons together? Each regency, like each succession, occurs in unique circumstances. Each is argued from existing norms, precedents and practices; each then becomes part of norm, precedent and practice for the future. The arguments about regency in late Saxon England have left scant traces in the sources, but arguments for female regency were made, and in some circumstances successfully.

* * *

Kingship by the tenth century was an office, a specialized role with a clear script and delimited duties defined by tradition; a highly restricted role, linked in a hierarchy with others and marked out by its uniqueness.[133] Its public functions were the defence of the Christian faith and the people,[134] not only through battle, but through the provision of justice and the maintenance of internal peace. It encompassed ideas of patrimonial

---

[132] Thus William of Poitiers, p 166.
[133] Nelson 1975 (1986), p 335. cf Weber, p 196; Linton 1936 (1971), pp 90–7; Goody 1966, Intro esp at p 2.
[134] Le Goff 1993, p 4.

family headship, arbitration and sacral leadership; of ruling and governing, of blood and family.[135] Kingship was a form of charismatic authority, though already institutionalized as a hereditary aspect of monarchy;[136] a development which creates a need for some other person, courtier, Grand Vizier or queen, to take responsibility for failure or unpopular actions. None of this was new in eleventh-century England; much of the idea of kingship as office and its unique and high status had, however, been recently stressed; especially in the context of ecclesiastical reforming movements and via Continental contacts.

Queenship too had risen alongside kingship. It too had acquired duties, if fewer and less clearly defined, but it had not achieved the same uniqueness. At a time when kingship was clarified as office, Queenship's official rather than wifely nature was to the fore. Yet whilst consecrated kingship was unique, consecrated Queenship remained tied to the female lifecycle. By the tenth century an English king had to die, be deposed or murdered before a rival could replace him in his own kingdom and certainly before another one could be consecrated; only a multiplication of the kingdom by division could allow a multiplication of kings. A Queen, by contrast, was deprived of some of her identity by the death of her husband and especially by the marriage of a new king and the consecration of his wife: Emma's survival did not prevent Edith's anointing. A late Saxon king's royal identity was his own. A late Saxon Queen's, even after consecration, remained tied to that of her husband or son. A king was not unmade by the death of his wife; a Queen was, if not unmade, at least threatened with demotion and dowagerhood by the death of her husband. This is not to say that consecration was irrelevant to her, or to the power she could exercise; that a consecrated Queen who had exercised much power necessarily became a cipher in retirement. Nor that the development of Queenship was not significant for Emma and Edith. But it is a reminder that however far the language of Queenship was from marriage and fertility, it never effaced the wife and mother in the women it described. Queenship like kingship was an office exercised by those who retained strong family identity and whose authority and power could still be conceived of in family terms. Office never annihilates other identities; but the alternative family ones remained stronger for Queens than for kings, a plurality which could be useful to women, though also threatening. It was through all of them that a woman like Emma sought and exercised power, justified it or was legitimized in it.

[135] Ibid pp 5–6 citing Benveniste on the fact that kingship comes from two roots *regere/recte* – with ideas of rule, governing; and *kuni/gens* – with ideas of blood, family; see also Weber 1970 and Wallace-Hadrill 1971.
[136] Cf Weber, p 251 'the king is everywhere primarily a warlord; kingship evolves from charismatic heroism' and ibid pp 262–3.

7

The Fluctuating Power of the Queen – Witnessing and Identities

One of the sharpest distinctions between the king and queen appears in the witness lists of charters. Once a king had succeeded, his witness in charters was almost invariable.[1] The unchanging aspects of his office and position were recognized. The queen, by contrast, comes and goes. Her recognition in the witness lists varies from queen to queen, and within any one queen's lifetime, as do the titles through which her position was described. These fluctuations seem to indicate changes in perceptions of the extent and nature of the queen's power. They will prove an important element in the rewriting of Emma's and Edith's stories in Part III. Their interpretation, however, is difficult and must be placed in a longer perspective. That perspective provides a final insight into the power of late Saxon queens, particularly by placing them in relation to other groups and office-holders in the kingdom.

The witness list of a royal diploma records a meeting of the royal court. The appearance of the queen in such lists has often been used as a measure of her power and status,[2] charted by the fluctuations of her attendance, the titles she is given and the position in which she is recorded *vis-à-vis* other witnesses. Use of the witness lists in this way is fraught with danger. It is easy to be lulled by the semi-uniform nature of the diplomas into thinking that they are a transparent window on the past, an unmediated view by contrast with the slippery narratives of chronicles and lives.[3] But those who produced diplomas had their own agendas. Doubt about the gift was to be dispelled and interests placated. The circumstances of the grant could be doctored, including the record of the meeting at which it was made and the descriptions of those whose

[1] The exception is a strange set of charters of Eadred, discussed Keynes 1994b, see also above p 187 n 121.
[2] See Barlow 1970, p 163 , Keynes 1980 pp 176–7 and especially A. Campbell, 'The status of Queen Emma and her predecessors', *Encomium*, pp 62–5.
[3] Huneycutt 1993, p 192 – though her discussion of the diplomatic sources is brief and it would be unfair to suggest that she would consider them unproblematic.

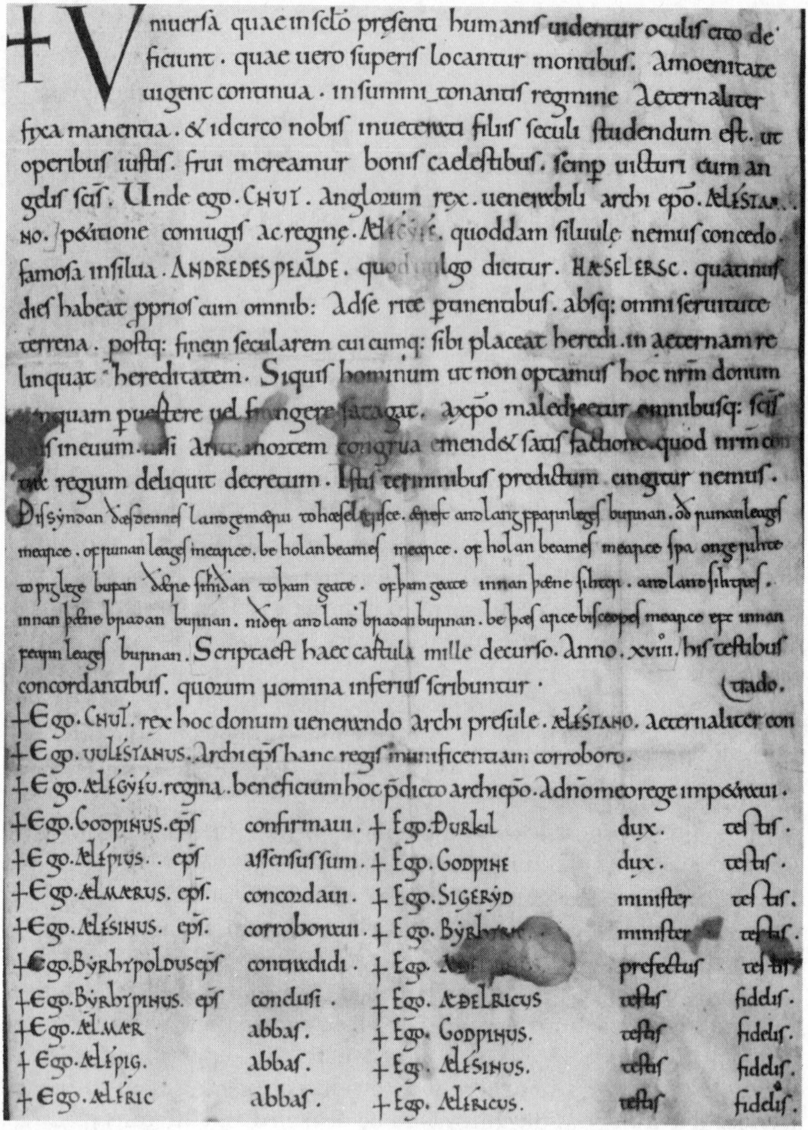

Figure 8 Original charter of AD 1018, in which Cnut grants land to Archbishop Lyfing of Canterbury, showing the witness of Ælfgifu/Emma as queen (*regina*) and, unusually, recording her petition in the body of the text. London, British Library, Stowe Charter 38. Reproduced by permission of the British Library

presence was acknowledged. The vocabulary available was stereotyped and limited, the room for manoeuvre narrow, but what leeway existed was exploited. The result is an edited story of power, though that very editing can increase its utility. A decision had to be made about the inclusion and description of the queen's witness. It is thus a sensitive indicator of some people's views of the queen and her power, and, since power cannot exist apart from its perception and recognition by others, of that power itself.

The lists record a variety of different types of meeting: some small and localized, often in Wessex, but also elsewhere; great meetings especially at the festivals of the ecclesiastical year; meetings in the context of campaign, or at least court movements determined largely by military needs. The composition of the group around the king was not uniform in all these sorts of meeting, though the presence of a group of ecclesiastical and secular office-holders and of the major court officials is regular and factors affecting status ranking seem to have remained the same in all. The relationship of the lists to the meetings of the court they describe are not straightforward. How far we can take them as a guide to all those at court, or only those judged to be important, whether the list records participation in particular court activities rather than mere presence, and, critically, whose judgement determines their composition and the description of the witnesses are all difficult questions. It is generally accepted that the witness lists give an accurate picture of at least some of the people gathered around the king on a particular occasion, and are not simply notional lists of all those considered as important at any one time.[4] It is far from clear that the list is exhaustive. Judgements of importance entered in, involving the balance and perhaps the geographical location of particular meetings;[5] even the size of the parchment could be relevant. And where, as in most cases, only cartulary copies have survived, mistakes, including the omission or repositioning of witnesses, can occur. Since the queen, when she appears, is usually near the top of the witness lists, the crucial questions for her are the general principles of inclusion, if any existed, and the identity of those who drafted the list.

The question of drafting leads into the vexed debate over the existence and nature of a late Saxon chancery, too large to be broached here.[6] The

---

[4] On this see Keynes 1980, esp pp 154–62.

[5] This may be especially important for the nobility. If a meeting was attended by fewer great men, for example, it is more likely that the lesser fry would be recorded; it may also have been the case that local men were more likely to be listed, even if of lesser general significance, if the meeting was held in their particular area, though, of course, it may simply be that they were more likely to have attended.

[6] Impossible to discuss this debate fully here, but some idea of its nature can be gained from Dumville 1993, Keynes 1980 and 1988, Chaplais 1966 and 1985. My own view is to incline to a set of flexible arrangements such as those proposed by Dr Chaplais; the

debate is between a view of central, chancery production of charters and one which argues for more diffused production in which beneficiaries played a major role in the drafting. If the scribes were chancery workers, then the witness list would reflect 'official' perceptions of importance, and of the appropriate titles to describe it. If the drafters and scribes were attached to one or other of the great ecclesiastical participants at court, in some cases the churchman or woman who was the beneficiary of the grant, then the list would reflect their perception of who should or should not be included. Different religious archives show different patterns of the queen's witness at certain periods, and give her different titles; an argument in favour of at least some diffused production. This has implications for interpreting the witness lists, and for judging the possible role of particular religious houses, or even particular clerics in promoting the queen's status. Whether the decision to include her was official chancery policy or the choice of a number of individuals, its very recording enhanced her status.

The lists were sensitive to changes. In general they display a uniform and status-conscious order: archbishops before bishops, sometimes with considerations of seniority whether of see or date of consecration; ealdormen with some attention to seniority or importance of office; king's thegns headed by the officials of the royal household, and all headed by the king. The order recalls the ranking in a political tract like Archbishop Wulfstan's so-called *Institutes of Polity*; it enshrines a view of the kingdom. It also mirrors a formal court life, with its order in seating, speaking and office. The order was not static. Individuals could move within it; meteoric rise in royal favour and political status is picked up immediately in the witness lists, as in the case of ealdorman Eadric's rise in the last decade of Æthelred's reign.[7] The appearance of the queen in these lists might thus indicate her formal inclusion in the kingdom and its orders, her position at court or the fluctuations of importance of individual queens; probably all three.

Some groups are invariably recorded in tenth- and eleventh-century witness lists: the king himself, the archbishops and bishops, the ealdormen and the lay nobility. The queen is not among them. These are the office-holders of the kingdom. The lay nobility appear primarily as *ministri*, king's thegns, that is, in their capacity as royal servants in the household or elsewhere, though this capacity was connected to their noble status. Insofar as she held an office, the queen did not count among these groups. Her witness is far less regular. Doubts about the nature of her office are reinforced. She is not, however, the only irregular witness.

---

witnessing of the queen and its recording fit better with such a view than with the idea of a single chancery responsible for the bulk of charter production from the early tenth century.

[7] Keynes 1980, p 214.

In the hierarchy of the witness lists of the tenth and eleventh centuries, four groups display a more or less irregular pattern: abbots and male ecclesiastics other than bishops, abbesses, the æthelings, and the queen.[8]

In the mid tenth century the witness lists betray uncertainty as to whether abbots should be included and which ones, and whether other lesser churchmen were also of sufficient importance to merit inclusion;[9] by the later part of the century, with a hiccup in the late 980s, abbots had become a normal and expected group. Other churchmen had not; until the reign of Cnut when household priests become more regular witnesses from the mid 1020s until 1066. Abbesses make a brief appearance mid tenth century[10] and then disappear, though the chronicles and other land documents show them still to have had a high profile in other respects. The æthelings/princes, like the queen, come and go, sometimes together with her but sometimes to different rhythms.[11] These exceptional groups, amongst whom she herself was counted, throw much light on the queen and the significance of her witness.

The tenth century saw a movement for change and reform in the English church which affected abbots, abbesses and in many ways the queen herself. One of the central issues of reform was the definition of monasticism, within wider questions of lay/clerical divisions. The status of abbots was first thrown into question, then, as reform of individual abbeys resolved it, that of 'true' abbots was confirmed, to some extent at the expense of the secular priests and other clergy. The link between reformers and the court in the tenth century ensured that this contested status was reflected in the view of the kingdom and its orders in the witness lists. The king's priests underwent a different development. A royal chapel already existed in the tenth century, but the strong monastic reforming influence tended to misprize non-monastic churchmen. Priests disappear in the late tenth century. The greater formalization of all aspects of the court in the eleventh, and the waning influence of monastic-centred reform gave them more recognition in witness lists now. Reforming ideas and the organization of the royal household both raised the status and profile of the queen.

Abbesses stood to benefit from reforming ideas which enhanced the

[8] This discussion covers the period from c. 940 onwards and ignores the question of the Welsh kings in English lists.

[9] Keynes 1995, Tables XXXVII, XLI, XLIV, XLVIII.

[10] S 1178 , AD 966, a Croyland charter, has Merwenna abbess of Romsey, after the abbots and before the ealdormen; S 1179, AD 966, also Croyland, has Merwenna and Wulwina *Mercamensis* (?Werhamensis). Both charters are highly suspect. But it is very strange for a forger to include abbesses, who so rarely appear in witness lists, and I am tempted to suggest that these were taken from some list or lists adapted. The witness of the abbess/ *magistra* of Wilton, Ælfgyth, S 582, AD 955, is far more secure.

[11] Keynes 1995, Tables XXXIa–c.

standing of the monastic life, and seemed to offer women a degendered ideal which equalized them with men.[12] They had the particular advantage of being monastic office-holders, the only female office-holders in tenth- and eleventh-century England apart from the queen. But unlike abbots, abbesses found no permanent place in the conception of the kingdom which witness lists seem to enshrine, a contrast with their higher profile in charters produced in the kingdoms of the conversion period and after, in the seventh and eighth centuries. Ironically Christianity's potential to degender had been realized in the earlier period precisely because of the closer association of ecclesiastical institutions and family at that date. The early abbesses were in witness lists as office-holders but also as daughters and sisters of kings, rulers of houses which were intimately connected to their founding families and their lands; the earlier witness lists recorded a kingdom which was still a family writ large. By the tenth century the tensions present in that situation had elicited a powerful critique of lay involvement and demands for stricter enclosure of religious men, but especially women. Conceptions of the kingdom itself were changing. Abbesses were now office-holders rather than daughters or sisters. Ironically, as a result the full potential of their office was unrealized, even though tenth-century reform had offered these celibate female monks near equality. Their clearer separation from the status of their lay families left them more vulnerable as women. The abbesses suggest that a gendered identity, especially within strong family connections, is not necessarily a drawback for a female office. The difficulties encountered in separating Queen, Mother and Wife were as much to the queen's advantage as her disadvantage.

The æthelings are different; they come and go. The most prominent princely witnesses, Eadred and Edgar in the mid tenth century, went on to become kings. Designation, anticipation of a future royal status, the mantle of regality spread by fraternal succession over all sons may thus account for their witnessing. It is as a royal woman that the queen, virtually the only woman ever included in the lists, appears. But the æthelings' appearances seem to be political rather than constitutional. Æthelings do not merely come and go, they prowl;[13] and their prowling is contained or encouraged by opportunities as much as by the desires of ruling kings. Potential heirs, foci of discontent, their pattern of witnessing charts the crises and practices of a politics which, whatever the theoretical conceptions of the kingdom, were still partly family politics. Debate about the succession and the need to demonstrate family unity brought them into prominence. The structure of the family itself, its

[12] I hope to deal with this more fully in a forthcoming article on 'The Queen, the nunneries and Churchmen'.

[13] To borrow Kenneth Harrison's inimitable description, Harrison 1976, p 92.

relative ages, marriage patterns and inheritance practices combined with court and wider issues in forefronting or sidelining them. The æthelings are a forceful reminder of the importance of family politics in tenth- and eleventh-century England. The queen's appearances trace her own part in those politics.

The appearances of tenth-century queens before 1002 were far from random. Eadgifu emerged to sudden prominence in the 940s after a long period in which West Saxon royal women had been virtually invisible.[14] She was the mother of the king and of a potential future king. She appeared regularly between 940 and 946 in the reign of her older son Edmund, and even more so from 946 to 952 in the first half of the reign of her son Eadred. In Edmund's reign she witnessed almost invariably in the company of her younger son Eadred, the ætheling.[15] Eadgifu's last appearances were in the company of her grandsons. In 952 she had temporarily disappeared, emerging again at the very end of Eadred's reign in 955, with her grandsons Eadwig and Edgar.[16] Ælfthryth appeared as the king's mother between 979 and 984,[17] and would also appear with the æthelings, her grandsons, in the 990s.[18] At that date, she, like Eadgifu before her, emerged from a temporary obscurity or retirement for a final swansong. These parallels between Eadgifu and Ælfthryth throw the contrast between them into sharp relief. As the wife of Edgar from 964 to 975 Ælfthryth's witnesses pale beside those of Eadgifu in the 940s. She appeared in less than one fifth of all possible grants.[19] The two queens' place within the rank order of witnesses also varied. Eadgifu was usually high: in Edmund's reign normally after the king, or after both her sons;[20] from the accession of Eadred until 951 almost invariably immediately after the king.[21] Ælfthryth in Edgar's reign

---

[14] Stafford 1981.

[15] The only exception is, perhaps significantly, a grant to a woman, a nun, probably of Wilton: S 493.

[16] S 565, 566, 569.

[17] She appears in 10 of the 21 surviving charters dated 979 to 984.

[18] She appears in no charter without them, and they appear in only one in which she is not also a witness: S 893, the Bromley charter for Rochester, AD 998.

[19] 19 out of 103. This figure includes all grants in 964, some of which were probably before the marriage, and those impossible to date more precisely than 963–75, some of which again are probably earlier. Excluding all the latter, the figure is still 19 out of 89. The 19 includes S 783 and 671, forgeries dated to Edgar's reign but calling her *regis mater*. NB no attempt has been made to exclude any other than the most blatant forgeries, but the general proportions are unlikely to be thereby greatly distorted.

[20] Exceptions where she appears after the archbishops are S 475 and 505, from Old Minster and New Minster archives respectively, though other charters from both archives place her in the more usual position.

[21] The exceptions are S 546, the Reculver charter, not above suspicion, and in any case one in which she and Dunstan are recorded low down but with very elaborate witnessing formulae to mark them out, and S 544, an alliterative charter.

was listed after the bishops, or rather at the head of the abbots.[22] From 979 to 1000 her position varied, sometimes after the bishops, sometimes listed immediately after the king.

On closer inspection these patterns look more complicated, especially in their relationship to other witnesses. In Edmund's reign the role of his brother Eadred is even more striking than that of his mother. It was the narrow royal family not merely the king's mother which was prominent. In 955 Eadgifu reappeared alongside the æthelings; Ælfthryth appeared in the 990s along with her grandsons, but her witnessing was not connected with that of her sons before Edgar's death. Edgar's sons were rare witnesses in the 960s and early 70s; the æthelings never appeared in a witness list of any credibility except in 966.[23] In the 990s Ælfthryth normally appeared in the company of the princes, and the whole family group after the bishops.[24] Between 979 and 984 there were no æthelings, and Ælfthryth's position varies. A close scrutiny which combines appearance, position and title with charter beneficiary introduces even further nuances. Between 979 and 984 Ælfthryth was given the title *regina* in four charters and placed after the bishops;[25] in the others she was *mater regis*, in one even *mater basilei* (mother of the emperor). On all but one occasion when a maternal title was used she was after the king or between the archbishops.[26] On the whole, Old Minster, Winchester, charters stressed her as *regina*, three out of four, and invariably place her after the bishops.

The importance of family and family politics in bringing the queen to the fore is the first conclusion from this pattern, along with the significance of maternity as opposed to marriage in a tenth-century English queen's power. A woman was more likely to play a large part in the rule of a son than in that of a husband. She was identified with the fortunes of her male descendants, even in the generation of her grandchildren. This is the general message of Eadgifu's and Ælfthryth's witnessing, and an explanation of some of the detailed pattern. Even as a wife, Ælfthryth's appearances in the charters are often tied to her fertility. She may have received a gift of land about the time

[22] This latter may be the primary factor, especially given the significance the *Regularis Concordia* gives her in relation to nunneries and abbesses, and the description of the coronation feast of 973, in which she appears as feasting separately from the king with the abbots and abbesses. The consistency of her placing suggests it is not simply the result of miscopying by cartulary scribes.

[23] S 774, and 798 are unacceptable lists, and S 783, allegedly dated 971, has in addition to Edward clito the incredible witness of Ailgiva the king's mother, who had been dead since 944.

[24] except S 891.

[25] S 835, 840, 843; in 837 she is among the bishops which may be a result of copiest's error, Keynes 1980, p 239.

[26] The exception is S 849, a grant to Bishop Æthelwold in the Old Minster archive.

of her marriage,[27] but her first appearance in the witness lists was in connection with the birth of her eldest son[28] and her next appearances very likely in the year of the birth of the second.[29] Her association with them is borne out by the wills which name her along with her sons.[30] Between 979 and 984 where she was *mater regis*, the stress on her close association with the king himself affected her position in the lists and took her to the top of the witnesses next to him.[31] Maternity stressed the blood relationship as the source of her share in his status if not his office.

The family politics which brought æthelings to prominence did the same for queens. Succession, fraternal succession and an unmarried king all provided the context in which Eadgifu as queen-mother could flourish. 955, for example, saw the reigning king's illness, and questions of the succession; the young æthelings emerged and along with them their grandmother, the mother of an unmarried king and the most suitable guardian of his nephews, now his imminent heirs.[32] The issues of family politics were not always the same, and apparently similar appearances of the queen read differently in context. Ælfthryth in the 990s, like Eadgifu in 955, witnessed along with her grandsons. The 990s, however, were a period of reorganization by a king at the height of his power,[33] involving perhaps the succession but also the place of the king's burgeoning family of young sons, providing for their household and lands. Their grandmother was part of this reorganization, but as much a victim as an orchestrator; neither queen nor æthelings took pride of place in the lists, but appeared after the bishops.

Motherhood may have been the most important family identity of a queen, but it was not the only one which gave her power. Ælfthryth's first appearance in Edgar's reign was in connection with the birth of her

---

[27] S 725, conceivably a dower or similar bridal gift, see above pp 70–2, thus having implications for not only Ælfthryth herself and her position at court, but for the legitimacy of her sons.

[28] S 739, where she appears only with her stepson, Edward, and S 745, the famous New Minster charter in which she and her infant son appear, and the legitimacy of both is stressed – either as a clarification of the superior claims of her sons, or to stress their disputable legitimacy in the friendly environment of a Winchester charter. In both this and the Burton charter of this year Ælfthryth appears higher in the witness list than in almost any other charter. Was this too a stress on her importance in the all-important year of her son's birth?

[29] S 767 and 806; for the date of Æthelred's birth above p 189 n 127.

[30] See will of Ælfheah, *Wills* 9.

[31] S 838, which places her between the archbishops could be a copiest's error.

[32] S 811 for the relationship between Eadgifu and Edgar whilst he was an ætheling. The enormous bequests to Eadgifu in the will of Eadred presumably belong to this final stage of her career. The scale of them fits an attempt to arrange a role for his mother in the early stages of the reign of the new young king.

[33] Keynes 1980, pp 186–208.

child; her later witnesses, unlike Eadgifu's from 940 to 946, were independent of those of her sons. Edgar did not forefront his sons in the 960s and early 70s. Ælfthryth was a Queen and wife during her husband's reign, though that role never made her as prominent as Eadgifu had been as a mother. The witnesses of Eadgifu and Ælfthryth as wife, mother and grandmother derive from the same family relationships, but expressed in differing family and political contexts.

Both queens show a pattern of retirement and re-emergence in association first with son then with grandson which recalls the Empress Adelaide in tenth-century Germany and Europe. The maternal imagery in which contemporaries described Adelaide's enormous power as 'the mother of kingdoms' seems to echo the maternal role as a basis of Eadgifu and Ælfthryth's power and the authority found in contemporary notions of motherhood. Family politics surrounding succession and regency brought all three women to the fore. Adelaide also had a landed significance in Italy as a basis for her power; the lands and household which were so important in the identity of an English Lady affected the pattern of her witnessing.

Three-fifths of Eadgifu's witnesses in Eadred's reign up to 951 are in connection with land in Kent and Sussex, her own ancestral area,[34] or in Northamptonshire[35] and Berkshire,[36] mostly in the Lambourn/Wantage/Newbury area with which earlier and later queens were involved, or north east of Wallingford, again in an area of the Thames valley where later queens would hold land. Of Eadgifu's witness in grants to laymen late in the reign of Edmund, at least two involved land which was later associated with the queen in some way,[37] and two concerned land in Thanet, where Eadgifu had landed interests.[38] The pattern can be extended to encompass the royal lands more broadly and the royal household(s).[39] Ælfthryth, for example, may have emerged as a grandmother in the 990s, but she appeared in only 6 of the 22 charters of this decade. Three of them were ecclesiastical restoration charters which were

---

[34] S 528, 527, 1631, 525, 535, 551, 546.

[35] S 533.

[36] S 517, 523, 529, 542, 552, 544, 578, 558, 559, 567.

[37] S 475 Pitminster, Som, cf S 1006 and perhaps S 491; S 855; S 495, a grant to Bishop Ælfric of land in Northants is concerned with the same land which Emma is later involved in granting, cf S 957 and 977.

[38] S 512 and 497. In S 489 Edmund granted to Eadgifu his mother North Minster in Thanet. She may have held other lands there, see Eadred in his will leaving his mother all his booklands in Kent and Sussex; in this context the grant to the bishop of Selsey S 506 should perhaps be seen not simply as a grant to an ecclesiastic but of land in Sussex. Eadred made a specific grant to his mother in this county, perhaps after she retired to a religious life, see S 562. It should, however, be noted that even in Kent her position is not so dominant that she is recorded in all gifts, see S 464 and 519.

[39] Most of Eadgifu's other witnesses were in areas with concentrations of royal land.

concerned with former royal lands.[40] Two were grants to a layman, Wulfric Spott, whose family seems in other ways to be associated with the æthelings and their household.[41] Whether dower, ancestral royal land, or brought in by marriage, the queen's lands were one basis of her power. They and her place in the royal households ensured some of the perceived need for her consent or consultation.

A need to record the queen's presence to signal her consent may be a factor in a third aspect of this pattern. Whether as wives, as mothers or as grandmothers, the witnesses of Eadgifu and Ælfthryth were affected as much by the identity of the beneficiary of the diploma as by their roles in family and court. Eadgifu from 940 to 946 appeared overwhelmingly in charters granting land to ecclesiastics rather than laypeople.[42] One sign of her greater importance in the early years of Eadred is not simply that she appeared in a larger proportion of witness lists now, but that she appeared in far more grants to the laity than before 946; but her witness of ecclesiastical diplomas was still a higher proportion.[43] Ælfthryth between 979 and 984 showed the same pattern. Although she witnessed about a half of all diplomas for these years she appears in all grants to ecclesiastical beneficiaries except two,[44] but in only two grants to lay beneficiaries.[45] Her 'disappearance' from court between 984 and the early 990s

---

[40] S 876 and 896 concerned with lands and privileges of Abingdon, and perhaps to be associated with S 937, undated and lacking a witness list, which is concerned with the compensation of Abingdon for the loss of lands rightly belonging to the æthelings which had been given to Abingdon by Edgar. And S 891, AD 997 which restores to Winchester the much-contended 100 hides of Downton.

[41] S 878, 879, AD 996. For the association of this family and the æthelings see the Will of Athelstan and grants in it, *Wills* 20. The sixth is a grant of land and privileges to St Albans, S 888, AD 996.

[42] Thirteen out of her 20 appearances are in such charters. She does not appear in the three grants to religious women/kinswomen S 462, 474 and 482; the first two are from the Glastonbury cartulary, where witness lists were rarely copied in full, but the third is from the Abingdon cartulary and has a full witness list. Nor does she appear in the grant to Abbot Dunstan, S 466, another defective Glastonbury copied list, nor in the suspect Bury privileges, S 507. The deficiencies of the Glastonbury lists makes it unfortunately impossible to test the allegedly close link of the queen-mother with Dunstan, or her association with religious women, though S 482 suggests that this was not invariable.

[43] Allowing for defective witness lists, she appears as a witness in over half of Eadred's charters. Eadred, in spite of his later reputation as a friend of churchmen, made proportionately far more grants to laymen than his brother had done, and his mother witnesses well over half of them until 951: 1 out of 4 in 946; 7 out of 9 in 947; 5 out of 6 in 948; 5 out of 9 in 949; 2 out of 5 in 951.

[44] S 836, a grant to Old Minster which is difficult to explain, and S 850, AD 984, a grant to Shaftesbury, of land associated with an earlier queen, Ælfgifu, which may itself be queen's land, and may thus signal her waning influence. Shaftesbury, where Edward the Martyr was buried, was one of the first religious houses to receive a grant after her death.

[45] S. 840, to Leofric, and S 855. The latter, a grant to Brihtric, involves land near Lambourn which may well be queen's land and so have needed her permission.

may partly be an illusion created by this pattern; the charters of these years are overwhelmingly for the laity.[46] The same association with ecclesiastical grants had marked her appearances during her husband Edgar's reign.[47] Such a pattern may be affected by the sort of meeting in which ecclesiastical grants were likely to be made – the great court occasions which the queen was more likely to attend and at which her presence might be formally acknowledged, rather than the day-to-day meetings. It may derive from the specific religious functions given a tenth-century English Queen; like family politics it may indicate that a queen's importance is related to what are seen as the political issues of the day and how legitimately she is considered to be concerned in them. It may signal a sympathetic attitude of many contemporary ecclesiastics, especially reformers, towards the queen and her role, and her involvement with them Conversely the motive may be healthy wariness. Many churchmen and churchwomen could have felt it prudent to secure the queen's witness for grants of land which could be seen as royal family land, which so often passed backwards and forwards between churches, royal servants and members of the royal family.

If much of her witnessing associated her with family and its lands, other aspects showed her as Queen: indeed her landholding already confounded these two aspects of her position. Eadgifu's high place in the witness lists fits the view of a ruling family trinity in the 940s; Ælfthryth's place after the bishops appears as a demotion in line with her less frequent witnessing. Another interpretation is possible. Whether associated with abbots or merely placed between bishops and abbots, she was being aligned with the orders of the kingdom rather than with the royal family itself. What might appear as demotion may rather express the Queen's place as an office-holder in a conception of the kingdom which appealed to the reformers of the later tenth century. Even as Queen-mother between 979 and 984, in sympathetic Winchester charters, she was *regina* – and after the bishops. Queenship placed her among those sacramentally consecrated, provided her with a body politic of her own, one lower in the hierarchy, after the clerical elite, though always before the abbots. A clearer definition of queenship may be one real change between Eadgifu and Ælfthryth. The new alignment which laid stress on her own office rather than her link to the king's body was potentially a dangerous move. In the ecclesiastical order enshrined in the New Minster *Liber Vitae* queens were classed with abbesses and noblewomen as 'Illustrious women'. Detached from the king's body they were illustrious,

---

[46] Sixteen of the 20 surviving.

[47] Out of 17 witnesses, where she is the king's wife (i.e. excluding those later forgeries dated to his reign but calling her the king's mother) 11 are for ecclesiastics, though note that her marriage was later than the flurry of grants to the laity at the beginning of the reign.

but above all women, and as such could rank, as here, after kings, princes, bishops, lay nobles and abbots – after all men.

Comparison with the other transients and vagrants of the witness lists places the queen's role within some of the wider themes of the tenth- and eleventh-century English Play. Unlike the abbots she achieved no permanence in the conception of the kingdom which the lists enshrine; but when men as important as the æthelings were impermanent we are reminded that the witness lists tell only part of the story. It is particularly the office-ial one. Abbots, abbesses and queens were all offices in flux; if the abbots' success suggests that office combined most effectively with male gender, the abbesses' failure underlines the strengths as well as the weaknesses of a combination of office, female gender and family. The meeting of court, family and wider politics gave the æthelings their occasional place in the sun. Ecclesiastics in general, and reformers in particular, were the recorders, but in the process actively involved as script writers of the various parts. As the drafters of witness lists they included or excluded the queen, placed her now next to the king, now after the archbishops, now with the æthelings, sometimes at the head of the abbots, telling us much about the part they felt queens could, should and did play, most notably that it was a varied, changing and ambiguous one. The general pattern of the queen's witnessing before Emma's arrival illuminates the traditions which she and Edith inherited, leading us to expect fluctuation, even in the careers of the most powerful women, whilst reminding that the variation may entail promotion towards ever greater power as well as demotion to lesser significance.

A discussion of the witness lists is no complete guide to any queen's career. They must always be interpreted in context. They are at best a partial picture, especially as long as such uncertainty shrouds their compilation. But that partial picture is an interesting one, which points forward to the detailed narratives of a queen's career and back to the structures which require study to understand that career. The witness lists revealed no once and for all changes, whether in individual careers or in the general pattern, no status which overrides or even seems more important than the political circumstances in which it is expressed; no simple pattern of development over time. Eadgifu may have overcome the apparent reluctance of the West Saxon kings and court to forefront women, but she created no status to hand on. The next three women at court may have been politically important in their marriages, but they never appear in witness lists.[48] Political circumstances, the lifecycles of

---

[48] Ælfgifu, wife of Eadwig, appears uniquely in R 31, a vernacular record of an exchange of lands, which is also witnessed by her mother, a woman apparently of some importance, see e.g. the *Life of Dunstan*, Auctore B, cf Hart 1992c; Ælfgifu never appears in a Latin diploma witness list, nor do Æthelflæd the shadowy first wife of Edgar and Wulfthryth his second.

families and individuals were as significant as any unilinear advance of queenship. At the same time, the witness lists tell a continuous if faltering story of queens from the 940s onwards. The long eleventh century of English queenship begins then. However many their faces and however tentative some of their roles, queens had made an appearance on the political stage. Emma and Edith were the last late Saxon performers.

Part III

The Lives

8

Emma

1 1002: The Arrival of a Queen

On 17 November 1000 or 1001, the dowager English queen Ælfthryth died. In the spring of 1002, before Easter, Emma, a young Norman woman, crossed the Channel to become the bride of an English king, Æthelred. Hers was no common journey. English princesses had crossed in the opposite direction to wed French or German rulers, though not recently, but we must look to the generation of the groom's great-aunts for the last such marriages. And to find an English king marrying a non-English wife, we must go back to his great-great-great-grandfather, almost a hundred and fifty years before, to Æthelwulf's marriage to Judith, the daughter of Charles the Bald. The marriage of Emma and Æthelred had an English context (in the death of an ageing queen-mother and the pressures of Viking attack) and a Norman one (in a ruling family confident if not entirely secure in its place in the world and beset by the usual family tensions). Emma's arrival in England was not unprecedented, but it was unusual. Like Judith before her, she came as the second if not the third wife of an English husband many years her senior. Unlike Judith, this young Norman woman was to play a central part in English history for the next half century.

Emma was the sister of the count/duke of Normandy, Richard II, and like him one of the offspring of Count Richard I and Gunnor.[1] By 1002

[1] William of Jumièges, vol I, pp 128–30. Emma's name might be thought to make her the daughter not of Richard I and Gunnor, but of Richard I and his first legitimate wife, Emma, sister of Hugh Capet, in spite of Dudo's insistence that the marriage of Richard and Emma was sterile 'absque liberis'. Jackman 1991, argued on onomastic grounds that Mathilda and Hadvise, Emma's sisters, were the daughters not, as later alleged, of Gunnor, but of the Capetian Emma, and his doubts concerning Dudo's total reliability on tenth-century Norman genealogy seem well founded. The same arguments and doubts might extend to Emma herself. There were, however, other routes by which Frankish names like Emma could have entered the Norman namestock. Jackman argues that the marriage of Lieutgard

her father Richard had been dead for over five years. He had died on 20 November 996 after nearly forty-five years as count of Rouen, or as his panegyrist Dudo termed him 'duke of the Norman region'.[2] For Dudo he had been a great man, the more than worthy son of a martyr father, William Longsword, and the grandson of Rollo, the Aeneas-like builder of what would become Normandy.[3] Others had a different view. When Richer of Rheims recorded his death he was brief but pointed: 'Richard the leader of the pirates died of lesser apoplexy.'[4] Richer could recall Richard's inviting in of Scandinavian Vikings to help him in the 960s, and their ravaging in Northern France. Dudo was well aware of Richard's Scandinavian roots, but more inclined to see them as admirable. Through Richard Emma was the great-granddaughter of a Viking warrior, Rollo, and granddaughter of William, whom Dudo at least saw as the ruler of Northmen, Bretons and Danes.[5] The Norman ruling family c. 1000 were in many ways French, but took pride in their Northern ancestry. Richard I was given a Christian burial, but on the heights above the harbour of Fécamp like a Viking warrior.[6]

Richard's marriages reflected this duality. His first, and undoubtedly full and legitimate one, was to Emma, daughter of Hugh the Great, duke of the Franks, and sister of Hugh Capet.[7] She died in or perhaps soon after 966/8.[8] At some stage, however, Richard contracted a union with Gunnor, Emma's mother, a Danish-born woman.[9] That union began as less than full marriage, and was only later given what legitimacy it had, according to Dudo at the insistence of Richard's followers, who were anxious to have an heir. By the 960s or later Richard's followers might

of Vermandois and William Longsword may have produced offspring, even Richard I himself. Keats-Rohan (forthcoming) notes the possibility of the borrowing of such names for prestige reasons and argues that the earlier fertile marriage of Rollo was to a high-born Frankish woman, Poppa. In view of this, I have accepted the later Norman chroniclers' claim that Emma was Gunnor's daughter.

[2] Dudo, p 293 'dux Northmannicae regionis'. For the tenth-century counts as counts of Rouen, the relatively late notion of 'Normandy', and the comital/ducal title see Werner 1976, Bates 1982, pp 56–64 and 148–51 and Fauroux, no 15. For the sake of convenience I have adopted the title 'duke' since it is the one by which the Norman rulers are now most commonly known.

[3] Searle 1984 on Rollo and Aeneas.

[4] Richer, Bk IV, cap 108, vol II p 328.

[5] Dudo, pp 183 and 196 on William. Rollo is usually considered to be Norwegian in origin, though Dudo makes him a Dane, a change appropriate to the context of Dudo's work c. 1000 AD and the conception of Normandy and its origins by now, see Douglas 1942, and Searle 1984 and 1988.

[6] Searle 1988, p 124.

[7] Flodoard, s.a. 960.

[8] van Houts, in William of Jumièges, p 129, n 6 states that she was still alive in 966, at the time of Fauroux no 3; the latter, however, is dated to 968.

[9] Dudo, p 289.

have been wise to suggest regularizing an heir-producing union, though tenth-century Norman history had not suggested that such a step was necessary to inheritance. Neither William Longsword nor Richard himself had been born of certainly full marriages.[10] It is impossible to date Richard's first union to Gunnor, though its regularization is placed c. 989; nor can we be certain whether Gunnor was Richard's 'concubine' during his full wife's lifetime, or only after her death.[11] It is ironic that Emma's own mother was joined in exactly the sort of debatable union of which Emma herself later accused her rival, Ælfgifu of Northampton.

Emma's own birth cannot be precisely dated. Tenth-century Norman sources are sparse, but tenth-century sources, full or sparse, rarely record the birth of children, male or female. She was one of nine children, and probably not the eldest, but beyond that we are in the realms of speculation. The latest date of her birth is c. 990, assuming that she is unlikely to have been younger than twelve when she arrived in England.[12] The early 980s are probably the earliest date, since she had a baby in arms in 1023, and was surely not much more than forty at that date. Emma was at most in her early twenties at the time of her marriage.

Her early upbringing is even more obscure. Her grandfather William Longsword was entrusted at some stage for his upbringing to a member of Rollo's military household; he was still in Botho's care when he was a young man (*adolescens*).[13] Richard I, Emma's father, was born at Fécamp, and if Dudo is to be believed, his own father, William, may not have seen him for several years. His birth was reported on by two members of William's household, and it was only later that he gave the boy a detailed visual and physical inspection before proclaiming him a worthy successor.[14] Richard was then entrusted to Botho, and sent to Bayeux. After his father's untimely death Richard was brought up in his

[10] Dudo, pp 173, 218 does not describe either of their mothers in ways which would suggest full marriage, whilst Jumièges brands both unions 'more danico', vol I, pp 58 and 78. Note, however, Jackman's suggestion that Richard was Lieutgard's son.

[11] Prentout 1915, pp 390–2 and Musset 1959, p 31 argued that the union was regularized c. 989, on the basis of Robert of Torigni's statement that Robert Archbishop of Rouen could not become Archbishop because of his birth of an irregular union, thus implying that the union was regularized a year or so before he became Archbishop in 990; printed William of Jumièges, Bk viii cap 36, vol II, pp 266–8. Torigni's story has no earlier basis in Dudo or Jumièges. Dudo, pp 288–9 makes it a prohibited union 'prohibitae copulationis' regularized at an unspecified date, but since Archbishop Robert was one of his patrons he might not be expected to record any problems concerning his episcopal appointment.

[12] Cf Searle 1989, pp 283–4, making her the youngest surviving daughter, and placing the birth of the eldest son in the early 960s; this is surely stretching Gunnor's fertility to the biological limits, but we do not know that Richard II was born as early as this. The birth of Edward c. 1004/5 means that she cannot be much younger than twelve in 1002.

[13] Dudo, pp 179 and 181.

[14] Dudo, pp 219–20.

father's household, though Louis IV plotted his kidnap, allegedly on the grounds that a royal household was a better place to rear him.[15] None of this suggests a close physical or even geographical relationship between the children of the Norman family and their parents, but it is dangerous to argue from Dudo's omissions, impossible to know at what age some of these arrangements took effect, and especially doubtful whether the upbringing of either was in any way typical of sons, let alone of daughters.[16]

In the absence of evidence about her age and rearing, it is impossible to say what Emma might have learnt from observing her mother. From 996 until 1002 she could have imbibed her first lessons in female power and regency. Evidence for Richard I's reign and for Gunnor's activity then is sadly lacking, but as his widow she, like many other noble and royal women at this date, exercised considerable influence. She appears in the witness lists of charters until the 1020s.[17] In the flattering mouth of a Rouen court poet, she is described virtually as a regent in the 990s, 'at the head of the kingdom after the rule of her husband . . . the lady countess' before whose feet the suppliant wept.[18] Since Richard II was almost certainly of age when he succeeded in 996, there is some exaggeration here. The court poet in question, Garnier of Rouen, dedicated his satire to Robert, Gunnor's son, and to her, Robert's 'exalted mother', and ended it with the hope that she, the glory of the kingdom, would along with Robert flourish for ever as shining lights for their followers.[19]

Gunnor and her son Robert were patrons of learning, as was her brother-in-law Rodolfus (Ralph d'Ivry). The three of them were responsible for the commissioning of Dudo's celebratory history of the Normans in general and of the family line in particular.[20] Rodolfus acted as Dudo's informant, so too did Gunnor, a woman of 'enormous memory, lavishly rich in the treasure of recollection'.[21] What she remembered especially was information about the family, about her own marriage and about the death of Richard's previous wife without children. Dudo's story of a tenth-century line of descent from father to single son, culminating in the marriage of Richard and Gunnor and moving immediately from that to Richard I's deathbed and the designation of Richard II is almost unbelievably conflict-free. The story told so as to leave no

---

[15] Dudo, pp 224–5, 227.
[16] It is, for instance, possible that Richard was not originally considered a possible or likely heir.
[17] Fauroux, nos 14bis, 15, 16, 17, 18, 19, 20, 21, 29, 32, 43, 47.
[18] Garnier of Rouen, Satire against Moriuht, p 203, lines 237–40.
[19] Ibid p 197 line 2 and p 210, lines 237–40.
[20] Searle 1984, and see Dudo, pp 123–5, 125–6, 126–8 and 214–17.
[21] Dudo, p 289.

rival to Richard II was also one in which Gunnor's marriage and its legitimacy were unassailed.[22] It was in part Gunnor's narrative, and it stuck. By the twelfth century Gunnor would be matriarch of the line, her son Richard 'Gunnorson', *Gunnoridae*, the Norman aristocracy tracing their descent from her and her sisters.[23] History and accident assured to Emma's mother what they denied to her, the role of 'mother of the dynasty', though with a little help from Gunnor's own selective memory. At the court of Rouen in the 990s the young Emma could have had in her mother an example of a widow's power, and could have learnt from her the value of shaping and editing as well as celebrating family history. But it is not necessary to argue for such individual tuition. The recurring patterns and problems of family politics taught such lessons.

The family history which Gunnor had told took pride in its Danishness, even imposing a Danish pattern on the Norman past (see above n 5). Gunnor was herself of Danish birth, the daughter of recent Danish settlers, and Dudo made much of the fact. She was a worthy mother for the heir to Normandy since she would make him Danish-born on both sides.[24] Although she apparently had a Frankish Christian name, Albereda, she was virtually never referred to by it in surviving sources.[25] Her sisters were all remembered by their Frankish names,[26] though not until the twelfth century. At Chartres as in Normandy c. 1000 Gunnor's brother Arfast was unashamedly Danish. Whereas her daughter Emma took an English name, Gunnor apparently kept the Danish one of her birth. Yet all her children were given Frankish names. Gunnor may have felt especially free to resume her Danish identity in widowhood; all the evidence comes from then, though Emma was to feel no such freedom to be Norman after 1016 or 1035. But Emma had little need or encouragement to resume such an identity. If Gunnor was able to glory in her Danish ancestry, it was because that was acceptable and desirable to her son the duke and his followers. Gunnor expressed Northern origins which were a part, but only a part, of Norman self-identity c. 1000. Women, as we have seen, can take on this function of expressing ambiguity and unifying difference, whether in families or in wider groups. Gunnor articulated and recognized the Danishness of Normans in Frankish Northern France. Emma, with her borrowed identity and changed name, would be able to play a similar role for the English after 1016.

---

[22] Cf Searle 1988, p 96, Jackman and Keats-Rohan (forthcoming) for the possible unreliability of Dudo's family history.
[23] Orderic Vitalis, volume II, Bk 3 p 8 for Richard. For her importance in wider descent Douglas 1944, White 1921, Searle 1988 pp 100–7 and especially van Houts 1989.
[24] Dudo, p 289.
[25] Only in the *Translation of St Ouen*, p 824; there is no compelling reason to provide Richard with a third wife to account for this *uxor Albereda*, though it is possible.
[26] van Houts 1989, p 233.

The Danish birth which she gave the Norman heir, Gunnor also transmitted to the English king's bride. Emma was Danish as well as Norman born. When William Longsword entrusted the young Richard to Botho, he sent him to Bayeux, where he would learn to speak fluent Danish as opposed to the more Romanized speech of Rouen.[27] Dudo exaggerates the linguistic Frankisization of the Norman court.[28] Dudo himself promised Richard a bilingual work,[29] and his sensitivity to the issue of language may result partly from his experience in a bilingual environment. It was his experience at court which alerted him to the linguistic patterns of courtiers, to 'the mellifluous sweetness of palace discourse' which Richard learnt as a hostage at Louis IV's court.[30] But even here Dudo was aware that the prolonged and enforced contact of captivity changed language. The Saxon duke Heriman could speak to William Longsword in Danish because of his imprisonment in Denmark, though it is rather less credible that William himself could understand the German speech of Saxons mocking him at the court of Henry I.[31] The literal truth of these stories is unimportant. Dudo had lived at court long enough to be aware of the language issues which court life raised, perhaps especially in a bilingual court. If Emma were raised at court, she probably spoke Danish, a tremendous advantage in 1016/17.

This cannot have made her transition to the English-speaking court of Æthelred any easier. Goscelin would later feel that the linguistic alienation of such a royal bride, sent to a court where she could not even speak the language, was a metaphor for his own sense of exile.[32] But efforts could be made to teach an incoming foreign bride. In Germany a generation before, the duty of teaching Theophanu, the Greek bride of Emperor Otto II, Latin had been taken on, perhaps by her mother-in-law, the dowager Empress Adelaide, if not her sister-in-law, Abbess Mathilda of Quedlinburg.[33] Emma's mother-in-law and sister-in-law were dead, but there must have been others to teach her the language of her new home. Like other hostages and captives, a foreign bride would have learnt.

The self-image of Emma's family was Norman and Northern, but it was already rooted in France, not least by marriage. Norman rulers c. 1000 AD were proud of their Scandinavian ancestry and its fierce warrior

[27] Dudo, pp 221–2.
[28] See Bates 1982 p 21, though Dudo seems to be concerned more to combine elements of a Northern and Frankish identity than to be a 'campaign to diminish the province's debt to its Northern heritage'.
[29] Dudo, p 120.
[30] Dudo, p 230.
[31] Dudo, pp 196, 197.
[32] Goscelin, *Liber Confortatorius*, p 41.
[33] McKitterick 1993, p 63. The Trier Psalter, for example, a Latin text without any abbreviations and with a Greek interlinear translation, looks like a teaching aid.

image, but they were firmly entrenched players in the politics of northern and western France. Through her long life Emma would count among her relatives the counts of Blois/Chartres, of Flanders, of Rennes, those of Mantes and Boulogne, the dukes of Brittany and more remotely those of Aquitaine, not to mention a constellation of lesser lights in Northern France, like the counts of Eu, Brionne, Arques, Ponthieu. Her ramifying connections do not constitute a mobilizable political faction but they conferred status and sometimes tangible aid. In 1037 she could take refuge with a step-great-nephew and his wife, who was perhaps a widow of her own nephew. It comes as no surprise that she and Cnut were remembered as patrons in France as well as in England. Emma was the daughter of a mother born of recent Danish settlers, and a father who was both 'leader of the pirates' and a Northern French count. The English descriptions of her as 'Richard's daughter', or later as 'Norman-born' simplified, to say the least.

The immediate Norman context of the marriage was continuing nego-tiations with the English king over Viking activity in the Channel, and a Norman family settlement. At the time of Richard I's death, none of his children were apparently married. In a series of matches around the turn of the millennium Richard II, perhaps with Gunnor's help, settled his own and his sisters' futures. In a double match his sister Hadvise married Geoffrey count of Rennes, son of Conan of Brittany, whilst Richard himself married Geoffrey's sister Judith.[34] Another sister, Mathilda, was married to Eudes, count of Chartres.[35] Emma's marriage to Æthelred belongs as part of this series. It has no obvious connections with the earlier agreement between Richard I and Æthelred, concluded in 991; both the delay and Richard I's apparent reluctance to marry off any of his daughters argue against that. It belongs with Richard II's attempts to establish his rule, enhance the prestige of his family and negotiate with his most powerful neighbours.

But the Viking activity which prompted the 991 agreement was a factor in the match. As before 991, the fleets which were attacking England were finding refuge in Norman harbours and buyers for their loot in Norman markets. Rouen itself was a market through which British and presumably English slaves were sold, like the wife of the Irish

---

[34] The marriages are normally dated 996 × 1008, see e.g. Judith's undated dower docu-ment, Fauroux, no 11; the negotiations were between Geoffrey and Richard II, see William of Jumièges, Bk V cap 5, vol II, p 14. Geoffrey died in 1008. Van Houts 1984, p 91 following Prentout prefers 1003, a date deduced by rereading Robert of Torigni's MXIII as MIII. Douglas 1950, pp 289–91 dates the marriage no later than 1008, 'possibly consider-ably earlier' and p 291 n 3 feels Prentout may be 'approximately correct'. 1002 is just as likely, and negotiations for this marriage and that of Æthelred and Emma were probably contemporaneous.

[35] Again the date is after 996, when both Eudes and Richard became counts, and before Mathilda's death in 1005, see Jumièges, Bk V cap 10, vol II, p 22 and n 1.

poet Moriuht whom he tracked down there.[36] Raids on England in the 980s and 990s came especially from the Irish Sea and the Channel. In 1000 AD the fleet which had been attacking England wintered in Richard's land.[37] The Channel, like the Irish Sea, was an area of recurring Viking activity during the tenth century, and there was easy movement between the two. Around 1000 AD Æthelred dealt with them both, through military expeditions in the Irish Sea and the negotiation of a Norman marriage. The match did not end Norman help to Viking fleets. Richard made an agreement with Swein of Denmark, apparently after 1002, providing for peace, succour for Danish raiders far from home, and, as ever, the disposal of booty. William of Jumièges' horrific account of Æthelred's massacre of settled Danes on St Brice Day, 1002, seems designed to excuse Richard's behaviour.[38] It would not have been so easy for Emma in England to smooth over her brother's actions.

The Viking context brought England and Normandy together, made them neighbours, albeit uncomfortable ones, and ensured that a Norman duke and an English king would see Emma and her marriage as an answer to their needs at the turn of the millennium. The precise timing of the marriage, however, owed much to English royal family developments. Æthelred's mother, Ælfthryth, died on 17 November in either 1001 or 1000.[39] At about the same time, in 1001 or 1000, Æthelred's wife died, or was disposed of.[40] The latter event could have been engineered to make way for a new queen; in the former nature took its course. It was surely the death of the consecrated dowager queen, Ælfthryth, who had overshadowed his previous wife/wives, which opened the way for Æthelred to contemplate an important political marriage which would bring a new queen to court. By late in 1001 the king and his court were in Kent. They remained there, or returned, in the early months of 1002 and were at Canterbury on 11 July that year.[41]

[36] Musset 1954, p 254.

[37] ASC, C, D and E s.a.

[38] William of Jumièges, Bk V caps 6–7, vol II, pp 14–18.

[39] BL Egerton 2104A, fo 43r, a Wherwell book, dates her death to 17 November AD 1002, 'millesimo secundo'. However, Æthelred was making a grant to Wherwell, after her death, between 8 January and 23 April 1002, see Keynes 1980, p 258. Ælfthryth's last appearance as a witness was in S 896, dated 999.

[40] Her youngest son, Edgar, first appears in charters in 1001, S 899, but was not present with his brothers in 998, S 891 and 893. Although we cannot be certain what delay occurred between the birth of a prince and his first apperance in charters, it could be very little, see e.g. Edmund in 966, following his parents' marriage only a year or so earlier.

[41] For Kentish nobles at court after 7 October 1001 and after 8 January 1002 and before 23 April 1002, and the probability that the meetings were in Kent, see Keynes 1980, pp 257–9 and 132–4. The differences in the witness lists may point to two separate visits, though a long stay is also possible. S 905 is dated 11 July at Canterbury, the year is given as 1003, but the witness list of this original charter shows that this was a mistake for 1002.

Negotiations with Richard, waiting for Emma's arrival if not personally conducting her across the Channel, and a marriage at Canterbury, by the Archbishop, would account for a protracted stay or a series of visits hard on each other's heels. The making of the first foreign marriage in seventy years or more, and the arrival of the first foreign queen in a century and a half called for careful preparation. If Ælfthryth's death occurred in November 1000, advance planning could have been leisurely; if in 1001 the move to Kent before the end of the year must have involved unseemly haste.

On his side Richard would have been anxious for full recognition of his sister's, and thus his own, dignity. The match was socially unequal. Emma's name was changed, just as Bertha, daughter of Hugh of Arles, became Eudoxia on her upwardly mobile marriage to the Emperor Romanos II.[42] But Richard had enough to offer to exert pressure. His own marriage to Judith involved extensive dower, and an elaborate document recording it, which effectively underlined its full and Christian nature. He would have wished for no less for his sister and may have insisted on her coronation and consecration as Queen. The practice was common enough in France by now, and Richard must have been aware that Robert the Pious' wife Bertha, his own brother-in-law's mother, had not been consecrated, a fact possibly linked to the survival of Robert's mother, the dowager Adelaide.[43] Waiting for Ælfthryth's death may have been Richard's idea as much as Æthelred's. Full Christian marriage, consecration, even assurances about the likely inheritance of Emma's future sons are all plausible conditions of the negotiations in 1001–2. So too would have been dower and dowry. Æthelred assigned dower which included at least Exeter, land in Winchester and the North East Midlands. Dowry would have been expected in return. The wives of previous

---

[42] McKitterick 1993, pp 66–7.

[43] The precise status of Adelaide and Bertha, whose lives overlap at Robert's court, poses problems. Adelaide's consecration is possible, even likely, but there is no contemporary evidence for it. No contemporary or later account of Hugh Capet's consecration in 987 mentions a consecration of Adelaide. Two later forgeries, Newman, nos 121 and 124, call Adelaide *regina*, and the dating clause of no 124 speaks of a joint rule or regency of Adelaide and Robert. Normally Adelaide is *mater*, though, as with Emma, this can co-exist with consecrated queenship and often seemed a preferable title. Adelaide's influence in the late 990s was strong, witness her involvement in the important issue of the Rheims archbishopric in 997, see Gerbert, *Letters*, no 181; the view of the modern editors that her direction of this affair was 'étonnant', p 457 n 1 at least indicates her power. There is, however, little doubt that Bertha was not consecrated. In royal charters she is never anything other than *coniunx*, and once, Newman no 119, even *comitissa*. In a grant to Marmoutier in 1003–4 she is *regina*, and Pope John so referred to her in 1004, see Duby 1978, pp 124–5, though since both documents seem to be in the context of the repudiation their titles may be strategic usage. Constance, Robert's second wife, was consistently *regina*. Bertha's status certainly left her vulnerable, though there were other factors in her repudiation.

Norman counts had brought dowry, and dowry had been provided for outmarrying daughters.[44] Land as well as movables was involved. Richard gave Eudes of Blois half the castle of Dreux and land on the River Avre with Mathilda, a dowry which caused trouble when Mathilda died without children.[45] Was land in the Cotentin Emma's dowry? Did it lead to friction between the brothers-in-law, as Mathilda's dowry led to war between Richard and Eudes? Æthelred certainly led a strange expedition to the Cotentin, perhaps to secure Emma's dowry.[46] If trouble over dowry did occur, it can have made Emma's position at Æthelred's court no easier.

The arrival of a new queen was a dramatic event. It could be spectacular. Emma may have arrived, like her great-aunt Gerloc in Poitou, 'fittingly decked out with an abundance of wedding gifts, carried by female horses laden with showy harness and gold and silver strappings, with an innumerable crowd of servants of either sex, and an abundance of chests filled and weighed down with silk clothing worked in gold.' Emma brought some followers with her. But the deeper impact of her coming was felt in the English court and in the royal family. Late in 1001, whilst the king and court were at Canterbury, the nunnery of Shaftesbury received a grant of land earmarked for the preservation of the relics of the king's martyr-brother Edward.[47] Early in 1002 the abbess of Wherwell received a general confirmation of privileges, and a grant of land hitherto held by Ælfthryth but connected to the æthelings; the abbess or her representatives travelled to Kent to secure this.[48] Early in 1002, and before Emma's arrival, the ealdorman of Essex, Leofsige, was disgraced and exiled for killing a king's high reeve, Æfic, previously if not still the steward of the princes' household. These apparently unconnected events are drawn together by a thread which links them all to the death of the old queen and the changes to be anticipated from the arrival of the new one. Leofsige had risen through the æthelings' household. His appointment had been secured through the petition of a female relative, Æthelgifu, to Ælfthryth, and his subsequent promotion to ealdorman of Essex had occurred in the early 990s when the dowager queen was more politically active, if not emerging from a period of retirement.[49] His fall now, in a dispute with a man

[44] Dudo, pp 288–9 for that of Emma, Hugh's daughter, which Richard I offered to return when she died without children; Dudo, p 192 for Gerloc's marriage to the count of Poitou. Some hyperbole may be suspected in this account.

[45] William of Jumièges, Bk V cap 10, Vol II, p 22.

[46] William of Jumièges Bk V cap 4, Vol II, pp 10–14, told in relation to the marriage to Emma. Douglas 1944 and Fauroux, no 214 suggest that Gunnor's own family held land in this area, but van Houts 1989 argues persuasively for their origins in Upper Normandy.

[47] S 898.

[48] S 904.

[49] See Will of Æthelgifu.

who had himself been close to Ælfthryth and the æthelings in the 990s,[50] is no coincidence. It was connected with the uncertainties which a change of queen at court entailed: the removal of old protections and the jockeying for new positions. Others may well have been involved.[51] At a more mundane level, there were opportunities for those who served the new queen, like perhaps the Godwine who received a land grant late in 1002, and a rippling effect, on, for example, the royal servants who held land cheek-by-jowl with Bradford on Avon, granted to Shaftesbury in the interregnum between queens.[52] The beginning of a new reign in tenth-century England was normally marked by a flurry of land grants, as a new king established himself, his household and his servants. The arrival of a new queen was less far-reaching, but, as with kings, it brought its own opportunities just as the passing of the old regime left uncertainties. The years 1002–6 were a turning point in Æthelred's reign.[53] The revolution began close to the palace and in connection with a change of queen.

Most intimately involved were the members of the royal family itself. The princes were unusually prominent in 1001–2. They were with their father in Kent late in 1001 and early in 1002. They were there when Shaftesbury received land to harbour their murdered uncle's relics; a man killed in the interests of an ætheling's claim to the throne, of whose murder their grandmother had been suspected. They were there when Wherwell received a confirmation of land belonging to the nunnery which Ælfthryth had held in her own hands, and of the Æthelings' Dean, which Ælfthryth had also held. In the interregnum between queens, Wherwell sought to protect itself in the face of the loss of its patroness, both against a new queen, and against other members of the royal family. Now if not earlier the æthelings' sister, its future abbess, joined the Wherwell community. Shaftesbury sought to capitalize on the death of Ælfthryth, a woman whose feelings for the nunnery which

---

[50] See R 66.

[51] Amongst Leofsige's relatives, a woman Leoftæt had forfeited her land by 1005, when the king sold it for the foundation of Eynsham abbey, S 911. Leoftæt is an unusual name, found in the will of Æthelgifu, in a context which suggests it belongs to a relative of the testatrix, again in S 911, but also in S 877, a vernacular record, where her son is a witness, listed in a record associated with a later grant of lands to Queen Ælfthryth. This record is unusual in its use of matronymics, which may be linked to the fact that it records land which passed to the queen. If the matronymics indicate women associated with her in some way, then Wulfric Spott, who here appears as 'Wulfric Wulfrune's son', should perhaps be linked to Ælfthryth and her household or that of the æthelings; some of his surviving relatives were associated with the ætheling Athelstan later. It is possible that Wulfric Spott's family's fall begins from this change of queens, though their connections may be not merely with Ælfthryth, but also with Æthelred's first wife.

[52] S 867.

[53] See Stafford 1979, and Keynes 1980, p 209ff.

sheltered the relics of her murdered stepson could never have been warm.[54] Waiting for the arrival of Emma was a time for fears and claims among the royal family and the religious houses closely associated with its female members.

In 1001–2 family politics and national concerns chimed closely together. Æthelings' Dean, the site of the traumatic encounter of the Hampshire forces and the Viking fleet in May 1001, was given, perhaps with the king's own daughter, to Wherwell. The protectors of the bones of a murdered brother were enriched. These were offerings for victory, expiation, with the old queen as a useful scapegoat. Emma's marriage was a part of all this. She came as an expression of peace agreements against the attackers. She was given the name of Ælfgifu, a saintly ancestress, and one who lay beside Edward the Martyr at Shaftesbury. And her first son was named Edward, after the son of Alfred, victor against Danish settlers, and after his great-grandson, the martyr king. She was a peace-maker, of a particular kind, but one whose arrival had already provoked tension and fear.

'And then in the spring the Lady, Richard's daughter, came to this land.'

How much was hidden behind the Chronicler's bald statement.

2 1002–1016: Wife of the King and Mother of his Children

The successful attack on Exeter by the Danes in 1003 was blamed on Emma's French reeve, Hugh. The scapegoating is obvious and the judgement retrospective, but the Chronicler's linking of the attack and the queen may not be wide of the mark. Swein's attack was allegedly in retaliation for the death of his sister in the St Brice day massacre in November 1002. Exeter's connections with queens and royal child-rearing were already established. Part of the dower of the new queen, to which Danish connections with Normandy if not England would have alerted Swein, it was an especially apposite target.[55] The attack may have been a deliberate response to the marriage which had been designed to cut off the Danish armies from Norman harbours. A peace-making marriage may, as so often, merely have stimulated new violence. Within England a new queen stood in danger of retaining the suspect identity of an outsider, a situation frozen in the later memory of her

[54] Shaftesbury's only other grant of land in Æthelred's reign was in 984, when Ælfthryth retired from court, S 850 wrongly dating it to 983. The land in question had belonged to a former queen.

[55] Cf Conner 1993, p 30, stressing the link between the town and the sons of Edgar.

French reeve. But in 1004 or 1005 Emma gave birth to a son. A new queen became a more assured member of the family when she produced its children.

Emma's life during Æthelred's reign seems to be dominated by marriage and children. There are no records of her patronage from this date, or of her action or intervention on behalf of followers. Her appearance in witness lists cluster in 1002, and in 1004–5, 1007–8 and 1011–12. 1002, 1007 and 1012 saw the augmentation or re-arrangements of her lands: in 1012 she received a holding in Winchester, in 1002 and 1007 reeves with responsibility for her lands may have been appointed.[56] The year 1002 is obviously the year of her marriage, perhaps the others signal the births of her three children: Edward born by 1005; Alfred by 1013,[57] perhaps her daughter Godgifu c. 1007. Ælfthryth's first appearance in witness lists had been connected to childbirth. The birth of children was perhaps marked by new land grants, as by gifts from mother to child. Westminster later claimed that Emma had given Edward Islip and Marston as a first gift on the day of his birth.[58] If inclusion and ranking in witness lists is a guide, from 1004–7 Emma was more important than Ælfthryth had been by the 990s,[59] though like Ælfthryth then her importance is firmly linked to that of the royal family more widely; Emma was invariably in the company of the princes. The most likely date for the marriage of two if not three of her stepdaughters to leading nobles is 1007.[60] It is the royal family as a whole which is prominent in these years. During the turbulent changes in court and kingdom now, the unity of the royal family was emphasized or demanded. The new regime was cemented by a series of marriages of Emma's stepdaughters. The stress on the royal family, like the changes at court, began in the period of negotiations about Æthelred's remarriage; unlike those changes, it continued for the rest of the reign.

The presence of a new queen and the birth of a new potential heir are keys to this emphasis. It was later claimed that an oath was sworn whilst Emma carried Edward, that if the child were a boy, he would be awaited as the king who would rule over the whole race of the English.[61] The

[56] S 925, 1012; Godwine, the recipient of land in S 902 may have been her servant, similarly perhaps Ælfgar the reeve, receiving land in 1007, S 915.

[57] S 925, 1012 may have special reference to Alfred's birth. The charter is concerned with legitimacy and birth; it refers to the legitimacy of her marriage, and its dating clause speaks of the birth of the Lamb of God 'de utero parthenali'.

[58] *Writs* 104.

[59] Judged by the proportion of charters in which she appears and position in the witness list; Ælfthryth and the princes were usually after the bishops in the 990s, whereas Emma and the princes from 1005 are usually immediately after the king.

[60] The husbands of two of them, Eadric and Uhtred, were appointed about now.

[61] *VitaEd*, pp 7–8.

circumstances of Emma's marriage were certainly favourable to the making of some provision for her sons, and previous practice supported the affirmation of her sons as throneworthy, but nothing in Æthelred's reign itself suggests such a firm promise of the succession. Any hints of precedence or designation after 1004 pointed to Athelstan, the eldest son, not Edward, and after Athelstan's death to his eldest surviving brother, Edmund. When Athelstan died he was buried in the Old Minster, Winchester, the first non-king to be buried at Winchester since Edward the Elder's brother, Æthelweard.[62] His special royal status was as marked in death as in life. Yet all of this underlines rather than excludes family tension. The history of the tenth-century royal family did not foster fraternal love, especially not among stepbrothers. Athelstan was singled out, but especially by his own supporters, for example at Burton in the North Midlands.[63] If his death was marked as kingly, that was in the circumstances of 1014, in what was undoubtedly a developing family crisis. We do not need to argue for a firm promise to Edward to recognize that a stepmother at court and new princes introduced doubt and suspicion into the royal family. Edward and Alfred were both given kingly names, they were æthelings, and their mother's queenship and the legitimacy of her marriage to Æthelred was stressed in what seem to have been the years of their births.[64] Their older brothers had reason to fear them, and may have acted to exclude them from succession. There is a strange late story that Edward was brought to Ely as a child by Æthelred and Emma, offered on the altar, and then raised for some time there, learning the psalms and hymns with the other boys.[65] This may simply garble Edward's fostering at Ely in the light of later traditions of his celibate sanctity. But monastic profession was a time-honoured way of side-tracking claimants to the throne and someone may have attempted to point the young Edward in that direction. Emma's arrival inevitably opened up succession questions; all the arguments may not have gone her way.

The question of royal succession was complicated by the increasing military pressures of the latter part of Æthelred's reign. Emma's eldest son was named Edward and her second Alfred, both named for successful military ancestors who had been victorious against the Danes. The pattern of Emma's appearances at court in these years is a family one, but in the context of increasing warfare. The military nature of the court and

---

[62] See above p 91.

[63] See above p 86.

[64] Emma is *regina* in 1005, S 910 and 911, the first charters in which Edward occurs as a witness, also in S 916, 1007 and S 926, 1012. For S 925, also 1012, see above nn 56 and 57.

[65] *LE*, Bk 2 cap 91, pp 160–1. The story was attested to by old monks who had witnessed it, Barlow 1970, pp 32–3.

its activities separated her from it, just as it recast the relationship between Æthelred and his eldest sons.[66] There are not one but two royal families at this date, divided less by different mothers than by age. The older princes, young men of warrior age, were with their father, involved in military planning and action. The younger remained with their mother and stepmother, the queen, or more correctly with foster parents, but attached in some way to her and her household.[67] In 1013, the family split along different lines. When Swein conquered England, Emma and her sons were sent to Normandy, apparently separately: Emma with the abbot of Peterborough, Ælfsige, Edward and Alfred with the bishop of London. Æthelred followed them, but the older princes, including Eadwig, hitherto rarely associated with his older brothers, remained behind. If the two royal families had hitherto been divided along lines of age and military capacity, they were now split into rival groups of stepbrothers. Whatever earlier tensions had existed in the royal family, they took particular shape in the critical years 1013–14.

Æthelred's flight could have been seen as a temporary retreat, or an abdication. The death of Swein on 3 February 1014 merely exacerbated the doubt. Was Æthelred to return, was Swein's son Cnut to be king, or was one or other of the princes, still in England, to press his claims? Æthelred returned in the spring, Cnut was chosen as king by the Danish army, and almost certainly Athelstan or his brother Edmund made moves in the early months of the year which in retrospect after their father's return looked treacherous. Whilst Athelstan or Edmund had tasted power, their father had been in Normandy, a guest of their stepmother Emma's brother, accompanied by their stepbrothers, whose claims their mother's family would have been free to press. Edward was entrusted with his father's response in the negotiations between Æthelred and the English counsellors. Now, if not before, Æthelred would have been made aware of his older sons' actions in his absence; any growing preference for Edward, fostered by his Norman uncles, could have become firmer. The actions of those older sons are lost, and thus all interpretations of 1014 are conjectural.[68] But within a year of his father's return Edmund was in open rebellion, marrying the widow of a man who had been accused of a crime sufficient to lead to his disappropriation. His older brother Athelstan had died unmarried; Edmund's taking of a bride and his specific choice signalled his rejection of whatever accord had existed between father and older sons. The succession and family politics were central to all this. The burial of Athelstan at the Old Minster at this juncture was a symbolic recognition of his and his full brothers'

[66] Cf Nelson 1991b for similar suggestions re Alfred's later years.
[67] *Writs* 93 for Edward the Confessor's fostermother, Leofrun.
[68] For different interpretations cf Stafford 1979 and 1989 and Keynes, 1980 and 1986.

throneworthiness, if not an act of reconciliation between father and older sons. The funeral in June or July 1014 must have been a tense family affair.[69]

The years 1013–14 introduced new arguments into the inheritance question. Whatever the Norman interlude did for the claims of her sons, it affirmed Emma's importance to her husband. She returned with him to England.[70] There, on 23 April 1016 he died, leaving her a widow for the first time.

Later sources paid scant attention to the years 1002–16 as a period of Emma's life; even in her own account they were irrelevant. It has proved possible to supply some of their detail: to fill with meaning her identity as 'Richard's daughter'; to understand the circumstances of her marriage and the significance of her arrival in England; to appreciate the problems of her family situation and her relations with her stepsons. It has been less easy to flesh out her political activity in these years. From 1002 to 1016 Emma appeared as a wife and mother; even her title in the charters of these years is most frequently *conlaterana regis*, she who is at the king's side. Her association was with princes and family, with childbirth and child-rearing, albeit at one remove. Family politics in which she would have played a part are to the fore, but she was the mother of a possible, but at this stage unlikely, future king. Marriage and childbirth may be one of the more passive stages of a woman's life, though they had not prevented a tenth-century French queen like Gerberga from playing a full, even a military, role. Emma's situation also included her Norman/Danish birth. This had been critical in her marriage, but may have been a source of trouble and suspicion in the years 1002–16 as England came under ever increasing Danish attack. That suspicion would be masked in sources written in or after 1016, in whose eyes Emma was now primarily an English queen. A military court and military politics were no help to a queen's influence, perhaps particularly one 'Danish born on both sides', whose peace-making marriage had proved singularly ineffective in closing off Norman aid to England's Danish attackers. The years 1002–16 are arguably the stage of Emma's career when she was most strongly gendered as a woman, in marriage, childbirth and military incapacity, when she was most feminine, though it was the combination of circumstances, not her gender alone, which were her weakness. The first decade or so of Emma's career, like the last, were her least powerful. The years 1013–14 may have begun to change that. Æthelred's death certainly was no ending for his widow, but an important new beginning.

[69] Keynes 1980, p 267 for date.

[70] For the question of whether or not she was in England in 1014–16 see Keynes 1991, pp 176–7. It is extremely unlikely that she would have been absent at this critical juncture.

3 1016–35: Queen and King's Wife

The struggle for the throne which ensued on the death of Æthelred was between Edmund and Cnut. Earlier promises or hints or changes of plan there may have been; but the eleven- or twelve-year-old Edward had no chance of making good a claim to a throne disputed by an external attacker with a Danish fleet. Emma remained in London, where her husband had died and Edmund had been chosen king. The city was besieged twice in the course of the year before Edmund and Cnut's decision to divide the kingdom after the battle of Ashingdon, on 18 October. The division left London at Cnut's mercy, to buy peace for itself and still to serve as winter quarters for his army. Emma's role in these events is unknown. In all accounts in which she is mentioned, she is associated with London whose heroic resistance was remembered in the North, as well as in England; but how actively or passively we cannot tell. We do not know whether she fled the city, was spirited away to safe keeping or, perhaps more likely, was captured during the temporary or final occupation. Her son Edward had left England and was at Ghent by Christmas 1016.[71] Edmund had died on November 30 and Cnut had seized the rule of all England.

Emma's situation in 1016–17 was a difficult one. Her husband was dead, and his English successor was her stepson, with whom relations after 1014 cannot have been easy. That stepson had a wife, whose family came from precisely that North Midlands area where a large part of Emma's dower lands lay, and whose surviving relatives had little reason to feel loyalty to Æthelred or his widow. Edmund already had one if not two sons, Edmund and Edward; his choice of recent dynastic names for both asserted both his and their claims to the throne.[72] Edmund's rival for the throne was a Dane, who had also married into the same North Midlands family as Edmund. Both men saw the importance of this area for holding North–South communications, a motive for the queen's own endowment here. Emma's sons had apparently fled the country before the end of 1016. Æthelred's death left his second wife a widow and a stepmother; even without the complications of Danish conquest the history of the tenth-century royal family meant that the situation facing Emma would have been fraught with problems. In the event, the normal uncertainties of widowhood were compounded by foreign conquest, by the passing of the throne to her stepson's line and by the specific threats to a large section of her dower lands.

Edward was wise to flee in 1016. Cnut was ruthless in his actions towards Æthelred's surviving male line. Edmund's full brother and the

---

[71] Keynes 1991, pp 177–81.
[72] Unless they were twins one at least of these sons must have been born before his death.

only remaining son of the earlier marriage(s), Eadwig, was exiled in 1017, and murdered at some later date after his return to England. He was buried at Tavistock, the family foundation of his grandmother Ælfthryth,[73] possibly after attempting to rally some resistance in the South West. The young sons of Edmund were despatched to the king of the Swedes, to be disposed of there. In these circumstances we might have expected Emma to return, like many royal widows before her, to her native family. That she did not may be an indication that Cnut had her closely guarded in 1016–17. He may already have decided to follow the example of his own father, Swein, who marked his superiority over Olaf, king of the Swedes, by marrying Olaf's father Erik's widow.[74] Such an arrangement could have been in his mind even before Edmund's death. Edmund, like Olaf, appears as a tributary king; the kingdom was divided but payment was made, apparently from the whole kingdom, for Cnut's army.[75] Forced marriage was a metaphor for conquest in the skaldic verse sung at Cnut's court.[76] In 1016 forced marriage might seem a way of underscoring conquest for the Danes; forced marriage with Edmund's stepmother underlining superiority over a king whom they saw as tributary. If Emma fell into Cnut's hands during or after the siege of London, she was a God-sent opportunity to make his point.

The marriage, however, did not take place until 1017, when Cnut ordered Emma to be fetched. By now his conquest had taken a different turn, and the meaning of the forthcoming marriage changed with it. Edmund's death had allowed Cnut to take all the kingdom under his control. A meeting of the English nobles late in 1016 or early in 1017 in London had confirmed the disinheritance of Edmund's sons and the other æthelings;[77] oaths had been sworn and payments promised. Later in 1017 another meeting took place at which a peace was made between Cnut and the great men and all the people, promising firm friendship and the setting aside of all enmities, again sealed with oaths.[78] Possibly on the same occasion, possibly at yet another meeting in 1017, Archbishop Lyfing consecrated Cnut as king.[79] Since these meetings are not datable, we cannot know which if any of them was associated with the marriage to Emma, an event which took place before 1 August, presumably late in July 1017.[80] Meetings and marriage, however, belong not to the stage of conquest, division and overlordship, but rather to the acceptance of Cnut

[73] William of Malmesbury, *DGRA*, Bk I, cap 180, p 218 and cf Finberg 1946.
[74] Sawyer 1994, pp 14–15.
[75] *ASC*, MSS C, D and E s.a. 1016.
[76] Frank 1994, p 122.
[77] *Fl Wig* s.a. 1016.
[78] *Fl Wig* s.a. 1017.
[79] Ralph de Diceto, I p 169.
[80] See *ASC*, MSS C, D and E s.a.

as king of all England and the establishment of peace and friendship, however constrained, between the English and their conqueror. It is associated also with the coronation of Cnut and of Emma herself. By the time the marriage occurred it thus signified not merely the domination of a conqueror over the conquered, but the friendship and peace between them.[81]

It should be read alongside the legal documents which record aspects of that peace.[82] Their precise relationships to any decisions made at meetings between 1016 and 1018 is difficult to establish,[83] but they represent at least an edited version of those decisions as seen through the eyes of Archbishop Wulfstan of York, at most the agenda of the English leaders and bishops in a form acceptable to Cnut. They are remarkable for their reiteration of the laws of Æthelred and Edgar. They are a bridge and continuity between the English kingship of Æthelred and a foreign conqueror now English king. The text known as 'D', which seems to represent the outcome of a particularly important meeting between king and English leaders, 'fully established peace and friendship between the Danes and the English and put an end to all their former enmity'.[84] Peace and friendship were affirmed against a background of continuing tension and insecurity: the text moves from the general statements about loyalty to the king in Æthelred's laws to a specific injunction of personal loyalty to Cnut and it ends with a general admonition to allow foreigners to live in peace.[85] It promulgates the feast of Edward the Martyr, Æthelred's brother, whose murder ushered in Æthelred's reign. The memory of Edward simultaneously connected Cnut's reign with the traditions of English kingship whilst undermining Æthelred's prestige and that of his surviving progeny, claimants to the English throne.[86] This legal text is

---

[81] For the opposite view, that the marriage could not have been part of the reconciliation of the English, see Keynes 1991, p 183 and n 32, following A. Campbell.

[82] These include the record in CCCC 201, known as 'D', usually dated to 1018 on the basis of the fact that both it and the meeting at Oxford in that year were concerned with the agreement to observe the 'Good old law' of King Edgar, the two codes I and II Cnut, and probably the compilation Edward and Guthrum, whose prologue associates it with the time 'when the English and the Danes fully established peace and friendship between themselves'. With its reference to two kings who ruled different parts of England it is tempting to place this very early and see it as Wulfstan's version of or commentary on the division between Edmund and Cnut. 'D' may belong to 1018, but an association with one or other of the meetings of 1017 is possible. All are printed Liebermann, except 'D' for which see Kennedy 1983. Kennedy passim but esp p 69 n 61 and 70 for 'D' as a political rather than a legal witness to these years.

[83] See e.g. Stafford 1982, Kennedy 1983 and Lawson 1994.

[84] Kennedy 1983, p 72.

[85] Kennedy 1983, pp 72 and 80–81; cf Garnett 1986a, p 129 for the later derivation of William I's law from D and I Cnut 1.

[86] Discussed Rollason 1989, pp 143–4, and cf Ridyard 1988, pp 154–71. Rollason's arguments might make more allowance for simultaneous, differing meanings of the cult.

datable within a year of the marriage with Emma and may even have accompanied it. The marriage too established peace between English and Dane, through a woman who could embody the continuity which the legal texts sought. That continuity was with Æthelred's reign, but also with a longer English past, through a woman whose name change in 1002 had linked her to a sanctified dynasty. The negotiations between English and Cnut which took up much of 1017 delayed the marriage, which was part of them. It may be no coincidence that the legal text D included a section on the marriage of widows, no earlier than a year and a day after their husband's death and with their own consent. Emma would later stress that her marriage brought peace, that it was an equal union, freely chosen. Such statements are hindsight, but they capture some of the hopes and aspirations of the participants at the time.[87]

Some Norman sources later claimed that Emma's Norman family had consented to the marriage and supported it,[88] but their attitude at the time is not so clear. They may have been embarrassed by it, and particularly by their failure to control it; the contemporary satirist who wrote *Semiramis* played on that. It was presented by the historian of the dukes, William of Jumièges, as almost a marriage by capture,[89] which served to salvage some dignity from the situation. There is certainly no reason to believe that Emma was in Normandy, wooed and brought from there in 1017.[90] There is, nonetheless, a Norman dimension to the match, half recognized by chroniclers like Ralph Glaber, who felt that the Norman duke must have been involved. Emma was the sister of the Norman ruler, and her sons had taken refuge there. From Cnut's point of view, a marriage to her, especially one which produced children, might neutralize or inhibit Norman support for their claims. The Normans may have been consulted, even though the match should not be seen as one negotiated with them. The English Chronicler who recorded it at the time certainly felt that Emma was married as Æthelred's widow *and* as Richard's daughter. But it is as part of his negotiations with the English that Cnut's marriage with Emma should chiefly be seen; and it is in this context that the likelihood of promises concerning the succession and in relation to Cnut's existing wife and children should largely be weighed.

[87] Van Houts 1984, p 88 suggested that the marriage was delayed because of the laws about widow remarriage. I agree with Lawson 1993, p 86 that the circumstances make this unlikely. However, I do think that the inclusion of this section on widows, by no means necessary, indicates that widow remarriage had some significance for its drafters.

[88] See *Inventio . . . sancti Vulfranni*, van Houts 1989b, p 251 in the early 1050s and cf Ralph Glaber, Bk II cap 3, p 54 suggesting that the marriage sealed a peace between Cnut and Richard.

[89] William of Jumièges, Bk 5 cap 8, vol II, pp 20–1 and n 6.

[90] Contra my statement, 1982 p 183. See Keynes 1991 for further discussion.

When Cnut married Emma in 1017 he already had a wife, Ælfgifu of Northampton, and one or more sons. Archbishop Wulfstan included a section on the remarriage of widows in the legal texts of these years, but maintained a tactful silence on the issues of divorce, concubinage and polygamy.[91] Ælfgifu was an Englishwoman, daughter of a murdered English ealdorman and member of a powerful North Midlands family. She had been a desirable bride for Cnut when he and his father were conquering England, even when he was briefly king of its northern and eastern parts. But she and her sons, present or future, did not have the same meanings and significance for the English or for Cnut in 1017 as Emma did. If John of Worcester's account of the events of 1016 can be trusted, the succession was certainly a question in 1016–17. It took the pressing form of overriding the division between Edmund and Cnut in favour of Cnut holding all England after Edmund's death, but this entailed disinheriting and disposing of existing æthelings. The negotiations and peace-makings of 1017 are likely to have included a forward look to the succession. In the circumstances, the promise to a son of Emma and Cnut, which Emma later claimed, was probably made. Whether Ælfgifu of Northampton was then dismissed is more debatable. She remained sufficiently in favour to be sent with her son Swein to rule Norway in the latter part of the reign. Emma's path and hers were, as we shall see, to cross again.

Emma would claim in 1040–1 that her marriage to Cnut had been one of equals, in which she had exercised considerable bargaining power and freedom. The woman whom Cnut 'ordered to be fetched' in 1017 was not, however, the woman of the early 1040s. Emma was important to Cnut: she could offer expertise in English politics, some form of link with her natal family, and if, as seems probable, she had learnt Danish in her native Normandy, that can only have been an advantage to the new conqueror. Moreover in 1017 as opposed to 1002 the age balance was more in Emma's favour. This was not a marriage of a young foreign woman to an established middle-aged king, but of a woman of thirty or more to a man no older, and possibly substantially younger. This has potential for the development of the partnership between husband and wife *during* the marriage rather than for the circumstances of its *inception*. Emma's freedom in 1017 was minimal; the order to fetch her even hints at her imprisonment.[92] In 1002 and 1017 Emma was at her most powerless, was most a pawn of others' politics and interests – though it was precisely as a result of those politics and interests that she was placed and remained in a position of future power.

[91] Though some of these do feature in the latest of the legal texts of these years, I and II Cnut, see II Cnut 50, 50.1, 54.1 and especially 55 on the irregular marriages of foreigners.
[92] Keynes 1991, p 182.

The marriage of a predecessor's widow was relatively common in the early middle ages. Brunhild had been sought by the young Merovech for the claims she carried to her former husband Sigibert's kingdom; Theudechild is alleged to have offered herself and her treasure to King Guntram; in early Lombard Italy the marriage of a widow to the next claimant was a regular occurrence.[93] Nearer in date, the marriage of Adelaide, daughter of a king of Burgundy and widow of a king of Italy, to Otto I, Ottonian king and future emperor, was one of the most important political unions of the tenth century and played a role in the Ottonian taking and control of Italy. Foreign brides were especially likely to be remarried in this way, both for the alllliances they represented and perhaps because their natal kin were more remote and less able or willing to offer protection. Brunhild like Emma was a foreign bride remarried, and Anne of Kiev would be another later in the eleventh century. One of Athelstan's sisters, Eadgifu, married to Charles the Simple, became the wife of an aspiring great noble in her widowhood. The last foreign bride in England, Judith, daughter of Charles the Bald and widow of Æthelwulf of Wessex, was married in her widowhood by Æthelwulf's rebellious son, her own stepson Æthelbald. He took over the whole kingdom at his father's death. In taking his father's widow he took over the prestige of the Carolingian Imperial match and outmanoeuvred brothers with strong claims.

Swein's taking of his enemy Erik's widow in a gesture of domination was thus only one form of such matches. All must be read in context and with close attention to the meanings they have at the time and those they acquire as time goes by. Marriage is a flexible and protean diplomatic instrument. In the early eleventh century it could simultaneously be conceived as a partnership of equals, as a hierarchy, or as a conquest and acquisition resulting in domination. It could be alliance or subordination. The woman involved could symbolize and represent her family of birth, but marriage itself identified her increasingly with her family of adoption. As a widow she could carry both identities, and retained some of those of her former husband.[94] United with her husband but always separate in some respects, she could represent the different, could symbolize their subjection, but also reconcile them to the new regime. Emma meant all these things in 1016–17 depending on who was looking at her marriage and when. Marriage is not a once and for all event. It inaugurates a union whose balance and significance changes over time. Different aspects of the original union can thus assume importance in retrospect, and Emma, in the later perspective of the *Encomium*, might be accused of editing 1017. But the meaning of Emma's marriage was not fixed in 1017, for

---

[93] Discussion of all this in Stafford 1983 and see also Nelson 1978.
[94] Cf for this Nelson 1978 on Brunhild, esp p 40ff.

her or for others. The freedom and self-determination she claimed to have exercised in the original match seem very unlikely, though there can be little doubt that she was important to Cnut and the establishment of his conquest. There can, however, be no question that Emma's importance grew during Cnut's reign: all the evidence points to this as the period of greatest power and influence in her career. The potential for such development was already present in 1017, in the marriage and its meanings and in the coronation which followed if it did not accompany it.

For sections of the English in 1017 Emma was especially an English queen. Already crowned and anointed in 1002, Emma was, perhaps like Ælfthryth in 973, crowned again along with Cnut in 1017. The coronation and consecration finally established Cnut as an English king, and remained important in his eyes and in the eyes of others. Cnut was later represented at Winchester receiving the crown from heaven, and his first coinage issue, Quatrefoil, shows him wearing a crown, the first coinage so to present an English king since Edgar's issue about the time of his Imperial coronation.[95] Crowns were important to Cnut. He gave crowns to Winchester if not Canterbury, and may have had the English crown remodelled on German Imperial lines.[96] A revised version of the coronation *ordo* was produced for this Danish conqueror, and for his Queen. In it Emma was glorified as Queen, of the English and the Anglo-Saxons; the English identity so important in her marriage was highlighted. So too was her share in Cnut's rule. No earlier version of the English Queen's *ordo* affirms Queenly power so openly. The coronation no more handed Emma ready-made power than her marriage did. But like the marriage, it offered potential meanings which in the right circumstances she might later develop.

Emma's appearances in the witness lists, together with the titles used of her now, mark her out among early English queens. In 1018–19 she is listed after or between the archbishops, and twice as the king's wife;[97] from then on she is after the king, and in Winchester charters of 1033 jointly associated in his witness and grant: 'I Cnut king of the

[95] Lawson 1993, pp 82–3. Unfortunately Quatrefoil cannot be securely dated, so cannot throw any more light on the precise date of Cnut's coronation; for an argument for Autumn 1017 and a survey of other proposed dates, see Jonsson 1994, pp 200–201.

[96] Lawson 1993, pp 136–8.

[97] S 955 and 956 for her as *thoro consecrata regio* and *eiusdem regis conlaterana*. Keynes 1991 n 57 sees this as indicating a lower status than at the end of Æthelred's reign, though at that time, in S 916 and 923, she had been after or between the archbishops, and was not often *regina*. The æthelings and their importance have an impact on her placing in Æthelred's reign. It may be that we should especially note the prominence and importance of the archbishops at the beginning of Cnut's reign. There is also a SW pattern here, five of the charters in which she appears after the archbishops, including the only examples from later in the reign, are from Exeter/South West, S 951, 953, 962, 963, 971.

English with my Queen Ælfgyfu confirm my own gift with royal confirmation.'[98] *Regina*, Queen, is her regular title;[99] during Cnut's reign she is
only rarely called a consecrated wife, and never the mother of future
kings, never dependent on the æthelings for her position.[100] She appears
in lay as well as ecclesiastical grants, and for a range of beneficiaries. We
must return to Eadgifu during her sons' reigns for any approach to this
predominance; and no earlier woman had been accorded such recognition during her husband's lifetime. Nor is that recognition confined to the
diploma witness lists. The bulk of Emma's traceable patronage is datable
1017–35; and it is a patronage which parallels rather than complements
that of her husband. It is now that her influence is sought or acknowledged in a range of transactions, from land purchases and the confirmation of episcopal appointments to the making of wills.[101] It is now that
she is presented visually at Winchester as a parallel of Mary on earth; it
is now that Mary herself is presented as a Queen treading Arius under-
foot as Emma had been adjured to root out heresy at her consecration.
Early medieval queens often achieved the height of their power and
influence as the mothers of royal sons. At this stage of her career, and in
these circumstances, Emma demonstrates the potential power of a wife
and Queen.

At the beginning of the reign, circumstances meant continuing tension
between the English, or some of them, and Cnut. Emma's public appearances were often at gestures of conciliation designed to defuse political
opposition. She may have been present at the consecration of the church
at Ashingdon in 1020, celebrating Cnut's victory, but also commemorat-
ing the English dead.[102] She and her infant Harthacnut played a major
role in the movement of Archbishop Ælfheah's relics from London to
Canterbury in June 1023. She and her son met the body at Rochester and
accompanied it with glory, joy and songs of praise on its journey to the
cathedral.[103] Once arrived there she offered precious gifts in recognition

[98] S 970 and 972.
[99] She is *conlaterana regis* at New Minster and Abingdon, S 956, 964 and 967 – cf
Abingdon usage during Æthelred's reign. Yet by 1034 she is *regina* in the Abingdon charter,
S 973.
[100] Only in the strange witness list of S 936 does Harthacnut appear. His absence is
exaggerated by the lack of charters between 1023 and 1026, he may have been sent to
Denmark around the latter date. Whatever the reason for his absence, it is clear that
Emma's position is not associated with his.
[101] E.g. *Wills* 23, 27; R 81, 86; *Writs* 27; K 733. All this reinforces Heslop's arguments for
her patronage of manuscripts now along with Cnut.
[102] Much depends on the date of the royal family group, which includes her, listed in the
later copy of the *Thorney Liber Vitae*, BL Additional 40000, fo 10r. Its inclusion of
Harthacnut as king shows it may represent more than one visit or royal association, but
Thorkell and other earls date one important visit recorded in the *Liber Vitae* to 1020; see
Gerchow 1988, pp 190 and 326.
[103] *ASC*, MS D, s.a.

of Ælfheah's sanctity.[104] Here she was the English Queen receiving the body of an English martyr murdered by Danes in 1011. She was also Cnut's wife and his heir's mother, associating the new dynasty in expiation and conciliation. Already that new dynasty was ruling Denmark as well as England, and Emma's new circumstances included a husband often absent in Scandinavia. The arrangements for that may have given Emma a form of regency, as Richard of Devizes later claimed; though if so it was alongside the archbishops and great earls like Thorkell and Godwine, who are more clearly identifiable as acting in the king's name. The role of such regency in enhancing Emma's position is impossible to calculate.

Emma's circumstances placed her as a symbol of reconciliation, and a co-ruling wife, but also, once again, as a second wife. The royal family groups which visited Thorney in the 1020s may have included Ælfgifu of Northampton as well as Ælfgifu/Emma.[105] Emma in the *Encomium* dismissed Ælfgifu as a nameless concubine, but in reality she was not so easily set aside. It was far from unprecedented for a polygamous or serial monogamous king to keep his first wife or return to her after a second marriage. In 1009–10 Bertha, Robert the Pious' first wife, had come close to returning to Robert's bed, even though he had been married to Constance for four or five years and she had already borne him a son.[106] Whether or not Ælfgifu of Northampton was so openly in evidence after 1017, she was still alive, and unlike Bertha she had sons by the king, sons who were not easily ignored.[107] Both had been given Danish royal names: the eldest, Swein, named for Cnut's father, the second, Harold, for his grandfather. When Emma bore Harthacnut, it was to his great-grandfather's generation that Cnut had to turn to recognize the boy's inclusion in the dynasty. Ælfgifu's own union had stronger claims than Emma's propaganda allowed. 'Concubine' is a term of abuse as much as a technical description of marital status. Its abusive potential derives from the doubt it sows about inheritance claims on behalf of a woman and her children. When it is used retrospectively and partially, as Emma used it in the *Encomium*, it cannot be taken as a cool legal appraisal.

---

[104] *Translation of Saint Ælfheah* by Osbern, p 312. I have followed the Chronicle for the overall account, since it is less *parti pris* towards Canterbury than Osbern, but have assumed that his details of her role at Canterbury are accurate.

[105] An Ælfgifu is one of the royal family group in BL Additional 40000 fo 10r. Whitelock identified this as a gloss on Emma, but Gerchow p 190 suggests it is Ælfgifu of Northampton and points to the inclusion of her son Harold, *rex*. Unfortunately we cannot be sure whether this Harold is her son, or Harold Cnut's brother; nor whether the list conflates a visit in the 1020s with one after 1037, when Harold and his mother could have visited together. Cf Lawson 1993, pp 131–2.

[106] Duby 1978, p 46 and n 75.

[107] Lawson 1993, p 131 suggests she was established at Northampton.

Ælfgifu of Northampton was the daughter of a powerful North East Midlands family and Cnut's needs for English allies at the time of the union point to some formalities to protect her and her children. Her children's naming is perhaps the best indication of their father's intentions to recognize their claims at the time of the match. But her union with Cnut probably lacked some property exchanges, and was vulnerable both in 1017 and later. The marriage of Emma and Cnut itself redefined that of Ælfgifu and Cnut, but it did not destroy all the claims of its children. Ælfgifu was sent with her son Swein to rule Norway after the battle of Sticklestad in July 1030. Whatever promises were made about Emma's sons in 1017, they had not disinherited Ælfgifu's. Harthacnut may have been recognized as a more throneworthy heir. In the promises made in 1017 his throneworthiness applied especially to England, of which his father was conqueror and his mother Queen. Cnut's acquisition of the patrimonial inheritance of Denmark and then of Norway changed the succession argument. Harthacnut, as the most legitimate son, was now in line for the rule of Denmark, where he was sent in 1026-8.[108] From now if not before Emma must have worried whether he was still in line for the English throne, especially once Ælfgifu's son was sent to rule Norway. By the later 1020s England was not the conquest with which a young king was coming to terms, but the acquisition of a ruler who was now in control of his Danish patrimony. England as the other acquired kingdom was an obvious inheritance for Harold, Ælfgifu's second son. There is no record of Cnut's arrangements and rearrangements about the succession, but Harold's presence in England at the time of his father's death may point to this as his share of the inheritance. At the very least it gave powerful *de facto* strength to his claims.

Emma's problems with princes did not stop at her new batch of stepsons. Her own sons by Æthelred were still alive, well and living with her brothers in Normandy. The Normans may actively have supported their claims, perhaps as early as 1022, more certainly in 1033.[109] In 1033 the young Henry I of France was in short-lived exile in Normandy. Duke Robert brought him to Fécamp. There Emma's sons in exile, Edward and Alfred, were given special precedence and included in the witness lists of charters, Edward as 'king'. Robert gathered a naval force at Fécamp, ostensibly to attack England on Edward and Alfred's behalf. In the event nothing came of it. The fleet was detained in Jersey and ended up at Mont St Michel, from where it proceeded to attack Brittany.[110] The seriousness

---

[108] See his coinage minted there for this date, Becker 1981, p 125 and Jonsson 1994, p 226.
[109] Keynes 1991 argues for continuous support, and at p 185 for a military threat as early as 1022; however, cf Lund 1994, p 36 suggesting that the expedition to the Isle of Wight of this year may have been to East Prussia, *Witland*, and against Thorkell not the Normans.
[110] William of Jumièges, Bk VI cap 9, vol II, pp 76–9; Keynes 1991 for a reconstruction of the charter evidence.

of this military support for Edward and Alfred must be open to question. It cannot be coincidence that this show of force occurred during Henry I's brief exile and in his presence. The refuge in Normandy of an exiled French king prompted the Norman duke to wheel out his other exiled kings-in-waiting and mount a suitable show of strength in their favour, one which, unsurprisingly, proved abortive. There had been better moments to attempt an attack on Cnut's England had that been a serious intention; the whole business was more for French consumption than English.

But such gestures have many audiences. News must have reached England; indeed Robert probably intended that it should. Marriage negotiations between Cnut and Robert in which Cnut's sister Estrith was joined to the Norman count may date from this time rather than from 1027.[111] At either date its aim was to neutralize claimants to the English throne, of whom Cnut was acutely aware in the late 1020s. In 1027 he had been in Rome, and had perhaps taken the opportunity to negotiate with the emperor about the grandsons of Æthelred still at large in central Europe. Negotiations may have begun now for the marriage of his daughter by Emma, Gunnhild, to the emperor's son Henry.[112] The year 1033 fed fears of princes-across-the-water and their would-be supporters, and not necessarily simply in Cnut's mind. Invasion from Normandy was not something English nobles would relish, and this political posturing on the other side of the Channel can have done little to win friends or support for Edward or Alfred on their attempted return in 1036.

Its impact on Emma herself is unknown, but must be conjectured. In similar circumstances in 1030, Gisela, empress and wife of Conrad II, was driven to take a public oath that she would not support the sons of her first marriage.[113] Her eldest son Ernst had led a revolt in an attempt to regain his duchy, and Gisela, 'holding her ill-advised son in less esteem than her wise husband', gave public assurances that she would not act against anyone on his behalf. Gisela like Emma found that serial marriage pitted motherhood against wifely duty, and she chose the latter 'a thing pitiable to recount, but praiseworthy to do'. Perhaps Emma like Gisela made some public display of her unity with her husband's not her sons' interests. The Winchester charters which join her witness most closely to that of Cnut date from 1033. In Wipo, Gisela had a sympathetic recorder of the quandaries of a woman caught between maternal feeling and wifely duty, or rather a recorder who was

[111] See Lawson 1993, pp 109–10; my suggestion of 1027 in Stafford 1989, p 75 should thus be hedged.
[112] See Adam of Bremen, Bk II cap 56, pp 116–17 and cap 65 p 125 speaking of negotiations for the marriage which involved a journey of Cnut and Conrad to Italy.
[113] Wipo, p 85.

convinced that a woman's loyalty to her husband should, in spite of
her divided loyalties, win through. Emma would have to make her own
arguments in the face of a more complicated outcome. We can only
speculate how far 1033 affected Emma's ability to help her sons in
1036, though it is likely to have made life more difficult for her and
more dangerous for them. The events of that year must have taught
their own lesson to Edward. Henry I's exile in Normandy, in flight
from rebellions in which *his* mother Constance had played a role
against him, had their own message about the reliability of maternal
feeling.

Emma during Cnut's reign seems to show us two separate and contradictory faces: on the one hand the powerful Queen, on the other the wife
and mother embroiled in family politics. Marriage showed Emma once
again a transacted and passive symbol, but even more than in 1002 it was
the source of that power and near-equality in terms of which Emma
herself redefined it in 1041–2. Emma's natal family may look sometimes
like a problem for her in these years, but it was also a web of relationships stretching from Poitiers to Rouen across which she and Cnut spun
their reputations as patrons and powerful givers. Emma's queenship at
this stage is not readily separable from her wifehood. It bears little or no
relationship to the careers of her sons, which diverged from hers to the
extent of geographical separation by the North Sea and the Channel.
Emma was, however, always closely connected with Cnut, and if anything her status rose during the marriage. Although no regency can be
demonstrated, it is difficult not to see this as linked to Cnut's position
first as a foreign conqueror, and increasingly as an absent king of several
kingdoms. Like the years 1002–16, Emma's life from 1017 to 1035 is
virtually unchronicled. In this case, however, the silence has hidden a
period of power and action. Her witnessing and patronage indicates the
political woman the details of whose activity have forever been lost. It
was now that she laid the basis without which her prominence between
1035 and 1042 is incomprehensible. Her weakness remained: the vulnerability of her own sons' claims, the binding up of her future survival with
theirs and the complications multiple marriages were storing up for
relations between her and them. These complications were to dominate
the next phase of her life, when motherhood was both her trump card
and her weakest suit.

4 1035–52: Widow and Mother

On 12 November 1035 Cnut died at Shaftesbury. Ensuing events demonstrated the doubts his marriages and his rule of many kingdoms had left
over the succession. Any arrangements he had made were challenged

amid questions of whether his death had left an interregnum for a known but absent king either in the whole of England or in part of a divided kingdom, of who was the best and rightful heir, and thus of who should be regent and for what.

Immediately after Cnut's death, Harold, his son by Ælfgifu of Northampton and the only claimant on the spot in England, took the throne. His coup is attested by the simple statement that Cnut died and Harold 'came to the throne',[114] by the calculations of his reign made once he had secured the throne in 1037, which dated it from two weeks after Cnut's death,[115] and by the coinage.[116] He straightaway sent to Winchester, where Emma had remained after the burial of Cnut, and had her deprived of the greater and best part of the treasures which Cnut had left.[117] But although Harold began to rule as if he were the 'just heir', he was not accepted by all, and he was not as powerful as Cnut had been. It was perhaps now that he sought consecration from Archbishop Æthelnoth. If the crown was among the treasures at Winchester, the sceptre was in the archbishop's keeping. Æthelnoth neither refused nor acceded, but with a dramatic gesture placed crown and sceptre on the altar and forbade Harold or any bishop to remove them.[118] Arguments against Harold, based on his birth, had already begun. It was claimed that he was not a son of Ælfgifu and Cnut, but that Ælfgifu, wishing for a son by Cnut but unable to bear one, had tricked the king by having a child brought to her bed. In the earliest versions, this was said to be the child of a serving-maid; later the father was specified as having been a cobbler.[119] Harold's swift action had not succeeded.

Opinion was clearly divided on his claim and that of his rival Harthacnut; at this stage there is no evidence that either Edward or Alfred were considered, or commanded any support. A meeting of all the

[114] *ASC*, MS D, cf also *Fl Wig* 1035 s.a. who has Harold take the royal dignity in 1035.

[115] *ASC*, MS E, he died on 17 March 1040 and had reigned for four years and sixteen weeks. Given that 1040 was a leap year this is exactly four years and eighteen weeks to the day after 12 November.

[116] Cnut's last issue was Short Cross. A few coins of this type were issued in Harold's name, i.e. some mints recognized Harold as king immediately after his father's death, Talvio 1986, p 275.

[117] John of Worcester in his detailed account places this action now, *Fl Wig* s.a., agreeing with *ASC*, MS C which also places this in 1035. A would-be king should have immediately seized the treasure.

[118] *Encomium*, p 40. The timing is uncertain, but the *Encomium* places these events soon after Harold had been chosen by certain of the English. Alternatively this refusal of consecration may belong in the aftermath of Oxford and the choice there.

[119] *Encomium*, p 40 for the serving-maid, *Fl Wig*, 1035 for the cobbler's child. At Worcester by the early twelfth century Ælfgifu's other son, Swein, was made a child of the same trickery, this time the son of a priest's concubine, *Fl Wig*, s.a. 1035. All MSS of the *ASC* note the doubts raised about Harold's birth.

great men was held at Oxford soon after Cnut's death.[120] This was the
meeting at which a new king would have been chosen and approved.
Harold's actions preceded it, but could not pre-empt it. The questions
about his birth were perhaps first raised in debates here. The final
decision at Oxford was in favour of division: Harold became king of
Mercia and Northumbria, Harthacnut of Wessex. Harold's major supporters seem to have been Leofric, earl of Mercia, the nobility north of
the Thames and the fleet in London.[121] The division made both men
kings, and a new coinage issue was struck in both their names, with mints
north of the Thames on the whole striking in Harold's name, and those
to the south and in Gloucester, in that of Harthacnut.

The division, however, was far from straightforward and accepted.
London, Oxford and Southwark struck coins in the names of both kings;
York and Lincoln struck a few in Harthacnut's name, and some
moneyers, at Cambridge, Bristol, Dover, Exeter, Salisbury, Southwark,
Wallingford and London hedged their bets by striking in the name of
'Cnut' which could be interpreted either as acknowledgement of
Harthacnut, even a deliberate association of him with his father, or as a
wariness of the holding-power of the Oxford decision, or a refusal to
accept the arrangements of late 1035/early 1036 as anything other than
provisional.[122] There were those who sought to overturn or undermine
the arrangements made at Oxford. During 1036 opinion was moving
towards Harold.[123] By August 1036 news had reached Emma's daughter
Gunnhild at the German court that her 'unhappy and unjust stepmother'
(i.e. Ælfgifu of Northampton) was working to deprive her brother
Harthacnut of his kingdom, holding great feasts, trying by argument and
gifts to persuade the great men to swear loyalty to her and her son. News
of this had been sent to Harthacnut begging him to return quickly.[124]
Either Harthacnut himself or Emma or both had sent this news to
Gunnhild after her arrival at the German court in 1036.

Emma, meanwhile, sat at Winchester. Some if not all members of the
royal household had apparently transferred their allegiance to
Harthacnut; she stayed there with the housecarls of the king, her son.
The Oxford meeting had agreed that she should remain there with them
and that they should hold Wessex for Harthacnut. Godwine, along with

[120] Fl Wig places it in 1035; ASC, MS E in 1036; both agree in placing it either shortly after
Harold seizure of the throne, Fl Wig, or shortly after Cnut's death, MS E.

[121] Thus Fl Wig s.a. 1035 and 1037 on the division; MS E has Leofric and others choose
him as regent over all England for himself and his brother, thus implying a division between
the brothers.

[122] The exact interpretation of this depends also on determining the movement of moneyers
and the sources of die supply, which cannot always be done precisely.

[123] ASC, MS C s.a.

[124] See Stevenson 1913, printing the letter from the court of Conrad II to the bishop of
Worms at p 116.

the elders of the West Saxons, had resisted either the decision to divide the kingdom or to give Harold some control of his brother's share. Godwine was Emma's and Harthacnut's most loyal man.[125] Æthelnoth, Archbishop of Canterbury, should perhaps also be placed in Emma's and Harthacnut's camp. He frustrated Harold's consecration in 1035–6, and may have influenced the South Eastern support which Harthacnut commanded.[126] But Emma must have been painfully aware of the insecurity of the situation and of her own position. Harold's actions against her left little doubt of his determination to be king, and the support he commanded at Oxford could only have bolstered it. As the weeks went on in 1036, support for Harthacnut wavered, as it became apparent that his absence was undermining the Oxford decisions. When Harold finally became king in 1037 it was said to have been because Harthacnut lingered too long in Denmark,[127] and Gunnhild's informant made it clear that he was being begged by his supporters to return in 1036. Gunnhild herself was perhaps contacted in the hope that she might add her voice to those urging the need for his presence in England. Into the midst of this uncertain situation at some time in 1036 came Edward and Alfred.

Both made their way towards their mother at Winchester. Edward seems to have come directly from one of the Norman ports, with many Norman soldiers;[128] Alfred came via Boulogne, where he enlisted the aid of his new brother-in-law Eustace.[129] Their separate journeys may indicate some tension between them, or that the Normans backed Edward's return, leaving Alfred to seek help where he could. The arrival of two new claimants to the throne, each with a band of armed men, threatened Harold, if it did not disturb Godwine and other English nobles. Edward made his way straight to his mother at Winchester. There he stayed until after his brother's capture. Alfred ended up in the custody of Earl Godwine, at Guildford to the south west of London. Whether he had lost his way avoiding ambushes en route to his mother at Winchester[130] or was for some reason hurrying to a meeting with Harold in London,[131] he and his comrades here met a terrible fate; his followers captured and many summarily murdered, he himself was taken into East Anglia where he was blinded and died. Events at Guildford were the subject of suspicion and accusation as late as 1051. Whether any or all of this was done

---

[125] *ASC*, MS E 1036; the phrase 'heoldan . . . to handa' suggests regency, see discussion above p 189 n 129.

[126] See the Table in Talvio, p 284 for the mints of this area striking in Harthacnut's name.

[127] *ASC*, MS C and *Fl Wig* s.a.

[128] *Fl Wig* s.a. 1036, though this Worcester source has Edward and Alfred come together.

[129] The *Encomium*, p 42 claims that he was offered help by Baldwin and refused, but crossed with a 'few' men from Boulogne.

[130] Ibid.

[131] *Fl Wig* s.a. 1036.

by Godwine on his own initiative, as a supporter of Harthacnut or as a man unwilling to follow Emma in this stage of her plans, or by Harold, with Godwine turning a blind eye or offering less than full protection, cannot now be determined. What is clear is that there was some form of trial, at least of Alfred.[132] If the *Encomium* is not merely indulging in literary artifice when it described the fate of Alfred's companions, his 'few' followers were a sufficient band to be lodged by twenties, twelves and tens at Guildford. Emma could not admit it in the *Encomium* but she had played a part in luring her sons into a dangerous venture in which in many eyes they would appear as invaders and stirrers of rebellion rather than legitimate claimants to the throne. Such is the nature of a succession dispute of this complexity.

Some commentators were clear that Godwine had prevented Alfred reaching his mother because opinion was swinging heavily in Harold's favour.[133] If Alfred was hastening to a meeting with Harold, the situation was becoming extremely complicated. Harold may have been trying to exploit division between the brothers or to drive a wedge between them, attempting to negotiate with Alfred whilst Edward was with his mother. With so many claimants in play outcomes were increasingly hard to predict. Whatever the legacy of 1033, 1036 was unfolding in ways which left Godwine's position increasingly uncertain. By the end of 1036, Harthacnut was still in Denmark, Alfred was dead, Edward was returned to Normandy and Godwine unsure of his allegiances. The move towards Harold had become a landslide. In the latter stages of the coin issue which had begun with the inauguration of the joint rule of Harold and Harthacnut, all coins were struck in Harold's name, even at Winchester. 1037 saw the fall of Winchester, the driving out of Emma, the choice of Harold as king of all England. Two years into her second widowhood Emma was in exile in Flanders.

As in all succession disputes, the situation in 1035–7 was open to different interpretations. Harold claimed that he was king immediately on the death of his father, and vindicated that judgement during his own brief reign when its length was calculated from a fortnight after Cnut's death. On this interpretation, the seizure of the treasure and the attempt to gain consecration were entirely justified. The Oxford division was a forced compromise, against which he would naturally struggle, and the continued efforts of himself and his mother in 1036 merely attempts to recover a kingdom rightly his. Emma's resistance was illegitimate; she could certainly not be a candidate for regency of the whole kingdom on behalf of her absent son Harthacnut, and should have retired as a dowager widow to her lands. In Harold's view, he would have been

---

[132] *Encomium*, p 44 Alfred was judged (*diiudicatur*) by appointed judges (*judices constituti*).
[133] *ASC*, MS C 1036.

acting justly and honourably in leaving her with a portion of the treasure in late 1035 which could be seen as her widow's share. Emma, on the other hand, judged Harold a tyrannical usurper without a claim on the throne, which should have gone to her son Harthacnut, or in his absence to her as regent, as mother of the king and widow of his father. Her holding of Winchester and the royal treasure was but a fraction of what should legitimately have been in her hands.

In some eyes this was a succession dispute between candidates both with strong and arguable claims: that at least was the opinion which emerged from the deliberations at Oxford. It was decided to divide the kingdom, but that decision was complicated by Harthacnut's absence. This raised the questions of who should control his share until his return, and who should take general responsibility in a divided kingdom one of whose rulers was in Denmark. Harold, it was decided, would hold the whole, but on behalf of himself and his brother, whilst Emma and Godwine were left in control of Wessex as Harthacnut's share. This difficult arrangement gave Harold considerable advantage, and was a recipe for trouble. Those who argued for division had 1016 and even the 950s as precedents. In both cases division had been resolved by the sudden death of a young king; neither precedent could induce peaceful sleep in the major protagonists. The Oxford decisions did not resolve the problems left by Cnut's death, they stoked them; there was resistance. Among those who resisted were perhaps some who had a different view of 1035–6; who believed at the time what was claimed later, namely, that nothing had been settled, that this was an interregnum, the division not a solution but merely a stage in a dispute which would only be ended when a single king of the English was chosen.[134]

Each of these interpretations of 1035–6 allotted a different role to Emma: a maximum one as regent in her own view; a more limited and debatable one as mother for those who argued division; possibly a role as caretaker widow in an interregnum, though her motherhood of one of the candidates rendered her partisan, but hardly any place in Harold's picture. For him Emma could only be a dowager widow, facing a living queen-mother if not queen who would require their own endowments.[135] Emma was playing for high stakes.

She was not the passive woman she chose to present in the *Encomium*. She is the most likely source of the rumours about Harold's birth, which she gave in detail in the *Encomium*. And in 1036 it was surely she who brought Edward and Alfred to England. That they were summoned to

[134] Hermann, p 47.
[135] Stevenson 1913 for evidence of a son of Harold Harefoot later in exile in France. The marriage may have occurred in or after 1037, but it is possible that Harold was already married in 1035–6.

England by a letter in their mother's name is clear.[136] Whether she sent it or whether it was sent by Harold to lure these claimants to England is more debatable, though Emma must be the chief suspect. As she herself realized in the *Encomium*, this letter and its intent are central to the understanding of her plans and aims.

Emma 'Queen in name only' sent her maternal greetings to her sons. One of them was to come quickly but privately to her to receive her counsel concerning how this business (by implication the realization of their claim on the throne, since many would prefer that one of them ruled) should be brought to a conclusion.[137] The letter presents a picture of Harold going about with gifts, threats and arguments to win over the great men. Its argument and presentation have some notable similarities to the news sent to Gunnhild. The two appeals were appropriately angled, but clearly connected. Edward and Alfred were reminded of their inheritance of which another was depriving them; Gunnhild of a stepmother's activities against her brother. But in both there is the same urging that Emma's sons' delay and absence is giving Harold the advantage, the same begging that those sons come to England. The parallels add to the arguments for the letter's genuineness and link both to Emma. She and her supporters were thus in contact with four of her children in 1036, and perhaps also with the fifth, Godgifu, remarried in that year to Eustace of Boulogne,[138] who also played a part in the drama.

The similarities between the two appeals might suggest that both were sent at about the same time, that Emma called simultaneously on all her sons, reinforcing her later contention that she always worked for the interests of them all. A mother's desire to back all her sons and their claims is certainly a credible argument. Yet it is doubtful whether Emma could realistically have backed them all in 1036, or even late in 1035. If 1033 had raised fears in England, she might already have given assurances that she would never give backing to Edward and Alfred, and would certainly have had a chance to gauge their likely, more probably unlikely, support. Before or after Oxford, the claims of any son were only as good as the backing he could mobilize, and the division decided on there had effectively excluded Edward and Alfred. Whatever Emma's personal preference, Harthacnut was the only serious candidate apart

---

[136] Keynes 1991, p 196 agrees that Emma encouraged their return, but believes the letter was forged later to distract attention from Emma's involvement in the whole affair. To forge a letter in her own name summoning her sons is an odd way of deflecting attention from herself; in what was clearly an apologia she had to acknowledge the existence of a letter which must have been common knowledge, especially to Edward the Confessor, one of its recipients and one of those who was intended to hear his mother's arguments in 1041.

[137] *Encomium*, pp 40–42.

[138] See Barlow 1970, pp 307–8 and Bates 1987, pp 38–9.

from Harold in late 1035/early 1036. It was the unfolding of events in 1036 and the growing support for Harold which drove Emma to summon one of her sons by Æthelred. The presence of one or other of her sons in England was becoming imperative to her. By the time the appeals were sent to her children, their simultaneity was more an indication of her desperate predicament than evidence of her even-handedness. By now her strategy and that of Earl Godwine had parted company. The E Chronicle leaves little doubt that the support of Godwine, if not of all the West Saxon nobility, was for Harthacnut. There is no sign of a party in favour of Æthelred's sons, or of any warm reception for them when they arrived. The 1033 threat could have damped any lingering enthusiasm, and Godwine himself had no reason to feel any. In the letter Emma alleged that many would back Edward and Alfred's claims. There may have been some opinion in favour of the old dynasty. Archbishop Æthelnoth may, as Emma later claimed, have backed her and all her sons; but the *Encomium* had obvious reasons for stressing that he did, since it enhanced Emma's own prestige as an arbiter of the succession and reinforced the line she was arguing in 1041. The arrival of Edward *and* Alfred perhaps threw any support into confusion, and may have been the last straw for men like Earl Godwine.

The year 1035–6 was a crisis of family politics. It involved and drew in much else, as the critical role of nobles like Godwine and Leofric demonstrate; and it was as much a product of the rule of many kingdoms as of steprelations and complicated marriage politics. But Leofric's stance may itself partly have been determined by kin ties; he was possibly a relative of Ælfgifu of Northampton.[139] And many kingdoms merely exacerbated an inheritance question which was ultimately a family one. In such politics women are actors, and it is no surprise to find two women, Emma and Ælfgifu of Northampton, to the fore. Emma, as we have seen, acted for her children and with them, though it is not always possible to work out for which and when. Ælfgifu is one of the 'holes' in our understanding of these years. MS E of the Anglo-Saxon Chronicle acknowledges her significance, giving her an identity and a name accorded to few earlier English queens, let alone 'concubines'. Emma chose to dismiss her in the *Encomium*; but the letter which went to Gunnhild in the heat of 1036 told a different story. Both Ælfgifu and Harold deployed prayer and gift in the battle for support. The accusations and reports of their actions can be read as gender specific: in the *Encomium* Emma accused Harold of using his 'masculine' threats, whilst Ælfgifu's feasts, reported to Gunnhild, appear 'feminine'. His threats are certainly meant to discredit him with the unacceptable face of masculinity; but her

[139] *Burton Charters*, p xliii.

feasts are only debatably feminine. They remind us that power is sought and exercised by much more than brute force. Threats and prayers, gifts and feasts were geared to the same ends.

The prize at stake for Ælfgifu as for Emma was a role as queen, one which Ælfgifu temporarily filled between 1037 and 1040.[140] This was what Emma stood to lose. Queenship may have helped Emma in 1036. Archbishop Æthelnoth had reason to be grateful; Canterbury had been among the favoured recipients of Cnut's and Emma's patronage. The pattern of support for Harthacnut in some ways matches that of Emma's dower lands. Her dower borough of Winchester, on the evidence of coinage and chronicles, was the staunch centre, and it is no surprise to find Exeter minting Harthacnut's coins, nor perhaps Gloucester as a centre of support north of the Thames given the importance of eleventh-century queens in the Marches. The slightly ragged look of the 1036 division might find some explanation in the geography of Emma's supporters and servants throughout the country. Lincoln and Stamford were among the few mints north of the Thames which struck for Harthacnut. Some of this pattern is, of course, Godwine's earldom as much as Emma's influence, though the court and household were the place where Godwine would have become her 'most loyal man'. The power of a queen could not overcome all other forces. Given Ælfgifu of Northampton's family connections, it was unlikely that Emma's dower lands in the North East Midlands proved a solid centre of support. But being queen was important; to lose the position was to lose, among other things, control of patronage and influence. One of the few acts which can be dated to Harold's reign is the appointment of Grimketel as bishop of Selsey. Grimketel was no friend of Emma. When she fell again, dramatically, in 1043, it was he who was chosen to replace her close adviser Stigand at Elmham. Emma struggled to retain a powerful position not an empty title.

In 1035–6 Emma acted as a powerful woman, with a strategy of her own and some of the means to enact it. Part of that power derived from her motherhood which enabled her to call on all her children. Not surprisingly Emma found 1036 and especially the death of Alfred difficult to explain. The most detailed sections of the *Encomium* dealt with the events surrounding Alfred's death. Her generous patronage of Ely found one motive in his burial here. Motherhood was one of her best arguments for power, but it was also potentially her Achilles' heel. At the time and since she was judged as a mother, and it was as a sorrowful mother that she presented herself in the *Encomium*. The personal feelings

---

[140] See *Wills* 26 where Bishop Ælfric makes a payment to 'the Lady' as well as to Harold. This may be Harold's wife, though Ælfgifu is perhaps more likely in view of her importance to him in 1036. For the possible later fate of women connected with Harold, see Beech 1990.

between the players in 1035–6 are now almost irrecoverable. It is easy to see Emma distanced from her sons by Æthelred and closer to Harthacnut; her attitudes determined by maternal preference. Emma had been separated from Edward and Alfred for nineteen years; Alfred had been little more than five when he left England. But her ties with Harthacnut were not necessarily closer. The infant of 1023 had been sent to Denmark by 1026–8; there may have been contact in the meantime, but not necessarily prolonged. Four of Emma's five children were out of England in 1035, and though Gunnhild was probably with her then,[141] she left in 1036 to become the bride of Conrad II's son Henry. If Emma is to be judged by the standards of motherhood, it must be by eleventh-century standards. Maternal feeling at this social level entailed working in the best interests of children. Eleventh-century idealizations of motherhood did not, however, accommodate her difficult family and political situation, with sons by two fathers, all of whom could claim the throne but whose support was far from equal and with a stepson who had taken the initial advantage and kept it. Ælfgifu of Northampton had a straightforward task, to raise support for Harold. Emma's choices were much more complicated, especially as 1036 advanced. In her letter Emma called Edward or Alfred to *her*, to discuss her plans in private, though there can be little doubt that she wanted one of them in England as a claimant to the throne – she reminded them of their inheritance. The response of *both* sons had not been her intention, and was at least in part responsible for Alfred's death. But her appeal to them was probably less than honest when she suggested that they would find support in England.

No judgement on Emma can be made without an appreciation that the ideals of family relations were a partial ideology in relation to the circumstances of much eleventh-century family politics, nor without full realization of her predicament. Nor should she be judged, overtly or implicitly, for inappropriate ambition. Emma was a queen in 1035 and it was queenship she struggled to retain. In doing so she reaped the harvest of queenship's ambiguities. She was queen, parallel to the king with an official role in the kingdom, yet so placed through the family role of wife, which was threatened by widowhood, and only able to retain her official status through motherhood. For an eleventh-century political woman with no room to manoeuvre outside of family the dilemmas are obvious. We must sympathize with a woman so placed, but not without recognizing that the confusion of private and public from which her problems arose was precisely the source of her power. If Emma did not always work for all her sons, circumstances explain it, and maternal ideals, twentieth- or eleventh-century, are an unfair yardstick by which to assess

---

[141] There is some doubt since Annalista Saxo, p 680, s.a. 1036 has Gunnhild come from Dania to marry Henry, but since she was met by the court at Nijmegen a journey from England rather than Denmark may be indicated.

her. If she struggled to retain her power and position, it is no more than should be expected from a queen. If she used her sons to do so, the family politics within which she operated left her no option. But if her strategy involved inviting her sons back into a dangerous situation in which they lacked support she was culpable. Her appeal to them was at best sanguine, possibly self-deluding and at worst politically immoral.

In 1037 Emma was driven out into exile; she had failed in the first round of the family struggle. She did not return to her natal family in Normandy. The fate of Edward and Alfred in 1036 cannot have strengthened family ties. At the same time Normandy in 1037 was not the most secure court in Northern France, and Emma could turn to other relatives, a niece's stepson and his wife, Baldwin and Adela in Flanders. She sought a refuge popular with later eleventh-century English exiles, one where they were well placed for a comeback.[142] In 1037 Emma was much more an English queen than a Norman count's daughter. It was as a queen that she wished to be remembered in her sojourn there. In Bruges she continued her efforts to secure her intertwined aims, a son on the throne and her own continuation as queen-mother. Edward was understandably reluctant to risk another attempt on the English throne, if, indeed, he was seriously asked. Emma in 1041 stressed that she had discussed the option with him;[143] that need not imply that at the time it was mooted as a truly viable course of action. As long as Harold was on the throne any challenge to him had to be accompanied by military strength.

That military strength and its possible deployment posed its own problems for Emma. In the *Encomium* in 1041 she may have tried to give the impression that she was aware only of the ten ships Harthacnut brought to Bruges to his parley with her. But he had left a large fleet in an inlet and had Harold's death not intervened it would have been needed.[144] Harthacnut was more important than the *Encomium* allows. The plans and strategies of 1037–9 were not all hers. Emma came back on his coat tails as much as under her own steam. But if she was plotting a comeback in 1037–9, she must also have been considering the possibility of an invasion and show of military might, a fact she was reluctant to acknowledge in the *Encomium*. To be a wife and woman in the eleventh century was to be a peace-maker. To be a political actor was, on occasion, to be a force-user. There was no representation which could easily reconcile the two.

Harold's death obviated the need for invasion, though Emma and Harthacnut still returned with their fleet. In 1041, probably at Emma's instigation, Harthacnut invited Edward back from Normandy; he re-

---

[142] Tenth-century examples are of churchmen, like Dunstan. In the eleventh century Godwine, Osgod Clapa, and after 1066 Godwine's widow Gytha all came here.

[143] *Encomium*, p 48.

[144] Ibid p 48.

turned accompanied by Emma's grandson, Ralph, Godgifu's son.[145] Edward returned to share rule. How this uncomfortable end was to be achieved, without the division which was anathema to Emma if not to Harthacnut, is not clear. Edward took some sort of royal oath as king in 1041.[146] Perhaps Edward was to be a regent whilst Harthacnut was in Denmark. Perhaps Harthacnut was already ill, and Edward being promised the succession: although only in his early twenties, Harthacnut died of convulsions at a marriage feast on 8 June 1042. Edward's popularity in England may also have been increasing as an unknown but native prince, in contrast to Harthacnut who now seemed to many a high-taxing, oath-breaking Danish king. Edward's return created the triangle through which Emma or Harthacnut or both may have sought to bolster a slumped popularity. Emma presented it through the strong image of a trinity of power on earth to match that in heaven. Emma may have at last attained the advancement of all her sons which she claimed she had always sought and which circumstances now permitted. She must also have hoped that she had secured the continuation of her own queenship.

During Harthacnut's reign, and for the first year or so of Edward's, Emma exercised considerable power in the role she had fought for, that of mother of the king. In the witness lists of these years, admittedly sparse for Harthacnut's reign, her high status during the last decade of Cnut continued. She was no longer Queen, *regina*[147] but as *mater regis*, the king's mother, she was still invariably placed after the king. A different not lesser type and source of authority was recognized. A mother, like a wife with her husband, could exercise a joint rule with her son.[148] There were precedents for the importance of a mother alongside full-age royal sons: in England, Eadgifu's dominant role during stages of the reign of Eadred; in late tenth-century France, Emma, widow of Lothar, alongside her son Louis V. The French nobility swore oaths after Lothar's death to Emma and Louis together.[149] Edward had just returned from a Northern France where a trinity of king, queen and designated son had recently been emphasized.[150] The English Emma described her own idealized view of such rule in the trinity of mother and sons she invoked at the end of the *Encomium*.

Here Emma used the idealization of motherhood to her own advantage, but with a degree of wishful thinking. The Capetian trinity was of husband wife and son, and after Robert's death family unity here had

---

[145] According to *Chron Ram*, pp 171–2; cf Bates, 1987, p 39.
[146] *ASC*, MS C s.a.
[147] Except in S 998.
[148] See *Writs* 57 in which Harthacnut and Emma together address the writ to Ramsey.
[149] Gerbert, *Letters*, no 74, sping 986.
[150] See Lemarignier 1965, pp 75–6 who calls the 'Capetian Trinity' in the last years of Robert the Pious from c. 1030 'une sorte de gouvernement familiale'.

broken up in a struggle which pitted mother against son. The precedents for mother–son rule were not encouraging. Louis V acted against Emma in 986, joining in the accusations which linked her with Adalbero, bishop of Laon.[151] This earlier Emma fell from power, attacked and abandoned by her son. The letter to *her* mother, the great dowager Empress Adelaide, in which she remembered the oath of the great nobles, began 'Emma, once queen, now deprived of the light of the Franks', and two years later, released from captivity, she would lament that she 'who had commanded so many thousands' had no faithful servants to accompany her to her meeting with Hugh Capet.[152] Like Emma in 1040, Eadgifu had emerged in the 940s and 950s alongside first sons then grandsons. But Eadgifu fell, after 956 attacked by her own grandson and deprived of her property.[153] In her relations with Harthacnut and Edward in the early 1040s Emma did not face the challenges which contributed to the fate of some earlier women. Neither Harthacnut nor Edward had a wife in 1040–42 and Eadgifu's fall had coincided with the arrival of a new queen, her grandson's bride, at court. Prospects of long-term survival in 1040 were nonetheless slim. Few if any early medieval queens maintained an important position alongside a full-age king securely established who had no need for a regent,[154] and especially not alongside one who was married, as one or other of her sons was bound soon to be. Neither family nor female lifecycle was on Emma's side by 1041.

In 1043 her son Edward moved against her. She was attacked without warning at Winchester by Edward and earls Godwine, Leofric and Siward, and deprived of untold treasure in gold and silver. All the land she had was taken into the king's hands; he returned to her only enough for her needs. She was ordered to remain quietly in Winchester. Meanwhile Stigand was deprived of his bishopric and the king took all his possessions.[155] Emma's deprivation took effect. The Thingoe hundreds, a substantial part of her landed wealth in East Anglia, was granted to Bury St Edmunds.[156] A fallen queen was in a dangerously exposed position. It was during her despoiliation that a goldsmith attached to her household stole the head of St Ouen from her treasury and gave it to Malmesbury.[157] This was the sort of fate Emma had feared in 1016 and 1035.

[151] See discussion in Sassier, pp 188ff.
[152] Gerbert, *Letters*, no 147, AD 988.
[153] See Stafford 1981 and 1983.
[154] Adelaide in the tenth century maintained her importance, though with some difficulty, largely because of her role in Italy.
[155] See *ASC*, MSS C and D and *Fl Wig* s.a.
[156] *Writs* 9 datable to 1043–4 by the brief pontificate of Grimketel at Elmham.
[157] William of Malmesbury, *DGP*, p 419.

Various reasons were adduced for her disgrace. Contemporary chroniclers alleged that 'she had withheld it (the land and treasure) previously from him (Edward)', and that 'she was previously very hard to her son the king and did less for him than he would have wished, before he was king and after'. Stigand was deprived 'because he was closest in his (the king's) mother's counsels and it was felt that she did whatever he advised.' A generation or more later she was accused at Canterbury of offering aid to Magnus of Norway for an invasion of England, for which she had provided him with her enormous treasures. Hence she was deprived of all she had, at Winchester where she was staying.[158] At a generation's distance again, William of Malmesbury enlarged on the idea of ill-feeling between son and mother, but also saw her as an unjust hoarder of wealth.[159] Over a century later, the attack was on her and the bishop of Winchester, and the accusation one of sexual liaison and consequent neglect of her sons' welfare.

The death of Harthacnut had changed the situation. The year 1042 had replaced the rule of a man in his early twenties alongside Emma, a fifty- to sixty-year-old woman, by that of Edward, a man of thirty-eight or so. There is no need of Freudian explanation to admit that Edward would have felt ready to rule alone. Contemporary references to animosity should not be ignored. Eleventh-century maternal feeling needs to be judged against the pursuit of the best interests of children, but this left scope for differing assessments. Emma's *Encomium* was a self apologia which was necessary because she recognized the need to counter alternative views. That was in 1041; 1043 was only two years later. Edward may well have felt aggrieved. The mood at the beginning of his reign was likely to have been one of suspicion and there are hints of rash, or at least ill-thought-out action soon repented or undone. Emma was restored to some at least of her dignity and Stigand to his bishopric within a year. Perhaps Edward's action had achieved its main aim, the cutting down of Emma from her pre-eminent position to a more normal widowhood. The pretexts may thus be simply that; excuses to act against a woman who had been queen for forty years, and of undoubted power and prominence for almost twenty of them. The contemporary ones are accurate in placing the fall of such a woman in a context of family feeling, though rather economical in their presentation of the full family context.

At its most straightforward, this was the deprivation of a queen who had attempted to buck the female lifecycle, the forcible retirement of a dowager, the reduction of her to widowhood by a king who would marry within eighteen months or so. It has obvious similarities to Harold's

---

[158] Goscelin, *Translation*, pp 176–8.
[159] William of Malmesbury, *DGRA*, Bk 2 cap 196 p 237.

comparable attempt to reduce Emma to such a status in 1035. In both cases she was to be left at Winchester, on her dower land, with enough to live out her widowhood. Understood in terms of the female and family lifecycle, she was being cut down to the minimum rights of widowhood, whereas she had since 1035 played for the maximum interpretation of the role. Once again queenship is revealed as bound up with these lifecycles. Yet Emma had been a powerful woman. Reduction to widowhood was an acceptable and defensible way to treat her, but the pretexts and the scale of the attack suggest that there was more to her fall, and that more was needed to remove such a woman than merely an appeal to the natural cycle of family life. Not all widows required three earls and a king to make them go gracefully. Nothing measures Emma's power like her leaving of it.

Some later interpretations of 1043 are clearly anachronistic, affected by the greater critique of wealth which the twelfth-century chroniclers articulated, and their greater obsession with female sexual misdemean-ours, not to mention the fact that distance allowed Emma to become less of a person, more of a stereotype to be bent to their purposes. But some of them may contain a memory of earlier accusations and rumours showing us the queen as well as the mother who was attacked in 1043.

Emma's fall was later attributed to adultery with a bishop closely attached to the royal household. Such accusations were not unusual and could be strictly contemporary, as in the case of Emma's namesake the French queen and Adalbero, bishop of Laon. In the English Emma's case some confusion of the stories of Emma and Edith has occurred which cannot now be disentangled. But at the time Emma was linked to a bishop, Stigand; she and Stigand fell together, a queen and a court priest/ bishop. The accusations were not, however, of sexual liaison, but of shared involvement in the exercise of power. Stigand's later career marks him out as a political court-bishop of the type who came to be especially vilified. The man accused of being too close in the dowager queen's counsels was the man who, it has been suggested, ran the royal adminis-trative machine by 1066.[160] Emma had not surrounded herself with nonentities.

In 1043 the treasure she held was royal treasure, guarded and control-led by a queen. By the time William of Malmesbury wrote she was accused of its misuse. Only the poor and the church would have been its worthy recipients. There were other more positive attitudes to her wealth in the mid eleventh century (sometimes shared by William when the question was of his contemporaries). Taxation and royal oppression were, however, issues in the 1030s and 1040s. Harthacnut was remem-

[160] Campbell 1987, p 218.

bered especially for his heavy taxation; and William of Malmesbury himself had heard popular songs expatiating on the pomp of Gunnhild's marriage preparations and the scale of the dowry with which she left England.[161] Events which had in fact occurred in 1036 had by the twelfth century if not before become associated with the reign of the unpopular high-taxing Harthacnut. Emma was the mother of both bride and king. An attack on Emma's wealth, as wealth, as greed, as unacceptable amassing of riches, is a possible factor in 1043: the chroniclers insisted on its fabulous scale, 'beyond telling'. Gunnhild's dowry may have caused problems for Emma in 1036, and a mood of criticism of Harthacnut and Emma could have been fruitfully tapped in 1043 to justify her downfall. The politics of the mid eleventh century began to give a voice to critics of the high costs of queens as of kings.[162] Emma herself was sensitive to the question. She insisted that she lived with suitable royal dignity in Flanders, but that it had not been at the expense of the poor. And the *Encomium* tried to suggest that the huge fleet, whose size and cost later caused such trouble, was not known to her when Harthacnut came to meet her in Bruges.

The story of Emma helping Magnus is difficult to judge. It emanated from eleventh-century Canterbury and was believable within living memory of her. In 1042 Magnus was unlikely to have been planning an invasion of England when his attention was absorbed in Scandinavia. Magnus attacked Denmark on the death of Harthacnut. If there is any basis for the accusation against Emma it may lie here. Swein of Denmark, the claimant to the Danish throne, was Earl Godwine's nephew. The relations of Emma and Godwine, especially after 1036 are unknowable; we cannot know whether she would have backed Magnus out of enmity with Godwine. Magnus himself sent a fleet against England in the 1050s, and the later coupling of Emma with his hostile intentions may tell us no more than the extent to which she was identified with Scandinavian dynasties and interests in some eleventh-century English minds. 'Backing Northern kings who cost England dear' is the closest we may come to finding any basis for this strange accusation. It is an unlikely pretext in 1043. It may witness how far Emma in some eleventh-century English eyes was seen as 'the wife and mother of Danish kings', after being in 1017 an English queen and before her identity was reworked as a 'Norman gem'.

Emma returned to court in 1044. But she was never again to exercise great power. It is tempting to see her hand in the appointment of her old

---

[161] William of Malmesbury, *DGRA*, Bk 2 cap 188, p 229. Some confusion has occurred, however, since this woman was allegedly accused of adultery, was repudiated and retired to a nunnery. All other evidence has Gunnhild die young, soon after the marriage, as the result of the heat of Italy.

[162] Cf Clanchy 1983, pp 52–5 and Stafford 1989, pp 22, 80–82 and 105–9.

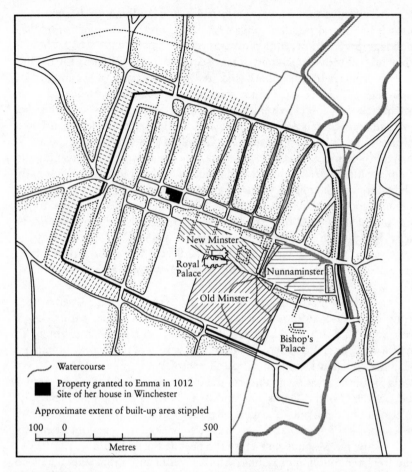

Figure 9 Winchester in the eleventh century, showing the churches and royal palace and the probable site of Queen Emma's house. Adapted from *Winchester in the Early Middle Ages*, eds F. Barlow, M. Biddle, O. von Feilitzen and D. J. Keene, Winchester Studies Vol 1, ed. M. Biddle

ally Stigand as bishop of Winchester in 1047 and perhaps in that of her grandson, Ralph, as earl in the Marches at about the same date. She virtually disappears from the witness lists and other sources; only the landed arrangements made for her servant Wulfweard and his burial, and provision for bequests to Bury seem to date from now.[163] For the third time silence envelops the details of her life, but during this last decade or so it is near total. Emma now became as shadowy as the wives and widows of the tenth century, recalling Eadgifu in her

---

[163] R 114 and *Writs* 16 and 17.

final years. As with Eadgifu a political life ended with a period of quiet retirement, the other face of widowhood. Emma retired almost certainly to Winchester, where perhaps, like Henry the Fowler's Mathilda, she tended her husband's grave, one of the accepted and acceptable activities of widowhood. Emma did not spend her final years surrounded by children and grandchildren. The 'mother of kings' had been predeceased by three if not four of her five children[164] and though her daughters Godgifu and Gunnhild had produced sons and daughters, Emma had no grandchildren in the male line.[165] She died in Winchester on 6 March 1052, in the city where she had been given land as dower fifty years earlier when she arrived in England as a young bride. She was in her sixties or early seventies, and was buried next to Cnut in the church of St Swithun, the Old Minster.[166] Her memory remained green there. Her death was commemorated in Winchester in the later eleventh century[167] and the house where she had lived was still identified as hers in the twelfth.[168] It was here, as the eleventh century turned, that Prior Godfrey wrote the poem which could serve as a partial epitaph for her:

> She had kings as sons and kings as husbands
> She shone forth in the glory of her progeny of kings
> She excelled in virtue even the ranks of her glorious ancestors[169]

To Daughter, Wife and Mother Emma had added Lady and Queen, playing all the parts of queenship. On these family roles she had built one of the great political careers of eleventh-century England.

* * *

During the twelve months before and after Emma's death her son-in-law, Eustace of Boulogne, and her great nephew, William of Normandy, came to England. The daughter of the duke of Normandy retained her French connections. Perhaps Eustace came to pay his last respects to his mother-in-law and both he and William to settle the questions of inheritance her death raised. Perhaps they came to debate the English succession with her son Edward the Confessor.[170] Eustace's visit became part of the drama of

---

[164] Gunnhild, Alfred and Harthacnut definitely and perhaps Godgifu, on whose marriage and death see Barlow 1970, p 308 and Bates 1987, pp 38–9.

[165] On Godgifu's children, see Bates 1987 and Barlow 1970.

[166] ASC, MS C 1051, recte 1052 and Annals of Winchester, p 25.

[167] See London BL MS Vitellius E XVIII, the Vitellius Psalter, fo 3r and cf e.g. BL Cotton Titus D XXVII fo 4v. Her death was also commemorated at Ely and Canterbury, see Gerchow 1988.

[168] Winton Domesday, printed Biddle 1976 at p 46.

[169] Godfrey of Winchester, p 148.

[170] Barlow 1970, p 117 for the connection with Emma's death, and in distinction from almost all writers on the Norman Conquest and succession who have seen William's visit if not Eustace's as connected to the succession.

Godwine's fall, and thus of Edith's. The lives of mother-in-law and daughter-in-law touched at the last.

There are few other known contacts between them, apart from a meeting in 1045. In that year Emma made her last appearance in a witness list, along with Edith. The document is extremely suspect. [171] But if this witness list is genuine,[172] 1045 would join 901 and 966 as the only occasions in tenth- and eleventh-century England when two queens witnessed together.[173] The earlier witnessings signalled meetings of great moment. In 901 Edward the Elder's mother and wife joined him at the dedication of his new foundation at Winchester, intended as a new family mausoleum. It was an expression of unity in which Edward the Elder reinstated his mother after the suspicion which had surrounded her and him late in Alfred's reign, and marked his own accession as a new dynastic beginning.[174] In 966, Eadgifu, Edgar's grandmother, came out of the obscurity of her final retirement to join Edgar and his third wife Ælfthryth at a meeting which granted great privileges to that same New Minster, but also celebrated the birth and legitimacy of Ælfthryth's first son. Both were family events centred on a church closely linked to the royal family. Both were occasions of dynastic arrangement or rearrangement, looking to the family's past generations with an eye to its future.

The meeting in 1045 was of similar significance. It took place in London, and privileges were granted to Edward's favoured Westminster, the new mausoleum where he would later be buried. Edward was accompanied by his mother, and by his new bride of seven months' standing, Edith. The meeting celebrated the return of the old dynasty; the charter was dated not from Edward's consecration in 1043 but from his return to England in 1041. It is appropriate that Emma should make her last known public appearance at such a family gathering. It is tempting to suggest that prayers were offered for Edith's fertility; prayers were requested for the king himself and for the stability of the kingdom. Through this marriage the restored dynasty's succession was to be assured. Such a family meeting would have looked to the future and the hoped-for birth of a son. The fate of that aspiration is, however, part of Edith's not Emma's story.

---

[171] S 1011.
[172] It is defended by Keynes 1988, pp 198–9 and 206.
[173] S 364 for the 901 meeting and S 745 and 746 for 966.
[174] Cf Nelson 1991b for the need for this.

9

Edith

1 Godwine's Daughter

Towards the end of Æthelred's reign his eldest sons gathered a household and military following around them. Among these young men was a certain Godwine, Wulfnoth's son, to whom the ætheling Athelstan left land at Compton in his will.[1] This Godwine was probably the future earl of Wessex and father of Edith.[2] His own father Wulfnoth was a noble-man of the South Saxons, remembered for his quarrel in 1009 with Brihtric, ealdorman Eadric's brother.[3] Eadric was the most prominent of Æthelred's counsellors in the last decade of his reign; in the *Encomium Emma* recalled his valued skills. Godwine's father was accused to the king in 1009 by Eadric's brother, and then took twenty ships and ravaged the south coast, later burning the large naval force sent against him. What he was accused of, whether he was suspect because of his association with the princes, or whether his son's association with them resulted from Wulfnoth's disgrace, is unclear. The first appearance of Edith's family is as noble, military leaders in southern England, em-broiled in the factional politics of the last stages of the reign of Æthelred, her future husband's father, at loggerheads with the king's closest advis-ers and attached to the following of her future husband's stepbrothers.

Godwine was of English noble birth but his rise to power came under the new Danish dynasty, during the reign of Cnut. By 1018 he had been appointed as an earl of part of England south of the Thames, but it was as a result of his prowess in Denmark in the suppression of rebellion in 1019 or 1022–3 that Cnut advanced him higher.[4]

---

[1] *Wills* 20; see DB I fo 24r for an estate of this name held by Earl Godwine in West Sussex.
[2] Freeman, Vol I, Appendix, Note ZZ; Raraty 1989, esp pp 4–5 and n 4; Keynes 1994, pp 70–1.
[3] *ASC*, MSS C, D and E s.a.; MS F notes that this Wulfnoth was the father of Earl Godwine.
[4] Keynes 1994, pp 72–3; cf Williams 1995, p 11 for the suggestion that Cnut took Godwine to Denmark in 1017–18.

Godwine was his inseparable companion in the whole journey. Here the king tested more closely his wisdom, here his perseverance, here his courage in war, and here the strength of this great nobleman. He also discovered how profound he was in eloquence, and what advantage it would be to him in his newly acquired kingdom if he were to bind him more closely to him by means of some fitting reward. Consequently he admitted this man, whom he had tested in this way for so long, to his council and gave him his sister (Gytha) as wife. And when Godwine returned home, having performed all things well, he was appointed by him earl and guardian of almost all the kingdom.[5]

Thus the author of the *Life* of Edward described Godwine's rise, and the marriage of Edith's parents, in terms which would please his daughter, and perhaps on the basis of information from Edith herself. Gytha was not, in fact, Cnut's sister, but loosely speaking his sister-in-law. She was the sister of Jarl Ulf, who was in England c. 1022,[6] and who had himself married Cnut's sister, Estrith. The marriage was part of the cementing of loyalties to the new regime through time-honoured matrimonial alliance. It also brought to England the sister of a great Danish leader at a time when Cnut was far from sure of loyalty in the North. Edith's mother, like Emma, was a kind of hostage. Edith, like Emma, was Danish-born on her mother's side. Through her mother she was the niece of Ulf, later the Danish regent for Harthacnut, and would be the cousin of Swein Estrithson, who would later follow Harthacnut as king in Denmark. At the time when Emma's marriage was providing a bridge between the English and their Danish conquerors, that of Godwine and Gytha confirmed the new reign and its English supporters.

The marriage took place some time between 1019 and 1023, and Edith was one of its nine or more children, six sons and three daughters.[7] The date of her birth and her place in the birth order can be fixed no more precisely than that of Emma. At a time when even deaths are only rarely recorded, and then only with the date rather than the year, births pass almost without comment. Identities were acquired in life not securely fixed at birth. Doubt over the succession meant that even future kings were not always known as such when they were born. Future queens were certainly not identifiable, though the chroniclers' reticence in giving any account of most of them suggests that their births would not have been noted even had they been known. Four of Edith's brothers were old enough to be at court by 1044;[8] Harold was there by the early

---

[5] *VitaEd*, pp 5–6.
[6] Keynes 1994, p 63; on Ulf in the North, see Campbell, *Encomium*, pp 82–7; on the marriage Freeman, Vol I, Note EEE.
[7] Freeman, Vol II, Note F on the children of Godwine.
[8] S 1003.

1030s.[9] Unless he was brought to court as young as ten, Godwine's marriage can hardly have been as late as 1023.

Edith is normally assumed to have been the eldest child.[10] Yet all the older sons of this marriage had Danish names; it was only for the youngest that Godwine and Gytha chose English ones, Leofwine and Wulfnoth. In the early stages of Cnut's reign we might expect the couple to demonstrate their loyalty by Danish names. Edith should have been the eldest daughter, if not the eldest child, since she was the one chosen to marry Edward. Her English name comes as a surprise, especially since another of Godwine's daughters, Gunnhild, was given a Danish one.[11] The choice of 'Edith' may indicate that the naming of daughters was less critical than that of sons, or, as was the case in the royal family, was used to other ends. Daughters' names could keep alive the memory of a wider family, or perhaps in this case temporarily less favoured ancestry. The mix of names within the family, like Godwine and Gytha's marriage, could express the union of Dane and English, with the Danish names of its sons a reminder of the inequality of conqueror and conquered. Edith in her name like Emma in her marriage would thus have embodied some of the English past. Her English name may, however, raise doubt as to how early Edith's birth should be placed. It could belong to the later phase of the family, when English names were chosen for its sons. A date range for her birth as wide as 1020–30 or later is possible; and it is even possible that the delay in Edward's marriage until early 1045 was to allow Godwine's eldest daughter to attain marriageable age.

'Edith/Eadgyth' need not, of course, have been her original name; she, like Emma, may have changed her name at marriage. 'Edith' would have been an appropriate choice: if Emma was named for a saintly ancestress, Edith would be called for Edward's saintly aunt, the patron saint of Wilton. Edith was raised here in one of the richest and most royal of the English nunneries.[12] Wilton was one of the group of royally-connected nunneries which clustered around Winchester in the heart of Wessex. In Domesday Book the value of its landed property placed it second only to Shaftesbury with an income of over £274 p.a.[13] It had housed royal as well as noble women. King Edgar's daughter, Edward's aunt, Edith, had become a nun there whilst her mother, Wulfthryth, Edgar's repudiated

---

[9] If, as is likely, he is the Harold of S 964, 965, 968.

[10] Thus Freeman, op cit; on the basis of the poem in the *VitaEd*, p 15 'Prodit gemma prior . . .' Barlow 1970, p 80 accepts that she was the eldest child. The *Life*, however, is dedicated to Edith and celebrates her throughout. Its statement of her precedence may not be intended as an indication of birth order.

[11] It is possible that her birth is to be dated 1040–42 and her name would thus represent Godwine's anxiety to affirm his loyalty.

[12] *VitaEd*, p 23.

[13] Thus Crick forthcoming, correcting Knowles, p 136 n 1 and 702. His second mention of Winchester, New Minster, just above Shaftesbury, seems to be a mistake for Wilton.

second wife, was abbess. Two of the daughters of Edward the Elder and one of his wives were buried there.[14] Edith's own niece, Gunnhild, Harold's daughter, would be placed there for safekeeping after 1066.[15] It was here that Edith acquired the learning for which she was later known. In the early twelfth century Wilton would boast the first known English woman poet, Muriel.[16] Already in the late tenth century foreign artists, Radbod of Rheims and Benno of Trèves, had been brought in to embellish it; the latter especially was a noted artist and taught Edgar's daughter.[17] That same daughter, Edith's namesake, was skilled in painting, writing, and working textiles in gold and gems,[18] all of which she presumably learnt at Wilton.

The nunnery was already enclosed. Abbess Wulfthryth built a wall around it,[19] but its inmates were far from cut off from the world and their lifestyle was a noble one. Its nuns moved among the great and the great visited them. One nun muttered complaints about losses to the nunnery's possessions whilst staying at Salisbury with Bishop Hermann.[20] Cnut and Emma came to Wilton and apparently regularly; Cnut out of respect for the place always dismounted before he entered its holy precinct.[21] It boasted some of the luxuries of high noble life, including a tenth-century zoo. Saint Edith had collected a large number of wild animals, and an enclosure against the south wall housed them.[22] And although she wore goats' hair next to her skin, she dressed externally like the princess that she was.[23] Not all the nuns were of royal birth, but all those of whom we know were noble or connected to the royal household and its service.[24] Eleventh-century Wilton must have resembled tenth-century Quedlinburg where Henry the Fowler's widow, Mathilda, lived surrounded by well-born nuns, the absence of low-born persons guaranteeing, in the view of its inmates, the high standards of the house 'since the well-born rarely and with difficulty degenerate'.[25] Godfrey of Winchester remarked on Edith's knowledge of measures, numbers, music, grammar and languages, whilst to Goscelin of St Bertin she was 'a most learned'

[14] William of Malmesbury, *DGRA*, Bk II, cap 126, p 137, Edfleda and Ethelhilda, daughters of Edward Elder.
[15] Coleman, *Life of St Wulfstan*, p 34.
[16] Tatlock 1933.
[17] Goscelin, *Life of St Edith*, p 50.
[18] Ibid pp 68–9.
[19] Ibid p 274.
[20] Ibid p 298.
[21] Ibid pp 280–1, 278.
[22] Ibid p 65.
[23] Ibid p 70.
[24] The Danish father and Lotharingian mother of the nun Eve may have been so connected, Goscelin, *Liber Confortatorius* p 41 and Wilmart 1938, p 62.
[25] *Annals of Quedlinburg*, s.a. 936.

queen.[26] If Edith learned Danish from her mother, her other languages and accomplishments would have been acquired at Wilton. To be reared in such a house was an indication of the status of Edith's family and their connection to the king and court; after the Danish conquest Wilton remained royal as much as English. To be reared there was not, however, necessarily to be destined for the religious life; and even those so destined could be removed for marriage.[27] Edith's rearing there is no indication that her parents intended her to become a nun, though it did not preclude that option. The accession of Edward the Confessor and the importance of her father in the early 1040s ensured that she would leave.

When Edward the Confessor married Edith on 23 January 1045 he married Godwine's daughter. Wilton may have made her a peculiarly fitting royal bride, but her choice was determined by the importance of her family, especially of her father. Edward returned to the normal tenth-century pattern, where kings had taken English noble brides. Never before, however, had a bride and her father and brothers formed such a powerful family group in the English kingdom, and in Edith Edward chose a half-Danish daughter of the man whose career had been built under the foreign king who had replaced his own father. The freedom of Edward's choice of wife is doubtful; women may appear powerless in their marriages, but men too were constrained in their choices. Godwine was the richest and most powerful man in England at the time of Edward's return from exile, and many sources make Edward in 1042 reliant on him. Her husband's biographer, surely recording Edith's own view of the situation, made Godwine a king-maker, responsible for urging the choice of Edward as king.[28] This was an interpretation shared by the Worcester chronicler: 'Edward was raised to the throne in London, chiefly by the exertions of Earl Godwine and bishop Lyfing of Worcester.'[29] Edward may, as William of Malmesbury later claimed, have considered returning to Normandy in 1042, dissuaded only by Godwine;[30] more likely William here reports later anti-Godwine stories which had the king fall into his control early in the reign. Edward's situation was not desperate, but the earl's support was a bonus. It was only six years since Edward had made his abortive attempt to return from Normandy to find no welcoming party awaiting him. His brother, Harthacnut, whose rule he had shared had not been popular. The back-

---

[26] See Goscelin's *Vita Kenelmi*, Oxford, Bodley MS 285, fo 80v 'doctissima regina Edgyde nobis exposuit que de ipso legisse dicebat preclara indicia', *Three Eleventh-century Anglo-Latin Saints' Lives*, p 52.

[27] For the problems of definition of such houses see Parisse 1978, 1990, 1992.

[28] *VitaEd*, p 9.

[29] *Fl Wig* s.a. 1043.

[30] William of Malmesbury, *DGRA*, Bk I cap 196, p 236.

ing of the powerful earl was desirable, and Godwine was only too willing to erase the past. The earl gave Edward a fully armed ship, a present similar to that he had made to Harthacnut. In 1043–4 his sons Swein and Harold received earldoms and in early 1045 his daughter married the king. No tenth- or eleventh-century king's marriage was free in the sense of unpolitical. Edward may have felt that the field of choice was a very narrow one.

In 1045 Edward was forty or nearing that age; Edith no more than twenty-five, possibly considerably younger. Such age gaps were not unusual. Henry I of France, whom Edward had met in 1033, had at that date been about twenty-four. In 1033/4, after taking his throne, he married a ten-year-old girl. The marriage lasted until her death in 1044 when the king was thirty-five.[31] Nor, as the case of Henry shows, was it unusual for a king or noble to remain unmarried until he had secured his inheritance. Edward's biographer recorded a famous vision in which Bishop Brihtwold saw St Peter consecrate a seemly man as king, mark him out for a chaste life (*celibem . . . vitam*) and determine the years of his reign. Edward, like the German Emperor Henry II, would later be sanctified for his chastity. The combination of that fact with a late and childless marriage and the story of the vision has led many, starting with twelfth-century chroniclers, to deduce that Edward never consummated his marriage to Edith, even producing speculation, as in William of Malmesbury's case, that the king's hatred of Godwine extended to revulsion against his daughter.

The deduction is an unwise interpretation of both the marriage and the vision.[32] The fact that the vision was included in Edith's own narrative of the eleventh century has lent it a special significance; a celibacy reported by the very queen and wife who should have known. The vision is not, however, a tale of chaste marriage. It was clearly remembered in the 1060s, but it purports to date to the period of Edward's absence during the rule of the Danish kings. Brihtwold was bishop of Ramsbury from 1005 to 22 April 1045. The vision was designed to underline the fitness of Edward to be king; it is primarily a designation of him as such by the prince of the apostles himself. His chaste life was part of that fitness, not necessarily to continue when he returned to England. The decision to include the vision in Edward's *Life* must indeed have been Edith's own. By the 1060s time had put a different angle on it. Hints at celestial reasons for her childless marriage now fitted Edith's needs especially well. It suited her purposes to present her husband as a saint and designated by a saint. It was as Edward's widow that Edith manoeuvred in 1066–7. The particular pattern of royal sanctity within which he

[31] Bautier 1985 and de Vajay 1971.
[32] For similar conclusions to the following on Edward's chastity see Barlow 1970, pp 81–5.

was cast had contemporary parallels in France, in Helgaud of Fleury's Robert the Pious, a 'monk in a crown'.[33] It allowed for local variation and adjustment. If rumours were being spread of Edward's chastity as early as the 1060s, his wife was one person behind them. They were part of her strategy then, rather than a simple account of his – or her – married life. It is futile to speculate on the sex lives, sex drives or sexuality of eleventh-century kings from such sparse and partial evidence. When the first wife of Henry I of France died, he remained seven years unmarried, in spite of having no heir. Yet he married again to Anne of Kiev, and a son Philip I was born.[34] The marriage of Edward and Edith should be taken at face value: the binding of a king–noble friendship in the most traditional of ways and a search for an heir. The latter was a primary duty of a king, and personal preference need play little part in it. The precedents for the family gathering with Emma and Edith both present at London in high summer 1045 suggest a king looking to his dynasty's future.

The marriage and consecration were seen as important. A contemporary chronicler mentioned and even dated them. The new queen was immediately recognized in charters for Winchester and Wilton in 1045–6. Her standing was high, next to the king himself in the witness lists. Neither Ælfthryth's nor Emma's first royal marriages had been given such recognition. Edith's father is one key. Here in the centre of Godwine's West Saxon earldom his queenly daughter was given her due place. The presence of Emma in the background is another. The position of the new queen could be left in no doubt whilst the power of her mother-in-law was so recent. With the exception of the Wilton charter, Edith is '*conlaterana regis*' in these years: the king's wife, she who is at his side. The title differentiated her from Emma and stressed her marriage. There is also a Winchester connection and a dynastic one. The Old Minster did well from royal patronage in 1045. Lands were recovered or restored or given for the first time to consolidate its holdings.[35] These are the last years of the pontificate of Bishop Ælfwine, the bishop later associated with Emma/Edith in the story of the ploughshares; he was replaced by Stigand in 1047. Perhaps Ælfwine had consecrated Edith. Perhaps Winchester, together with Wilton where she had been raised, had been rewarded by a grateful royal couple with gifts of land. Perhaps the new queen's status was especially marked out in these gifts, as

[33] Helgaud, Introduction, e.g. pp 33–8 on the image of royal sanctity fitted to its monastic audience; see also Folz 1984.
[34] Bautier's suggestions, 1985 p 549, that Henry I was effeminate, traumatized by his mother Constance and had personal problems, his assertion that 'il faut bien avouer que les faits, en ce qui le concerne, sont troublants' do not allow for some of the problems of finding suitable brides in eleventh-century France, see Duby 1984, p 79.
[35] S 1008, cf previous grants here in S 440 and 475; similarly cf S 1007 and S 942.

Godwine's daughter, but especially as the king's wife and the bearer of his hoped-for children. They, like the meeting to grant privileges to Westminster in 1045, may express hopes for the fertility of the couple. Whatever the case they are followed by a long period in which neither the queen nor her mother-in-law appear in witness lists. Edith disappears from them until the mid to late 1050s. Between then and the flurry of importance around her marriage, the dramatic events of 1051–2 had intervened.

2 1051–1052: The King's Wife and Godwine's Daughter

In 1051 Edith was sent from court and from the king's side. It was not an unusual event in late Saxon England. Edward's grandfather Edgar had disposed of one if not two wives; his father Æthelred may have acted in like fashion.[36] It was, however, uncommon to be rid of a wife whose family were as powerful as Edith's. In 1051 Edward acted not only against her, but against her father and brothers, all of whom were forced to flee the country in that year. The drama, and particularly the triumphant return of the family in 1052 against the king's will, ensured that this royal separation, unlike any of the others in tenth- and eleventh-century England, was recorded by contemporaries. Edith gave her own version, in which the fall of her family and herself was the work of Archbishop Robert who had become dominant in royal counsels.[37] According to her, it was Robert who urged the king to separate from him the daughter of the earl, against the law of the Christian religion, so that no member of that family should remain at his side to provide for the country's good. Edward agreed, but preferred a more honourable course. Edith was sent to Wilton to await the peaceful outcome of the storms which were stirring up the kingdom. Her leaving was mourned by the courtiers more than that of the earl himself. After the family's return and reconciliation with the king, the queen, the earl's daughter, was led back to the royal bedchamber. Edith's own version links her fall firmly to that of her father and family; she is the queen, but also the earl's daughter. Such an interpretation shifts attention away from her own marriage as a major factor. Others emphasized the fall of a 'consecrated queen' in 1051, a measure of the enormity of events.[38] The full context and ramifications of the affair are not relevant to a story of queens; but those aspects which make it a crisis of court-centred politics, of family and succession, are. Whether it was Godwine's daughter or the barren wife of the king who was caught up in that drama is a question relevant not only

[36] Stafford 1981 and above Chapter 4.
[37] VitaEd, pp 17–28.
[38] ASC, MS E s.a.1048, recte 1051.

to this crisis of Edward the Confessor's reign, but to the identity of Edith herself.

The crisis developed in the counsels and councils of the king and involved the patronage of religious office, especially the appointment to the Archbishopric of Canterbury. These appointments were decided by the king and governed by his desires, but were inevitably the subject of local pressure, which sought backing amongst those powerful at court.[39] The monks of Canterbury must have felt secure in choosing Ælric, a relative of Earl Godwine, and then enlisting the earl's aid on their side. In the circumstances of 1050–1 they were mistaken. The king was acutely sensitive to episcopal appointments in the wake of recent problems with Pope Leo.[40] Robert of Jumièges was given the archbishopric. He was a monk, a bishop already and a close counsellor. The issue was an ecclesiastical one, but also a question of court patronage and influence, as Edith later portrayed it. In the world of court politics surrounding the king, it sent out a strong message that Godwine's influence was far from all-engrossing. The appointment placed an archbishop in enmity with an earl and allowed longstanding disputes over Canterbury land to come sharply into focus. The rapid escalation of the crisis in the autumn of 1051 shows that Godwine felt that he had lost favour and power at court. It was in Edith's own interests to present the events as a result of Robert's dominance in the king's counsels; the split between her husband and family was an embarrassment to Edith after 1066 just as it was disastrous at the time.

Provocations and disputes came to a head when Godwine was publicly accused of the murder of Alfred in 1036 and asked to clear himself. The crisis of Edith's marriage thus meshed with Emma's career, and it would be interesting to have known the aging queen-mother's response to this dredging up of the past. Alfred's death was the *cause célèbre* of the mid eleventh century, and an obvious trump card to use against Godwine. In raising it, however, king and archbishop raised the ghosts of the succession dispute of which it was a part.

In the course of 1051 Edward received visits from his brother-in-law, Eustace of Boulogne, son-in-law of Emma and grandfather of a claimant on the English throne, and William of Normandy, his cousin once removed and Emma's great-nephew. Meanwhile the king's brother-in-law, Tostig, Edith's brother, was negotiating a marriage with Judith, half-sister of the count of Flanders and Emma's great-niece. At Winchester the dowager queen Emma was close to death. Edward, like many early medieval rulers, appointed his kin to office and utilized their marriages for his own ends. c. 1050 the defence of England may have been

[39] Discussed Brooks 1984, pp 303–4 linking the trouble with plans for a Norman succession.
[40] Barlow 1963, pp 216 and 300–2.

uppermost in his mind, and these family affairs related to that.[41] But when families meet, and especially when one of their oldest members is nearing death, their thoughts often turn to inheritance. By 1051 the king had been married for six years without living issue. The uncertainties of 1035–7 were on people's minds in England; Alfred's death was being openly talked about at court. Someone, everyone, may have been discussing the succession in 1051. And the succession involved Godwine because it involved Edith. If Edith was the earl's daughter, Godwine was the queen's father. Edith, putting her own slant on 1051, linked her fall to that of her father and brothers. If their fall was somehow connected to hers, if inheritance, succession and thus the childless marriage were on the agenda alongside disputes over Canterbury land and favour at court, we would not expect her to tell us about it.

One of Edward's primary aims in 1051 may have been to divorce Edith as so many kings before him had done when seeking an heir. Whether this was the origin of the crisis, or a course of action which hardened as events unfolded, it was surely part of it. News from abroad concentrated the mind on royal marriages and children. In 1050 the six-year-old marriage of Agnes of Poitou and Emperor Henry III had at last produced a son, baptized at Easter 1051; Henry III was 32 and twice married.[42] On 19 May, 1051, Henry I of France, seven years a widower and heirless, had remarried to Anne of Kiev.[43] Kings could remarry and remarriages could produce heirs. There was even a recent reminder of how kings might go about achieving such ends. In 1049 Leo IX had translated the bones of the Empress Richardis, divorced wife of Charles the Fat, at the request of Abbess Mathilda of Andlau near Strasbourg.[44] The childless Richardis had been set aside and her royal husband had claimed a *mariage blanc* and accused his wife of adultery with a high-ranking ecclesiastic at his court. Edith later showed herself acutely aware of both types of accusation. Both may have been pretexts in a royal divorce begun now.

Edith later tried to present 1051 as little more than a temporary separation. She claimed that Edward had mitigated Robert's severity by sending her to Wilton, with royal pomp and ceremony. At the time chroniclers said she had been delivered into the custody of the king's sister, the abbess of Wherwell. Nunneries were favoured places for divorced wives; Richardis had been sent to one. Edith admitted that Robert had sought a full separation 'against Christian law', which Edward mitigated when he sent her to Wilton. What she does not tell us is whether the divorce was avoided because the tide began to swing back

[41] Stafford 1989, pp 86–9.
[42] Bulst Thiele 1933, pp 25–6.
[43] Bautier 1985, p 550.
[44] Folz 1992, p 48ff.

towards Godwine; whether she was sent first to Wherwell, in what was intended to be a divorce, and then brought to Wilton as it became clear that Godwine's return, and hers, were likely. A judicious telescoping of events could make Edward's mitigation look like the free choice of a royal husband, rather than the enforced act of an unwilling king. If Edward attempted to divorce Edith in 1051, we may even have some inkling of the charges against her. Edith on her deathbed cleared herself of charges of adultery.[45] Richard of Devizes later ran together a story of Emma's fall in 1043 with that of Edith, instigated by Archbishop Robert in 1051; the resulting composite queen cleared herself by walking over burning ploughshares, as Richardis had done before. William of Malmesbury reported rumours that the marriage of Edward and Edith had never been consummated. Stripped of the later gloss that Edward's sanctification would put on this, non-consummation and adultery sound like the accusations which could end an eleventh-century marriage. And the queen was deprived of her property in land, gold and silver. Such property symbolized marriage itself, which was made through its allocation and exchange; its acquisition and its loss signalled the turning points of the female lifecycle. When Emma was deprived in 1043 it marked her demotion to widowhood; when a woman was so deprived in the life of her husband, the end of the marriage was surely signified.[46] This was intended as no temporary retirement of a queen to await the passing storm. The divorce may, of course, have been intended to complete the fall and disgrace of Godwine and his family through the dismissal of his daughter. It is impossible at this remove to disentangle the relationships of the 'king's great matter' to the fall of Godwine. But context and comparative circumstances indicate that there *was* a 'king's great matter' in 1051; that succession, an heir to the throne, divorce and remarriage were at issue. Edith was, however, the earl's daughter. If she did not cause or contribute to his fall, his return restored her. She was to have been divorced as king's wife; she was returned as Godwine's daughter. In 1052 she was back in the king's bedchamber and the divorce aborted.

These dramatic events easily overshadow the career of Edith; even more than 1035–40 engross attention in Emma's, since Edith's life as a whole is so sparsely chronicled. Coupling them with the charter witness lists can give a picture of a queen forefronted as a great noble's daughter and heir-producing wife at the time of her marriage, then insignificant as the marriage failed to produce the desired sons, finally almost divorced in 1051; a plaything of forces to a large extent outside her control. That picture captures some of the circumstances of Edith's early married

[45] William of Malmesbury, *DGRA*, Bk 2 cap 197, p 239.
[46] ASC, MS E uses the verb *forlætan* which means 'abandon, release, let go, give up'.

life, but is not entirely accurate. Whatever the circumstances which led to it, or which threatened its continuation, Edith's marriage and consecration made her a Queen, the legatee of the traditions and powers of eleventh-century Queenship.

Edith disappeared from charter witness lists after 1046, but she had not ceased to be active. Between 1045 and 1049 she presided over a grant of land by a nun, Ælfwyn, to Westminster, a queenly responsibility for religious women which dated back at least to Ælfthryth's time.[47] In 1050 when a new diocese was created centred on her dower borough of Exeter it was done on divine authority, on the king's authority but also on the authority of the king's wife and Queen, Edith. She, along with the king and the new bishop, Leofric, were at the heart of the rituals. Edward laid the charter on the altar, and then the king leading the bishop by the right arm and his queen Edith leading him by the left they placed him on the episcopal throne.[48] Her dower lands, the defined duties of a Queen, her place in the household gave Edith a continuous importance, occupying a position in the kingdom which is only occasionally recognized in the sort of sources which have survived, but clear from the unique and precious evidence of Domesday Book. Charter witness lists record only part of this activity; they are a significant but potentially misleading source. Edith does not even appear in the witness list of the Exeter charter of 1050, whilst the rituals it describes are usually hidden behind the formulaic composition of these documents. The *Life* of King Edward claimed that her absence left a void at the heart of rule. The claims are doubtless exaggerated but not incredible, and should be taken seriously when they place her power in the context of the court and its life. Her removal in 1051 was a dramatic event in its own right.

Gaps in her witnessing are not a straightforward sign of disappearance from political activity and the exercise of power. The later 1040s are the most sparsely documented period of Edward the Confessor's reign. Edith's absence from the few sources which have survived may thus tell us little. Charter witness lists are, however, some guide to public recognition and in some circumstances to the influence a queen was felt to have over and above her established activities. The Exeter rituals were a dramatic enactment of the power a queen's solid landed base gave her; without futher context they cannot tell us whether Edith c. 1050 was able to translate that base into wider influence. When she begins to appear again regularly in the witness lists, as she does in the last decade and especially the last years of the reign, and when those appearances coincide with other indications of her influence and activity, we can feel more certain of her power and suspect that a real shift had occurred.

[47] See *Writs* 79.
[48] S 1021.

3 1052–January 1066: Wife and Queen and the Earls' Sister

From the mid 1050s records are fuller and Edith's role is well established. It is now that she appears as a regular witness of charters. Of the 22 charters, genuine and spurious, which have survived with witness lists from 1055 onwards, Edith witnesses 14, always at the top of the list after the king, usually as queen/*regina*.[49] Like Emma's in the reign of Cnut, Edith's help was sought and her patronage exercised. It was now that she influenced episcopal appointments, perhaps that of Hermann to Sherborne in 1058, more certainly those of Giso to Wells and her chaplain Walter to Hereford in 1060.[50] It is now that we find her witnessing gifts and exchanges made by lay nobles or churchmen.[51] It is now that she issues a writ and grants land in her own name.[52] It was c. 1060 that she invalidated Archbishop Cynesige of York's gifts to Peterborough, and in that year that she disputed the will of the woman Leofgifu with the abbey. On that occasion Abbot Leofric had to 'turn her power' with the help of the king and her brothers.[53]

Edith's importance mirrors that of her brothers. Between 1053 and 1066 first Harold, then Harold and Tostig, finally Harold, Tostig, Leofwine and Gyrth received earldoms which gave them control of all England except Mercia, and along the Welsh Marches extended their power even there. Edith, with her holding at Leominster, her appointee in the bishopric of Hereford, her interference to prevent the dilapidation of the York archbishopric to Peterborough's advantage, was active in areas where Harold and Tostig ruled. The *Life* of Edward paints a picture of a kingdom at this date guarded by the two brothers, and ruled by the royal couple. Edith was still Godwine's daughter and the earls' sister.

All these areas, however, are areas of royal activity where queens were already established actors. Edith's activities meshed with those of her brothers and may have drawn strength from their position, but it was her roles as queen which were now reinforced, extended and acted out. The

---

[49] In four she is *regis conlaterana*; two from Westminster S 1031 and 1040, the latter spurious as it stands, and in two for French abbeys, S 1028 for St Denis and 1033 for Rouen. In the definitely spurious York charter, S 1037a, she is *regina Anglorum*, a title rarely used for pre-1066 queens in witness lists of charters, though cf K 805, S 1408 a grant by Ealdred of Worcester.

[50] For Sherborne see William of Malmesbury, *DGP*, p 183 where she is said to have promised the bishopric to Hermann; in 1066 she held Sherborne, DB I, fo 77r; for Giso, see *Ecclesiastical Documents*, p 17; for Walter, *Fl Wig* s.a. 1060.

[51] *Writs* 69, R 115 and 117; S 1235, 1238, 1408, 1479, 1475, 1480.

[52] *Writs* 70.

[53] Hugh Candidus, p 71 for Cynesige; S 1029 for Leofgifu's bequest, where Leofric 'potentiam (reginae) flexit'.

second half of Edward the Confessor's reign saw an affirmation of his kingship. The court seems to have undergone formalization and reorganization in this last decade of the reign, datable particularly to c. 1060, the year which saw a peak of Edith's activity. In the mid 1050s Edward appeared in enthroned majesty on his coins.[54] Edith had some responsibility for all this. Her concern for the presentation of Edward's kingship may have extended throughout the reign. If she was behind the designing of the new royal seal, it was cast either in the early 1050s, soon after her reinstatement as queen, or in mid decade when other evidence shows her influence growing.[55] An increase in the power and prestige of a queen during the course of her marriage is a normal pattern. 1051 disrupted that, though its effects were to some extent counteracted by the death of Emma in 1052, after which Edith stood to increase her wealth if she now secured all the lands available to endow queens. An affirmation of kingship in the 1050s might well entrain that of queenship, particularly if Edith was involved in the former. She would have been anxious to expunge any cloud over her status left by 1051.

At this stage of Edith's career the queen and the earls' daughter and sister are inseparable identities. The crisis of 1051–2 had watered if not sown the seeds of enmity between the sons of Godwine and those of Earl Leofric of Mercia. Appointments to ealdormanries in the 1050s exacerbated the tensions. The woman at odds with the abbot of Peterborough, who was also Earl Leofric's nephew and namesake, was Tostig's and Harold's sister. She was also the queen protecting a lay position against an increasingly independent abbey, exploiting her royal powers even as she defended them. The clashes between her and the abbey were exaggerated by the aftermath of 1066; but whether clashes or merely the entangling of queenly and abbatial interest they came where we would expect them, over royal servants' land, and over a widow whom she might claim to protect, if not over an ecclesiastical dynasty in Grantham and Lincoln whose male and female members were associated with her.[56]

The *Life* of Edward presented the last stage of the reign as a rule of Godwine's sons and the royal couple. Harold and Tostig were the king's brothers-in-law. If Edith's connections with her brothers remained strong, that was in part because of their great power, in part because her own lack of children did not knit her as closely into her marital family as Emma. The absence of children meant that both Edward and Edith turned outwards to wider kin. The power of Harold and Tostig is an exaggeration of the general role of the wider royal family in Edward's reign. Edward and Edith had no children but many relatives. From 1057

[54] Dolley and Elmore Jones, esp p 224.
[55] Harmer, *Writs*, pp 99 and 104 for the earlier date, cf Rezak, pp 61–2 and 65, dating it to 1057.
[56] See Appendix 2 on Earnwine the priest.

at least, the court included some of the children of Edward's nephew, Edward the Exile, who had returned to England and died in that year: his son Edgar if not his daughters Margaret and Christina.[57] By the end of the reign the son of Earl Ralph, Harold, who was another great-nephew of Edward and another great-grandson of Æthelred II, was under Edith's protection and wardship.[58] According to the *Life* of Edward, Edith 'reared, taught, adorned and showered with maternal love' the boys of royal birth.[59] Edgar was given special prominence. Edward allegedly named him *ætheling*, giving him hope and expectation of the throne.[60] Edgar was singled out as an ætheling during Edward's lifetime. Although he never appears in the witness lists of charters, his name was entered, as 'Edgar clito', along with that of Edward and Edith in the New Minster, Winchester's *Liber Vitae*.[61] They were a royal family group. With the attempt to divorce her aborted, Edith recovered the roles of queen, and even extended them in a surrogate family. Though lacking children of her own, Edith was nevertheless responsible for the potential future heirs at a time, in the last decade of Edward's reign, when the succession to the throne was a burning political question. Although she could not have foreseen the precise outcome of 1066, she must already have been aware that the succession to her childless husband would have serious implications for her own future.

The years 1064–5 present us with the two faces of Edith: the builder and patron of the nunnery at Wilton, and the accused murderess of a great noble at court; the queen alongside her husband and the sister aiding her brother Tostig. In the last years of the reign she and Edward concentrated their efforts on completing their proposed building works at Wilton and Westminster. Edith's plan was to replace the nunnery church in stone; Edward's to construct a royal mausoleum. In this dual act of patronage they followed the injunctions of the *Regularis Concordia*: he to care for the men, she for the women. He honoured a London whose importance had grown in the politics of the eleventh-century kingdom: she affirmed the old dynastic connections with Wessex. It was a finely judged pairing, in which the royal couple expressed the holy kingship of a unified kingdom. Edith, like Edward, was also looking forward, in her case to widowhood. Wilton was completed first, and

[57] One or other of the daughters may have been reared in a West Saxon nunnery: Christina was later a nun if not abbess of Romsey.

[58] DB I, fo 129v.

[59] *VitaEd*, 2nd ed, p 24, from Richard of Cirencester.

[60] Leges Edwardi Confessoris, Liebermann, *Die Gesetze*, vol I, p 665, para 35 1c, a post-1066 source.

[61] BL Stowe 944, fo 29r (47) 'Eadweard rex, Eadgyð regina, Edgar clito'. His lack of witness is not unusual, see above discussion of æthelings. Edith's uncle Ælfwig was abbot of New Minster and may have been responsible for this association of king, queen and heir in the manuscript.

finally consecrated on 3 October 1065. Details of the splendid gathering which accompanied it were later recalled by Goscelin of St Bertin writing to the nun Eve. Bishop Hermann presided and the young nuns were not automatically present at the festivities. Goscelin secured Eve's attendance and sent her a fish, just as he would later ensure that she was at the dedication of Westminster where she and the black-clothed nuns stood out among the purple- and jewel-clad women.[62] The audience for the queen's dedication involved many more exalted than the young nuns of Wilton. Wilton was an act of religious patronage but also a political one, and, as perhaps was always intended, the endowment of a dowager retreat. In some later eyes the need for that retreat had been hurried on by Edith's own actions at the end of 1064.

Edith's power was centred at court and it was at court that she stood accused of its abuse. There, it was claimed, she was responsible for murder. On the fourth night of the Christmas festival 1064, so it was alleged, acting on behalf of her brother Tostig, she engineered the death of Gospatric the noble Northumbrian thegn.[63] The identity of Gospatric is not certain, but it is likely that he was a member of the old Bamburgh family which had ruled Northumbria, almost independently, since the early tenth century. He was probably the last surviving son of Uhtred earl of Bamburgh who had married Æthelred II's daughter. If so he was the half uncle of a claimant on the English throne, of his namesake, Gospatric, Uhtred's grandson, great-grandson of Æthelred II and great-nephew of Edward the Confessor, later earl of Northumbria from 1068–72.[64] In 1060–1 Tostig had been accompanied on his visit to Rome by Gospatric the younger, the kinsman of King Edward.[65] Gospatric may simply have been a fellow pilgrim, but a journey to Rome together could signify peace and friendship. Carl and Ealdred had proposed just such a joint pilgrimage as sworn brothers before 1038.[66] Theirs was an ominous precedent: the plan was abandoned and Carl killed Ealdred instead. Gospatric may have accompanied Tostig to Rome as a follower, as a sworn brother, or as a hostage, because Tostig was afraid of what might happen in the North during his absence; maybe for all these reasons. Pilgrimage, unfortunately, was a dangerous undertaking, pilgrims a source of loot and ransom, and Gospatric was captured by robbers as the

---

[62] Goscelin, *Liber Confortatorius*, pp 28–9.

[63] *Fl Wig* s.a. 1065.

[64] For doubts see Barlow 1970, p 235 n 3, though the elder Gospatric's obvious importance weighs against his argument that the assassination of a man fifty years after his father's death was unlikely. For acceptance of him as Uhtred's son, see Kapelle 1979, pp 94–5, Morris 1992, Williams 1995, p 69.

[65] Gospatric the elder is possible but unlikely. He would by now have been well turned fifty, and *VitaEd*, pp 35–6 makes the Gospatric in Rome an *adolescens* and a kinsman of King Edward.

[66] Symeon of Durham, *De Obsessione Dunelmi*, ed Hodgson Hinde, p 156.

party left Rome. There was already tension between Tostig and the Northern nobility. The appointment of Tostig, the king's brother-in-law and the first West Saxon to be earl of Northumbria, fuelled Northern resentments. In this atmosphere the capture of a scion of the Bamburgh house whilst in the following of Earl Tostig was unlikely to be seen as an accident, doubly unlikely by 1065, by which time the same man's uncle had died at court. Edith found it necessary to explain in the *Life* of Edward what happened on the road from Rome. She was driven to do so by the accusation against her and her brother of murder.

Since the death of Æthelred II the relationships of the Bamburgh family with the southern court had been unhappy and violent. Uhtred had met his own death whilst ostensibly under Cnut's protection. His son Ealdulf had been murdered at court by Earl Siward in 1041, betrayed by Harthacnut who had assured him of his safety. Another son, Ealdred, had been killed in 1038 by Carl, in a feud which was caught up in the southern kings' attempts to rule the North.[67] That Uhtred's last surviving son should meet his death by violence at the southern court and that the then earl of Northumbria, Tostig, should be suspected of complicity merely adds another repeat to the pattern. By the 1060s the family had an additional significance. Along with the grandson of Godgifu and Eustace of Boulogne, Gospatric the younger was one of the two male descendants of Æthelred II not being safely reared at the royal court. In their geographical remoteness and their links North to Scotland, Uhtred of Bamburgh's descendants were now a factor not merely in the control of Northumbria but in the fate of the English throne. They were of concern to Edith in more ways than one.

At this remove in time it is hard to judge the truth of the accusation. The previous history of relations between the southern court and Northumbria invited suspicion and accusation, but also lend them credibility. Murder was part of English political life between 1002 and 1066. Several occurred at court or with suspected royal connivance. Few can be pinned with total certainty to a particular suspect. Edith was powerful at court, concerned with the succession. The Bamburgh family, with English royal blood in its veins, had a potential say in the succession to the throne with which her own fate was bound up, but were remote and less than friendly. As her actions concerning Archbishop Cynesige's bequests and Peterborough demonstrate, she was far from indifferent to what was happening in the North, and her interests here as queen and as her brothers' sister were inextricably entwined. We may suspect that Edward himself had a part in the murder which his later reputation whitewashed, leaving Edith with the blame. The age-old archetype of disaster which

[67] Details of all these murders are in *De Primo Saxonum Adventu, De Obsessione Dunelmi* and Symeon of Durham's *Historia Regum*, ed Hodgson Hinde, pp 212–13, 156–7, 91–3.

began with the action of a woman gave strength and conviction to a story which fingered her alone.[68] But Edith should not be removed entirely from the list of suspects. She and Tostig were closely identified, by English and Normans after 1066. The patron of Wilton was not *ipso facto* incapable of involvement in political murder. Like Emma in the 1030s Edith was a political actor and court politics had a nasty side in eleventh-century England, from which her gender did not exclude her. If nothing else, the accusation is further proof of where Edith's power was seen to lie. Emma, a queen whose career followed the cycle of family politics, had to clear herself of culpability in a son's death. Edith, in her own self-image the queen-in-the-household *par excellence*, rebutted accusations of complicity in court murder.

Neither Edith nor Edward could have foreseen the consequences which would flow from that murder. Tostig's imposition of southern methods of rule on the North meant that the murder of Uhtred's last surviving son had an impact far beyond that of the earlier ones which had devastated the family.[69] The ensuing Northern rising of 1065 divided Tostig and Harold and demonstrated the limitations of Edward's own power. The sense of despair and foreboding which the *Life* of Edward expresses in Edith's tears is influenced by a retrospective view from beyond the battle of Hastings, but accurately captures her situation by late 1065. With Edward old and sick in mind and perhaps already close to death,[70] Tostig in exile, and Harold possibly planning a bid for the throne and contemplating taking the sister of earls Edwin and Morcar as his wife and future queen,[71] Edith faced the sort of prospects which Emma confronted in 1035.

Edith, however, lacked even an absent son. Her role as queen and in the upbringing of the royal heirs gave her some claim on regency, but Edgar was probably already old enough to rule alone,[72] and her brother Harold certainly was. Recent experience would have shown her the dangers of widowhood. She could be a second Cunigund, childless like

---

[68] Cf Bak 1993: Gisela, wife of St Stephen, became a legendary murderess as her increasingly saintly husband was exonerated. Edith was eventually subsumed into Edward's sanctity, but in the early stages when her reputation after 1066 was more debatable, this development may have begun around her too.

[69] Discussed Stafford 1989, pp 95–9.

[70] *VitaEd*, p 53 'egrum trahebat animum'.

[71] The date of this plan is not certain. It may belong either to 1065 and the accommodation Harold reached with her brothers, or to 1066 and his search for support after his coronation.

[72] The date of Edgar's birth is difficult to calculate, see Hooper 1985, esp p 211 where it is argued that he was in his 70s c. 1125, giving a date of birth c. 1050 × 55. If, however, he is the Edgar Ætheling recorded mid twelfth century, a later date of birth might be argued, though this reference would make him extraordinarily old at the date of his death and should perhaps be discounted.

Edith but who had played a part in the transition after the death of her husband, the Emperor Henry II. Cunigund's was a role limited in time to the interregnum, and she had had her brothers to help her, whereas Edith's were now divided and at odds. The recent example of Anne of Kiev in France demonstrated that even with a son and a formal role in regency a queen's position *vis-à-vis* a powerful noble regent like Baldwin of Flanders was far from certain. Further afield the dowager Empress Agnes had lost control of her son and regency in 1062, though in 1065 she was back in Germany playing a significant role at court.[73] Edith could have had diverse models in mind as the prospect of widowhood and a succession crisis loomed, none of them a straightforward guide to her own situation. The exile and deprivation of her own mother-in-law were recent English reminders of the fates which awaited widowed queens.

Edith has left us the only detailed account of her husband's deathbed and of the final arrangements which would determine her fate as well as that of the English crown. Roused from sleep, the king had summoned the group who would be witness to his last wishes: Harold, Robert the highest ranking member of the royal household, Archbishop Stigand, and Edith herself, unless she was already by his bedside, warming his feet in her lap.[74] In his wife's version of his deathbed utterances, his statements concerning the English and their leaders, especially the English church and its leaders, were received with a measure of scepticism and opposition by those assembled. But there was no debate about Edward's words concerning the fate of the kingdom, although they have proved anything but clear to later historians. Edward's wife, a woman who had been as a daughter to him, was commended with the kingdom to Harold, as his Lady and sister, not to be deprived as long as she lived of any due honour received from Edward himself.[75] Edith claimed that she had been guaranteed against precisely the fates that Emma had suffered in 1035 and again in 1043, and at her saintly husband's insistence. At the very least she was not to be despoiled of her honour, and of the possessions of a queen which were essential to its preservation.

But Edward's words were sufficiently general to admit of a broader interpretation. In Edith's version Harold was not appointed king or given the throne unambiguously. The roles given to Harold deliberately recalled the tutelage Henry I had earlier given Baldwin, emphatically a sort of regent.[76] Edith as 'wife, daughter, Lady' was given the material out of which to construct arguments which were left suitably unformulated. Edith carefully did not claim that she had been left as regent, or as arbiter

---

[73] See Bulst Thiele 1933, pp 89–92 for Agnes' activities in Germany in these years, though with a tendency to make her too simply a pawn of papal politics.

[74] *VitaEd*, p 76.

[75] Ibid p 19.

[76] Ibid p 54.

of the fate of the kingdom, nor did she say that she had not. In 1066–7 it was still not clear what Edith could hope to salvage out of 1066. At least she hoped for the preservation of her position, in itself an achievement beyond Emma's after 1042, though one which the latter had fought for after 1035. But she might have hoped for more – a recognized role in the new court and kingdom, unprecedented but arguable if she could maintain some identification as queen with the kingdom and its fate, as widow with her dead husband or most daringly, or desperately, as his spiritual daughter, with a daughter's claims on inheritance. The role she was given in the Norman stories of 1066 half acknowledges her right as a dowager queen and widow to have a say. Edith may have hoped for more than that; her own narrative put together a year or more later was still almost studiedly ambiguous.

4 1066 to 1075: Edward's Widow

In 1066 Edith faced the sort of reduction in status which Emma had feared and suffered. Immediately after Edward's burial Harold had taken the throne. He already had adult sons and a wife of some years' standing, though apparently one who could be disposed of in the interests of a better match. Now or in 1065 he married Ealdgyth, the sister of Edwin and Morcar and widow of Gruffudd the Welsh king. Edwin and Morcar would have wanted full recognition, including dowering, for their sister. A new king with a wife to endow and adult sons to provide for would have looked hungrily at Edith's rich landed possessions. There could be no automatic loyalty of sister to brother in 1066. If Edith was associated more with Tostig than with Harold in later English and Norman eyes, the alignments between brothers and sister, like the divisions between brothers, may date from 1065–6. This would not necessarily make her a supporter of the Norman claim. The Norman stories had their own logic and their own need to include Edith, and they have eclipsed other accounts of 1066. She came to terms with the Normans after Hastings, though not necessarily in quite the way they described; but earlier in the year her options are likely to have been more open. Edith's cousin, Swein Estrithson, was another candidate, and joint Danish–English monarchy had opened a powerful role for Emma earlier in the century. In the final version of the Norman story, Edith was Edward's widow, legitimately transferring to William a crown which was his from the day Edward died. This was not the way 1066 was, nor even the way the Normans themselves first saw it.[77] Edith's manoeuvrings in 1066 are one of the lost stories of that year.

[77] Garnett 1986b.

By the end of it she had reached at least a preliminary agreement with William, handing over the keys of Winchester to him. Edith as a powerful woman having contact through the court with the administration was useful to him and had a bargaining position; her skill in languages should not be discounted as an additional advantage. Her own narrative belongs to these early inchoate stages of conquest when it was far from clear that the English nobility were finished. A tale which gloried in aspects of the recent English past could still be told to political advantage and an apologia still needed not merely to appeal to Normans but to meet internal English criticism and recrimination. Godwine's daughter and Edward's wife and queen, inextricably united in the person of Edith, determined the shape of the tale she told.

The practical success of her arguments is now difficult to determine. Never, however, had a widow been protected so well as Edith was after 1066. Edith was one of the most successful of all early queens in her retention of land and property in widowhood. She was to be one of the few English whose situation improved as the Norman story took final shape, partly because of her role in that story. The more William was stressed as Edward's immediate and automatic heir, the more respect for his widow became *de rigueur*. The dispossessions after Hastings made it easier for William to provide for his own wife and queen without appropriating Edith's lands, but even so Edith's dowager holdings were enormous. Of the three royal widows who attempted to buck the female lifecycle through their queenship in tenth- and eleventh-century England, Eadgifu and Emma were finally deprived and reduced, Edith died in possession of much of her land. The Norman Conquest, far from destroying Edith, secured for her a prosperous widowhood. What part her version of the eleventh century played in her survival across the critical early stages is debatable, though a stress on her position as Edward's widow was one of its central planks. The picture of her as the sorrowing wife in the Bayeux Tapestry is her own; perhaps it suggests that she established her case.

Her survival ensured her continued patronage and protection of her servants. She made gifts to Giso of Wells,[78] arranged the marriage of Wulfweard the White's daughter and gave land in Essex to Walter the Deacon. She was still at court occasionally, as in March 1071, when she witnessed the appointment of Walcher to Durham. At Wilton in 1072 she was surrounded by a gathering of survivors from the old regime. And Wilton's retention of English abbesses across the early years of the Conquest if not later may be due in part to her influence.[79] But her power seems to have been waning. The woman whom once an abbot

[78] *Writs* 72.
[79] Williams 1995, p 132.

of Peterborough had had to petition through her husband and brothers now found her rents withheld by the man whom she had put in charge of her horses. She appealed to the local hundred for help.[80] Servants must always have been recalcitrant and difficult to control, but dowager queens may have found them a particular problem; dowager queens in a new regime, even a sympathetic one, especially so.

Emma survived 1016 as a symbol of some sort for the English nobility. What did Edith symbolize after 1066? For some of the English she was a last reminder of the old regime. For the scribe of the Combe charter, recording the meeting in the westworks of Wilton in 1072 where Edith was surrounded by the remnants of the pre-1066 royal household, she was defiantly 'the Lady, King Edward's widow', whilst William the Conqueror's wife, Mathilda, was no more than William's 'bedfellow'; like the use of Old English not Latin for the charter this looks like a first stirring of English nationalism.[81] The same note, if now more nostalgic, was struck by the Northern author of the Anglo-Saxon Chronicle when in 1075 the death of 'the Lady . . . King Edward's wife' was noted. But outside the pages of Domesday Book these are two rare mentions of Edith in the years following 1066. In general the dowager queen is remarkable for her absence from the accounts of rebellion and resistance during these years, in marked contrast with her mother. Edith's fate and that of her mother diverged, and so in many respects did their significance for English survivors.

Edith's mother, Gytha, lived at Exeter in the years immediately following 1066.[82] Exeter had been one of the residences of Earl Godwine, so she was there as his widow, but it was also one of her daughter's dower boroughs. Gytha was respected as a widow, perhaps at her daughter's insistence. Yet Gytha was suspect. Her grandsons, Harold's sons, attacked the South West and in 1068 Exeter itself and other South Western towns rose against William. Gytha's presence may have been important to this resistance. Gytha's actions at the time and her treatment in later chroniclers point to her as a symbol of resistance. At Abingdon it was remembered that her breach with William led Abbot Ealdred to withdraw his loyalty.[83] When the author of the D manuscript of the Anglo-Saxon Chronicle told the story of the aftermath of the Conquest, he gave Gytha a tragically noble role, fleeing to the island of Flatholme in the Bristol Channel, 'with many good men's wives'. From there she fled, like Emma before her, to Flanders, where the presence of her and her daughter was another of William's worries after 1066. The Danish-born Gytha, like Emma before her, acquired an English identity

---

[80] Writs 72.
[81] Pelteret no 56, printed Dickinson 1876.
[82] Williams 1995, pp 20–21.
[83] Thus Williams 1995, p 20 and Chron Abing, vol II, p 283.

through her marriage, and was fully assimilated as the mother and grandmother of claimants to the English throne. Her part after 1066 was thus relatively straightforward. She played a part in rebellion and had the potential to become a symbol of English resistance if not of English survival.

Edith played no such role, a fact which tells much about an English queen and much about English resistance. Exeter was Edith's town, and Edith may have intervened to obtain its pardon,[84] but her name was never linked with its fate after 1066. As Harold's sister she could have been associated like Gytha in what was a family as much as a national resistance. But 1065–6 had driven wedges among Godwine's children. Even more significant, Edith had always been Edward's queen as well as Godwine's daughter; Edward's widow was the identity increasingly important to her after 1066. After 1066 the role of an English queen differed from that in 1016. Her links in the South West were with the opponents of resistance. Her brother Harold's sons were driven off by Eadnoth the staller and by the men of Bristol. Eadnoth was a household official, and father of Edith's steward, Harding, who was still with her in 1072; the family may already have held land in Bristol where Harding's descendants would be so important by the twelfth century. Edith's servants, if not Edith as a queen, were tied to kings of the English and their rule. After 1066 resistance to that was rebellion, albeit in support of English claimants against a Norman king. Edith remained in contact with English survivors. Some remnants of the pre-1066 court still gathered around her at Wilton in 1072, and she visited Archbishop Stigand in prison after his deposition.[85] Her role at court linked her with the group of servants and administrators who were accommodated most effectively in the early stages of the Conquest at least.[86] If she had significance as a symbol for any group after 1066 it was for these, for whom her own survival in the new regime made her a good individual protector and mistress and offered the hope of their own.

In England more generally Edith was an unlikely symbol. Whereas struggles against the Danes before 1016 had helped produce a unified English identity which Emma could embody, 1066 was an unexpected conquest which in its immediate aftermath merely served to open up English divisions. In 1016–17, for those who came to terms with Cnut, that is, for the upper ranks of the English leadership, Emma and her marriage were part of the negotiations and settlement. In the fragmented responses after 1066 Edith had no clear place. In the *Life* Edith had tried to associate herself with the kingdom and its fate. But when that fate

---

[84] Williams 1995, p 20.
[85] William of Malmesbury, *DGP*, p 37.
[86] See Williams 1995 chap 4 and especially 5.

turned to resistance it was the disunities of the English which emerged. The queen could not articulate them; nothing in her previous career fitted her to do so. During the tenth and eleventh centuries the queen had become an integral part of the unification of England, and had helped negotiate its divisions, but Edith's resulting actions in the North, her role in the Welsh Marches and in the North East Midlands identified her with a southern English monarchy rather than equipped her with the identity which might have provided a rallying call in the greatest centres of resistance after 1068. Like Emma in 1036 her most secure powerbase lay in Wessex, in the dynasty's traditional heartland. Insofar as resistance fanned residual separatism as much as English feeling, a West Saxon queen was an unlikely heroine. 1066 revealed how far the king and queen of the English had still been the king and queen of the West Saxons. In the end the experience of the Norman Conquest would forge a strong sense of Englishness, but by this time Edith's very success in negotiating 1066 and its aftermath made her unlikely to become its figurehead.

From what records remain it seems that Edith lived out her life in and around the heart of Wessex, perhaps largely at Winchester and Wilton. Chaste widowhood had been a belated fate for Emma; circumstances if not choice forced it on Edith. It is tempting to see the learned Edith leading a quiet retirement in the nunnery where she had been raised, perhaps even reading the lives of the English saints, if it was now that she gave Goscelin of St Bertin information about Saints Kenelm and Edward.[87] But Godwine's daughter who had been raised at Wilton was now but a shadow; nothing after 1066 had linked Edith to the fate of her surviving natal family. The coincidence of the year of her death and that of the last rebellion was exactly that. The queen of the English had played no known part in the rebellions after 1066. She died a rich woman, though uncoupled from her identities as mistress of a royal household, queen and king's wife her wealth brought her only limited power. Her most important achievement after 1066 had been survival, not a fate from which heroes are made but one which many English nobles by 1075 would have envied her. Already she was as important to the Normans as to the English; it was William who arranged her burial. It was at Winchester that she died on 19 December 1075, according to a later tradition after a long illness on the brink of death,[88] and was taken to be buried near Edward at Westminster. She was no older than fifty-five or so. By the twelfth century she would be an ambiguous figure for the English looking back on 1066. In 1075 the English Northern chronicler recorded her death with just a hint of nostalgia.

---

[87] Above n 26 and Goscelin, *Liber Confortatorius*, p 16.
[88] Matthew Paris, p 20.

Edith the Lady died seven nights before Christmas in Winchester, she was King Edward's wife, and the king had her brought to Westminster with great honour and laid her near King Edward, her lord.[89]

---

[89] *ASC*, MS D s.a.

Appendix I   The Lands and Revenues of Edith in Domesday Book

Totals have been calculated under three headings

a) Lands which were unquestionably held by Edith herself
b) Lands held by her tenants, 'men' and others holding of her (excluding those who held in commendation)
c) Lands said to be held by the 'Queen', or to be of the Queen's fee, or held by 'Edeva', possibly Edith.

In each shire the totals have been given at the end of the first shire entries, though they include lands listed later in the table as debatably Edith's.

Overall totals

a) £1573 12s 11d p.a. (If Wilton land in Sussex is included this rises to £1659 12s 11d)
b) £299 2s 6d p.a. (excluding Wilton lands in Sussex)
c) £93 9s

Miscellaneous annual payments to the Queen

£15 as gifts/gersuma
10 ounces of gold and one gold mark
5 ores

Domesday statistics present many problems. First, there is the problem of identification of landholders who are not always consistently identified throughout the Survey; the calculation under c) above tries to deal with this. Second, details are inconsistently recorded from area to area or circuit to circuit. Thus in many shires or in individual entries, it is not clear whether the value applies to 1066, 1086 or both; where only one value is given, that has been used in the calculations, though with the obvious possibility that it may have risen or declined between 1066 and 1086. Thirdly, some shires, like Bedfordshire and Buckinghamshire, record overlords and tenants for 1066; in others it is only the tenant or only the overlord who is listed. This can distort by underestimating a great lord's estate where only tenants are listed, but by overestimating it if tenants' lands should be excluded from it. To allow for this the calculations of the values of Edith's lands have been made both with and without those of her tenants. This runs the risk of exaggerating her landholding, especially in the South East Midlands and East Anglia; and it fails to draw a distinction between lands whose revenues were entirely hers and those where she merely called on the loyalty or some other non-monetary return from her men. It is not, however, clear that Domesday

itself is consistent in making this distinction. Its reasons for listing sometimes tenants and sometimes overlords are obscure and certainly bear no
simple relationship to patterns of estate management and revenues. In
some respects the differences are a feature of different circuits and thus
perhaps of regional differences in tenurial patterns, in others of the
existing lists and evidence the commissioners and scribes had before
them. But they are also determined by the evidence presented to the
commissioners in 1086 and the disputes and strategies of those who
named their predecessors, even in some areas a factor of the disruption of
landholding since 1066 and thus of the need for detail in arguments
about the pre-existing situation. Finally, there are problems of omissions;
some shire totals may be gross underestimates. Lincolnshire, for example, contains no adequate valuation of Edith's substantial urban holdings
in Stamford and Torksey. It is possible that the high values of the
Rutland manors include Stamford, some at least of the payments from
here are said to lie in Rutland. A proportion of the renders listed for both
boroughs have been added in the totals, but they may significantly
underassess Edith's income.

LAND	1066 Val	1086 Val	1066 Holder	1086 Holder	Comment
KENT					
Canterbury, fo 2r	25d		Edith		No royal soke over Edith's lands
Canterbury, fo 8r			Edith of king Edward	William s of Robert, of Odo of Bayeux	Belonged to Shelve
?Shelve, fo 8r	£4		Edith, ?the Queen	William s of Robert, of Odo of Bayeux	
Newington, fo 14v	£40		Sigar, of Edith	Albert the Chaplain	Customary dues of cheeses and other payments from royal manor of Milton belong here
?Hartanger, fo 11r	40s		Edith, ?the Queen	Ralph s of Robert, of Odo of Bayeux	
TOTALS a) £4 2s 1d b) £40 c) £2					
SUSSEX					
Beddingham, fo 18v	20s		Edith	Ct of Eu	
Frog Firle, fo 21v	£3		Edith	Abbot of Grestain, of Ct of Mortain	TRE Edith gave it to St John's, Lewes
Parrock, fo 21v	52s		Edith	Ct of Mortain	never paid geld; 1 virgate Earl Harold had held, taken from St

Place (folio)	Value	1066 holder	Tenant-in-chief	Notes
Eckington and Chelvington, fo 22r	40s	Edith	Ct of Mortain	John's, where Ct of Mortain has a hall
Iford, fo 26r	£50	Edith	Wm of Warenne	26 burgesses in Lewes attached here. Following lands in Sussex held by Wilton nunnery in 1066, possibly held by Edith earlier in her lifetime
West Firle, fos 19rv and 21r	£65 3s	Wilton	Ct of Eu, Ct of Mortain, Walter son of Lambert	
Falmer, fo 26r	£20	Wilton	William of Warenne	
Arlington, fo 19r	7s	Wilton	Walter son of Lambert	
Alciston, fo 19v	10s	Wilton	Ct of Eu and Walter son of Lambert	

TOTALS
a) £58 12s
a/b) £86
(=Wilton land)

SURREY

Place (folio)	Value	1066 holder	Tenant-in-chief	Notes
Reigate, fo 30r	£40	Edith	King	
Fetcham, fo 30v	60s	Edith	King	
Shere, fo 30v	£15	Edith	King	
Dorking, fo 30v	£18	Edith	King	'From the 3 (sic) manors which Queen Edith had in Surrey, the sheriff has £7 because he aids them when they need it'

LAND	1066 Val	1086 Val	1066 Holder	1086 Holder	Comment
TOTALS					
a) 76					
HAMPSHIRE					
Anstey, fo 38r	50s		Edith	King	
Greatham, fo 38r	60s		Edith	King	
Selborne, fo 38r	12s 6d		Edith	King	
Upton, fo 38v	£4		Edith	King	
Wootton, fo 40r		£3	Edith	King	
Alton, fo 43r	£6		Edith	St Peter, Winchester	County testifies unjustly exchanged for a house of the king
King's Clere, fo 43r	£7		Edith	St Peter, Winchester	Kg Wm gave in exchange for land on which domus regis is
Hayling Island, fo 43v	£15		Wulfweard White of Edith in alodium	St Peter, Jumièges	Monks of Bishopric of Winchester claim
Penton, fo 43v	£10		Edith	Grestain Abbey	
Tunworth, fo 45r	£3		Alfred, of Queen Edith	Hugh of Port	
Candover, fo 49v	£4		Osbern, of Queen Edith	Chipping	land of the king's thegns
Shoddesden, fo 50r	15s		Agemund, of Queen Edith	Agemund	land of the king's thegns
TOTALS					

a) £36 2s 6d
b) £22 15s

DEVON				
Exeter, fo 100r	£12	Edith	King	Exeter renders £18 p.a.; Baldwin the sheriff has £6 and Colwin £12 'ad numerum in ministeriis Edded reginae'
Lifton, fo 100v	£15	Edith	King	'The lands written below Queen Edith held; now the king holds' Exon DB Colwin holds Lifton from the king at farm
Kenton, fo 100v	£30	Edith	King	
North Molton, fo 100v	£45	Edith	King	
Wonford, fo 100v	£18	Edith	King	
TOTALS				
a) £120				
CORNWALL				
Landinner, fo 121v, and fo 100v	?60s	Edith	Ct of Mortain	The two lands at Landinner and Trebeigh belong to Lifton, Devon
TOTALS				
a) £3 10s				
SOMERSET				
Milverton, fo 87r	£12	Edith	King	'Queen Edith held the lands written below'

LAND	1066 Val	1086 Val	1066 Holder	1086 Holder	Comment
Martock, fo 87r	£80	£70	Edith	King	
Keynsham, fo 87r			Edith	King	8 burgesses in Bath pay 5s p.a.; various people held and hold of this manor including Wulfweard, succeeded by Bishop of Coutances and by his own wife; Exon DB 113 b i acquired by Wm Hosatus, ?Wm of Mohun, sheriff of Somerset, for the *firma*; cf DB I fo 99r for his lands listed with those of other royal servants, including Hugolin the Interpreter, who also held land in Batheaston.
Chewton Mendip, fo 87r	£30		Edith	King	4 burgesses in Bath
Batheaston, fo 87r			Edith	King	'these two hides were and are *de dominica firma* of Bath'
Bath, fo 87r		£60 plus 1 gold mark plus 100s from mint	Edith		Wulfweard White's lands of Corton, Whitcomb Pitney and Mudford follow immediately after Edith's; perhaps held of her.

		Alfred, of Edith	A man of Bp of Coutances	Exon DB Alfred the Steward
Twerton, fo 88v	60s			Exon DB Alfred the Steward
Puriton, fo 91r	£12	Edith	St Peter, Rome	
Luccombe, fo 97r	£3	Edith	Ralph of Limesy	
Selworthy, fo 97r	20s	Edith	Ralph of Limesy	
Combe, fo 99r	20s	Edith	Agelric, a king's thegn	
?Crewkerne and Easthams, fos 86v–87r	£46 / 50s	Eddeva / Eddeva	King, men of the Ct of Mortain	Eddeva's lands are listed among those of the Godwine family. Is this a mistake for Eddid, though in Somerset royal lands which had been Edith's are listed separately

TOTALS
a) £262
b) £3
c) £48 10s

WILTSHIRE

Wootton Rivers, fo 65r	£26	Edith	King	
Westbury, fo 65r	£100	Edith	King	
Winterbourne Stoke, fo 65r	£33	Edith	King	
Lavington, fo 73r	£20	Edith	Robert Marshall	
?Kingston Deverill, fo 68v	40s	Eddeva	Canons of Lisieux	For Eddeva see above. Nearby Brixton Deverill held by Brictric then Queen Mathilda

LAND	1066 Val	1086 Val	1066 Holder	1086 Holder	Comment
TOTALS a) £179 c) £2					
DORSET Sherborne, fo 77r		£50 £27 £6 10s £6	Edith, before her bishop Ælfwold	Bishop of Sherborne	land held by thegns, monks and milites; what bishop holds worth £50, milites, £27, monks £6 10s, thegns £6
TOTALS a) £89 10s					
BERKSHIRE Waltham, fo 56v	£12		Edith	King	
Warfield, fo 57r	£12		Edith	King	
Wargrave, fo 57r	£31		Edith	King	
Remenham, fo 57r	£15		Edith	King	
Winterbourne, fo 58r	£6		Lank, of Edith	King	
Long Wittenham, fo 60r	£20		Edith	Walter Giffard	8 hagae in Wallingford belong here
Burghfield, fo 60v	20s		2 alodarii	Henry of Ferrers	One of two alodarii served the Queen TRE; 20s = half value
Shottesbrook, fo 63v	£7		goldsmith held	Ælfweard the	Ælfweard's father held of Edith

Place, folio	Value	of Queen Edith		Notes
Carswell, fo 63v	£4	Edith	Goldsmith	TRE, the land is geographically close to Waltham, Warfield, Wargrave, Remenham
Burley, fo 63v	20s	Ælfgifu	Ælfwold chamberlain Harding, of Edith, now Harding	Harding held and still holds; Ælfgifu held TRE
TOTALS a) £94 b) £15				

GLOUCESTERSHIRE

Place, folio	Value	of Queen Edith		Notes
Marshfield, fo 163r Cirencester, fo 162v	£35	Edith	King	Queen had the sheep's wool
TOTALS a) £35				

WORCESTERSHIRE

Place, folio	Value	of Queen Edith		Notes
Elmley, fo 176r	£10	Ælfwold, of Queen Edith	Ralph of Tosney's man	
Stanford, fo 176v	50s	Godric, of Queen Edith	Roger of Lacy	
Stanford, fo 176v	20s	Brictric, a thegn of Queen Edith held	Osbern, son of Richard	
TOTALS b) £13 10s				

HEREFORDSHIRE

LAND	1066 Val	1086 Val	1066 Holder	1086 Holder	Comment
Stanford, fo 180r	100s		Edith	King	It is leased for £60, should be £120; 26 lands belonged here TRE, one piece now in hands of the Abbess at Fencote, 40d; there is a render from Leominster *ad victum monialium*. Land worth £12 11s held by others in 1086; Stanford and Much Marcle belonged here TRE worth £30
Leominster, fo 180r		£60 £30 £12 11s	Edith	King	
Martley, fo 180v		£24 and 12s	Edith	King	The £24 and 12s *de gersuma* paid to Hereford; it has three houses attached to it in Worcester
Leinthall, fo 183v	50s		Edith	Ralph of Mortimer	
?Shobdon, fo 183v	£6		Edith, ? the Queen	Ralph of Mortimer	
Frome, fo 184r	60s		Tostig of Queen Edith	Roger of Lacy	

TOTALS
a) £140 13s
b) £3

OXFORDSHIRE				
Hempton, fo 157v	£6	Edith	Walter Giffard	Total value 100s
Horley, fo 159r	50s	Queen Edith held half	Berengar of Tosney	
Gt Haseley, fo 159r	£15	Edith	Miles Crispin	
TOTALS a) £23 10s				
BUCKINGHAMSHIRE				
Amersham, fo 144r	20s	Ælfwine, Queen Edith's man	Bp of Bayeux	
Hughenden, fo 144v	£7	Edith	Bp of Bayeux	
Marlow, fo 144v	£4	Edith	Bp of Bayeux	
Worminghall, fo 145r	£7	Eddeva/ Eadgifu, wife of Wulfweard White, of Edith	Bp of Coutances	
Ludgershall, fo 145r	£6	Eadgifu, wife of Wulfweard White, of Edith	Bp of Coutances	Edeve/Eadgifu also held Water Eaton and Linford
Simpson, fo 145r	£8	Edith	Bp of Coutances	
Addingrove, fo 147r	£4	Wulfweard, Edith's man	Walter Giffard	
Winchendon, fo 147r	£12	Eadgifu of Queen Edith	Walter Giffard	'tenuit Eddeda de regina Eddeva', ?recte 'Eadgifu held of Queen Edith'
Lillingstone, fo 147v	50s	Syric, Queen Edith's man	Walter Giffard	
Bradwell, fo 148r	30s	Ælfgeat, Queen Edith's man	Walter Giffard	

LAND	1066 Val	1086 Val	1066 Holder	1086 Holder	Comment
Upton, fo 148r	60s		Ælfwine, Queen Edith's man	William Peverel	
Iver, fo 149r			Toki	Rbt D'Oilly	Of 3 freemen on this large manor one was Queen Edith's
Wycombe, fo 149r	£12		Brictric of Queen Edith	Rbt D'Oilly	
Amersham, fo 149v	£16		Edith	Geoffrey de Mandeville	
Waddesdon, fo 150r	£30		Brictric, Queen Edith's man	Miles Crispin	
Wingrave, fo 150r	100s		Brictric, Queen Edith's man	Miles Crispin	
Linslade, fo 150v	£10		Ælfwine, Queen Edith's man	Hugh of Beauchamp	
Chesham, fo 150v	£12		Brictric, Queen Edith's man	Hugh of Bolbec	
Calverton, fo 150v			Queen Edith's man plus other	Hugh of Bolbec	Most of the land held by a thegn of Edward; 2 hides by a man of Queen Edith
Eton, fo 151r	£6		Edith	Walter son of Ohthere	
Nashway, fo 151v	50s		Azor son of Toti, Queen Edith's man	Roger of Ivry	

Place, folio	Value	Holder TRE	1086 holder	Notes
Wolverton, fo 152r	?£2 10s	Ælfric, Queen Edith's man, 1 of 3	Mainou the Breton	2 other holders TRE, one a man of Harold, one a housecarl of Edward; Edith's man held 2 and half hides of 20; hence £2 10s of £20 value
Claydon, fo 153r	£11	Edith	Alric the Cook	
Chesham, fo 153r	100s	Edith	Ælfsige	Chesham, Shortley and Shipton given by Edith TRW to Ælfsige with Wulfweard's daughter
Shortley, fo 153r	£3	Wulfweard	Ælfsige	
Shipton, fo 153r	20s	?Wulfweard	Ælfsige	
Milton Keynes, fo 153r	£8	Edith	Godric Cratel	Land of various men, cf lists of 'king's thegns' in other shires

TOTALS
a) £65
b) £115

MIDDLESEX

Place, folio	Value	Holder TRE	1086 holder	Notes
Ebury, fo 129v	£12	Harold son of earl Ralph	Geoffrey de Mandeville	Harold held it and Edith 'custodiebat' him and the manor; then Wm the chamberlain held of the Queen for £3 p.a., after Queen's death he held of the king; Wm lost the manor 4 years ago

TOTALS
a) £12

HERTFORD SHIRE

LAND	1066 Val	1086 Val	1066 Holder	1086 Holder	Comment
N. Mimms, fo 135r	£10		3 thegns, men of Queen Edith	Bp of Chester	The land is not *de episcopatu*; it belonged to the bishop's father, Rayner.
Wigginston, fo 136rv	£3		Brictric, Edith's man held half	Ct of Mortain	Estimated value on basis of half the holding
Broadfield, fo 137v	10s		Gode of Queen Edith	Earl Roger	
Hoddesdon, fo 139v	60s		Gode of Queen Edith	Edward of Salisbury, sheriff	
Bushey, fo 139v			1 freeman there was a man of Queen Edith TRE	Geoffrey de Mandeville	Queen Edith's man has been added to this manor, see below
Cassio, fo 139v	20s		Ælfwine the hunter, Queen Edith's man	Geoffrey de Mandeville	G de M has placed this land in Bushey where it does not belong; the freeman of Edith in Bushey was not there TRE
Welwyn, fo 140r	£6		Gode and her son of Queen Edith	Geoffrey of Bec	
Hoddesdon, fo 142r	30s		Gode, Queen Edith's man (*sic*)	Peter, a burgess (king's thegn)	
TOTALS ab) £25					

Sewell, fo 209v	20s	Walraven, Edith's man	King	Ralph Taillebois has added this land to royal manor of Houghton
Eaton, fo 209v	£20	Ælfsige, Queen Edith's man	Bp of Bayeux	
Bromham, fo 213v	£4	Ælfsige, Queen Edith's man	Hugh of Beauchamp's man Serlo	
Biddenham, fo 213v	10s	Ælfsige of Bromham, Queen Edith's man	Hugh of Beauchamp's man Serlo	
Thurleigh, fo 213v	30s	Moding, Queen Edith's man	Hugh of Beauchamp's man, Leofgeat	
Sharnbrook, fo 216v	60s	Ælfgar, Queen Edith's man	Albert of Lorraine	
Carlton, fo 218v	1s 6d	Alli a thegn of Edward and Ketelbert, Queen Edith's man	Ketelbert, Queen Edith's man	Listed under *Terra praepositorum et elemosinarum*; Ketelbert held 1 hide TRE – he has appropriated 2½ virgates; next entry, 5 bros and their mother hold 3 virgates, Lank their father held – ? man who elsewhere appears as Edith's man. 1s 6d = half TRE value

TOTALS
b) £29 11s 6d

LAND	1066 Val	1086 Val	1066 Holder	1086 Holder	Comment
LEICESTERSHIRE					
Dishley		40s			
+?Thorpe	£3		Edith	Godwine of the king	Godwine held Whatborough, with 1½ carucates in Burgo, Thorpe and Dishley ad firmam. Were all three held by Edith? and Saddington? fo 230r 2 houses in Leicester belonged to Saddington and Thorpe
Whatborough	10s				
Saddington fo 230v	£4				
TOTALS					
a) £9 10s					
c) 19s					
ESSEX (DB II)					
Rivenhall, fo 27r	£9		Edith	Ct Eustace	
Wix, fo 54r		10s	Edith	Hugh de Montfort's man	the Queen had the soke
Wix, fo 87r	£6		Edith	Walter the deacon	
	10s				
Little Bromley, fo 87r	£5		Edith	a *miles*, of Walter the deacon	Queen Edith gave this land to Walter after William's arrival
Little Chesterford, fo 87r	100s		Edith	a *miles*, of Walter the deacon	

TOTALS
a) £26
c) £36

SUFFOLK (DB II)					
Ipswich, fo 290r	?⅔ of £4 paid by moneyers	?⅔ of £40	Regina Edeva/ ?Edith		Queen held ⅔ TRE and earl Gyrth ⅓, 1066 value included a render in kind, 1086 one taken for calculations
Ipswich, fo 427r	20d		Edith	Walter the deacon	Walter has 5 houses and 3 vacant *mansurae* which Queen held
Belstead, fo 306r	£4		Godwine, son of Ælfsige, a thegn of Queen Edeva/ ?Edith	Robert Malet	In all these Edeva/Edith entries the Queen's name is given as Edeva, although elsewhere it is 'Edid'; is this Edith or Eadgifu the Fair, probably the wife of Harold?
Playford, fo 314v	£8		Godwine son of Ælfhere, of queen Edeve/ Edith had commendation only	Robert Malet's man	
Bricett, fo 393v			Bondi, freeman, regina Edeve/ Edith	Richard s of Ct Gilbert	Richard claims it *ad feudum Wisgari*, i.e. Wihtgar son of Ælfric
Ixworth Thorpe, fo 421r			Sparrowhawk, man of Queen Edith (Edit)	Peter of Valognes	'She gave him to Peter. After her/his (*eius*) death, the king gave it to him'
Bildeston, fo 426r	£8		Queen Edith (Edid)	Walter the deacon	

LAND	1066 Val	1086 Val	1066 Holder	1086 Holder	Comment
Swilland, fo 426rv Otley, fo 433r	50s		Queen Edith (Edid) Leoflæed under commendation of Rbt Malet's predecessor	Walter the deacon Humphrey the Chamberlain	Queen had soke On this manor a freeman, Brihtwold, under the commendation of the queen – which one unclear
Bayhlam, fo 448v		2s	Queen Edeva/ ?Edith	Edeva/ ?Edith as long as she lived; then Wm of Bonneville	Half the church and 12 acres. Does the reference to survival of Edeva/?Edith after 1066 here suggest here and elsewhere this Edeva a mistake for Edith, rather than Harold's wife, Eadgifu/Edeva?
Chediston, fo 332r		10s	Godwine, freeman of the Queen	man of Roger Bigot	
Chediston, fo 332v		5s	Wulfsige	man of Roger Bigot	Wulfsige, Ulf and Anund had 13 acres each, valued in total at 4s. The Queen had had commendation of Ulf, half that
Chediston, fo 332v			Ulf	man of Roger Bigot	of Wulfsige and probably half that of Anund
Chediston, fo 332v Chediston, fo 332v			Anund 2 freemen, in commendation of the king and queen TRE	man of Roger Bigot man of Roger Bigot	these 2 held 30 acres

Place, folio	Value	Holder		Notes
Baylham, fo 337v				Warengar holds from Roger Bigot a freeman, Brun, reeve of Ipswich, and in commendation of the Queen, ?Mathilda, ?previously Edith/Eadgifu?
Cretingham, fo 433rv	?20s	Brictwold, in commendation of Queen	Amund	It is now part of lands of Humphrey the Chamberlain
Helmingham, fo 433v		Grimwulf, under commendation of queen	Humphrey the Chamberlain	It belonged to Otley and is part of Otley's *pretium*
Barton Mills, fo 435v	£8	Ælfgeat held, then William of the queen	Ælfgifu	Is the queen Edith or Mathilda?
TOTALS a) £37 3s 4d b/c) £20 16s				
LINCOLNSHIRE Stamford, fo 336v	£4 ?+ half of £15	Edith	King	Queen Edith had 70 *mansiones* (i.e. c half the *mansiones*) which lay in Rutland with all *consuetudines*, except the bakers'; 2 $\frac{1}{2}$ carucates of land are attached, 1 plough and 45 acres of meadow outside the town – worth £4. £15 = TRE render

LAND	1066 Val	1086 Val	1066 Holder	1086 Holder	Comment
Torksey, and adjacent manor of Hardwick, fo 337r	£18-to king and earl		Edith		plus two carucates, which did not pay geld, outside the town; does the value TRE equal the queen's revenue, or exclude it?
Grantham, fo 337v	£52		Edith	King	no-one had sake and soke except nun Ælfswith; Edith had a hall, 2 carucates and 3 ploughs without geld.
Great Ponton, fo 337v			Edith	King	attached to Grantham along with many other lands
Nettleham, fo 338r	£24		Edith	?King	many attached lands
Gayton-le-Wold, fo 338v	£15		Edith	?King	extensive soke
Horncastle, fo 339r	£20		Edith	?King	extensive soke
Colsterworth, fo 371r	20s		a thegn of the queen	?same	land of king's thegns
Fillingham, fo 371v	4s		Earnwine the priest held of the Queen; then Godric the deacon	King, Asketill holds; Roger of Poitou got it 'sine liberatore'	

TOTALS
a) £140
b) £1 4s

RUTLAND				
Oakham, fo 293v	£40	Edith	King	with 5 berewicks, churchsoke
Hambleton, fo 293v	£52	Edith	King	with 7 berewicks, churchsoke
Ridlington, fo 293v	£40	Edith	King	with 7 berewicks, churchsoke
RUTLAND listed in Northants				
Ketton, fo 219r	£10	Edith	King	Hugh of Port holds *ad firmam de rege*
Barrowden, fo 219r	£3	Edith	King	Hugh of Port holds *ad firmam de rege*
Luffenham and *Scaulthorp*, fo 219r	30s	Edith	King	Hugh of Port holds *ad firmam de rege*
TOTALS a) £146				
NORTHAMPTONSHIRE				
Finedon, fo 220r	£20 *ad numerum*	Edith	King	many lands attached here
fo 219r	£40 at 20 to the ora			Among general shire payments, *De maneriis Eddid reginae* £40, presumably referring to Finedon.
TOTALS a) £20				

FOLLOWING LANDS ARE 'DE FEUDO REGINAE' OR 'REGINA' Identity unclear

LAND	1066 Val	1086 Val	1066 Holder	1086 Holder	Comment
SURREY					
Coombe, fo 36v	£4 then 20s	100s	Alfred, of the king	Humphrey Chamberlain *de feuo reginae*	After 1066 the woman who held placed herself in the queen's hands; Edith or Mathilda
ESSEX (DB II)					
Shalford, fo 3v	£22		Earl Ælfgar, then the queen	Otto the Goldsmith	Otto has 3 houses belonging to Shalford in Colchester which countess Ælfgifu held – '*hoc est de terra regina*', Edith and/or Mathilda; certainly Mathilda since the Queen gave land here to Richard Fitz Gilbert
Childerditch, fo 5r	£3		Harold, then the queen	Sheriff of Surrey	Edith or Mathilda; probably Mathilda
Finchingfield, fo 3v	£9		Earl Ælfgar, then the queen	Otto the goldsmith	Edith and/or Mathilda; as with Shalford, Mathilda is likely, though as there, this does not preclude Edith
Little Birch, fo 93v	20s		Wulfweard, then the queen	Hugh *de dono reginae*	If this is Wulfweard White, probably Edith
Middleton, fo 98r	?20s		9 freemen of Earl Ælfgar, then the queen	Gilbert the Priest claims *ex dono reginae*	Edith or Mathilda; cf Shalford and Finchingfield

NORFOLK (DB II) Burston, fo 155r	3s	1 freeman in commendation of Leofric of Thorndon	Robert Malet *ex dono reginae*	Robert's mother holds. Edith or Mathilda; if theories that Robert Malet's mother was English are correct, possibly Edith, though this does not preclude Mathilda later
SUFFOLK Occold, fo 450r cf fos 320v and 323v				Dispute between Robert Malet's mother and Bp of Bayeux; Stigand had this land, gave it to Robert's mother, she later held it from the Queen, now the bishop holds. Edith and/or Mathilda, see Burston above. Wulfeva held freeman here
Bedingfield, fo 310v	9s 4s	5 freemen under commendation of Stigand	Robert Malet's mother *de feudo reginae*	Edith and/or Mathilda, see above. Heading *Terra matris Roberti Malet de feudo reginae* – unclear whether this applies to more land
Finningham, fo 321r	30s	18 freemen, mostly under Leofric and Wulfeva	Robert Malet's mother of Robert and *de feudo reginae*	Edith and/or Mathilda, see above
Yaxley, fo 323v	4s	Hagris under commendation of Wulfeva	Robert Malet's mother *de feudo reginae*	Edith and/or Mathilda; note the possibility that Wulfeva ?Wulfeva Betteslau, was attached in some way to Edith, or were her lands used to endow Mathilda. Wulfeva's considerable lands have also passed to Robert Malet

LAND	1066 Val	1086 Val	1066 Holder	1086 Holder	Comment
Wickham, fo 323v	3s		2 freemen under commendation of Wulfeva	Robert Malet's mother *de eodem feudo*	Edith and/or Mathilda, see above
LEICESTERSHIRE					
Sharnford, fo 232r	12d	10s	Ælfwine	Hugh of Grandmesnil *de feudo reginae ut dicit*	
Newbold Verdon and Brascote, fo 232r	5s		?Queen	Hugh of Grandmesnil *de feudo reginae*	
Neulebi, fo 232v	2s		?Queen	Hugh of G *de feudo reginae*	
Market Bosworth, fo 233r	10s		Ælfwine	Hugh of G *de feudo reginae*	
Barton in the Beans, fo 233r	12d		Ælfwine	Hugh of G *de feudo reginae*	

Miscellaneous Payments which Domesday Records as Made to the Queen

Northamptonshire – fo 219r among miscellaneous components of shire farm, 5 ores *de dono reginae et de feno* – as gift to the queen and for hay

Warwickshire – fo 238r among various components of shire farm, 100s *reginae gersumam* to the queen; these payments appear to be only since 1066, when the renders consisted of cash, honey and honey dues

Gloucestershire – fo 162v Cirencester – the queen had the wool from the sheep

Bedfordshire – fos 209rv three great royal manors – Luton, owes among other renders 4 ounces of gold *ad opus reginae*; Leighton, among other renders, 2 ounces of gold *ad opus reginae*; Houghton, among other renders, 2 ounces of gold to the queen

Norfolk – DB II fo 117v Norwich used to pay various dues and renders in cash and kind; now a cash payment and 100s *de gersuma* to the queen

Lincolnshire – fo 337r Queen Edith is one of those who had sake and soke, toll and team in Lincolnshire

Worcestershire – fo 172r sheriff's payments *de comitatu* include 100s to the Queen.

Appendix II   Emma's and Edith's Household and Followers

The following is a listing of those certainly or possibly associated with Edith or Emma, through service or tenancy. The reconstruction of the queen's household pre-1066 is a hazardous undertaking, and many of the following identifications must be very tentative, nor can they claim to be exhaustive. A full study of the royal servants and royal lands is urgently needed. In Edith's case an attempt has been made to distinguish those in her service (group 1) from those who merely held from her or were her 'men' or followers (group 2). Given the expandable nature of the royal household, a distinction between 'servants' and 'followers' may be some-what arbitrary, but an attempt to make one helps to underline the numbers of people involved in royal service in eleventh-century England.

The following have been placed in group 1:

a) those specifically called Edith's servants
b) those given titles which indicate service (*camerarius* etc.) and who held land of her
c) those who held land of her and *either* are also listed among the servants or thegns of the king in Domesday Book *or* their successors or predecessors were king's or queen's servants
d) those associated with her through e.g. the Waltham or Combe charter (S 1036 and Pelteret no 56, printed Dickinson 1876) and whose landholding shows features associated with or links with royal or queen's service
e) those who are not specifically associated with Edith, but their land passed to the servants of Queen Mathilda, and who exhibit other features which link them to the pattern of pre-1066 royal service.

I am aware that c) and especially d) and e) may prove nothing more than that queens held royal land, and that such land was, over the years, turned to many different royal purposes, including provision for royal servants. It has nonetheless seemed worthwhile to gather the evidence here, in the hopes that it will contribute to the developing study of the English landholders in 1066.

1 Candidates for Edith's Close Household, Queen's Servants

e) ALBOLD cook – perhaps associated with Mathilda and more debatably Edith. He held two and a half hides at Mapledurham, Hants, which had been held by Mathilda, and before that by WULFGIFU/ WULFEVA. It was royal land in 1086, DB I, fo 38r. THEODGAR was his predecessor.

ALBERT OF LORRAINE, THE CHAPLAIN see SIGAR.

ÆLFGAR, CHAPLAIN OF QUEEN EDITH held Burghley from Peterborough, Hugh Candidus p 67.

ÆLFGIFU there are several women of this name in Domesday Book. The
following two or more women have some connections with Edith, but it
is unclear how many women we are dealing with and which, if any,
should be seen as Edith's followers:

a) A sister or close relative of Edith – Harold had a sister Ælfgifu; a man of hers
held land at Waldridge Bucks, DB I, fo 144v (other land there was held by a
man of Esgar the staller, fo 148v). Ælfgifu, who held Lewknor before 1066,
was a relative, *consanguinea*, of Queen Edith, *Chron Abing I*, p 459; she was
dead by 1066, but may still have been listed in Domesday. A woman of this
name was connected to the Godwine family in the Wiltshire Domesday. Here
the land of King Edward is followed by lands which had been held by various
members of the Godwine family. An Ælfgifu appears at the end of the list:
she is either the last of the Godwines or the first of a group consisting largely
of priests holding royal churches, DB I, fo 65r. Her holding is 30 hides in
Knoyle, the rest of which was held in 1066 by the nunnery of Wilton, fo 68r;
the size of this estate may suggest that she is an important person. An Ælfgifu
had held two of the 77 hides of Chalke, claimed by the abbess of Wilton in
1086, fo 68r. This woman may or may not be the same as one or more
Ælfgifu's with connections to the royal land, especially the queen's lands and
servants.
b) A woman of this name held land at Burley in Berks, which Harding then held
of Edith, fo 63v; in Devon the lands of a woman/women of this name went to
Walter de Claville, Gotshelm and Baldwin the sheriff – see COLWINE for
Gotshelm and his connections with the queen. An Ælfgifu is also one of the
predecessors of Aiulf the sheriff in Dorset, fo 82v. An Ælfgifu closely connected to the royal lands and their servants held two estates in Berkshire in
1066: Basildon, *terra regis* in 1086, fo 57r and Aston Upthorpe, which had
passed to Reinbald of Cirencester, i.e. Reinbald 'the Chancellor', fo 63v. This
latter had been queen's land in the 960s – Edgar gave it to Ælfthryth, perhaps
as part of the marriage settlement, S 725.
   One or more of the above may be Godwine's daughter, who, like other
members of her family, had acquired royally connected and nunnery connected lands. This acquisition was, however, through royal service, and she
may have gained land through her sister's patronage, and the royal household.
c) Countess Ælfgifu, widow of Earl Ælfgar, also held land which was *terra
reginae* in Colchester, DB II, fo 106v. She may be one or other of the women
of this name above.

ÆLFRIC a man of Queen Edith, held land at Wolverton, Bucks, DB I, fo
152r. He should perhaps be included amongst the men of Edith. The
likelihood that he was some sort of servant is increased by the fact that

the other two holdings in Wolverton were in the hands in 1066 of a man
of Earl Harold and a housecarl of the king.

ALRIC/ÆLFRIC THE COOK held Steeple Claydon, Bucks in 1086, held
by Edith in 1066, DB I, fo 153r. Had he been in her service? see Williams
1995, p 99.

ÆLFRIC OF KEYNSHAM according to the Winton Survey, Biddle
1976, p 38, Ælfric of Keynsham held a tenement in Winchester TRE
which lay behind the shops which belonged to Queen Edith. Keynsham
was Edith's land, and one of her servants and his widow held land of her
there, see WULFWEARD WHITE. The tenement had passed to Geoffrey,
son of Herbert, probably Herbert the Chamberlain.

ÆLFSIGE son-in-law of WULFWEARD THE WHITE, held three lands
in Bucks, all of which Edith had given him after 1066, two at least along
with WULFWEARD's daughter, DB I, fo 153r. One of these lands was at
Chesham, where Queen Ælfgifu had left land in her will in the tenth
century, Wills no 8. He follows ÆLFRIC THE COOK in the survey.
Both are placed between the lands of various women, including Queen
Mathilda, and a subheading 'Terra Lewini de Neweham' which begins
the listing of lands of royal servants, including, e.g. HARDING. Both of
them might be seen to be connected with the latter as royal servants. Like
the royal servants who precede and follow him he and his lands have
not been absorbed into a new Norman holding. Edith's gift had in some
way kept Ælfsige's land safe in his own hands without a Norman
overlord. Edith may have taken him into her service in succession to his
father-in-law.

ÆLFWEARD THE GOLDSMITH AND HIS FATHER the father of
Ælfweard the Goldsmith held land of Edith in 1066, at Shottesbrook in
Berks, DB I, fo 63v. The land is part of a large complex, including
Wargrave, Warfield, Waltham and Remenham to the east of Reading,
itself a tenth-century estate and nunnery held by a queen, see S 1494, the
will of the dowager Queen Æthelflæd. Much of this complex had been in
Edith's hands in 1066, see fos 56v, 57v. Just to the west, in Reading
hundred itself, Aubrey, the Queen's chamberlain, held Burley which
Ælfweard, (again the goldsmith?) had held in 1066; another hide in
Burley was held by HARDING from Queen Edith, though in 1066 it had
been held by ÆLFGIFU, fo 63v. Ælfweard the goldsmith may also be the
Ælfweard the moneyer in Winchester, whose successors were goldsmiths
and die-cutters; Biddle 1976, p 401 n 4. In the twelfth century
Shottesbrook Goldsmith provided for the upkeep of the royal
goldsmithies; tenure was by the service of providing charcoal for the

forging of the king's crown and regalia, *VCH, Berkshire*, vol 3, p 164. The moneyer of this name in the Winchester survey is otherwise unknown from Edward's coinage, but his successors were Odo and William Odo's son, a family of goldsmiths who provided dies for the coinage. The presence of an Ælfweard Goldsmith's father holding land by royal service in nearby Berks seems to enhance the possibility that he too held this as service land. For moneyer/goldsmith connections see Biddle 1976, p 421. It is very likely that Ælfweard's father was also a goldsmith. An Ælfweard married MATHILDA, a lady of Edith's bedchamber, possibly after 1066. Is this the same man? See also THEODERIC and GOLDSMITH.

ÆLFWEARD the third holder of land at Burley see also ÆLFGIFU and HARDING. By 1086 his land was held by Alberic the queen's chamberlain. Had Ælfweard held such a position? Is he, like ÆLFWEARD THE GOLDSMITH, a candidate for the husband of Edith's lady of the bedchamber, MATHILDA.

ÆLFWINE THE HUNTER (venator), a man of Queen Edith, added with his land at Cassio to Bushey, Herts by Geoffrey de Mandeville, DB I, fo 139v; see also A FREEMAN with whom he is presumably identical.

ÆLFWOLD BURþEN (chamberlain) present at Wilton as witness to the Combe charter in 1072, though it is possible that he was attached to the bishop, but see Ælfwold, chamberlain, *camerarius*, listed among the king's thegns who held land in Berkshire which had formerly been held by Edith, DB I, fo 63v.

ÆTHELRIC THE COOK present at Wilton as witness to the Combe charter in 1072.

ÆTHELSIGE STIWEARD (steward) present at Wilton as witness to the Combe charter in 1072, though it is possible that he was attached to the bishop or Azor.

ÆTHELSIGE THE GOLDSMITH present at Wilton as witness to the Combe charter in 1072 – see also ÆLFWEARD THE GOLDSMITH AND HIS FATHER.

AGEMUND among several of his holdings, all listed among the king's thegns in Hampshire, he had held Shoddesden of Queen Edith, DB I, fo 50v.

ALFRED held land at Tunworth, Hants, of Queen Edith, then of the sheriff, Hugh of Port, DB I, fo 45v.

ALFRED (THE STEWARD, *dapifer* according to the Exeter Domesday, *VCH Somerset*, I, p 452) held land of Edith in Twerton, Somerset, held in 1086 by a man of the bishop of Coutances, DB I fo 88v; is this the same man as Alfred *pincerna* who held land in Somerset, fo 92v and in Dorset, fo 78v; in both cases some of his lands were church land of Athelney and Winchester – see e.g. Bishopstone, Somerset, which he holds from the Count of Mortain and which had been Athelney land, fo 93r; Hele, which he held of the Count of Mortain, which in 1066 belonged to the bishop of Winchester's manor of Taunton, fo 92v.

ALFRED held land at Coombe, Surrey, in 1066 *de rege* which in 1086 was *de feudo reginae* and held by Humphrey the Chamberlain; after 1066 the woman who held this land placed herself in the queen's hand, DB I, fo 36v.

ALRIC ?ÆLFRIC cook – possibly to be associated with Edith. Held land at Claydon, Bucks formerly held by her, DB I, fo 153r.

AN ALODARIUS Burghfield, Berks, Reading Hundred, an alodarius 'servivit' the Queen; now holds from Henry de Ferrers, DB I, fo 60v.

ATHELSTAN a man of this name was given land at Ayston (= Athelstan's tun) in 1046, not long after the marriage of Edith and Edward (S 1014), land which should have been part of the soke of her land at Ridlington (see Hart 1992e, pp 194–9). Was he a part of Edith's estate organization in Rutland?

AZOR, THORED'S SON his land transaction with Giso of Wells, the Combe charter, was made before Edith at Wilton in 1072, Dickinson 1876. There are several Azors in Domesday Book. An Azor held land in Wiltshire. His successor was Earl Aubrey and then the king, DB I, fo 69r. All of Aubrey's other Wiltshire lands have connections with the queen or her service: six had belonged to Harding, one had been taken in part by Earl Harold from Amesbury, a tenth-century queenly estate and site of a queenly nunnery foundation. One of the three lands held by this Azor was in Gussage, which had been part of the (possibly dower) holdings of Queen Ælfgifu left in her will to the king, *Wills* no 8. Clarke 1994, p 253 identifies this man as Azor, Thored's son. However, an Azor in the same shire held land at Chitterne, where Harding also held land which had passed to Earl Aubrey; the successor of this Azor was Edward of Salisbury, the sheriff, DB I, fo 69v. Clarke, pp 253–6 distinguishes these two

Azors, though both may be the same man. Both have connections with land linked to royal service. Clarke 1994, pp 57–9 notes the peculiar scattering of three large estates, those of WULFWEARD White, Azor, Thored's son and WULFWYN OF CRESLOW. Royal service, and particularly the queen's service, is a possible link between all three. The scattering of land need not indicate a new man (Clarke) so much as a beneficiary of the opportunities of royal service, including queen's service.

BRICTRIC DODA'S (DODDA) SON present at Wilton as a witness to the Combe charter in 1072. A man/men called Brictric held land of Edith in Bucks etc, but this is unlikely to be the same. This may, however, be the Brictric who held part of the complex of Wimborne lands, most of which were in the hands of the crown or royal servants, DB I, fo 85v. His lands passed to Hervey the *cubicularius*/chamberlain, a *serviens regis*. The monk DODDA, listed before him in Wiltshire, may be his father, see DODDA.

BRUN, reeve at lpswich – possibly a reeve of the queen, though whether *the* reeve of lpswich and of which queen Domesday leaves us in doubt; see DB II, fo 337r; Warengar a man of Roger Bigot held him in the commendation of the queen.

COLWINE, the reeve of Queen Edith in Exeter, who administered her revenues there, DB I, fo 100r. He had also held at farm the old royal manor of Lifton, left in Alfred's will to Edward the Elder to which at that date extensive lands in Cornwall were attached. Some remained so attached in 1066 when Lifton was in Edith's hands in 1066, fo 100v. His successor as reeve at Exeter was Goscelin/Gotshelm, called Goscelm de Execestre in the last entry of his Devon holdings on fos 112v–113v. Goscelin farmed some of Mathilda's manors, Exeter Book fos 108 b2, 109 a2, 109 b1, and held land of Mathilda in Halberton, DB I, fo 101v. His lands, like those of Colwine, Queen Mathilda and other royal servants, went to form the Honour of Gloucester, whose common denominator is a connection with Brictric son of Ælfgar and/or the Queen, but probably at a deeper level with old royal lands which lie behind Brictric's holdings.

DODDA a man of this name had connections with the queen: Dodda held Edmondsham, Dorset, which had passed to Hugh son of Grip via Queen Mathilda, DB I, fo 75v; for Edmondsham's connections with the queen see EADGIFU. Edmondsham is next to Wimborne St Giles where Brictric Doda's son held land. It and other land held by Dodda may even have been given as almsland by Edith: a man of this name held land *in elemosina* in Hampreston, itself just outside Wimborne Minster, granted to him by 'the queen', which one unspecified; DB I, fo 84r. see BRIHTRIC, DODA'S SON; EADGIFU.

EADGIFU held land at Edmondsham, Dorset, of Humphrey the Chamberlain, DB I, fo 83r, a man who received a great deal of land with former queenly or royal service connections and seems to be a servant of Queen Mathilda. Queen Mathilda freed her land of geld in memory of her son Richard; DODDA may be her husband, see Williams 1995, pp 79–80 and n 40 and 41.

EADGIFU, mother of Godric, Lincoln lawman. Just possibly a connection of the queen – see below EARNWINE.

EADRIC held Queen Edith's manor of Dorking in Surrey and had given 2 hides from it to his daughters, fo 30v; a farmer of Edith's estates?

EARNWINE, THE PRIEST held land of the queen at Fillingham, Lincs, DB I, fo 371r. A priest of this name also held 7 plots in the queen's borough of Grantham, fo 337v. He held land in alms of King Edward at S Witham, fo 371r, and also at Owersby, fo 371r, both listed as lands of the thegns in Lincolnshire; at Owersby the bishop of Bayeux was claiming jurisdiction in 1086, fo 376r. He was a relative of Godric, son of Garwine and ?Eadgifu, a lawman of Lincoln, who had become a monk of Peterborough by 1086, and whose land Peterborough and Earnwine were claiming, fos 336r and 336r. This is presumably Godric the deacon who had succeeded Earnwine at Fillingham. Was Alswith the nun, who also held land in the queen's borough of Grantham, with full jurisdiction (cf Godric in Lincoln), a member of the same ecclesiastical dynasty; she too had allegedly given her land to Peterborough by 1086, fo 337v. Earnwine had fallen/been taken since 1066, see fo 347v. The whole family may be associated with the queen, and the use of a matronymic to describe Godric in Lincoln may be significant in this respect. The bishop of Durham, associated with Peterborough, and the abbot of Peterborough were claiming their lands in 1086, and this may be another case in which the queen and Peterborough had been potentially if not actually at odds.

GODE held of Queen Edith in Hertfordshire, DB I, fo 137v and 139r, and together with her son held of Edith, fo 140r. On fo 142r she is said to be a *homo*, man (*sic*) of Queen Edith; cf 137r where it is probably the same woman who is called a *homo* of King Edward. Edward of Salisbury, the sheriff was one of her successors, as was Peter, a *burgensis*, listed under the king's thegns. cf WULFWYN.

GODWINE SON OF ÆLFHERE held in Suffolk *sub regina* in 1066; 1086 Robert Malet the sheriff's man held, DB II, fo 316v.

GODWINE SON OF ÆLFSIGE Queen Edith's man, held land in Suffolk held in 1086 by the sheriff, Robert Malet, DB II, fo 306r.

GODWINE the queen's *dapifer*/steward according to the Waltham charter. Three if not four men of this name held land in 1066 of Edith: three in Suffolk, DB II, fos 306r, 316r, 332r, and the Godwine, who in 1086 held three lands in Leicestershire, which had been Edith's, at farm from the king, DB I, fo 230rv. This last may be the man of the Waltham charter, though geography is against the identification. A Godwine 'hos' was present at Wilton as witness to the Combe charter in 1072, and is possibly the same man. 'Hos' may, however, mean *hostiarius*, usher.

HARDING The Queen's *pincerna*/butler according to the Waltham charter. He held land of Edith in Domesday Book – see Burley in Berks, DB I, fo 63v, held by a woman ÆLFGIFU in 1066. Aubrey, the queen's chamberlain, also held a hide at Burley. Harding held land claimed by the bishop of Salisbury 'for life', fo 67r, and from Glastonbury, fo 90r; his father Eadnoth had held land from Winchester, and could not sell, fo 41r. Harding was present in 1072 at the meeting at Wilton among the group around the dowager queen Edith who witnessed the sale of land at Combe by Azor to Bishop Giso of Wells. Harding was the son of Eadnoth the staller on whom see Freeman, vol IV Appendix S and Clarke 1994, pp 281–83. Harding survived 1066 to found an important family in SW England. William of Malmesbury, *DGRA*, Bk III cap 254, p 313 associates Harding with skill in litigation. Like many royal servants he held ecclesiastical land, from Shaftesbury, see DB I, fo 67v, and Cooke ANS 12, 1989, p 35 makes him one of a 'circle of prominent administrators and royal officials of the south west' whose daughters entered Shaftesbury. Clarke 1994, p 38 ranks Harding and his father together as holding the sixteenth largest non-earlish estate in England in 1066. The scribe of the Combe charter thought him important and listed him first of the lay witnesses. He also witnesses Pelteret no 144, R Appendix I no 4, concerning dues owed from Taunton. For more details on him and his career see Williams 1995, pp 119–22 and Patterson 1989, esp n 2 and Finberg 1957.

KETELBERT, Queen Edith's man, held land in Bedfordshire, DB I, fo 218v, formerly held by himself and a thegn of King Edward, listed under the land of the reeves and almsmen.

LANK held Winterbourne in Berks of Edith DB I, fo 58r; it had been given to THEODERIC THE GOLDSMITH, who was also his successor at Hampstead, fo 63r. Probably the same man whose five sons and widow are listed as holding in Beds among the reeves and almsmen, fo 218v.

LEOFFLÆD in Suffolk – DB II, fo 433v largely on the grounds that her land passed to Mathilda's chamberlain Humphrey, who received a great deal of land with former queenly or royal service connections.

LEOFGEAT held as a royal servant by the service of producing 'aurifrisium', gold embroidered work, for the king and queen, which ones unspecified, DB I, fo 74r.

MATHILDA a Lady of Edith's bedchamber, who married Ælfweard a Worcestershire thegn. According to Hemming, BL Cotton Tiberius A iii fo 120r (=121r) Clopton had been held by Ælfweard, husband of Mathilda, a lady of the queen's bedchamber. The only land at Clopton listed in Domesday is one hide held by Brictmer of the church of Worcester in 1066, held in 1086 by Urse d'Abetot, fo 172v. Urse had ceased to render all service. It is possible that two different lands at Clopton are at issue, but if they are the same we seem to have a change of tenancy after 1066, from Brictmer to Ælfweard, associated with Edith and the marriage of a foreign member of her household. It is tempting to suggest that Edith took some Norman women into her household and then via their marriages continued a limited patronage of surviving members of the English nobility. See ÆLFSIGE, WULFWEARD WHITE'S son-in-law for another marriage arranged by Edith. The marriage may, of course, have taken place before 1066 if there were two Cloptons. In view of the tendency for royal servants to be holding church land, it is noteworthy that it was land claimed by Worcester which was used as dowry. See also ÆLFWEARD THE GOLDSMITH, ÆLFWEARD.

OSBERN, held Candover, Hants, DB I, fo 49v, from Queen Edith; it passed to Chipping and is listed among the Land of the King's thegns.

OTTO THE GOLDSMITH Shalford in Essex, held by Earl Ælfgar, then the queen, in 1086 by Otto the goldsmith; Otto held 3 houses which belonged to Shalford in Colchester, which Countess Ælfgifu used to hold – 'hoc est de terra regina', DB II, fo 3v, fo 106v. Otto married an English woman, ?Eadgifu, widow of a citizen of London, and acquired certain lands which were later held by hereditary serjeanty of keeping the king's money; see Gibbs, Early Charters of ... St Paul London, p 280, and p 136 n 1 and cf DB II fo 131v. Did Edith have a hand in this marriage? Or is the queen in question more likely to have been Mathilda? Note that two foreign moneyers married English women, cf THEODERIC. See also Edith's association with another London widow LEOFGIFU.

RABEL THE COOK present at Wilton as a witness to the Combe charter in 1072.

ROBERT MALET'S MOTHER in 1086 she held land *de feudo reginae*, Sk, DB II, fo 310v, 321r, 323v; STIGAND had given her land at Occold, Sk which she later held from the queen, ibid fo 450r. The Malets made one if not two marriages to English women, see Keats-Rohan 1995. It is conceivable, but unprovable, that Robert Malet's mother, William Malet's wife, was an English woman in the queen's service.

SÆRIC, held land at Winterbourne and Laverstock among the king's thegns in Wiltshire, DB I, fo 74r. His successors in the thirteenth century held the same lands by serjeanty for service in the royal court, see Campbell 1987, p 212; is he the Siric chamberlain in Hants, holding land which had been Wulfgifu's, fo 50r, and Enham, fo 50r, both listed under the Land of the king's thegns; and/or the Syric, *homo* of Queen Edith who had held Lillingstone, Bucks, before it passed to Walter Giffard, DB I, fo 147v.

SIGAR, CANON OF ST MARTIN'S DOVER had held Newington, associated with the royal manor of Milton, of Edith in 1066, DB I, fo 14v; note the food renders paid here from the great royal estate of Milton, one indication that this manor should be seen as still closely attached to the royal lands; cf Tatton Brown 1988, pp 107–8. The dues of the old queenly-connected nunnery of Minster in Sheppey (*Sexburgamynster*) were paid to Newington, *Domesday Monachorum*, VCH Kent, vol I p 256. Probably the representative of an old tenth-century noble family, even with connections to Queen Eadgifu. Sired/ Sigered and Siweard his brother occur frequently in documents of the late tenth, early eleventh century, see S 1455, 1456, 867, 885, 910, 911, 893, 877, 878, 899, 904, 905, 956 and 959. The similarity of the names, and with that of a fellow canon of St Martin's, Sired, e.g. DB I, fo 1v, suggests a connection among all these men. This is increased by the fact that S 875, AD 990, granted land at Sibertswold to Sigered; in 1066 Sigar and St Martin's held land here, DB I, fos 1v and 2v. On the evidence of names alone the family could be speculatively pushed back to Sigewulf, *pincerna regis*, of Alfred's day, who became an ealdorman in Kent, and/or Sigehelm, the father of Queen Eadgifu, both of whom were killed at the battle of the Holme, ASC, MS A 904. In this case then the queen's following had attracted a member of an established local noble family.

Albert the Chaplain held Newington in 1066. Albert's own connection with the lands of the queen is confirmed by his holdings in Rutland: he held the churches of Oakham, Hambleton and St Peter's, Stamford, DB I, fo 294r and cf fo 336v, where the church of St Peter's is said to lie in Rutland, in Hambleton; see Harvey 1977, p 404. Albert was a canon of St Paul's as was Sired, DB I, fo 127r. ALBERT and possibly Sigar should perhaps be associated with the queen as priests. See also Barlow 1963, p 133 n 4, and on Albert, Round 1899 and Brooke 1951.

SIRED see SIGAR.

THEGN OF QUEEN held Colsterworth, Lincs, DB I, fo 371r, among the lands of the king's thegns.

THEODERIC THE GOLDSMITH present at Wilton to witness the Combe charter in 1072. He and his wife appear in DB as holders in Oxfordshire, fo 160v; Surrey, fo 36v, and Berkshire; in the latter shire he is a tenant-in-chief, in the former two among the king's thegns. Was this marriage of a foreign royal servant arranged by the king or queen? A Theoderic held land in Winchester TRE, see Biddle 1976, Winton Survey, p 63 – not necessarily the same man – see e.g. a Theoderic the Cook who also held in Winchester, ibid p 59. Theoderic is usually associated with the cutting of Edward's great seal as well as the coin type in which the king appears enthroned in majesty; Dolley and Elmore Jones, p 220ff; cf Keynes 1988, pp 216–7 for Regenbald's possible association with the seal, and above pp 115–16 for Edith's – see MATHILDA and ÆLFWEARD THE GOLDSMITH for links between the queen and goldsmiths.

THEODGAR see ALBOLD THE COOK.

WALTER, THE LOTHARINGIAN, QUEEN EDITH'S CHAPLAIN was given the bishopric of Hereford in 1060, ASC, MSS D and E s.a., and FI Wig s.a. for the identification of him as the Queen's chaplain.

WIFE OF EALDRED in employ of Queen Mathilda as an embroideress, see Charters of Ste Trinité, no 16, for a chasuble made at Winchester by the uxor Aldereti. She held as dower (dos) land at Micheldever, a manor belonging to St Peter Winchester, of which a number of royal servants held, including her husband Ealdred and his brother Odo the steward, DB I, fo 42v; she may have worked previously for Edith; see Williams 1995, pp 115–16.

WIHTGAR, ÆLFRIC'S SON was not himself apparently a queen's servant, though his father had been, and the family's substantial wealth in 1066 probably owes something to that fact; for that wealth see Clarke, pp 357–63. Richard son of Ct Gilbert, who held queen's lands, claimed his land, see DB II, fo 393v. Is it significant that men like him, identified by some epithet, are common among the royal servants and former royal servants? Does this suggest lists of royal servants from pre-1086, cautious attempts to keep tabs on them and the lands they held?

WUDUMANN, KEEPER OF EDITH'S HORSES, *Writs* 72, Edith in her widowhood asks the hundred of Wedmore for a judgement on his withholding of her rent for 6 years.

WULFGIFU BETTESLAU, or perhaps more correctly *laf/lav* i.e. widow of Bette. She may be no more than a wealthy West Saxon widow, but her lands show strong connections with the lands of royal servants and particularly with those of the queen and her servants. Humphrey, Mathilda's chamberlain, was her successor in part of her Berkshire land, DB I, fo 63r; Robert, the son of Fulcred, Mathilda's chamberlain, held land in Winchester which had been hers, cf *Actes de Ste Trinité*, no 27 and the *Winton Survey*, Biddle 1976, p 42. Queen Mathilda herself and Albold the cook held her former land at Mapledurham, DB I, fo 38r. Mapledurham, now in Buriton, along with Chalton, made up Chalton hundred in 1066. The rest of the hundred had been in the hands of that most successful of royal servants, Earl Godwine. It lies next to the hundreds of East Meon and Meonstoke, with their strong royal and royal service connections. Ælfsige, *burchenistre* ?the valet, held two more of her former lands, fo 50r, and elsewhere in Hampshire she was succeeded by Siric the chamberlain, fo 50r. In Wilts Wibert, a *serviens regis*, held land at Clyffe Pypard which had been hers, fo 74v. Like so many royal servants she held land claimed by a royal church; after her death William 'restored' Laverstock, Hampshire to St Peter, Winchester, perhaps significantly for the soul of his wife as well as his own, fo 43r. The problems of Domesday identification make it impossible to know whether she is the Suffolk holder some of whose considerable lands were held in 1086 '*de feudo reginae*' by Roger Malet's mother; DB II, fos 321r, 323v. Clarke 1994 does not so identify her; if she is the same woman her ranking should be higher than 39th where he places her in the non-earlish estates, p 38. The fact that she is identified at all, by a by-name, may be significant for her status as a royal servant (above WIHTGAR SON OF ÆLFRIC). A woman of this name had held people in commendation on what was in 1086 the queen's fee in Suffolk. See STIGAND.

WULFWEARD HWITE (the White). Present at Wilton as a witness to the Combe charter in 1072. He held land of Edith in 1066: 1 and a half hides of land at Keynsham in Som (1 hide of which was held by his widow in 1086) DB I, fo 87r; Hayling Island, Hants, fo 43v; land at Addingrove, Bucks, fo 147r. Butterwick and Freiston, Lincs, fo 376v, held by a Wulfweard, may have been given him by the queen – Wulfweard the White had sake and soke in Lincs; Hart 1992, p 185. His son-in-law held three lands in Buckinghamshire given him by Edith with Wulfweard's daughter, fo 153v; see ÆLFSIGE. His widow Edeva / Eadgifu also held Worminghall, Bucks from Edith and perhaps Winchendon, fos 145r, 147r. In Somerset, four lands of his are listed in the *terra regis*, immediately after Edith's land, fo 87r. In addition he held land in Kent, Wiltshire, Hampshire, Dorset, Gloucestershire, Middlesex, Oxfordshire and Bedfordshire (in the latter shires two epithets have been surely wrongly transposed – the Wulfweard Levet whose lands passed to Arnulf of Hesdin, elsewhere a successor of Wulfweard, must be him, fo 212r). He had formerly been a servant of Queen Emma. She had given him a life tenancy of half the land in Hayling Island which she gave to the Old Minster; cf R 114 for the text of an agreement between him and Winchester. He also held land claimed by the bishop of Salisbury, fo 66r. In Dorset he had held land as pledge from one of his reeves, and had bought other lands from the Bishop of Exeter, fo 82v. He is called King Edward's thegn in Middlesex, fo 129r. Clarke 1994, p 38 ranks him eighth among the non-earlish estates in England in 1066; see also Williams 1995, pp 99–100.

WULFWYN OF CRESLOW a possible connection of Edith. There is a tenuous connection with earlier queens through the estate at Great Gaddesden which she held from St Albans and which had been left by Æthelgifu, who may have been connected to Queen Ælfthryth in the 990s, see the will of Æthelgifu. In many shires Edward of Salisbury the sheriff held land which had been hers, perhaps the sheriff's claim on widows, more likely she was Edward's mother, see Williams 1995, p 105. She held land at Chitterne, Dorset, DB I, fo 69v, where both HARDING and AZOR had held land. For similarities between the pattern of her estate and that of WULFWEARD and AZOR see Clarke pp 57–9 and 38; he ranks her estate 23rd.

2 Men of Edith, Tenants of Edith

A FREEMAN, *homo reginae Eddid*, had been added to Bushey, Herts, by Geoffrey de Mandeville, DB I, fo 139v cf ÆLFWINE THE HUNTER.

ÆLFGAR Bedfordshire, DB I, fo 216v, held 2+ hides at Sharnbrook, *homo Edid reginae*. It passed to ALBERT OF LORRAINE.

ÆLFGEAT, Queen Edith's man, held Bradwell, Bucks; in 1086 Walter Giffard, DB I, fo 148r.

ÆLFSIGE OF BROMHAM a man of Queen Edith held Eaton, Beds, passed to Odo of Bayeux, DB I, fo 209v; fo 213v Bromham, and Biddenham (where he is *de bruneham*, of Bromham, *homo Eddid reginae*) – both these lands passed to Hugh of Beauchamp.

ÆLFWINE *homo Eddid reginae*, held Soulbury, Bucks, DB I, fo 150v which passed to Hugh of Beauchamp; Amersham, Bucks, which passed to the bishop of Bayeux, fo 144r; and Linslade, fo 150v, in 1086 part of Leighton Buzzard, left by a tenth-century queen, Ælfgifu in her will, *Wills* 8, held in 1086 by Hugh of Beauchamp. It is probably the same man who held 7 estates which passed to William Peverel, fo 148r – all 7 are listed consecutively and in 6 cases he is described as a thegn of King Edward, but once as Queen Edith's man. A man of this name had held land in Leics, said to be *de feudo reginae*, fos 232r, 233r.

ÆLFWOLD held Elmley, Worcs from Queen Edith, DB I, fo 176r.

AZOR SON OF TOTI *homo reginae Eddid* held numerous lands in Buckinghamshire, Herts, Warwicks and Northants; he is called Queen Edith's man fo 151v; Clarke 1994, pp 253–4 for details of his estate valued at £66; p 39 he ranks him 55th of the non-earlish estates.

BRICTRIC called a *homo* of Queen Edith, DB I, fo 136v, 150rv in Herts and Bucks. He held land from Edith, Wycombe, Bucks, fo 149r, and perhaps the same man was a thegn of Queen Edith in Worcs, fo 176v. It is probably the same man who is called a thegn of King Edward, fo 149v (cf ÆLFWINE for such alternatives). He and his man held land at Chesham, fos 150v and 151r, and Masworth, fo 149v, which had been part of the bequests of a tenth-century queen, Ælfgifu, in her will, *Wills* 8; cf ÆLFSIGE, SON-IN LAW OF WULFWEARD and ÆLFWINE. He held an extensive estate in Hertfordshire, Buckinghamshire, Oxfordshire, Bedfordshire and Worcestershire; his holdings, exclusive of those of his men, were worth over £100 per annum, see Clarke 1994, pp 262–4 and p 38 where he is ranked 35th among the non-earlish estates. Edith herself held a considerable estate in this area and it is no surpise to find a follower or servant of hers ensconced here.

GODRIC held Stanford, Worcs of Edith, DB I, fo 176v.

GODWINE a freeman of the queen, probably Edith; held land in Suffolk held in 1086 by Roger Bigot, DB II, fo 332r.

GODWINE SON OF ÆLFHERE held land of the queen in Suffolk TRE, DB II, 314v.

GODWINE SON OF ÆLFSIGE a thegn of Queen Edith held land at Belstead Sk, DB II, fo 306r.

LEOFGIFU, THE LONDONER (LUNDONICA) S 1029, both Peterborough and Edith claimed that this woman had left Fiskerton to them; had she held it of Edith?

MODING, Queen Edith's man, held Thurleigh, Beds, DB I, fo 213v; in 1086 Hugh of Beauchamp.

SPARROWHAWK a man of Queen Edith, his land in Suffolk passed to Peter of Valognes after his death, DB II, 421r.

TOSTIG held Frome, Herefords, of Queen Edith, which passed to Roger de Lacy, DB I, fo 184r.

WALRAVEN a man of Queen Edith, his land in Beds had been added to the royal manor of Houghton, DB I, fo 209v. Such a move suggests how far the queen's lands were seen as part of the royal lands.

WALTER THE DEACON Edith gave him land at Wix in Essex, after the coming of King William. He, or rather a *miles* from him, held two other lands which had been Edith's in 1066, DB II, fo 87r; in Suffolk he held two lands which had been Edith's, and 5 houses and three empty plots in Ipswich which had been hers, DB II, fos 426rv, 427r.

MEN OF QUEEN EDITH see 3 at N Mimms, Herts, DB I, fo 135r; 1 at Calverton, Bucks, fo 150v.

PEOPLE UNDER THE QUEEN'S COMMENDATION see Bricett, Sk, DB II, fo 393v; Otley, Sk, DB II, fo 433r; Chediston, Sk, DB II, fo 332v; Cretingham, Sk, DB II, fo 433rv; Helmingham, Sk DB II, fo 433v.

3 Emma's Servants/Followers

ÆLFGAR THE REEVE, S 915, AD 1007 granting him land at Waltham, Berks; Queen Edith held land here, see DB I, fo 56v.

ÆLFRIC SON OF WIHTGAR administered the eight and a half hundreds of Thingoe for Emma, see S 1078. A relative of LEOFGIFU. According to Clarke, 1994, p 43, 30% of his manors passed to the church, perhaps in an arrangement similar to that of WULFWEARD THE WHITE and Winchester, perhaps as a result of more diverse and complex links between royal servants and church lands, for which see pp 153–4 and Appendix II passim. cf Clarke p 50 'it seems that the family did not necessarily lose the use of land which a layman had left to the church.'

EADSIGE the priest of Emma and Cnut, R 86.

FATHER OF RALPH THE STALLER a Breton who may have come to England with Emma in 1002, see Williams 1995, p 61 and notes 70 and 71. Ralph's East Anglian lands may be linked to the holdings which Emma had in this area, and cf STIGAND, ÆLFGAR and LEOFGIFU as her other connections here. If this identification is correct it provides another dynasty of royal service to place alongside HARDING and his father Eadnoth, and even more tentatively Robert Fitz WYMARC.

GODWINE S 902, dated 1002 i.e. the year of Emma's arrival, land granted to him at Little Haseley. In 1086 this was held by Hervey, DB I, fo 155v, who was a royal servant/*minister regis*, involved in taking profit from royal land, fos 156v and 160v – and see above BRICTRIC DODA'S SON for a Hervey *cubicularius*. The adjacent land at Great Haseley was held in 1066 by Queen Edith, DB I, fo 159v.

GOLDSMITH a certain goldsmith, who was '*ei a secretis*', a term which usually denotes close household service, took the head of St Ouen, which was kept in Emma's own treasure, '*in secreto suo*', and gave it to his brother who was a monk at Malmesbury, William of Malmesbury, *DGP*, p 419.

HUGH, FRENCH REEVE OF EXETER appointed by Emma c. 1002/3, see ASC MS C 1003.

LEOFGIFU relative of ÆLFRIC SON OF WIHTGAR left him land at Bramford in her will, S 1521, *Wills* no 29, AD 1035 × 44; 1086 the sheriff claimed that this land belonged to the royal manor of Bramford. ÆLFRIC'S service of Emma may have been via Leofgifu's links with the queen rather than vice versa; cf the Will of Æthelgifu for a woman in the 990s securing a place in the Ætheling's household for a male relative through the queen. Hers is the only early English will directed solely to the queen, and land at Belchamp is returned/left to Emma in it. Belchamp lies just outside Sudbury, which is arguably the southern borough of the Thingoe hundreds.

LEOFSTAN Emma's *cniht*, held Kirby, Norfolk, which she gave after his death to Bury, *Writs* 16.

STIGAND he and his family held extensive lands in East Anglia. Smith 1994 accepts a close link with Emma, chiefly on the grounds of *ASC*, MS C 1043, where he was her close advisor, and their rise and fall together. He first appears as the priest in charge of Cnut's new foundation at Ashingdon, and later as a priest in the royal chapel. In 1043 Stigand and Emma rose and fell together. In April, or soon after the coronation then, Stigand was appointed a bishop. In November the queen lost lands and treasures, and Stigand was deprived of his bishopric. If the attack on her was on a queen unwilling to relinquish her various household roles, was not the attack on Stigand on a man implicated in the same offence? Was Stigand the man responsible for Emma's household, either the queen's own steward or similar official, or a high-ranking official in the royal household with which she was associated? Barlow 1963, pp 77–81 and cf p 134 calling him 'a domestic archbishop'. Stigand went on to ever higher things, though his role in the royal administration may always have reflected his origins as the queen's priest. Campbell 1987, p 218 throws out the suggestion that by 1066 Stigand ran the whole administrative machine. His East Anglian links with land associated with the queen is evident from Domesday: DB II, fo 450r where he gave land to Robert Malet's mother which she later held from the queen; Bedingfield, Sk contained holdings in commendation of Stigand, later of Robert Malet's mother, listed as *de feudo reginae*, DB II, fo 310v. In 1066 he held Mildenhall, Sk, which had been Emma's, which she had lost in 1043, and which Edward had given to Bury, DB II, 288v–289r and *Writs* 9. See also R 92 a grant c. 1040 by him, which is witnessed by ÆLFRIC WIHTGAR'S SON, a queen's servant – and cf his witness again to R 97, an agreement between Stigand's brother and the abbot of Bury. Stigand was a beneficiary of the will of LEOFGIFU, one of Emma's connections. It might be noted that the areas where Stigand's personal wealth was concentrated, Beds, Oxon, Cantab, Dorset, Gloucs, Hants, Herts, Kent, Norfolk, Suffolk (Smith, p 219), cover his East Anglian origins, but also areas of royal lands and those of royal servants. In some there are also numerous followers of the queen, e.g. Beds and Herts.

WULFWEARD THE WHITE see above.

WYMARC a Breton woman of this name was the mother of the great royal servant of the Confessor's reign, Robert FitzWymarc. He may have come to England with Edward, but it is also possible that his mother came with Emma. On him see Barlow 1970, p 191 and n 1 and Williams 1995, p 63 and n 82.

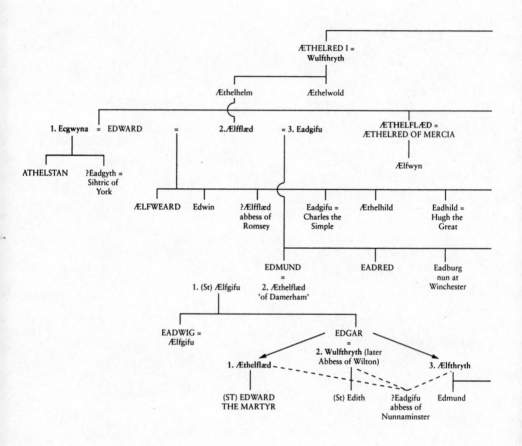

ÆTHELRED I =
Wulfthryth

Æthelhelm   Æthelwold

1. Ecgwyna = EDWARD = 2.Ælfflæd = 3. Eadgifu   ÆTHELFLÆD =
ÆTHELRED OF MERCIA

ATHELSTAN   ?Eadgyth =
Sihtric of
York

Ælfwyn

ÆLFWEARD   Edwin   ?Ælfflæd   Eadgifu =   Æthelhild   Eadhild =
abbess of   Charles the   Hugh the
Romsey   Simple   Great

EDMUND   EADRED   Eadburg
=   nun at
1. (St) Ælfgifu   2. Æthelflæd   Winchester
'of Damerham'

EADWIG =   EDGAR
Ælfgifu   =
2. Wulfthryth (later
Abbess of Wilton)

1. Æthelflæd   3. Ælfthryth

(ST) EDWARD   (St) Edith   ?Eadgifu   Edmund
THE MARTYR   abbess of
Nunnaminster

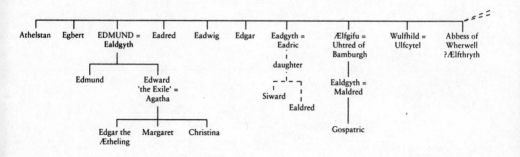

Athelstan   Egbert   EDMUND =   Eadred   Eadwig   Edgar   Eadgyth =   Ælfgifu =   Wulfhild =   Abbess of
Ealdgyth   Eadric   Uhtred of   Ulfcytel   Wherwell
                                         daughter   Bamburgh   ?Ælfthryth

Edmund   Edward   Siward   Ealdgyth =
           'the Exile' =   Ealdred   Maldred
             Agatha

Edgar the   Margaret   Christina   Gospatric
Ætheling

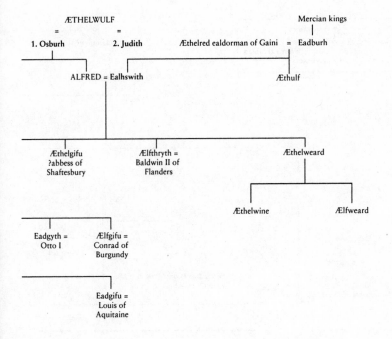

ÆTHELWULF

= 1. Osburh

= 2. Judith

Mercian kings

Æthelred ealdorman of Gaini = Eadburh

ALFRED = Ealhswith

Æthulf

Æthelgifu ?abbess of Shaftesbury

Ælfthryth = Baldwin II of Flanders

Æthelweard

Æthelwine

Ælfweard

Eadgyth = Otto I

Ælfgifu = Conrad of Burgundy

Eadgifu = Louis of Aquitaine

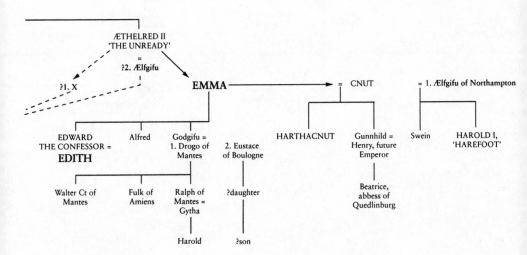

ÆTHELRED II 'THE UNREADY'

= ?2. Ælfgifu

?1. X

EMMA

= CNUT

= 1. Ælfgifu of Northampton

EDWARD THE CONFESSOR = **EDITH**

Alfred

Godgifu = 1. Drogo of Mantes

2. Eustace of Boulogne

HARTHACNUT

Gunnhild = Henry, future Emperor

Swein

HAROLD I, 'HAREFOOT'

Walter Ct of Mantes

Fulk of Amiens

Ralph of Mantes = Gytha

?daughter

Beatrice, abbess of Quedlinburg

Harold

?son

Emma's French Connections

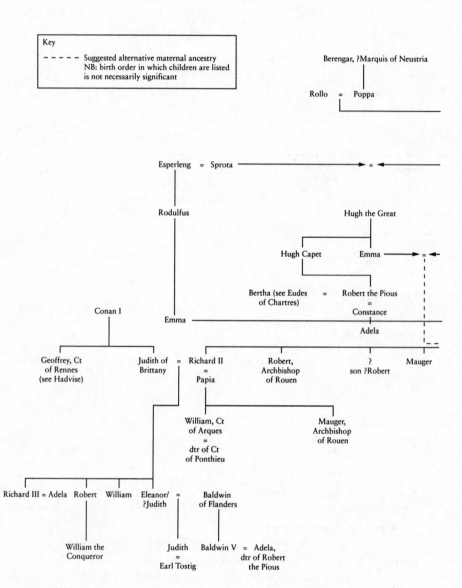

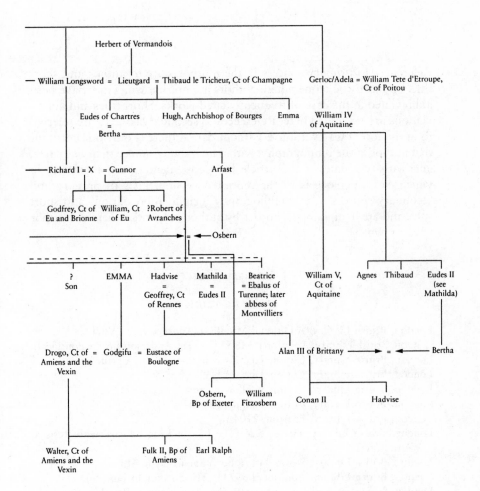

Bibliography

References to primary sources in the footnotes are to author and short title, or short title alone where authors are not known. Titles have been abbreviated in the case of frequently cited works. Short titles and abbreviations are expanded here. References to secondary sources are referred to in the footnotes by author: without date if there is only one entry for that author in the bibliography; with date if there is more than one entry, and with two dates if the article has subsequently been reprinted, in which case reference is to the reprinted version. Lists of primary and secondary sources in this bibliography include abbreviations and short titles and are in alphabetical order by author or by title where the author is unknown.

1 Primary Sources

a) Manuscripts

London, British Library, Additional MS 4000 (Thorney Liber Vitae).
London, British Library, Additional MS 57337 (The Anderson/Brodie Pontifical).
London, British Library, Cotton Tiberius A iii (Hemming's Cartulary).
London, British Library, Cotton Tiberius C i.
London, British Library, Cotton Vitellius A vii.
London, British Library, Cotton Caligula A viii.
London, British Library, Egerton, 2104A.
London, British Library, Harley 526 (The Life of King Edward who Rests at Westminster).
London, British Library, Stowe 944 (Liber Vitae of Hyde Abbey).
London, British Library, Additional 33241 (The Encomium Emmae).
London, Society of Antiquaries MS 60 (The Liber Niger of Peterborough).

b) Printed

A Pre-Conquest English Prayerbook (BL MSS Cotton Galba A xiv and Nero A ii, ff 3–13), ed. B.J. Muir, Henry Bradshaw Society, vol 103 for 1983–4 (London, 1988).

Actes de Ste Trinité, Les Actes de Guillaume le Conquérant et de la reine Mathilda pour les Abbayes Caennaises, ed. L. Musset, Mémoires de la Société des Antiquaires de Normandie, vol 37 (Caen, 1967).

Adam of Bremen, *Gesta Hammaburgensis Ecclesiae Pontificum, Adam von Bremen Hamburgische Kirchegeschichte*, ed. B. Schmeidler, *MGH Scriptores* (Hannover and Leipzig, 1917).

Ælfric, *Catholic Homilies I and II, The Homilies of the Anglo-Saxon Church, The Sermones Catholici or Homilies of Ælfric*, ed. B. Thorpe, 2 vols, Ælfric Society (London, 1844 and 1846).

Ælfric, *Glossary, Ælfrics Grammatik und Glossar*, ed. J. Zupitza, 2nd ed. H. Gneuss (Berlin, 1966).

Ælfric, *Grammar, Ælfrics Grammatik und Glossar*, ed. J. Zupitza, 2nd ed. H. Gneuss (Berlin, 1966).

Ælfric, *Homily for the nativity of the Blessed Virgin Mary, Angelsachsische Homilien und Heiligenleben*, ed. B. Assmann, Bibliothek der Angelsachsichen Prosa, vol 3 (Kassel, 1889), no 3.

Ælfric, *Lives of the Saints*, ed. W. W. Skeat, Early English Text Society, 2 vols (London, 1881–1900).

Ælfric, *Pastoral Letters, Die Hirtenbriefe Ælfrics*, ed. B. Fehr, Bibliothek der Angelsachsichen Prosa, vol 9 (Hamburg, 1914).

Ælfwine's Prayerbook, ed B. Günzel, Henry Bradshaw Society, vol 108 for 1992 (1993).

Aelred, *Vita S Edwardi Regis*, in Migne, *PL*, vol 195 (Paris, 1855), cols 737–790.

Æthelweard, *Chronicle, The Chronicle of Æthelweard*, ed. and trans. A. Campbell (Edinburgh, 1962).

Agrip, Agrip af Noregs Konunga Sogum, ed. F. Jónsson, Altnordische Saga – Bibliothek, vol 18 (Halle, 1929).

Aimo of Fleury, *De Miraculis sancti Benedicti libri duo*, in Migne, *PL*, vol 139 (Paris, 1880).

Alfred, Alfred the Great, Asser's Life of King Alfred and Other Contemporary Sources, trans. S. Keynes and M. Lapidge (London, 1983).

Alpert of Metz, *De Episcopis Mettensibus Libellus, MGH Scriptores*, vol IV, ed. G.H. Pertz (Hannover, 1841).

An Ancient Manuscript of the Eighth or Ninth Century, ed. W. de G. Birch, Hampshire Record Society (London and Winchester, 1889).

An Eleventh-Century Anglo-Saxon Miscellany, British Library Cotton Tiberius B V Part I Together with Leaves from British Library Cotton Nero D II, ed. P. McGurk et al., Early English manuscripts in facsimile (Copenhagen, 1983).

Anglo-Saxon Litanies of the Saints, ed. M. Lapidge, Henry Bradshaw Society, vol 106, for 1989–90 (London, 1991).

Anglo-Saxon Poetry, trans. R.K. Gordon (London, 1954).

Annalista Saxo, *MGH Scriptores*, ed. G.H. Pertz, vol VI (Hannover, 1844).

Annals of Hildesheim, Annales Hildesheimenses, MGH Scriptores, ed. G.H. Pertz, vol III (Hannover, 1839).

Annals of Quedlinburg, Annales Quedlinburgenses, ed. G.H. Pertz, *MGH Scriptores*, vol III (Hannover, 1839).

Annals of Winchester, 'Annales Monasterii de Wintonia', *Annales Monastici*, ed. H.R. Luard, vol II, Rolls Series (London, 1865).

ASC, MS A, The Anglo-Saxon Chronicle, a Collaborative Edition, Vol 3, MS A, ed. J. Bately (Cambridge, 1986).

ASC, MS C, ed. Conner, *The Anglo-Saxon Chronicle, a Collaborative Edition, Vol 10, The Abingdon Chronicle*, AD *956–1066 (MS C, with reference to BDE)*, ed. P.W. Conner (Cambridge, 1996).

ASC, MS F, The Anglo-Saxon Chronicle, a Collaborative Edition. Facsimile of MS F: the Domitian Bilingual, ed. D. Dumville (Cambridge, 1995).

ASC, (+MS letter) *Two of the Saxon Chronicles Parallel*, eds C. Plummer and J. Earle, 2 vols (Oxford, 1892 and 1899), translated in *English Historical Documents*, vols I and II.

ASPR, The Anglo-Saxon Poetic Records, eds G.P. Krapp and E.V.K. Dobie, 6 vols (New York, 1931–42).

Asser, Life of King Alfred, ed. W.H. Stevenson (Oxford, 1959).

Bede, *Venerabilis Baedae Opera Historica*, ed. C. Plummer (Oxford, 1896).

Beowulf, with the Finnesburg Fragment, ed. C.J. Wrenn (London, 1958).

Bishop, T.A.M. and Chaplais, P., *Facsimiles of English Royal Writs to* AD *1100* (Oxford, 1957).

Burton Charters, The Charters of Burton Abbey, ed. P.H. Sawyer (Oxford, 1979).

Cambridge Psalter, Der Cambridger Psalter (MS Ff 1.23, Univ Lib, Cantab), ed. K. Wildhagen, Bibliothek der Angelsachsichen Prosa, vol 7 (Hamburg, 1910).

Carmen, The Carmen de Hastingae Proelio of Guy Bishop of Amiens, eds C. Morton and H. Muntz (Oxford, 1972).

Chron Abing, Chronicon Monasterii de Abingdon, ed. J. Stevenson, 2 vols, Rolls Series (London, 1858).

Chron Ram, Chronicon Abbatiae Rameseiensis, ed. W.D. Macray, Rolls Series (London, 1886).

Chronicle of John of Wallingford, ed. R. Vaughan, Camden Miscellany, 21, Camden Soc, Ser 3, vol 90 (London, 1958).

Chronicle of St Maixent, La Chronique de Saint Maixent, ed. J. Verdon, Classiques de l'histoire de France, vol 33 (Paris, 1979).

Chronicon Abbatiae de Evesham, ed. W.D. Macray, Rolls Series (London, 1863).

Chronicon Roskildense, ed. M.C. Gertz, *Scriptores Minores Historiae Danicae Medii Aevi*, vol I (Copenhagen, 1917–18).

Chronique de Saint Pierre-le-Vif de Sens, dite de Clarius, eds R-H. Bautier and M. Gilles, Sources d'Histoire Médiéval (Paris, 1979).

Coleman, *Life of St Wulfstan, The Vita Wulfstani of William of Malmesbury*, ed. R.R. Darlington, Camden Soc, Ser 3, vol 40 (London, 1928).

Concordance, A Microfiche Concordance to Old English, eds A. diPaolo-Healey and R.L. Venezky (Toronto, 1980).

Coronatio Hermintrudis reginae, MGH Capitularia Regum Francorum, vol II (Hannover, 1897), no 301, pp 453–5.

Coronatio Iudithae Karoli II filiae, Benedictio super reginam quam Edelulfus rex accepit in uxorem, *MGH Capitularia Regum Francorum*, vol II (Hannover, 1897), no 296, pp 425–7.

Corpus Benedictionum Pontificalium, ed. M. Moeller, Corpus Christianorum, Ser. Lat., vol 162 (Turnhout, 1971–3).

Crawford Charters, *The Crawford Collection of Early Charters and Documents*, eds A.S. Napier and W. Stevenson, *Anecdota Oxoniensia* (Oxford, 1895).

D.O.II, *Diplomatum regum et Imperatorum Germaniae*, II, Pt i, Otto II, *MGH Diplomata* (Hannover, 1888).

DB, Domesday Book, various editions, cited here by folio from that of A. Farley, 1783, reproduced in the Phillimore edition, general editor J. Morris (Chichester, 1975–86).

De Villis, *MGH Capitularia Regum Francorum*, vol I (Hannover, 1883), no 32, pp 82–91.

Diplomatum regum et imperatorum Germaniae, II. Pt ii, Otto III, *MGH* (Hannover, 1893).

Domesday Monachorum, *The Domesday Monachorum of Christchurch Canterbury*, ed. D.C. Douglas, Royal Historical Society (London, 1944).

Du Cange, D., *Glossarium mediae et infimae latinitatis*, with supplements, ed. G.A.L. Henschel, 7 vols (Paris, 1840–50).

Dudo, *De Moribus et actis primorum Normanniae Ducum auctore Dudone Sancti Quentini decano*, ed. J. Lair (Caen, 1865).

Eadmer, *Concerning the Excellence of the Virgin Mary*, Eadmeri monachi, *De Excellentia virginis Mariae*, Migne, *PL*, vol 159 (Paris, 1903), cols 557–80.

Eadmer, *Historia Novorum in Anglia*, ed. M. Rule, Rolls Series (London, 1884) trans. *History of Recent Events*, G. Bosanquet (London, 1964); p refs are to the Latin text.

Eadmer, *Vita Dunstani*, in *Memorials of St Dunstan*.

Ecclesiastical Documents, ed. J. Hunter, Camden Soc, Old Series, vol 8 (London, 1840).

EHD I, *English Historical Documents*, vol I, c. 500–1042, ed. D. Whitelock, 2nd ed. (London, 1979).

EHD II, *English Historical Documents*, vol II, 1042–1189, eds D.C. Douglas and G.W. Greenaway, 2nd ed. (London, 1981).

Encomium, *Encomium Emmae Reginae*, ed. A. Campbell, Camden, Ser 3, vol 72 (London, 1949).

Fauroux, *Recueil des actes des ducs de Normandie de 911–1066*, ed. M. Fauroux, Mémoires de la Société des Antiquaires de Normandie, vol 36 (Caen, 1961).

Fl Wig, Florence of Worcester, *The Chronicle of John of Worcester*, eds R.R. Darlington, P. McGurk and J. Bray, vol II (Oxford, 1995), and for the period after 1066 the older edition, *Florentii Wigorniensis Monachi, Chronicon ex Chronicis*, ed. B. Thorpe, Vol II (London, 1849). For ease of reference, all citations are by year.

Flemish Chronicles, *Les Annales de Saint-Pierre de Gand et de Saint Amand*, ed. P. Grierson (Brussels, 1937).

Flete, *Westminster*, *The History of Westminster Abbey by John Flete*, ed. J. Armitage Robinson (Cambridge, 1909).

Flodoard, *Annales de Flodoard*, ed. P. Lauer (Paris, 1905).

Fulbert of Chartres, *The Letters and Poems of Fulbert of Chartres*, ed. F. Behrends (Oxford, 1976).

Gaimar, *Geffrei Gaimar, L'Estoire des Engleis*, ed. A. Bell, Anglo-Norman Text Society, vols 14–16 (Oxford, 1960).

Garnier de Rouen, H. Omont, 'Satire de Garnier de Rouen contre le poète Moriuht', *L'Annuaire Bulletin de la Société de l'Histoire de France*, vol 31 (1894), pp 193–210.

Gerbert, *Letters*, Gerbert d'Aurillac, *Correspondance*, eds P. Riché and J.P. Callu, 2 vols (Paris, 1993).

Gervase of Canterbury, *Gesta Regum, Historical Works of Gervase of Canterbury*, ed. W. Stubbs, vol II, Rolls Series (London, 1880).

Gesta Episcoporum Cameracensium, MGH Scriptores, vol VII, ed. G.H. Pertz (Hannover, 1846).

Gibbs, M., ed., *Early Charters of the Cathedral Church of St Paul London*, Camden Soc., Ser 3, vol 58 (London, 1939).

Godfrey of Winchester, *The Anglo-Latin Satirical Poets and Epigrammatists of the Twelfth Century*, ed. T. Wright, vol I, Rolls Series (London, 1872).

Goscelin, *Liber Confortatorius*, C.H. Talbot, 'The *Liber Confortatorius* of Goscelin of Saint Bertin', *Studia Anselmiana*, vol 37, *Analecta Monastica*, 3rd ser, fasc 37 (1955), pp 1–117.

Goscelin, *Life of St Edith*, A. Wilmart, 'La légende de Ste Édith en prose et vers par le moine Goscelin', *Analecta Bollandiana*, vol 56 (1938), pp 5–307.

Goscelin, *Life of St Wulfsige of Sherborne*, C.H. Talbot, 'The Life of St. Wulfsin of Sherborne by Goscelin', *Revue Bénédictine*, vol 69 (1959), pp 68–85.

Goscelin, *Life of Wulfhild*, M. Esposito, 'La vie de Sainte Vulfhilde par Goscelin de Cantorbéry', *Analecta Bollandiana*, vol 32 (1913), pp 10–26.

Goscelin, *Translation of St Augustine, Historia Translationis S. Augustini Episcopi*, in *Migne, PL*, vol 155, cols 13–46.

Goscelin, *Translation*, 'Goscelin of Canterbury's account of the translation and miracles of St Mildreth (BHL 5961/4), an edition with notes', ed. D.W. Rollason, *Medieval Studies*, vol 48 (1986), pp 139–210.

Hampson, McGurk, P., 'The metrical calendar of Hampson. A new edition', *Analecta Bollandiana*, 104 (London, 1986), pp 79–125.

Hariulf, *Chronique de l'Abbaye de Saint Riquier*, ed. F. Lot, Collection de Textes, vol 17 (Paris, 1894).

Helgaud of Fleury, *Vie de Robert le Pieux*, ed. and trans. R.H. Bautier and G. Labory (Paris, 1965).

Henry of Huntingdon, *Henrici Archidiaconi Huntendunensis Historia Anglorum*, ed. T. Arnold, Rolls Series (London, 1879).

Hermann, *Heremanni archidiaconi, Miracula Sancti Eadmundi, Ungedruckte Anglo-Normannische Geschichtsquellen*, ed. F. Liebermann (Strasburg, 1879), pp 203–81.

Hincmar, *De Ordine Palatii*, ed. A. Boretius, *MGH Capitularia Regum Francorum*, vol II (Hannover, 1897), pp 515–30, trans. D. Herlihy. *The History of Feudalism* (London, 1970), pp 208–27.

Historia Norwegiae, Monumenta Historica Norvegiae, Latinske Kildeskrifter til Norges Historie i Middelalderen, ed. G. Storm (Kristiania, 1880).

Homily on Esther, Angelsachsische Homilien und Heiligenleben, ed. B. Assmann, Bibliothek der Angelsachsichen Prosa, vol 3 (Kassel, 1889), no 8.

Hugh Candidus, *The Chronicle of Hugh Candidus*, ed. W.T. Mellows (Oxford, 1949).

Hugh of Flavigny, *MGH Scriptores*, ed. G.H. Pertz, vol VIII (Hannover, 1848).

Hugh of Fleury, *MGH Scriptores*, ed. G.H. Pertz, vol IX (Hannover, 1851).

I placiti del 'Regnum Italiae', ed. C. Manaressi, vol 2, Fonti per la Storia d'Italia, vol 96 (Rome, 1957).

K + number, Kemble, J.M., *Codex Diplomaticus Aevi Saxonici*, 6 vols (London, 1839–48) cited by number.

Kalendars, English Kalendars before AD *1100*, ed. F. Wormald, Henry Bradshaw Society, vol 72 (London, 1934).

Knytlinga Saga, Danakununga Sogur, ed. B. GuÐnason, Islenzk Fornvit, vol 35 (Reykjavik, 1982).

Lambert of St Omer, *Lamberti S Audomari Canonici, Liber Floridus*, ed. A. Derolez (Ghent, 1968).

Lampert of Hersfeld, *Lamperti Monachi Hersfeldensis, Opera*, ed. O. Holder-Egger, *MGH Scriptores Rerum Germanicarum in usum scholarum* (Hannover and Leipzig, 1894/1956).

Lanalet Pontifical, Pontificale Lanaletense, ed. G.H. Doble, Henry Bradshaw Society, vol 74 for 1936 (London, 1937).

Latham, R.E., *Revised Medieval Latin Wordlist from British and Irish Sources*, with supplement (Oxford, 1965).

Lauer, *Actes de Charles III, Recueil des Actes de Charles III le Simple, roi de France*, ed. P. Lauer (Paris, 1940).

LE, Liber Eliensis, ed. E.O. Blake, Camden Soc, Series 3, vol 92 (London, 1962).

Le Sacramentaire Grégorien, ses principales formes d'après les plus anciens manuscrits, ed. J. Deshusses, vol I, Spicilegium Friburgense, vol 16 (Fribourg, 1971).

Leges Henrici Primi, ed. and trans. L.J. Downer (Oxford, 1972).

Liber Monasterii de Hyda, ed. E. Edwards, Rolls Series (London, 1866).

Liebermann, F., *Die Gesetze der Angelsachsen*, vols I–III (Halle, 1903–16).

Life of Dunstan, Auctore B, *Vita Sancti Dunstani, Auctore B*, in *Memorials of St Dunstan*, pp 3–52.

Life of Henry IV, in *Imperial Lives and Letters of the Eleventh Century*, trans. T.E. Mommsen and K.F. Morrison (New York and London, 1962).

Life of Werburga, Vita Sanctae Wereburge Virginis, auctore Goscelino, in Migne, *PL*, vol 155 (Paris, 1880), cols 94–110.

LVH, Liber Vitae, Register and Martyrology of New Minster and Hyde Abbey, Winchester, ed. W. de Gray Birch, Hampshire Record Society (London, 1892). Page numbers refer to printed edition, folio to MS, BL Stowe 944.

Matthew Paris, *Historia Anglorum*, ed. F. Madden, vol I, Rolls Series (London, 1866).

Medieval Women's Visionary Literature, ed. E.A. Petroff (New York and Oxford, 1986).

Memorials of St Dunstan, ed. W. Stubbs, Rolls Series (London, 1874).

Memorials of St Edmund's Abbey, vol I, ed. T. Arnold, Rolls Series (London, 1890).

MGH, Monumenta Germaniae Historica.

Migne, *PL, Patrologiae Cursus Completus. Series (Latina) Prima*, ed. J.P. Migne, 221 vols (Paris, 1844–64).

Newman, *Catalogue des Actes de Robert II roi de France*, ed. W.M. Newman (Paris, 1937).

Niermeyer, J. and van de Kieft, C., *Mediae Latinitatis Lexicon Minus* (Leiden, 1976).

Odilo of Cluny, *Epitaph of Adelaide, Die Lebenschreibung der Kaiserin Adelheid von Abt Odilo von Cluny*, ed. H. Paulhart, M.I.O.G. Ergänzungsband XX heft 2, Festschrift zur Jahrtausendfeier der Kaiserkrönung Ottos der Grossen, Zweiter Teil (Cologne, 1962).

Old English Bede, The Old English Version of Bede's Ecclesiastical History, ed. T. Miller, vol I, Early English Text Society (London, 1890).

Old English Martyrology, Das Altenglische Martyrologium, ed. G. Kotzor, 2 vols, Bayerische Akademie der Wissenschaften, philosophisch-historisch Klasse, Abhandlungen, Neue Folge, Heft 88/1 and 2 (Munich, 1981).

Orderic Vitalis, *The Ecclesiastical History of Orderic Vitalis*, ed. and trans. M. Chibnall, 6 vols (Oxford, 1969–80).

Passion of Edward the Martyr, Fell, C., *Edward, King and Martyr*, Leeds School of English (Leeds, 1971).

Pelteret, D.A.E., *Catalogue of English Post-Conquest Vernacular Documents* (Woodbridge, 1990).

PRG, Le Pontifical Romano-Germanique du dixième siècle, eds C. Vogel and R. Elze, vol 2, Studi e Testi, vol 227 (Vatican City, 1963).

R + number, *Anglo-Saxon Charters*, ed. A. Robertson, 2nd ed. (Cambridge, 1956) cited by number.

Ralph de Diceto, *Historical Works of Master Ralph de Diceto*, ed. W. Stubbs, Rolls Series (London, 1876).

Ralph Glaber, *The Five Books of the Histories*, in *Rodulfus Glaber, Opera*, eds J. France, N. Bulst and P. Reynolds (Oxford, 1989).

Reading Abbey Cartularies, ed. B.R. Kemp, vol I, Camden Society, Ser 3, vol 31 (London, 1986).

Records of Romsey Abbey, H.G.D. Liveing (Winchester, 1906).

Recueil des Historiens des Gaules et de la France, ed. L. Delisle, vol 10 (Paris, 1874).

Regularis Concordia, trans. T. Symons (Edinburgh, 1953).

Richard of Cirencester, *Speculum Historiale de Gestis Regum Angliae*, ed. J.E.B. Mayor, Rolls Series (London, 1869).

Richer, *Histoire de France 888–995*, ed. and trans. R. Latouche, 2 vols (Paris, 1930 and 1937).

Roger of Wendover, *Flores Historiarum*, ed. H.R. Luard, vol II, Rolls Series (London, 1890).

Rouleaux, Rouleaux des morts de IXe au XVe siècle, ed. L. Delisle, Société de l'histoire de France, vol 135 (Paris, 1866).

S + number, *Anglo-Saxon Charters, an Annotated List and Bibliography*, P.H. Sawyer, Royal Historical Society Guides and Handbooks, no 8 (1968), cited by number.

Saxo Grammaticus, *Danorum Regum Heroumque Historia*, Books x–xvi, ed. E. Christiansen, British Archaeological Reports, International Ser (Oxford, 1980).

Schröer, A., ed., *Die angelsachsichen Prosarbeitungen der Benedictinerregel* (Kassel, 1888).

SEHD + number, F. Harmer, *Select English Historical Documents of the Ninth and Tenth Centuries* (Cambridge, 1914) cited by number.

Semiramis, Poetic Individuality in the Middle Ages, New perspectives in poetry, 1000–1150, ed. P. Dronke (1986), printed at pp 66–75.

Sigebert of Gembloux, *MGH Scriptores*, vol VI (Hannover, 1844).

St Olaf's saga, Snorri Sturluson, Heimskringla, Part One, *The Olaf Sagas*, trans. S. Laing, rev. J. Simpson, vol 2 (London, 1964).

St Paul's, Early Charters of the Cathedral Church of St Paul London, ed. M. Gibbs, Camden Ser 3, vol 58 (London, 1939).

Sven Aggeson, *Svenonis Aggonis filii, Brevis historia regum Dacie* ed. M.C. Gertz, *Scriptores Minores Historiae Danicae Medii Aevi*, vol I (Copenhagen, 1917–18).

Swanton, M.J., 'A fragmentary life of St Mildred and other Kentish royal saints', *Archaeologia Cantiana*, vol 91 for 1975 (1976), pp 15–27.

Symeon of Durham, *Symeonis Dunelmensis Opera et Collectanea*, ed. Hodgson Hinde, vol I, Surtees Society, vol 51 (Durham, London and Edinburgh, 1868).

Symeon of Durham, *Symeonis Monachi Opera Omnia*, ed. T. Arnold, 2 vols, Rolls Series (London, 1882–5).

Temple, *Anglo-Saxon Manuscripts, 900–1066*, ed. E. Temple (London, 1976).

The Benedictional of Archbishop Robert, ed. H.A. Wilson, Henry Bradshaw Society, vol 24 for 1902 (London, 1903).

The Canterbury Benedictional, ed. R.M. Woolley, Henry Bradshaw Society, vol 51 for 1916 (London, 1917).

The Claudius Pontificals, ed. D.H. Turner, Henry Bradshaw Society, vol 97 for 1964 (London, 1971).

The Durham Collectar, ed. A. Correa, Henry Bradshaw Society, vol 107 for 1991 (London, 1992).

The Durham Ritual, ed. T.J. Brown et al., Early English Manuscripts in Facsimile, vol 16 (Copenhagen, 1969).

The Law of Hywel Dda, Law Texts from Medieval Wales, ed. and trans. D. Jenkins (Llandysul, 1986).

The Leofric Missal, ed. F.E. Warren (Oxford, 1883).

The Missal of Robert of Jumièges, ed. H.A. Wilson, Henry Bradshaw Society, vol 11 for 1896 (London, 1896).

The Missal of the New Minster, Winchester (Le Havre Bibl Mun, MS 330), ed. D.H. Turner, Henry Bradshaw Society, vol 93 for 1960 (London, 1962).

The Pontifical of Egbert, ed. W. Greenwell, Surtees Society, 27 (London, 1853), new ed. *Two Anglo-Saxon Pontificals*, ed. H.M.J. Banting, Henry Bradshaw Society, 104 for 1985–7 (London, 1989).

The Pontifical of Magdalen College, ed. H.A. Wilson, Henry Bradshaw Society, 39 for 1910 (London, 1910).

The Will of Æthelgifu, a Tenth-century Anglo-Saxon Manuscript, ed. D. Whitelock (Oxford, 1968).

The Winchcombe Sacramentary (Orleans, Bibl Mun 127 (105)), ed. A Davril, Henry Bradshaw Society, vol 109, for 1993–4 (London, 1995).

Theodric the Monk, *Theodrici Monachi Historia de Antiquitate regum Norwagiensium, Monumenta Historica Norvegiae, Latinske Kildeskrifter til Norges Historie i Middelalderen*, ed. G. Storm (Kristiania, 1880).

Thietmar of Merseburg, *Die Chronik des Bischofs Thietmar von Merseburg und ihre Korveier Überarbeitung*, ed. R. Holtzmann, *MGH, Scriptores Rerum Germanicarum in usum Scholarum*, new ser., vol 9 (Berlin, 1935).

Thomas Rudbourne, *Historia Major Wintoniensis, Anglia Sacra*, ed. H. Wharton, vol I (London, 1691).

Three Coronation Orders, ed. J. Wickham Legg, Henry Bradshaw Society, 19 for 1900 (London, 1900).

Three Eleventh-century Anglo-Latin Saints' Lives, ed. and trans. R.C. Love (Oxford, 1996).

Toller, T.N. and Campbell, A., *Supplement to J. Bosworth, An Anglo-Saxon Dictionary* (Oxford, 1972).

Translation of St Ælfheah, Translatio Sancti Ælfegi Cantuariensis archiepiscopi et martiris, by Osbern, ed. and trans. A. Rumble and R. Morris, *The Reign of Cnut, King of England, Denmark and Norway*, ed. A. Rumble (London, 1994), pp 283–315.

Translation of St Ouen, Acta Sanctorum, August IV (Paris and Rome, 1867), pp 823–4.

Vita Mahthildis Reginae Posterior, MGH Scriptores, vol 4 (Hannover, 1841), pp 282–302.

Vita Mahthildis reginae antiquior, ed. D.R. Koepke, *MGH Scriptores*, vol 10 (Hannover, 1852), pp 573–82.

Vita Oswaldi, Vita Oswaldi Archiepiscopi Eboracensis, The Historians of the Church of York and its Archbishops, ed. J. Raine, vol I, Rolls Series (London, 1879), pp 399–475.

VitaEd, The Life of King Edward who Rests at Westminster, ed. F. Barlow, 1st ed. (Edinburgh, 1962), 2nd ed. (Oxford, 1992). References are normally to the first edition; those to the second are specified as such.

Vocabularies, Anglo-Saxon and Old English Vocabularies, eds T. Wright and R.P. Wulcker, 2 vols (London, 1884).

Wace, *Le Roman de Rou de Wace*, ed. A.J. Holden, Société des Anciens Textes Français, 3 vols (Paris, 1970, 1971, 1973).

Walter Map, *De Nugis Curialium*, ed. M.R. James, *Anecdota Oxoniensia*, vol 14 (Oxford, 1914).

Waltham Chronicle, The Waltham Chronicle, ed. and trans. L. Watkiss and M. Chibnall (Oxford, 1994).

William of Jumièges, *The Gesta Normannorum Ducum of William of Jumièges, Orderic Vitalis and Robert of Torigni*, ed. E.M.C. van Houts, 2 vols (Oxford, 1992 and 1995).

William of Malmesbury, *De Antiquitate Glastonie Ecclesie, The Early History of Glastonbury, William of Malmesbury's De Antiquitate Glastonie Ecclesie*, ed. and trans. J. Scott (Woodbridge, 1981).

William of Malmesbury, *DGP, De Gestis Pontificum Anglorum*, ed. N.E.S.A. Hamilton, Rolls Series (London, 1870).

William of Malmesbury, *DGRA, De Gestis Regum Anglorum*, ed. W. Stubbs, 2 vols, Rolls Series (London, 1887–9).

William of Poitiers, *Guillaume de Poitiers, Histoire de Guillaume le Conquérant*, ed. and trans. R. Foreville, Classiques de l'Histoire de France au Moyen Age, vol 23 (Paris, 1962).

Wills + number, *Anglo-Saxon Wills*, ed. D. Whitelock (Cambridge, 1930), cited by number.

Wipo, *The Deeds of Conrad II*, in *Imperial Lives and Letters of the Eleventh Century*, trans. T.E. Mommsen and K.F. Morrison (New York and London, 1962).

Writs + number, *Anglo-Saxon Writs*, ed. F. Harmer (Manchester, 1952), cited by number.

Wulfstan, *Æthelwold*, *Wulfstan of Winchester: The Life of St Æthelwold*, eds M. Lapidge and M. Winterbottom (Oxford, 1991).

Wulfstan, *Homilies*, *The Homilies of Wulfstan*, ed. D. Bethurum (Oxford, 1957).

Wulfstan, *Institutes of Polity*, '*Institutes of Polity, Civil and Ecclesiastical*' *ein Werk Erzbischof Wulfstans von York*, hgbn von K. Jost, Swiss Studies in English, vol 47 (Bern, 1959), trans. M. Swanton, *Anglo-Saxon Prose* (1975), pp 125–38.

2 Secondary Sources

Allen, P., 'Contemporary portrayals of the Byzantine Empress Theodora', *Stereotypes of Women in Power: Historical Perspectives and Revisionist Views*, eds B. Garlick, et al. (New York and London, 1992), pp 93–103.

Althoff, G., 1988, '*Causa scribendi* und Darstellungsabsicht: Die Lebensbeschreibungen der Königin Mathilda und andere Beispiele', *Litterae Medii Aevi. Festschrift für Johanne Autenreith*, eds M. Borgolte and H. Spilling (Sigmaringen, 1988), pp 117–33.

—— 1991a, 'Gandersheim und Quedlinburg: Ottonische Frauenklöster als Herrschafts- und Überlieferungszentren', *Frühmittelalterliche Studien*, vol 25 (1991), pp 123–44.

—— 1991b, 'Vormundschaft, Erziehrer, Lehrer – Einflüsse auf Otto III', *Kaiserin Theophanu*, eds A. von Euw and P. Schreiner (Cologne, 1991), pp 277–89.

—— 1993, 'Probleme um die dos der Königinnen im 10 und 11 Jahrhundert', *Veuves et Veuvage dans le haut Moyen Age*, ed. M. Parisse (Paris, 1993), pp 123–33.

Anderson, T.M., 'King's Sagas (Konungasögur)', *Old Norse-Icelandic Literature, a Critical Guide*, eds C.J. Clover and J. Lindon, Islandica, vol 45 (Ithaca, 1985).

ANS, *Anglo-Norman Studies*, eds R. Allen Brown, et al. (Woodbridge).

Appleby, J.T., 'Richard of Devizes and the Annals of Winchester', *Bulletin of the Institute of Historical Research*, vol 36 (1963), pp 70–7.

Armitage Robinson, J., 'The Passion of S. Perpetua', *Texts and Studies Contributing to Biblical and Patristic Literature*, vol 1.2 (Cambridge, 1891).

ASE, *Anglo-Saxon England*, eds P. Clemoes et al. (Cambridge).

Attreed, L.C., 'From *Pearl* maiden to Tower Princes: towards a new history of medieval childhood', *Journal of Medieval History*, vol 9.1 (1983), pp 43–58.

Aurell I. Cardona, M., 'Les avatars de la viduité princière: Ermessende (ca. 975–1058), comtesse de Barcelone', *Veuves et Veuvage dans le haut Moyen Age*, ed. M. Parisse (Paris, 1993), pp 201–32.

Bachrach, B., 'Henry II and the Angevin tradition of family hostility', *Albion*, vol 16 (1984), pp 111–30.

Backhouse, J., et al., *The Golden Age of Anglo-Saxon Art, 966–1066* (London, 1984).

Bak, J.M., 'Roles and functions of queens in Arpádian and Angevin Hungary (1000–1386 AD)', *Medieval Queenship*, ed. J.C. Parsons (New York, 1993), pp 13–24.

Barker, K., 'The early history of Sherborne', *The Early Church in Western Britain and Ireland*, studies presented to R.A. Ralegh Radford, ed. S.M. Pearce, British Archaeological Reports, British Ser, vol 102 (Oxford, 1982), pp 77–116.

Barlow, F., 1958, 'Two notes: Cnut's second pilgrimage and Queen Emma's disgrace in 1043', *English Historical Review*, vol 73 (1958), pp 649–55.

—— 1963, *The English Church, 1000–1066. A Constitutional History* (London, 1963).

—— 1970, *Edward the Confessor* (London, 1970).

Barrow, J., 'English Cathedral Communities and Reform in the late tenth and the eleventh centuries', *Anglo-Norman Durham*, eds D. Rollason, M. Harvey and M. Prestwich (Woodbridge, 1994), pp 25–39.

Bates, D., 1982a, *Normandy before 1066* (London, 1982).

—— 1982b, 'The origins of the justiciarship', *ANS*, vol 4 (London, 1982), pp 1–12.

—— 1987, 'Lord Sudeley's ancestors: the family of the counts of Amiens, Valois and the Vexin in France and England during the eleventh century', *The Sudeleys – Lords of Toddington*, The Manorial Society of Great Britain (London, 1987), pp 34–48.

Bautier, R.H., 1975 (1991), 'L'hérésie d'Orleans et le mouvement intellectual au debut du XIe siècle: documents et hypothèses', *Actes du 95e Congrès national des sociétés savantes Reims, 1970*. Section de philologie et d'histoire jusqu'à 1610, t.1 (Paris, 1975), pp 63–88. Reprinted *Recherches sur l'histoire de la France médiévale. Des Mérovingiens aux premiers Capétiens* (Hampshire and Vermont, 1991).

—— 1985 (1991), 'Anne de Kiev, reine de France, et la politique royale au XIe siècle: étude critique de la documentation', *Revue des études slaves*, vol 57 (1985), pp 539–64. Reprinted *Recherches sur l'histoire de la France médiévale. Des Mérovingiens aux premiers Capétiens* (Hampshire and Vermont, 1991).

—— 1992, 'L'Avènement d'Hugues Capet et le sacre de Robert le Pieux', *Le Roi de France et son Royaume autour de l'An Mil*, eds M. Parisse and X. Barral I Altet (Paris, 1992), pp 27–37.

Becker, C.J., 'The coinages of Harthacnut and Magnus the Good at Lund, c. 1040–c. 1046', *Studies in Northern Coinages of the Eleventh Century*, ed. C.J. Becker (Copenhagen, 1981), pp 110–74.

Beech, G., 'England and Aquitaine in the century before the Norman Conquest', *ASE*, vol 19 (1990), pp 81–101.

Bell, A., 'Gaimar and the Edgar–Ælfthryth story', *Modern Language Review*, 21 (1926), pp 278–87.

Bernhardt, J.W., *Itinerant Kingship and Royal Monasteries in Early Medieval Germany, c. 936–1075* (Cambridge, 1993).

Bernstein, D.J., *The Mystery of the Bayeux Tapestry* (London, 1986).

Bethell, D., 'The making of a twelfth-century relic collection', *Popular Belief and*

Practice, Studies in Church History, vol 8, eds G.J. Cuming and D. Baker (Cambridge, 1972), pp 61–72.

Biddle, M., 1966, 'Excavations at Winchester 1965, fourth interim report', *The Antiquaries Journal*, vol 46 (London, 1966), pp 308–32.

—— 1975, '*Felix urbs Winthonia*: Winchester in the age of monastic reform', *Tenth-century Studies*, ed. D. Parsons (London, 1975), pp 123–40 and 233–7.

—— 1986, 'Seasonal festivals and residence: Winchester, Westminster and Gloucester in the tenth to twelfth centuries', *ANS*, vol 8 (1986), pp 51–63.

Biddle, M., et al. *Winchester in the early Middle Ages, an edition and discussion of the Winton Domesday*, Winchester Studies, vol I (Oxford, 1976).

Binski, P., 'Reflections on *La estoire de Seint Aedward le rei*: hagiography and kingship in thirteenth-century England', *Journal of Medieval History*, vol 16 (1990), pp 333–50.

Bloch, H., *Medieval Misogyny and the Invention of Western Romantic Love* (Chicago, 1991).

Bloch, M., 'La vie de S. Édouard le Confesseur par Osbert de Clare', *Analecta Bollandiana*, vol 41 (1923), pp 5–131.

Blunt, C.E., Stewart, B.H.I.H. and Lyon, C.S.S., *Coinage in Tenth-century England, from Edward the Elder to Edgar's Reform* (Oxford, 1989).

Bouchard, C., 'Patterns of women's names in royal lineages, ninth–eleventh centuries', *Medieval Prosopography*, vol 9.1 (1988), pp 1–32.

Bouman, C.A., *Sacring and Crowning, The development of the Latin Ritual for the anointing of kings and the coronation of an emperor before the eleventh century*, Bijdragen van het Instituut voor middeleeuwse Geschiedenis der Rijks-Universiteit te Utrecht, vol 30 (Gröningen, 1957).

Boussard, J., 'Les éveques de Neustrie avant la reforme grégorienne', *Journal des Savants* (1970), pp 161–96.

Brooke, C.N.L., 'The composition of the chapter of St Paul's', *Cambridge Historical Journal*, vol 10 (1951), pp 111–32.

Brooks, N., 1971, 'The development of military obligations in eight- and ninth-century England', *England before the Conquest. Studies in Primary Sources Presented to D. Whitelock*, eds P. Clemoes and K. Hughes (Cambridge, 1971), pp 69–84.

—— 1984, *The Early History of the Church of Canterbury* (Leicester, 1984).

Brooks, N. and Walker, H.E., 'The authority and interpretation of the Bayeux Tapestry', *ANS*, vol 1 (1979), pp 1–34.

Brühl, C., 'Fränkischer Krönungsbrauch und das Problem der "Festkrönungen"', *Historische Zeitschrift*, vol 194 (1962), pp 265–326.

Buchholz, P., 'Die Ehe in Germanischen besonders altnordischen Literaturdenkmälern', *Il matrimonio nella società altomedievale*, Settimane di studio del centro Italiano di studi sull'Alto Medioevo, vol 24, 1976 (Spoleto, 1977), vol I, pp 887–900.

Bulst-Thiele, M.L., *Kaiserin Agnes*, Beiträge zur Kulturgeschichte des Mittelalters und der Renaissance, vol 52 (Leipzig and Berlin, 1933).

Bur, M., 1977, *La Formation du comté de Champagne, c. 950–1150*, Publications de l'Université de Nancy, vol 2 (Nancy, 1977).

—— 1992, 'Adalberon, archevêque de Reims, reconsidéré', *Le Roi de France et son Royaume autour de l'An Mil,* eds M. Parisse and X. Barral I Altet (Paris, 1992), pp 55–63.

Cadden, J., *Meanings of Sex Difference in the Middle Ages, Medicine, Science and Culture* (Cambridge, 1993).

Cahn, W., 'The Psalter of Queen Emma', *Cahiers Archeologiques,* vol 33 (1985), pp 73–85.

Callender, V.G., 'Female officials in ancient Egypt and Egyptian historians', *Stereotypes of Women in Power: Historical Perspectives and Revisionist Views,* eds B. Garlick et al. (New York and London, 1992), pp 11–35.

Cam, H.M., 1963a, 'Early groups of hundreds', *Liberties and Communities in Medieval England* (London, 1963), pp 91–106.

—— 1963b, 'The king's government as administered by the greater abbots of East Anglia', *Liberties and Communities in Medieval England* (London, 1963), pp 183–204.

Cambridge, E., and Rollason, D., 'Debate: The pastoral organisation of the Anglo-Saxon church: a review of the "Minster Hypothesis"', *Early Medieval Europe,* vol 4 no 1 (1995), pp 87–104.

Campbell, A., *Skaldic Verse and Anglo-Saxon History,* Dorothea Coke Memorial lecture (London, 1971).

Campbell, J., 1978, 'England, France and Germany: Some comparisons and connections', *Ethelred the Unready, Papers from the Millenary Conference,* ed. D. Hill, British Archaeological Reports, British Series, 59 (1978), pp 255–70.

—— 1987, 'Some agents and agencies of the late Anglo-Saxon state', *Domesday Studies,* ed. J.C. Holt (Woodbridge, 1987), pp 201–18.

Campbell, M.W., 1971, 'Queen Emma and Ælfgifu of Northampton: Canute the Great's women', *Medieval Scandinavia,* vol 4 (1971), pp 66–79.

—— 1973, 'Emma reine d'Angleterre: mère denaturée ou femme vindictive', *Annales de Normandie,* vol 23 (1973), pp 97–114.

—— 1979, 'The *Encomium Emmae Reginae*: personal panegyric or political propaganda?', *Annuale Mediaevale,* vol 19 (1979), pp 27–45.

Camus, Marie Thérèse, 'La reconstruction de Saint-Hilaire le Grand de Poitiers à l'époque romane. La marche des travaux', *Cahiers de Civilization Médiévale,* vol 25 (1982), pp 101–20 and 239–71.

Chance, J., 1986 (1991), 'Grendel's mother as epic anti-type of the virgin and queen', chapter 7 of *Woman as Hero in Old English Literature* (Syracuse, 1986) reprinted in *Interpretations of Beowulf, a Critical Anthology,* ed. R.D. Fulk (London, 1991), pp 251–63.

—— 1990, 'The structural unity of *Beowulf*. The problem of Grendel's Mother', *New Readings on Women in Old English Literature,* eds H. Damico and A. Hennessey Olsen (Bloomington, Indiana, 1990), pp 248–61.

Chaplais, P., 1966, 'The Anglo-Saxon Chancery, from the diploma to the writ', *Journal of the Society of Archivists,* vol 3, no 4 (1966), pp 160–76.

—— 1985, 'The royal Anglo-Saxon "Chancery" of the tenth century revisited', *Studies in Medieval History Presented to R.H.C. Davis,* eds H. Mayr-Harting and R.I. Moore (1985), pp 41–51.

Charles-Edwards, T., 'Early medieval kingship in the British Isles', *The Origins of Anglo-Saxon Kingdoms,* ed. S. Bassett (London, 1989), pp 28–39.

Clanchy, M., *England and its Rulers, 1066–1272* (London, 1983).

Clark, C., 'The narrative mode of *The Anglo-Saxon Chronicle* before the Conquest', *England before the Conquest. Studies in Primary Sources Presented to D. Whitelock*, eds P. Clemoes and K. Hughes (Cambridge, 1971), pp 215–35.

Clarke, P., *The English Nobility under Edward the Confessor* (Oxford, 1994).

Clayton, M., *The Cult of the Virgin Mary in Anglo-Saxon England* (Cambridge, 1990).

Clover, C., 'The Germanic context of the Unferþ episode', *Speculum*, vol 55 (1980), pp 444–68.

Clunies Ross, M., 1985, 'Concubinage in Anglo-Saxon England', *Past and Present*, no 108 (1985), pp 3–34.

—— 1992, 'Women and power in the Scandinavian sagas', *Stereotypes of Women in Power: Historical Perspectives and Revisionist Views* eds B. Garlick et al. (New York and London, 1992), pp 105–19.

Collins, R., 'Queens-dowager and queens-regent in tenth-century León and Navarre', *Medieval Queenship*, ed. J.C. Parsons (New York, 1993), pp 79–92.

Colman, R.V., 'The abduction of women in barbaric law', *Florilegium, Carleton University Annual Papers on Classical Antiquity and the Middle Ages*, vol 5 (1983), pp 62–75.

Conner, P., *Anglo-Saxon Exeter, a Tenth-century Cultural History* (Woodbridge, 1993).

Cooke, K., 'Donors and daughters: Shaftesbury Abbey's benefactors, endowments and nuns c. 1086–1130', *ANS* 12 (1990), pp 29–45.

Corbet, P., 1986, *Les Saints ottoniens: sainteté dynastique, sainteté royale et sainteté féminine autour de l'an Mil*, Beihefte von *Francia*, bd 15 (Sigmaringen, 1986).

—— 1993, '*Pro anima senioris sui*. La pastorale ottonienne du veuvage', *Veuves et Veuvage dans le haut Moyen Age*, ed. M. Parisse (Paris, 1993), pp 233–53.

Cowdrey, H.E.J., 'The Anglo-Norman *Laudes Regiae*', *Viator*, vol 12 (1981), pp 37–78.

Cox, B., *The Place-Names of Rutland*, English Place Name Society, vols 67, 68, 69 (1994).

Crick, J., 'The wealth, patronage and connections of women's houses in late Anglo-Saxon England' (forthcoming).

Cutler, K.E., 'Edith, Queen of England, 1045–66', *Medieval Studies*, vol 35 (1973), pp 222–31.

Danico, H., *Beowulf's Wealhtheow and the Valkyrie Tradition* (Madison, Wisconsin, 1984).

Darlington, R.R., 'Ecclesiastical reform in the late old English period', *English Historical Review*, vol 51 (1936), pp 385–428.

Darmstädter, P., *Das Reichsgut in der Lombardei und Piedmont, 568–1250* (Strasbourg, 1896).

Davis, H.W.C., 'The Liberties of Bury St Edmund's', *English Historical Review*, vol 24 (1909), pp 417–31.

de Vajay, S., 'Mathilde, Reine de France Inconnue', *Journal des Savants* (1971), pp 241–60.

Delogu, P., 'Consors regni un problemo carolingio', Bulletino dell'Istituto Storice Italiano per il Medio Evo et Archivio Muratoriano, vol 76 (1964), pp 47–98.

Deshman, R., 1976, 'Christus Rex et magi reges: Kingship and Christology in Ottonian and Anglo-Saxon art', Frühmittelalterliche Studien, vol 10 (1976), pp 367–405.

—— 1988, 'Benedictus Monarcha et monachus. Early medieval ruler theology and the Anglo-Saxon Reform', Frühmittelalterliche Studien, vol 22 (1988), pp 204–40.

Dhondt, J., 'Sept femmes et un trio de rois', Contributions à l'histoire economique et sociale, Univ. Libre de Bruxelles, Institut de Sociologie, Solvay, vol 3 (1964–5), pp 35–70.

Dickins, B., 'The day of the battle of Æthelingadene, ASC 1001, A'. Leeds Studies in English, first ser, vol 6 (1937), pp 25–7.

Dickinson, F.H., 'The Sale of Combe', Somerset Archaeological and Natural History Society Proceedings, vol 22 (1876), pp 106–13.

Dixon, S., 'Conclusion – the enduring themes: domineering dowagers and scheming concubines', Stereotypes of Women in Power: Historical Perspectives and Revisionist Views, eds B. Garlick et al. (New York and London, 1992), pp 209–25.

Dodwell, C.R., Anglo-Saxon Art, a New Perspective (Manchester, 1982).

Dolley, R.H.M. and Elmore Jones, F., 'A new suggestion concerning the so-called "Martlets" in the "Arms of St Edward"', Anglo-Saxon Coins, Studies Presented to F.M. Stenton, ed. R.H.M. Dolley (London, 1961), pp 215–26.

Douglas, D.C., 1932, Feudal Documents from the Abbey of Bury St Edmund's (London, 1932).

—— 1942, 'Rollo of Normandy', English Historical Review, vol 57 (1942), pp 417–36.

—— 1944, 'The ancestors of William Fitz Osbern', English Historical Review, vol 59 (1944), pp 62–79.

—— 1950, 'Some problems of early Norman chronology', English Historical Review, vol 65 (1950), pp 289–303.

Duby, G., 1978, Medieval Marriage, Two Models from Twelfth-century France, trans. E. Forster (Baltimore and London, 1978).

—— 1983, 'La matrone et la mal mariée', Mâle Moyen Age (Paris, 1988), pp 50–73 repr. from 'The matron and the mis-married woman: perceptions of marriage in Northern France circa 1100', Social Relations and Ideas: Essays in Honour of R.H. Hilton, eds T. Aston, P. Coss and C. Dyer (Cambridge, 1983).

—— 1984, The Knight, the Lady and the Priest: the Making of Modern Marriage in Medieval France (London, 1984).

—— 1991, 'Le Modèle Courtois', Histoire des Femmes en Occident, eds G. Duby and M. Perrot, vol 2, Le Moyen Age, ed. C. Klapisch-Zuber (Paris, 1991), pp 261–76.

Dumville, D., 1976, 'The Anglian collection of royal genealogies and regnal lists', ASE, vol 5 (1976), pp 23–50.

—— 1979, 'The ætheling: a study in Anglo-Saxon constitutional history', ASE, vol 8 (1979), pp 1–33.

—— 1992a, Wessex and England from Alfred to Edgar (Woodbridge, 1992).

—— 1992b, *Liturgy and the Ecclesiastical History of Late Anglo-Saxon England* (Woodbridge, 1992).

—— 1993, *English Caroline Script and Monastic History, Studies in Benedictinism*, AD *950–1030* (Woodbridge, 1993).

Dutton, P.E., *The Politics of Dreaming in the Carolingian Empire* (Lincoln, Nebraska and London, 1994).

Eames, E., 'Mariage et concubinage légal en Norvège à l'époque des Vikings', *Annales de Normandie*, vol 2, no 3 (1952), pp 196–208.

Eckel, A., *Charles le Simple* (Paris, 1899).

Edwards, G., 1956, 'The Normans and the Welsh March', *Proceedings of the British Academy*, vol 42 (London, 1956), pp 155–77.

—— 1963, 'Studies in the Welsh Laws since 1928', *Welsh History Review*, Special Number (1963), The Welsh Laws, pp 1–17.

Ehlers, J., 'Carolingiens, Robertiens, Ottoniens: politique familiale ou relations franco-allemandes', *Le Roi de France et son Royaume autour de l'An Mil*, eds M. Parisse and X. Barral I Altet (Paris, 1992), pp 39–45.

Elias, N., *The Court Society*, trans. E. Jephcott (Oxford, 1983).

Enright, M.J., 'Lady with a mead cup. Ritual, group cohesion and hierarchy in the germanic warband', *Frühmittelalterliche Studien*, vol 22 (1988), pp 170–203.

Erkens, F-R, 1991, 'Die frau als Herrscherin in ottonisch-frühsalischer Zeit', *Kaiserin Theophanu*, eds A. von Euw and P. Schreiner (Cologne, 1991), pp 245–59.

—— 1993, '*Sicut Esther regina*. Die westfränkische Königin als *consors regni*', *Francia*, vol 20/1 (1993), pp 15–38.

Facinger, M., 'A study of medieval queenship: Capetian France 987–1237', *Studies in Medieval and Renaissance History*, vol 5 (1968), pp 3–48.

Finberg, H.P.R., 1946, 'Childe's Tomb', *Report and Transactions of the Devonshire Association*, vol 78 (1946), pp 265–80.

—— 1957, 'Three studies in family history', *Gloucestershire Studies*, ed. H.P.R. Finberg (Leicester, 1957), pp 145–83, 'Berkeley of Berkeley' at pp 145–59.

—— 1964, *The Early Charters of Wessex* (Leicester, 1964).

—— 1969, *Tavistock Abbey: a Study in the Social and Economic History of Devon* (Newton Abbot, 1969).

Fischer, A., *Engagement, Wedding and Marriage in Old English*, Anglistische Forschungen, vol 176 (Heidelberg, 1986).

Fleckenstein, J., 'Hofkapelle und Kanzlei unter der Kaiserin Theophanu', *Kaiserin Theophanu*, eds A. von Euw and P. Schreiner (Cologne, 1991), pp 305–10.

Fleming, R., 1985, 'Monastic lands and England's defence in the Viking age', *English Historical Review*, vol 100 (1985), pp 247–65.

—— 1991, *Kings and Lords in Conquest England* (Cambridge, 1991).

Folz, R., 1984, *Les saints rois en Occident, VIe–XIIIe siècles*, Subsidia Hagiographica, vol 69 (Brussels, 1984).

—— 1992, *Les saintes reines du moyen âge en occident (VIe–XIII siècles)*, Société des Bollandistes, Subsidia Hagiographica, vol 76 (Brussels, 1992).

Foot, S., 'Anglo-Saxon minsters: a review of terminology', *Pastoral Care before the Parish*, eds J. Blair and R. Sharpe (Leicester, 1992), pp 22–5.

Förster, M., *Der Flußname Theme und seine Sippe*. Sitzungsberichte der Bayerische Akademie der Wissenschaften, Phil.-hist. Abteilung, Bd 1 (Munich, 1941).

Fradenburg, L.O., 1992a, 'Introduction: rethinking queenship', *Women and Sovereignty*, ed. L.O. Fradenburg, *Cosmos*, Yearbook of the Traditional Cosmology Society, vol 7 (Edinburgh, 1992), pp 1–13.

—— 1992b, 'Sovereign love: the wedding of Margaret Tudor and James IV of Scotland', *Women and Sovereignty*, ed. L.O. Fradenburg, *Cosmos*, Yearbook of the Traditional Cosmology Society, vol 7 (Edinburgh, 1992), pp 78–100.

Frank, R., 'King Cnut in the verse of his skalds', *The Reign of Cnut: King of England, Denmark and Norway*, ed. A.R. Rumble (London, 1994), pp 106–24.

Frantzen, A., *The Literature of Penance in Anglo-Saxon England* (New Brunswick, NJ, 1983).

Franz, A., *Die Kircklichen Benediktionen im Mittelalter*, vol II (Freiburg, 1909).

Freeman, E.A., 1870–79, *The History of the Norman Conquest, its Causes and Results*, 6 vols (Oxford, 1870–79).

—— 1875, 'The mythical and Romantic elements in English history', *Historical Essays* (London, 1875), pp 1–39.

Fried, J., 'Theophanu und die Slaven, Bemerkungen zur ostpolitik der Kaiserin', *Kaiserin Theophanu*, eds A. von Euw and P. Schreiner (Cologne, 1991), pp 361–70.

Gameson, R., 'Manuscript art at Christ Church Canterbury in the generation after St Dunstan', *St Dunstan, his Life, Times and Cult*, eds N. Ramsay, M. Sparks and T. Tatton-Brown (Woodbridge, 1992), pp 187–220.

Gamillscheg, E., 'Zoe und Theodora als Träger dynastischer Vorstellungen in den Geschichtsquellen ihrer Epoche', *Kaiserin Theophanu*, eds A. von Euw and P. Schreiner (Cologne, 1991), pp 397–401.

Garlick, B., Dixon, S. and Allen, P., eds, *Stereotypes of Women in Power: Historical Perspectives and Revisionist Views* (New York and London, 1992).

Garnett, G., 1986a, ' "Franci et Angli": The legal distinctions between peoples after the Conquest', *ANS*, vol 7 (1986), pp 109–37.

—— 1986b, 'Coronation and propaganda: some implications of the Norman claim to the throne of England in 1066', *Transactions of the Royal Historical Society*, ser 5, vol 36 (1986), pp 91–116.

—— forthcoming, 'The Third Recension of the English Coronation Ordo: the manuscripts', *Journal of Ecclesiastical History*, forthcoming.

Gaudemet, J., *Le mariage en Occident* (Paris, 1987).

Gem, R., 1975, 'A recession in English architecture during the early eleventh century and its effects on the development of the Romanesque style', *Journal of the British Archaeological Association*, ser 3, vol 38 (1975), pp 28–49.

—— 1980, 'The Romanesque rebuilding of Westminster Abbey (with a reconstruction by W.T. Ball)', *ANS*, vol 3 (1981), pp 33–60.

—— 1986, 'The origins of the abbey', *Westminster Abbey*, eds C. Wilson et al. (1986), pp 6–21.

Gerchow, J., 1988, *Die Gedenkenüberlieferung der Angelsachsen*, Arbeiten zur Frühmittelalterforschung. Schriftenreihe des Instituts für Frühmittelalterforschung der Universität Munster, vol 20 (Berlin, 1988).

—— 1992, 'Prayers for Cnut, the liturgical commemoration of a conqueror', *England in the Eleventh Century*, ed. C. Hicks (Stamford, 1992), pp 219–38.

Gillingham, J., 1994, '1066 and the introduction of chivalry into England', *Law and Government in Medieval England and Normandy, Essays in Honour of Sir James Holt*, eds G. Garnett and J. Hudson (Cambridge, 1994), pp 31–55.

—— 1995a, 'Thegns and knights in eleventh-century England: who was then the gentleman?', *Transactions of the Royal Historical Society*, ser 6, vol 5 (1995), pp 129–53.

—— 1995b, 'Henry of Huntingdon and the twelfth-century revival of the English nation', *Concepts of National Identity in the Middle Ages*, eds S. Forde, L. Johnson and A.V. Murray, Leeds Texts and Monographs, New ser, vol 14 (Leeds, 1995), pp 75–101.

Gneuss, H., 'A preliminary list of manuscripts written or owned in England up to 1100', *ASE*, vol 9 (1981), pp 1–60.

Goody, J., *Succession to High Office*, Cambridge Studies in Social Anthropology, 4 (Cambridge, 1966).

Goody, J. and Tambiah, S.J., *Bridewealth and Dowry*, Cambridge Papers in Social Anthropology, 7 (Cambridge, 1973).

Gransden, A., 1974, *Historical Writing in England c. 550 to c. 1307* (London, 1974).

—— 1985 (1992), 'Legends and traditions concerning the origins of the Abbey of Bury St Edmund's', *English Historical Review*, vol 100 (London, 1985), pp 1–24 reprinted *Legends, Traditions and History in Medieval England* (London, 1992), pp 81–104.

Green, J., 1983, 'The sheriffs of William the Conqueror', *ANS*, vol 5 (1983), pp 129–45.

—— 1986, *The Government of England under Henry I* (Cambridge, 1986).

—— 1990, *The English Sheriffs to 1154*, Public Record Office Handbooks no 24 (London, 1990).

Grierson, P., 1940, 'Grimbald of St Bertin', *English Historical Review*, vol 55 (1940), pp 529–61.

Guillot, O., *Le Comte d'Anjou et son entourage au XIe siècle* (Paris, 1972).

Hare, M., *The Two Anglo-Saxon Minsters of Gloucester*, Deerhurst Lecture, 1992 (Deerhurst, 1993).

Harmer, F.E., 1938, 'Anglo-Saxon Charters and the historian', *Bulletin of the John Rylands Library*, vol 22 (1938), pp 339–67.

—— 1959, 'A Bromfield and a Coventry writ of king Edward the Confessor', *The Anglo-Saxons, Studies in some Aspects of their History and Culture Presented to Bruce Dickins*, ed. P. Clemoes (London, 1959), pp 89–103.

Harrison, K., *The Framework of Anglo-Saxon History to AD 900* (Cambridge, 1976).

Hart, C., 1992a. 'The East Anglian Hundreds', *The Danelaw* (London, 1992), pp 76–82.

—— 1992b, 'Oundle: its province and eight hundreds', *The Danelaw* (London, 1992), pp 141–76.

—— 1992c, 'The will of Ælfgifu', *The Danelaw* (London, 1992), pp 455–65.

—— 1992d, 'Athelstan Half King and his family', *ASE*, vol 2, revised and reprinted in *The Danelaw* (London, 1992), pp 569–604.

—— 1992e, 'The northern dowry of Queen Edith', *The Danelaw* (London, 1992), pp 194–9.

—— 1992f, 'The eastern Danelaw', *The Danelaw* (London, 1992), pp 23–113.

Harvey, B., *Westminster Abbey and its Estates in the Middle Ages* (Oxford, 1977).

Head, A., '"The gift of elves", Queen Emma', *Hatcher Review*, vol 3 pt 30 (1990), pp 471–9.

Heningham, E.K., 1946, 'The genuineness of the *Vita Ædwardi regis*', *Speculum*, vol 21 (1946), pp 419–56.

—— 1975, 'The literary unity, the date and the purpose of the Lady Edith's Book, "The Life of King Edward who Rests at Westminster"', *Albion*, vol 7 (1975), pp 24–40.

Herlihy, D., *Medieval Households* (Cambridge, Ma., 1985).

Heslop, T.A., 1980, 'English seals from the mid ninth century to 1100', *Journal of British Archaeological Association*, vol 103 (1980), pp 1–16.

—— 1990, 'The production of *de luxe* manuscripts and the patronage of King Cnut and Queen Emma', *ASE*, vol 19 (1990), pp 151–95.

Hill, D., *An Atlas of Anglo-Saxon England* (Oxford, 1981).

Hill, J., '"þæt wæs geomuru ides!" A female stereotype examined', *New Readings on Women in Old English Literature* , eds H. Damico and A. Hennessey Olsen (Bloomington, Indiana, 1990) pp 235–47.

Hillaby, J., 'Early Christian and pre-Conquest Leominster: an exploration of the sources', *Transactions of the Woolhope Naturalists' Field Club*, vol 45, pt 3 (1987), pp 557–685.

Hillard, T., 'On the stage, behind the curtain: images of politically active women in the late Roman republic', *Stereotypes of Women in Power: Historical Perspectives and Revisionist Views*, eds B. Garlick et al. (New York and London, 1992), pp 37–64.

Hofmeister, A., 'Studien zu Theophano', *Festschrift Edmund E. Stengel* (Münster, Cologne, 1952), pp 223–62.

Hohler, C., 'Some service books of the later Saxon church', *Tenth-Century Studies*, ed. D. Parsons (London, 1975), pp 60–83 and 217–27.

Hollister, C.W., 1978 (1986), 'The origins of the English treasury', *English Historical Review*, vol 93 (1978), repr. *Monarchy, Magnates and Institutions in the Anglo-Norman World* (1986), pp 209–22.

Holt, J.C., '1086', *Domesday Studies*, ed. J.C. Holt (Woodbridge, 1987), pp 41–64.

Hooper, N., 1985, 'Edgar ætheling, Anglo-Saxon prince, rebel and crusader', *ASE*, vol 14 (1985), pp 197–214.

—— 1994, 'Military developments in the reign of Cnut', *The Reign of Cnut, King of England, Denmark and Norway*, ed. A. Rumble (London, 1994), pp 89–100.

Huisman, G.C., 'Notes on the manuscript tradition of Dudo of St Quentin's *Gesta normannorum*', *ANS*, vol 6 (Woodbridge, 1984), pp 122–35.

Huneycutt, L.L., 1989, 'Images of high medieval queenship', *Haskins Society Journal*, vol 1 (1989), pp 61–71.

—— 1990, 'The idea of the perfect princess: the *Life of St Margaret* in the reign of Matilda II, 1100–1118', *ANS*, vol 12 (1990), pp 81–97.

—— 1993, 'Female succession and the language of power in the writings of twelfth-century churchmen', *Medieval Queenship*, ed. J.C. Parsons (New York, 1993), pp 189–201.

Hurnard, N., 'The Anglo-Norman franchises', *English Historical Review*, vol 64 (1949), pp 289–327.

Jackman, D., 'Review of E. Searle, *Predatory Kinship and the Creation of Norman Power, 840–1066*', *Ius Commune, Zeitschrift für Europäische Rechtsgeschichte*, Veroffentlichungen des Max-Plank-Instituts, vol 18, ed. D. Simon (Frankfurt am Main, 1991), pp 374–7.

Jaeger, C.S., *The Origins of Courtliness, Civilizing Trends and the Formation of Courtly Ideals, 939–1210* (Philadelphia, 1985).

Jäschke, K-U., *Notwendige Gefährtinnen, Königinnen der Salierzeit als Herrscherinnen und Ehefrauen im römisch-deutschen Reich des 11. und beginnenden 12. Jahrhunderts* (Saarbrücken-Scheidt, 1991).

Jenkins, D., 'Legal and comparative aspects of the Welsh Laws', *Welsh History Review*, Special Number (1963), The Welsh Laws, pp 53–9.

John, E., 1979, 'Edward the Confessor and his celibate life', *Analecta Bollandiana*, vol 97, pt 1–2 (1979), pp 171–8.

—— 1980–1, 'The *Encomium Emmae reginae*: a riddle and a solution', *Bulletin of the John Rylands Library*, vol 63 (1980–1), pp 58–94.

Jones, K.B., *Compassionate Authority: Democracy and the Representation of Women* (New York and London, 1993).

Jonsson, K., 'The coinage of Cnut', *The Reign of Cnut, King of England, Denmark and Norway*, ed. A. Rumble (London, 1994), pp 193–230.

Joyce, G.H., *Christian Marriage: an Historical and Doctrinal Study* (London, 1933).

Jussen, B., 'Der "Name" der Witwe. Zur Konstruktion eines Standes in Spätantike und Frühmittelalter', *Veuves et Veuvage dans le haut Moyen Age*, ed. M. Parisse (Paris, 1993), pp 137–75.

Kantorowicz, E., 1947, 'The Quinity of Winchester', *Art Bulletin*, vol 29 (1947), pp 73–85.

—— 1957, *The King's Two Bodies. A Study in Medieval Political Theology* (Princeton, NJ, 1957).

Kapelle, W.C., *The Norman Conquest of the North. The Region and its Transformation, 1000–1135* (London, 1979).

Kay, S., and Rubin, M., *Framing Medieval Bodies* (Manchester, 1994).

Keats-Rohan, K.S.B., 'The parentage of Countess Lucy made plain', *Prosopon, Newsletter of the Unit for Prosopographical Research*, no 2 (May, 1995).

—— (forthcoming), ' "Bilichildis" et "Poppa" – Problèmes et possibilités d'une étude de l'onomastique et de la parenté de la France du nord-ouest', in *Actes de la première table ronde 'Onomastique et parenté', Saint-Jean-d'Angely, 21–25 mars 1996*, eds K.S.B. Keats-Rohan and C. Settipani, Occasional Publications of the Unit for Prosopographical Research 1 (Oxford, 1996, forthcoming).

Kehr, P., 'Zur Geschichte Ottos III', *Historische Zeitschrift*, vol 66 (1891), pp 385–443.

Kelly, F., *A Guide to Early Irish Law* (Dublin, 1988).

Kemp, B.R., 1968, 'The monastic dean of Leominster', *English Historical Review*, vol 83 (1968), pp 505–15.

—— 1969, 'The churches of Berkeley Hernesse', *Transactions of the Bristol and Gloucestershire Archaeological Society*, vol 87, for 1968 (1969), pp 96–110.

Kennedy, A.G., 'Cnut's law code of 1018', *ASE*, vol 11 (1983), pp 57–81.

Keynes, S., 1978, 'The declining reputation of king Æthelred the Unready', *Ethelred the Unready, Papers from the Millenary Conference*, ed. D. Hill, British Archaelogical Reports, British Series, vol 59 (Oxford, 1978), pp 227–53.

—— 1980, *The Diplomas of King Æthelred the Unready, 978–1016* (Cambridge, 1980).

—— 1985, 'King Athelstan's books', *Learning and Literature in Anglo-Saxon England*, eds M. Lapidge and H. Gneuss (Cambridge, 1985), pp 143–201.

—— 1986, 'A tale of two kings: Alfred the Great and Æthelred the Unready', *Transactions of the Royal Historical Society*, Ser 5, vol 36 (1986).

—— 1988, 'Regenbald the Chancellor (sic)', *ANS*, vol 10 (Woodbridge, 1988), pp 185–222.

—— 1991, 'The æthelings in Normandy', *ANS*, vol 13 (1991), pp 173–205.

—— 1994a, 'Cnut's earls', *The Reign of Cnut, King of England, Denmark and Norway*, ed. A. Rumble (London, 1994), pp 43–88.

—— 1994b, 'The "Dunstan B" charters', *ASE*, vol 23 (1994), pp 165–93.

—— 1995, *An Atlas of Attestations in Anglo-Saxon Charters, c. 600–1066* (Cambridge, privately circulated).

Kidd, J., 'The Quinity of Winchester reconsidered', *Studies in Iconography*, vols 7–8 (1981–2), pp 21–33.

Klaniczay, G., *The Uses of Supernatural Power, The Transformation of Popular Religion in Medieval and Early Modern Europe*, trans S. Singerman (Princeton, NJ, 1990) for 'From sacral kingship to self-representation: Hungarian and European royal saints', pp 79–94; 'Legends as life-strategies for aspirant saints in the later Middle Ages', pp 95–110; and 'The cult of dynastic saints in Central Europe: fourteenth-century Angevins and Luxemburgs', pp 111–28.

Knowles, D., *The Monastic Order in England* (Cambridge, 1966).

Konecny, S., *Die Frauen des karolingischen Königshauses: Die politische Bedeutung der Ehe and die Stellung der Frau in der frankischen Herrscherfamilie vom 7 bis zum 10 Jahrhundert*. Ph D dissertation, University of Vienna, 1976.

Korhammer, P.M., 'The origin of the Bosworth Psalter', *ASE*, vol 2 (1973), pp 173–87.

Körner, S., *The Battle of Hastings, England and Europe 1035–1066* (Lund, 1964).

Kristjánsson, J., *Eddas and Sagas, Iceland's Medieval Literature*, trans. P. Foote (Reykjavik, 1992).

Kuefler, M.S., ' "A Wryed Existence". Attitudes towards children in Anglo-Saxon England', *Journal of Social History*, vol 24.4 (1991), pp 823–34.

Lanoë, G., 1992, 'Les *ordines* de couronnement (930–1050): retour au manuscrit', *Le Roi de France et son Royaume autour de l'An Mil*, eds M. Parisse and X. Barral I. Altet (Paris, 1992), pp 65–72.

—— 1993, 'L'*ordo* de couronnement de Charles le Chauve à Sainte–Croix d'Orléans (6 juin 848)', *Kings and Kingship in Medieval Europe*, ed A. Duggan, King's College London Medieval Studies (London, 1993), pp 41–68.

Lapidge, M., 1982, 'The origin of CCCC MS 163', *Transactions of the Cambridge Bibliographical Society*, vol 8 (1982), pp 18–28.

—— 1992, 'B and the *Vita S. Dunstani*', *St Dunstan, his Life, Times and Cult*, eds N. Ramsay et al. (Woodbridge, 1992), pp 247–59.

Larson, L.M., *The King's Household in England before the Norman Conquest* (Madison, 1904).

Laudage, J., 'Das Problem der Vormundschaft über Otto III', *Kaiserin Theophanu*, eds A. von Euw and P. Schreiner (Cologne, 1991), pp 261–75.

Lauer, P., 1900, *Le Regne de Louis IV d'Outremer. Annales de l'histoire de France à l'epoque Carolingienne* (Paris, 1900).

—— 1910, *Robert I et Raoul de Bourgogne, Rois de France 923–36* (Paris, 1910).

Lauranson-Rosaz, C., 'Douaire et *sponsalicium* durant le haut Moyen Age', *Veuves et Veuvage dans le haut Moyen Age*, ed. M. Parisse (Paris, 1993), pp 99–105.

Lawson, M.K., 1993, *Cnut. The Danes in England in the Early Eleventh Century* (London, 1993).

—— 1994, 'Archbishop Wulfstan and the homiletic element in the laws of Æthelred II and Cnut', *The Reign of Cnut, King of England, Denmark and Norway*, ed. A. Rumble (London, 1994), pp 141–64.

Le Goff, J., 'Le roi dans l'Occident médiéval: caractères originaux', *Kings and Kingship in Medieval Europe*, ed. A. Duggan, King's College London Medieval Studies (London, 1993), pp 1–40.

Le Jan-Hennebique, R., 'Aux origines du douaire médiéval (VIe–Xe siècles)', *Veuves et Veuvage dans le haut Moyen Age*, ed. M. Parisse (Paris, 1993), pp 107–122.

Lemarignier, J.F., *Le Governement Royal aux premiers temps Capétiens, 987–1108* (Paris, 1965).

Lennard, R.V., *Rural England, 1086–1135* (Oxford, 1959).

Lewis, A., 'Successions ottoniennes et robertiennes: un essai de comparaison', *Le Roi de France et son Royaume autour de l'An Mil*, eds M. Parisse and X. Barral I Altet (Paris, 1992), pp 47–53.

Lewis, C., 'The Norman settlement of Herefordshire under William I', *ANS*, vol 7 (1985), pp 195–213.

Lexikon des Mittelalters, 7 vols (Munich and Zurich, 1980–1995).

Leyser, H., *Medieval Women. A Social History of Women in England, 450–1500* (London, 1995).

Leyser, K., 1979, *Rule and Conflict in an Early Medieval Society, Ottonian Saxony* (London, 1979).

—— 1983 (1994), 'The Ottonians and Wessex', *Communications and Power in Medieval Europe: the Carolingian and Ottonian Centuries*, ed. T. Reuter (London, 1994), pp 73–104 (fp 1983).

—— 1994a 'Theophanu dei gratia Imperatrix Augusta: western and eastern emperorship in the later tenth century', *Communications and Power in Medieval Europe: the Carolingian and Ottonian Centuries*, ed. T. Reuter (London, 1994), pp 143–64.

—— 1994b, '987, the Ottonian connection', *Communications and Power in Medieval Europe: the Carolingian and Ottonian Centuries*, ed. T. Reuter (London, 1994), pp 165–79.

Lifshitz, F., 'The *Encomium Emmae Reginae* a political pamphlet of the eleventh century?', *Haskins Society Journal*, vol 1 (1989), pp 39–50.

Lindquist, O., 'Encomium Emmae', *Scandia*, vol 33 (1967), pp 175–81.

Linton, R., 'On Status and role' from *The Study of Man* (1936) reprinted in Truzzi 1971, pp 90–7.

Lintzel, M., 1937, 'Königin Mathilde', *Westfälische Lebensbilder*, Hauptreihe 5 (1937), pp 161–75.

—— 1961a, 'Heinricus natus in aula regali, Miszellen zur Geschichte des zehnten Jahrhunderts no V', M. Lintzel *Ausgewählte Schriften*, vol II (Berlin, 1961), pp 276–82.

—— 1961b, 'Der Reichstag von Verona im Jahre 983', M. Lintzel *Ausgewählte Schriften*, vol II (Berlin, 1961), pp 291–6.

—— 1961c, 'Die Mathildenviten und das Wahrheitsproblem in der Uberlieferung der Ottonenzeit', M. Lintzel *Ausgewählte Schriften*, vol II (Berlin, 1961), pp 407–18.

Lobel, M.D., *The Borough of Bury St Edmund's* (Oxford, 1935).

Lot, F., 1891, *Les Derniers Carolingiens, Lothaire, Louis V, Charles de Lorraine* (Paris, 1891).

—— 1903, *Etudes sur le règne de Hugues Capet et la fin du Xe siécle* (Paris, 1903).

Loud, G.A., 'The "Gens Normannorum" – myth or reality?', *ANS*, vol 4 (Woodbridge, 1982), pp 104–16 and 204–9.

Loyn, H., *The Governance of Anglo-Saxon England, 500–1087* (1984).

Lund, N., 'Cnut's Danish kingdom', *The Reign of Cnut, King of England, Denmark and Norway*, ed. A. Rumble (1994), pp 27–42.

Mack, K., 'The stallers, an administrative innovation in the reign of Edward the Confessor', *Journal of Medieval History*, vol 12 (1986), pp 123–34.

Maitland, F.W., *Domesday Book and Beyond* (1960).

Martindale, J., 'Succession and politics in the Romance-speaking world, c. 1000–1140', *England and her Neighbours, 1066–1453*, essays in honour of Pierre Chaplais, eds M. Jones and M. Vale (London, 1989), pp 19–41.

Mason, E., *St Wulfstan of Worcester, c. 1008–1095* (Oxford, 1990).

Mason, J.F.A., 'William the First and the Sussex rapes', *1066 Commemoration Lectures* (London, 1966), pp 37–58.

Mauss, M., *The Gift: Forms and Functions of Exchange in Archaic Societies*, trans. I. Cunnison (London, 1954).

McCartney, W., 'The king's mother and the royal prerogative in early sixteenth-century France', *Medieval Queenship*, ed. J.C. Parsons (New York, 1993), pp 117–41.

McKitterick, R., 1989 (1994), 'Nuns' scriptoria in England and Francia in the eighth century', *Francia*, 19.1 (1989), pp 1–35, reprinted *Books, Scribes and Learning in the Frankish Kingdoms, 6th–9th Centuries* (Aldershot, 1994).

—— 1991 (1994), 'Women and literacy in the early middle ages', *Frauen und Schriftlichkeit in Frühmittelater*, ed. H.-W. Goetz (Köln, 1991), pp 65–118,

English translation *Books, Scribes and Learning in the Frankish Kingdoms, 6th–9th Centuries* (Aldershot, 1994).

—— 1993, 'Ottonian intellectual culture in the tenth century and the role of Theophanu', *Early Medieval Europe*, vol 2 (1993), pp 53–74.

McLaughlin, M.C., 'Survivors and surrogates: children and parents from the ninth to the thirteenth centuries', *The History of Childhood*, ed. L. deMause (New York, 1974 and 1988), pp 101–81.

McNamara, J.A. and Wemple, S., 'The power of women through the family in medieval Europe: 500–1100', *Clio's Consciousness Raised. New Perspectives on the History of Women*, eds M. Hartman and L.W. Banner (New York, 1974), pp 103–18.

Meritt, H., 'Old English entries in a manuscript at Bern', *Journal of English and Germanic Philology*, vol 33 (1934), pp 343–51.

Metcalf, D.M., 'Continuity and change in English monetary history, 973–1086, Part 1', *British Numismatic Journal*, vol 50 (1980), pp 20–49.

Meyer, M.A., 1977, 'Women and the tenth-century English Monastic Reform'. *Revue Bénédictine*, vol 87 (1977), pp 34–61.

—— 1981, 'Patronage of the West Saxon royal nunneries in late Anglo-Saxon England', *Revue Bénédictine*, vol 91 (1981), pp 332–58.

—— 1993, 'The queen's "Demesne" in later Anglo-Saxon England', *The Culture of Christendom*, ed. M.A. Meyer (London, 1993), pp 75–113.

Millinger, S., 'Anglo-Saxon nuns in Anglo-Norman hagiography: humility and power', *Distant Echoes, Medieval Religious Women*, vol I, eds J.A. Nichols and L.T. Shank (Kalamazoo, 1984), pp 115–29.

Moore, H.L., *Feminism and Anthropology* (Cambridge, 1988).

Mor, C.G., *'Consors regni*, la regina nel diritto pubblico italiano dei secoli ix–x', *Archivio Giuridico*, ser 6, vol 4 (1948), pp 7–32.

Morelle, L., 'Mariage et diplomatique: autour de cinq chartes de douaire dans le Laonnois-Soissonais, 1163–81', *Bibliothèque de l'Ècole des Chartes*, vol 146 (Jan–June, 1988), pp 225–84.

Morgan, D.A.L., 'The house of policy: the political role of the Plantagenet household, 1422–85', in Starkey et al., 1987, pp 25–70.

Morris, C.J., *Marriage and murder in eleventh-century Northumbria, a study of the 'De Obsessione Dunelmi'*, Borthwick papers, no 82 (York, 1992).

Musset, L., 1952, 'Review of *The Encomium Emmae*', *Annales de Normandie*, vol 2 (1952), pp 86–8.

—— 1954, 'Le satiriste Garnier de Rouen et son milieu (debut du xie siécle)', *Revue du Moyen Age Latin*, vol 10 (1954), pp 237–66.

—— 1959, 'Actes inédites du xie siécle, III: Les plus anciennes chartes Normandes de l'abbaye de Bourgeuil', *Bulletin de la Société des Antiquaires de Normandie*, vol 54 for 1957–8 (1959), pp 15–54.

—— 1974, 'Rouen et Angleterre vers l'an mil: du nouveau sur le satiriste Garnier et l'école litteraire de Rouen au temps de Richard II', *Annales de Normandie*, vol 24 (1974), pp 287–90.

Nelson, J., 1971 (1986), 'National synods, kingship as office and royal anointing: an early medieval syndrome', *Politics, Ritual and Reality* (London, 1986), pp 239–57 (fp 1971).

—— 1975 (1986), 'Ritual and reality in the early medieval *Ordines*', *Politics and Ritual in Early Medieval Europe* (London, 1986), pp 329–39 (fp 1975).

—— 1977 (1986), 'Inauguration rituals', *Politics and Ritual in Early Medieval Europe* (London, 1986), pp 283–307 (fp 1977).

—— 1978. 'Queens as Jezebels: the careers of Brunhild and Balthild in Merovingian history', *Medieval Women*, ed. D. Baker, Studies in Church History, Subsidia, I (Oxford, 1978), pp 31–77.

—— 1980 (1986), 'The earliest English royal *ordo*: some liturgical and historical aspects', *Politics and Ritual in Early Medieval Europe* (London, 1986), pp 341–60 (fp 1980).

—— 1982 (1986), 'The Rites of the Conqueror', *Politics and Ritual in Early Medieval Europe* (London, 1986), pp 375–401 (fp 1982).

—— 1986, 'The Second English Ordo', *Politics and Ritual in Early Medieval Europe* (London, 1986), pp 361–74.

—— 1988, 'Kingship and empire', *The Cambridge History of Medieval Political Thought*, ed. J.H. Burns (Cambridge, 1988), pp 211–51.

—— 1990, 'Perceptions du pouvoir chez les historiennes du haut moyen âge', *Les Femmes au moyen âge*, ed. M. Rouche (Paris, 1990), pp 77–85.

—— 1991a, 'La famille de Charlemagne', *Le Souverain à Byzance et au occident du VIIIe au Xe siécle: Hommage à la mémoire de Maurice Leroy*, eds A. Dierkens and J.M. Sausterre, *Byzantion*, vol 61 (1991), pp 194–212.

—— 1991b, 'Reconstructing a royal family: reflections on Alfred, from Asser, chapter 2', *People and Places in Northern Europe*, eds N. Lund and I. Wood (Woodbridge, 1991), pp 47–66.

—— 1993a, 'Women at the court of Charlemagne: a case of monstrous regiment?', *Medieval Queenship*, ed. J.C. Parsons (New York, 1993), pp 43–61.

—— 1993b, 'The political ideas of Alfred of Wessex', *Kings and Kingship in Medieval Europe*, ed. A. Duggan, King's College London Medieval Studies (London, 1993), pp 125–58.

—— 1997, 'Early medieval rites of queen-making and the shaping of medieval queenship', *Queens and Queenship in Medieval Europe*, ed. A. Duggan (Woodbridge, forthcoming, 1997).

Nolte, C., 'Die Königinwitwe Chrodechilde. Familie und Politik im frühen 6. Jahrhundert', *Veuves et Veuvage dans le haut Moyen Age*, ed. M. Parisse (Paris, 1993), pp 177–86.

O'Reilly, J., 'St John as a figure of the contemplative life: text and image in the art of the Anglo-Saxon Benedictine Reform', *St Dunstan, his Life, Times and Cult*, eds N. Ramsay, M. Sparks and T. Tatton-Brown (Woodbridge, 1992), pp 165–85.

Oleson, T., *The Witenagemot in the Reign of Edward the Confessor* (Toronto, 1955).

Olivier-Martin, F., *Les regences et la majorité des rois sous les Capétiens directs et les premiers Valois, 1060–1375* (Paris, 1931).

Oursel, R., *Haut Poitou Roman*, 2nd ed (Paris, 1984).

Owen, D.D.R., *Eleanor of Aquitaine* (Oxford, 1993).

Owen., G.R., 'Wynflæd's wardrobe', *ASE*, vol 8 (1979), pp 195–222.

Pacaut, M., *L'Ordre de Cluny* (Paris, 1986).

Painter, S., *French Chivalry* (Ithaca, New York, 1957).

Parisse, M., 1978, 'Les chanoinesses dans l'Empire germanique (IXe–XIe siècles)', *Francia*, vol 6 (1978), pp 107–26.

—— 1990, 'Les femmes au monastère dans le Nord de l'Allemagne du IXe siécle au XI siécle. Conditions sociales et religieuses', *Frauen in Spätantike und Frühmittelalter*, Lebensbedingungen, Lebensnormen, Lebensformen (Sigmaringen, 1990), pp 311–24.

—— 1992, 'Die Frauenstifte und Frauenklöster in Sachsen vom 10 bis zur Mitte des 12 Jahrhunderts', *Die Salier und das Reich*, Bd 2 Die Reichskirche in der Salierzeit. Hgbn von S. Weinfurter (Sigmaringen, 1992), pp 465–501.

—— 1993, 'Des veuves au monastère', *Veuves et Veuvage dans le haut Moyen Age*, ed. M. Parisse (Paris, 1993), pp 255–74.

—— ed., *Veuves et Veuvage dans le haut Moyen Age* (Paris, 1993).

Parisse, M., and Barral I Altet, X, *Le Roi de France et son Royaume autour de l'An Mil*, Actes du Colloque Hugues Capet, 978–1987. La France de l'An Mil, Paris-Senlis, 22–25 Juin, 1987 (Paris, 1992).

Parisse, M. and Oexle, O.G., *L'Abbaye de Gorze au Xe siécle* (Nancy, 1993).

Parkes, M.P., 'A fragment of an early tenth-century Anglo-Saxon manuscript and its significance', *ASE*, vol 12 (1983), pp 129–40.

Parsons, J.C., 1992, 'Ritual and symbol in the English medieval queenship to 1500', *Women and Sovereignty*, ed. L.O. Fradenburg (London, 1992), pp 60–77.

—— 1993a, 'Introduction: Family, sex and power: the rhythms of medieval queenship', *Medieval Queenship*, ed. J.C. Parsons (New York, 1993), pp 1–11.

—— 1993b, 'Mothers, daughters, marriage, power: some Plantagenet evidence, 1150–1500', *Medieval Queenship*, ed. J.C. Parsons (New York, 1993), pp 63–78.

—— 1995, *Eleanor of Castile, Queen and Society in Thirteenth-century England* (New York, 1995).

Patterson, R.B., 'Robert Fitz Harding of Bristol: profile of an early Angevin burgess-patrician and his family's urban involvement', *Haskins Society Journal*, vol I (1989), pp 109–22.

Peckham, W.D., 'The Bosham myth of Canute's daughter', *Sussex Notes and Queries*, vol 17 (1970), pp 179–84.

Pellaton, F., 'La veuve et ses droits de la basse Antiquité au haut Moyen Age', *Veuves et Veuvage dans le haut Moyen Age*, ed. M. Parisse (Paris, 1993), pp 51–97.

Perst, O., 'Zur Reihenfolge der Kinder Ottos II und der Theophano', *Deutsches Archiv*, vol 14 (1958), pp 230–6.

Peterson, C.M., *Studies in the Early History of Peterbrough Abbey, c. 650–c. 1066*, unpublished Birmingham Ph D thesis, 1995.

Pfister, C., *Etudes sur le règne de Robert le Pieux, 996–1031* (Paris, 1885).

Phythian-Adams, C., 1977, 'Rutland reconsidered', *Mercian Studies*, ed. A. Dornier (Leicester, 1977), pp 43–84.

—— 1980, 'The emergence of Rutland and the making of the realm', *Rutland Record, Journal of the Rutland Record Society*, vol 1 (1980), pp 5–12.

Pinoteau, H., 'Les insignes du roi vers l'an Mil', *Le Roi de France et son Royaume autour de l'An Mil*, eds M. Parisse and X. Barral I Altet (Paris, 1992), pp 73–87.

Pollock, F., and Maitland, F.W., *The History of English Law before the Time of Edward I*, 2 vols, 2nd edition (Cambridge, 1968).

Poly, J.-P. and Bournazel, E., *The Feudal Transformation, 900–1200*, trans. C. Higgitt (New York, 1991).

Poole, R., 'Skaldic verse and Anglo-Saxon history: some aspects of the period 1009–1016', *Speculum*, vol 62 (1987), pp 265–98.

Poulet, A., 'Capetian women and the regency: the genesis of a vocation', *Medieval Queenship*, ed. J.C. Parsons (New York, 1993), pp 93–116.

Poupardin, R., 1901, *Le Royaume de Provence sous les Carolingiens, 855–933* (Paris, 1901).

—— 1907, *Le Royaume de Bourgogne 888–1038. Etudes sur les origines du royaume d'Arles* (Paris, 1907).

Prentout, H., *Étude Critique sur Dudon de Saint-Quentin*, Mémoires de l'Academie Nationale des Sciences, Arts et Belles Lettres de Caen (Caen, 1915).

Prescott, A., 'The structure of English pre-Conquest Benedictionals', *British Library Journal*, vol 13 (1987), pp 118–58.

Prestwich, J.O., 'The military household of the Norman kings', *English Historical Review*, vol 96 (1981), pp 1–35.

Quirk, R.N., 1957, 'Winchester Cathedral in the tenth century', *Archaeological Journal*, vol 114 (1957), pp 28–68.

—— 1961, 'Winchester New Minster and its tenth-century tower', *Journal of the British Archaeological Association*, ser 3, vol 24 (1961), pp 16–54.

Ramsay, J.M., 'Political History to 1625', *VCH Rutland*, vol I (London, 1908), pp 165–84.

Rapp, R.R., 'Anthropology: a review essay', *Signs*, vol 4 (1979), pp 497–513.

Raraty, D.G.J., 'Earl Godwine of Wessex: the origins of his power and his political loyalties', *History*, vol 74 (1989), pp 3–19.

Reuter, T., 1979, *The Medieval Nobility, Studies on the Ruling Classes of France and Germany from the Sixth to the Twelfth Century* (Amsterdam, New York and Oxford, 1979).

—— 1990, *Germany in the Early Middle Ages* (London, 1990).

—— 1993, 'The origins of the German *Sonderweg*? The empire and its rulers in the high middle ages', *Kings and Kingship in Medieval Europe*, ed. A. Duggan, King's College London Medieval Studies (London, 1993), pp 179–211.

Reynolds, S., *Fiefs and Vassals, The Medieval Evidence Reinterpreted* (Oxford, 1994).

Rezak, B.B., 'The king enthroned, a new theme in Anglo-Saxon royal iconography. The seal of Edward the Confessor and its political implications', *Kings and Kingship*, ed. J. Rosenthal, *Acta*, vol 11, 1984 (Binghampton, New York, 1986), pp 53–88.

Richard, J., *Les Ducs de Bourgogne et la formation du duché, du XIe au XIVe siècle*, Publications de l'Université de Dijon, 12 (Paris, 1954).

Richlin, A., 'Julia's jokes, Galla Placidia and the Roman use of women as political icons', *Stereotypes of Women in Power: Historical Perspectives and Revisionist Views*, eds B. Garlick et al. (New York and London, 1992), pp 65–91.

Ridyard, S., *The Royal Saints of Anglo-Saxon England. A Study of West Saxon and East Anglian Cults* (Cambridge, 1988).

Ritchie, R.L.G., *The Normans in Scotland* (Edinburgh, 1954).

Ritzer, K., 'Le mariage dans les Églises chrétiennes du Ier au XIe siècle', *Lex Orandi*, vol 45 (Paris, 1970).

Rollason, D., 1978, 'Lists of saints' resting-places in Anglo-Saxon England', *ASE*, vol 7 (1978) pp 61–93.

—— 1982, *The Mildrith Legend. A Study in Early Medieval Hagiography in England* (Leicester, 1982).

—— 1989a, *Saints and Relics in Anglo-Saxon England* (Oxford, 1989).

—— 1989b, 'St Cuthbert and Wessex: the evidence of Cambridge, Corpus Christi College MS 183', *St Cuthbert, his Cult and Community to AD 1200*, eds G. Bonner, D. Rollason and C. Stancliffe (Woodbridge, 1989), pp 413–24.

Rosenstock, E., *Königshaus und Stämme in Deutschland zwischen 911 und 1250* (Leipzig, 1914).

Rosenthal, J., 'The Pontifical of St Dunstan', *St Dunstan, his Life, Times and Cult*, eds N. Ramsay, M. Sparks and T. Tatton-Brown (Woodbridge, 1992), pp 143–63.

Rosenwein, B., *To Be the Neighbour of St Peter: the Social Meaning of Cluny's Property, 909–1049* (Ithaca, New York, 1989).

Round, J.H., 1899, 'Ingelric the priest and Albert of Lotharingia', *The Commune of London and Other Studies* (London, 1899), pp 36–8.

—— 1904, 'The officers of Edward the Confessor', *English Historical Review*, vol 19 (1904), pp 90–2.

—— 1908, 'Introduction to the Domesday Survey', *VCH Herefordshire*, vol I (London, 1908).

Rumble, A., ed., *The Reign of Cnut, King of England, Denmark and Norway* (London, 1994).

Sassier, Y., *Hugues Capet* (Paris, 1987).

Sawyer, B., 1988, *Property and Inheritance in Viking Scandinavia: the runic evidence*, Occasional papers on medieval topics, 2 (Alingsås, 1988).

Sawyer, B. and Sawyer, P., *Medieval Scandinavia from Conversion to Reformation, c. 800–1500* (Minneapolis, 1993).

Sawyer, P., 1983, 'The royal *tun* in pre-Conquest England', *Ideal and Reality in Frankish and Anglo-Saxon Society*, Studies presented to J.M. Wallace-Hadrill, ed. P. Wormald et al. (Oxford, 1983), pp 273–99.

—— 1994, 'Cnut's Scandinavian Empire', *The Reign of Cnut, King of England, Denmark and Norway*, ed. A. Rumble (London, 1994), pp 10–22.

Saxonhouse, A., 'Introduction – Public and private: the paradigm's power', *Stereotypes of Women in Power: Historical Perspectives and Revisionist Views*, eds B. Garlick et al. (New York and London, 1992), pp 1–9.

Schmid, K., 1971a, 'Die Thronfolge Ottos des Grossen', *Königswahl und Thronfolge in ottonisch-frühdeutscher Zeit*, ed. E. Hlawitschka, Wege der Forschung, vol 178 (Darmstadt, 1971), pp 417–508.

—— 1971b, 'Neue Quellen zum Verständnis des Adels im 10 Jahrhundert', *Königswahl und Thronfolge in ottonisch-frühdeutscher Zeit*, ed. E. Hlawitschka, Wege der Forschung, vol 178 (Darmstadt, 1971), pp 389–416.

Schneidmüller, B., 'Ottonische Familienpolitik und französische Nationsbildung im Zeitalter der Theophanu', *Kaiserin Theophanu*, eds A. von Euw and P. Schreiner (Cologne, 1991), pp 345–59.

Schramm, P.E. 'Die Krönung im 9 und 10 Jahrhundert', *Kaiser, Könige und Päpste*, vol 2 (Stuttgart, 1968), pp 140–305 .

—— *Die Deutschen Kaiser und Könige in Bildern ihrere Zeit*, 2 vols (Leipzig, 1928).

Searle, E., 1984, 'Fact and pattern in heroic history: Dudo of Saint-Quentin', *Viator*, vol 15 (1984), pp 119–37.

—— 1988, *Predatory Kinship and the Creation of Norman Power, 840–1066* (Berkeley, 1988).

—— 1989, 'Emma the Conqueror', *Studies in Medieval History Presented to R. Allen Brown*, eds C. Harper-Bill, C. Holdsworth and J. Nelson (Woodbridge, 1989), pp 281–8.

Sharpe, R., 'The date of St Mildreth's translation from Minster-in-Thanet to Canterbury', *Medieval Studies*, vol 53 (1991), pp 349–53.

Shopkow, L., 'The Carolingian world of Dudo of Saint-Quentin', *Journal of Medieval History*, vol 15 (1989), pp 19–37.

Smith, M.F., 'Archbishop Stigand and the eye of the needle', *ANS*, vol 16 (1994), pp 199–219.

Smith, R.D., 'Anglo-Saxon Maternal Ties', *This Noble Craft*, Proceedings of the tenth research Symposium of the Dutch and Belgian University Teachers of Old and Middle English and Historical Linguistics, Utrecht, 19–20 January, 1989, ed. E. Kooper; *Costerus*, New Series, vol 80 (Amsterdam, 1991), pp 106–17.

Sonnleitner, K., 1987, 'Selbstbewußtsein und Selbstverständnis der ottonischen Frauen im Spiegel der Historiographie des 10. Jahrhunderts', *Geschichte und ihre Quellen*, Festschrift für Friedrich Hausman zum 70. Geburtstag, ed. R. Härtel (Graz, 1987).

—— 1988, *Die Annalistik der Ottonenzeit als Quelle für die Frauengeschichte*, Schriftenreihe des Institutes für Geschichte. Darstellungen, 2 (Graz, 1988).

Soullière, E., 'Imperial women in the history of the Ming dynasty (1368–1644)', *Stereotypes of Women in Power: Historical Perspectives and Revisionist Views*, eds B. Garlick et al. (New York and London, 1992), pp 121–40.

Southern, R.W., 'The first life of Edward the Confessor', *English Historical Review*, vol 58 (1943), pp 385–400 .

Stafford, P.A., 1978a, 'Sons and mothers, family politics in the early middle ages', *Medieval Women*, ed. D. Baker, Studies in Church History, Subsidia, I (Oxford, 1978), pp 79–100.

—— 1978b, 'The Reign of Æthelred II, a study in the limitations on royal policy and action', *Ethelred the Unready, Papers from the Millenary Conference*, ed. D. Hill, British Archaeological Reports, British Series, vol 59 (Oxford, 1978), pp 15–46.

—— 1980, 'The "Farm of one night" and the organization of King Edward's estates in Domesday', *Economic History Review*, 2nd ser, vol 33 (1980), pp 491–502.

—— 1981, 'The King's wife in Wessex, 800–1066', *Past and Present*, no 91 (1981), pp 3–27.

—— 1982, 'The laws of Cnut and the history of Anglo-Saxon royal promises', *ASE*, vol 10 (1982), pp 173–90.

—— 1983, *Queens, Concubines and Dowagers, the King's Wife in the Early Middle Ages* (Athens, Ga, 1983).

—— 1986, *The East Midlands in the Early Middle Ages* (Leicester, 1986).

—— 1989a, *Unification and Conquest, a Political and Social History of England in the Tenth and Eleventh Centuries* (London, 1989).

—— 1989b, 'Women in Domesday', *Medieval Women in Southern England*, eds K. Bate, et al., Reading Medieval Studies, vol 15 (Reading, 1989), pp 75–94.

—— 1993, 'The portrayal of royal women in England, mid-tenth to mid-twelfth centuries', *Medieval Queenship*, ed. J.C. Parsons (New York, 1993), pp 143–67.

—— 1994, 'Women and the Norman Conquest', *Transactions of the Royal Historical Society*, ser 6, vol 4 (1994), pp 221–49.

—— 1997a, 'Queen Emma, women and power in eleventh-century England', *Queens and Queenship in Medieval Europe*, ed. A. Duggan (Woodbridge, 1997).

—— 1997b, 'La mutation familiale: a suitable case for caution', *The Community, the Family and the Saint: Patterns of Power in Early Medieval Europe*, eds J. Hill and M. Swan (Leeds, 1997).

—— forthcoming, 'Cherchez la femme, the missing link in the foundation of Reading Abbey'.

Starkey, D., 1977, 'Representation through intimacy, a study in the symbolism of monarchy and court office in early modern England', *Symbols and Sentiments: Cross Cultural Studies in Symbolism*, ed. I. Lewis (London, 1977), pp 187–224.

—— 1987a, 'Court History in Perspective', *The English Court from the Wars of the Roses to the Civil War*, eds D. Starkey et al. (1987), pp 1–24 .

—— 1987b, 'Intimacy and innovation: the rise of the Privy Chamber 1485–1547', *The English Court from the Wars of the Roses to the Civil War*, eds D. Starkey et al. (London, 1987), pp 71–118 .

Starkey, D., et al., *The English Court from the Wars of the Roses to the Civil War* (London, 1987).

Stengel, E.E., 'Die Grabschrift der ersten Äbtissin von Quedlinburg', *Deutsches Archiv*, vol 3 pt 2 (1939), pp 361–70.

Stenton, F.M., 1908, 'Introduction to the Rutland Domesday', *VCH Rutland*, vol I (London, 1908), pp 121–36.

—— 1918, *The Early History of the Abbey of Abingdon* (Reading, 1918).

—— 1933, 'Medeshamstede and its colonies', *Essays in Honour of James Tait* (London, 1933), pp 313–26.

Stevenson, W.H., 'An alleged son of Harold Harefoot', *English Historical Review*, vol 28 (1913), pp 112–17.

Strathern, M., *The Gender of the Gift* (Berkeley, Ca, 1988).

Stroud, D., 'The provenance of the Salisbury Psalter', *The Library*, 6th series, vol 1 (1979), pp 225–35.

Talvio, T., 'Harold I and Harthacnut's *Jewel Cross* type reconsidered', *Anglo-Saxon Monetary History, Essays in Memory of Michael Dolley*, ed. M.A.S. Blackburn (London, 1986), pp 273–90.

Tatlock, J.S.P., 'Muriel the earliest English poetess', *Publications of the Modern Languages Association of America*, vol 48 (1933), pp 317–21.

Tatton-Brown, T., 'The churches of Canterbury diocese in the eleventh century', *Minsters and Parish Churches: the Local Church in Transition, 950–1200*, ed. J. Blair, Oxford University Committee for Archaeology, Monograph no 17

(Oxford, 1988), pp 105–18.

Taylor, C.S., 'Berkeley Minster', *Transactions of the Bristol and Gloucestershire Archaeological Society*, vol 19, for 1894–5, pp 70–84.

Thacker, A., 1982, 'Chester and Gloucester: early ecclesiastical organisation in two Mercian burhs', *Northern History*, 18 (1982), pp 199–211.

—— 1988, 'Æthelwold and Abingdon', *Bishop Æthelwold, his Career and Influence*, ed. B. Yorke (Woodbridge, 1988), pp 43–64.

Thompson, S., 'Why English nunneries had no history: a study of the problems of the English nunneries founded after the Conquest', *Distant Echoes, Medieval Religious Women*, vol I, eds J.A. Nichols and L.T. Shank (Kalamazoo, 1984), pp 131–49.

Truzzi, M., *Sociology, the Classic Statements* (New York, 1971).

Turner, R.V., 'The children of Anglo-Norman royalty and their upbringing', *Medieval Prosopography*, vol 11.2 (1990), pp 17–52.

Uhlirz, M., 1951, 'Studien über Theophanu, III. Die Interventionen der Kaiserin Theophano zugunsten der Nonnenklöster während der Regierungzeit Ottos II und ihre Bedeutung', *Deutsches Archiv*, vol 9 (1951), pp 122–35.

—— 1957, 'Die rechtliche Stellung der Kaiserinwitwe Adelheid in Deutschen und im Italischen Reich', *Zeitschrift der Savigny-Stiftung für Rechtsgeschichte, Germanistiche Abteilung*, vol 74 (1957), pp 85–97.

Uitz, E., Pätzold, B., and Bayreuther, G., *Herrscherinnen und Nonnen, Frauengestalten von Ottonenzeit bis zu den Staufen* (Berlin, 1990).

Van Houts, E., 1983, 'Scandinavian influence in Norman literature of the eleventh century', *ANS*, vol 6 (1984), pp 107–21.

—— 1984, 'The political relations between Normandy and England before 1066 according to the "Gesta Normannorum Ducum"', *Les Mutations socio-culturelles au tournant des XIe–XIIe siècles*, ed. R. Foreville, Actes du IVe Colloque Internationale Anselmien (Paris, 1984), pp 85–97.

—— 1989a, 'Latin poetry and the Anglo-Norman court 1066–1135; the *Carmen de Hastingae proelio*', *Journal of Medieval History*, vol 15 (1989), pp 39–62.

—— 1989b, 'Historiography and hagiography at Saint Wandrille: the "Inventio et Miracula Sancti Vulfranni"', *ANS*, vol 12 (1989), pp 233–51.

—— 1989c, 'Robert de Torigni as genealogist', *Studies in Medieval History Presented to R. Allen Brown*, eds C. Harper Bill, C.J. Holdsworth and J.L. Nelson (Woodbridge, 1989), pp 215–33.

—— 1992a, 'Women and the writing of history in the early middle ages: the case of Abbess Matilda of Essen and Aethelweard', *Early Medieval Europe*, vol 1 no 1 (1992), pp 53–68.

—— 1992b, 'A note on *Jezebel* and *Semiramis*, Two Latin Norman poems from the early eleventh century', *Journal of Medieval Latin*, vol 2 (1992), pp 18–24.

VCH Dorset, ed. W. Page, vol 2 (London, 1908).

VCH Hampshire and the Isle of Wight, ed. W. Page, vol 2 (London, 1903).

VCH Herefordshire, ed. W. Page, vol 1 (London, 1908).

VCH Rutland, ed. W. Page, vol 1 (London, 1908).

VCH Wiltshire, vol 3, eds R.B. Pugh and E. Crittall and vol 6, ed. E. Crittall (London, 1956 and 1962).

VCH, The Victoria History of the Counties of England.

Verdon, J., 1973, 'Les femmes et la politique en France au Xe siècle', *Economies et Sociétés au Moyen Age, melanges offerts à Edouard Perroy* (Paris, 1973), pp 108–19.

—— 1977, 'La femme et la vie familiale en France aux IXe–XI siècles', *TRAMES*, Travaux et Memoires de l'Université de Limoges, Coll. Histoire, vol 2 (1977), pp 63–83.

—— 1993, 'Les veuves des rois de France aux Xe et XI siècles', *Veuves et Veuvage dans le haut Moyen Age*, ed. M. Parisse (Paris, 1993), pp 187–99.

Vince, A., *Saxon London: An Archaeological Investigation* (London, 1990).

Vogel, C., 'Les rites de la formation du mariage: leur significance dans la formation du lien durant le haut moyen age', *Il matrimonio nella società altomedievale*, Settimane di studio del centro Italiano di studi sull'Alto Medioevo, vol 24, 1976 (Spoleto, 1977), vol I, pp 397–472.

Vogelsang, T., *Die Frau als Herrscherin im höhen Mittelalter* (Frankfurt, 1954).

von Euw, A. and Schreiner, P., eds, *Kaiserin Theophanu, Begegnung des Ostens und Westens um die Wende des ersten Jahrtausends*, Gedenkschrift des Kölner Schnütgen Museums zum 1000 Todesjahr der Kaiserin (Cologne, 1991), vol II.

Wainwright, F.T., 'Æthelflæd, Lady of the Mercians', *Scandinavian England, Collected Papers of F.T. Wainwright*, ed. H.P.R. Finberg (Chichester, 1975), pp 305–24.

Wallace-Hadrill, J.M., *Early Germanic Kingship in England and on the Continent* (Oxford, 1971).

Ward, E., 'Caesar's Wife: the career of the Empress Judith, 819–829', *Charlemagne's Heir, New Perspectives on the Reign of Louis the Pious (814–40)*, eds P. Godman and R. Collins (Oxford, 1990), pp 205–27.

Ward, P., 1939, 'The coronation ceremony in medieval England', *Speculum*, vol 14 (1939), pp 160–78.

—— 1942, 'An early version of the Anglo-Saxon coronation ceremony', *English Historical Review*, vol 57 (1942), pp 345–61.

Warner, M., *Alone of all her Sex, the Myth and Cult of the Virgin Mary* (London, 1976).

Weber, M., *From Max Weber: Essays in Sociology*, eds H.H. Gerth and C. Wright Mills (London, 1970).

Werner, K.F., 1976, 'Quelques observations au sujet des débuts du 'duché' de Normandie', *Droit privé et institutions régionales, Études historiques offertes à Jean Yver* (Paris, 1976), pp 691–709.

—— 1992, 'Les Robertiens', *Le Roi de France et son Royaume autour de l'An Mil*, eds M. Parisse and X. Barral I Altet (Paris, 1992), pp 15–26.

West, F., *The Justiciarship in England, 1066–1232* (Cambridge, 1966).

Westermann-Angerhausen, H., 'Spuren der Theophano in der Ottonischen Schatzkunst', *Kaiserin Theophanu: Prinzessin aus der fremde, des Westreichs grosse Kaiserin* (Cologne, 1991), ed. G. Wolf, pp 263–78, translated 'Did Theophano leave her mark on the Ottonian sumptuary arts?', *The Empress Theophano*, ed. A. Davids (Cambridge, 1995), pp 244–64.

Whitbread, L., 'Æthelweard and the Anglo-Saxon Chronicle', *English Historical Review*, vol 74 (1959), pp 577–89 .

White, G.H., 1921, 'The sisters and nieces of Gunnor, duchess of Normandy', *The Genealogist*, new ser, vol 37 (1921), pp 57–65 and 128–32.

—— 1948, 'The household of the Norman kings', *Transactions of the Royal Historical Society*, ser 4, vol 30 (1948), pp 127–55.

White, S., *Custom, Kinship and Gifts to the Saints, the Laudatio Parentum in Western France, 1050–1150* (Chapel Hill, 1988).

Whitelock, D., 'Wulfstan and the laws of Cnut', *English Historical Review*, vol 63 (1948), pp 433–52.

Wickham Legg, J., *The Coronation of the Queen*, The Church Historical Society, vol 42, SPCK (London, 1898).

Williams, A., 1979, 'Some notes and considerations on problems connected with the English royal succession, 860–1066', *ANS*, vol 1 (1979), pp 144–67 and 225–33.

—— 1986, 'The Knights of Shaftesbury Abbey', *ANS*, vol 8 (Woodbridge, 1986), pp 214–37.

—— 1989, 'The king's nephew: the family, career and connections of Ralph, earl of Hereford', *Studies in Medieval History Presented to R. Allen Brown*, eds C. Harper-Bill, C. Holdsworth and J. Nelson (Woodbridge, 1989), pp 327–43.

—— 1995, *The English and the Norman Conquest* (Woodbridge, 1995).

Wilmart, A., 'Eve et Goscelin, pt 2', *Revue Bénédictine*, vol 50 (1938), pp 42–83.

Wimmer, F.P., *Kaiserin Adelheid, Gemahlin Ottos des Großen in ihrem Leben und Wirken von 931–973* (Regensburg, 1897).

Wogan-Browne, J., 'Queens, virgins and mothers: hagiographic representations of the abbess and her powers in twelfth- and thirteenth-century Britain', *Women and Sovereignty*, ed. L.O. Fradenburg, *Cosmos*, The Yearbook of the Traditional Cosmology Society (Edinburgh, 1992), pp 14–35.

Wolf, G., 1989, 'Prinzessin Sophia (978–1039), Äbtissin von Gandersheim und Essen, Enkelin, Tochter und Schwester von Kaisern', *Niedersächsische Jahrbuch für Landesgeschichte*, vol 61 (1989), pp 105–23.

—— 1991a, 'Königinwitwe als Vormunder ihrer Söhne und Enkel in Abendland zwischen 426 und 1056', *Kaiserin Theophanu: Prinzessin aus der Fremde, des Westreichs grosse Kaiserin*, ed. G. Wolf (Cologne, 1991), pp 39–59.

—— 1991b, 'Theophanu und Adelheid', *Kaiserin Theophanu: Prinzessin aus der Fremde, des Westreichs grosse Kaiserin*, ed. G. Wolf (Cologne, 1991), pp 79–96.

—— 1991c, 'Kaiserin Theophanu und Europa', *Kaiserin Theophanu: Prinzessin aus der Fremde, des Westreichs grosse Kaiserin*, ed. G. Wolf (Cologne, 1991), pp 97–105.

—— 1991d, 'Versuch einer Skizze: die Skandinavien und England-Politik der Kaiserin Theophanu in den Jahren 984–99', *Kaiserin Theophanu: Prinzessin aus der Fremde, des Westreichs grosse Kaiserin*, ed. G. Wolf (Cologne, 1991), pp 141–5.

—— 1991e, 'Könige und Kaiser als liebliche Nachkommenschaft der Kaiserin Theophanu', *Kaiserin Theophanu: Prinzessin aus der Fremde, des Westreichs grosse Kaiserin*, ed. G. Wolf (Cologne, 1991), pp 180–211.

Wormald, P., 'Æthelred the lawmaker', *Ethelred the Unready, Papers from the Millenary Conference*, ed. D. Hill, British Archaeological Society Reports, British Series, vol 59 (Oxford, 1978), pp 47–80.

—— 1982, 'The age of Bede and Beowulf', *The Anglo-Saxons*, ed. J. Campbell (1982).

—— 1986, 'Charters, law and the settlement of disputes in Anglo-Saxon England', *The Settlement of Disputes in Early Medieval Europe*, eds W. Davies and P. Fouracre (Cambridge, 1986), pp 149–68.

—— 1993, 'How do we know so much about Anglo-Saxon Deerhurst', *Deerhurst Lecture, 1991*, Friends of Deerhurst Church (Deerhurst, 1993).

Wright, C.E., *The Cultivation of Saga in Anglo-Saxon England* (Edinburgh, 1939).

Wright, P., 'A change in direction: the ramifications of a female household, 1558–1603', *The English Court from the Wars of the Roses to the Civil War*, ed. D. Starkey et al. (London, 1987) pp 147–72.

Yorke, B., ' "Sisters under the skin"? Anglo-Saxon nuns and nunneries in Southern England', *Medieval Women in Southern England*, eds K. Bate et al., Reading Medieval Studies, vol 15 (Reading, 1989), pp 95–117.

Index

This index does not cover the material in the Appendices.